DEMOCRACY

DEMOCRACY

Edited by

**Ellen Frankel Paul, Fred D. Miller, Jr.,
and Jeffrey Paul**

CAMBRIDGE
UNIVERSITY PRESS

Published by the Press Syndicate of the University of Cambridge
The Pitt Building, Trumpington Street, Cambridge CB2 1RP, England
40 West 20th Street, New York, NY 10011, USA
10 Stamford Road, Oakleigh, Melbourne, Victoria 3166, Australia

First published 2000

Printed in the United States of America

Library of Congress Cataloging-in-Publication Data

Democracy / edited by Ellen Frankel Paul,
Fred D. Miller, Jr., and Jeffrey Paul.   p.   cm.
Includes bibliographical references and index.
ISBN 0-521-78620-7
1. Democracy.   I. Paul, Ellen Frankel.   II. Miller,
Fred Dycus, 1944-   .   III. Paul, Jeffrey.
JC423 .D439773   1999
321.8-dc21   99-051590
CIP

ISBN 0-521-78620-7 paperback

The essays in this book have also been published,
without introduction and index, in the semiannual journal
Social Philosophy & Policy, Volume 17, Number 1,
which is available by subscription.

CONTENTS

INTRODUCTION

Some twenty-four hundred years ago, Plato disparagingly described democracy as "a charming form of government, full of variety and disorder, and dispensing a sort of equality to equals and unequals alike."* Despite Plato's warning that democracy would degenerate into tyranny, the last decade of the twentieth century has demonstrated that the opposite is possible. Has democracy been vindicated, both in practice and in theory? Only time will tell, but this "charming form of government" has gained territory in the aftermath of the collapse of communist tyrannies around the world, while interest in democratic theory has enjoyed a corresponding renewal. In recent years, political theorists have reexamined traditional themes in democratic theory and given them novel interpretations. The nature of popular sovereignty, the limits of democratic political authority, and radical forms of democracy that involve greater levels of citizen participation have all been subjects of intense debate.

The twelve essays in this volume—written by prominent philosophers and political theorists—explore these issues and related topics. Some essays discuss the appropriate ends of government or examine the difficulties involved in determining and carrying out the will of the people. Some address questions relating to the kinds of influence citizens can or should have over their representatives, asking, for example, whether individuals have a duty to vote, or whether inequalities in political influence among citizens (measured in terms of campaign contributions) can be morally justified. Other essays analyze democratic institutions, discussing what role deliberation should play in the democratic process, or asking whether it is legitimate to use laws and public policies to express approval or disapproval of various kinds of conduct. Still others examine the relationship between democracy and value pluralism, or consider the suitability of democracy as a form of government in non-Western societies.

In the collection's opening essay, "The Very Idea of Popular Sovereignty: 'We the People' Reconsidered," Christopher W. Morris observes that the sovereignty of the people is often thought to be the foundation of modern democracy. The truth of this claim depends on whether it is plausible to attribute sovereignty to "the people," and Morris argues that it is not. He begins by setting out the complex notion of sovereignty, and suggests that appeals to popular sovereignty may be understood in many different ways. The claim that the people should be sovereign might express any one of a number of ideals. It might mean, for example, that

* Plato, *The Republic*, Book VIII, 558c.

the ends of a polity should be determined by the interests of its citizens, or that the consent of the governed is necessary for legitimate rule, or that the institutions of government should encourage citizen participation. Morris discusses these and several other interpretations of popular sovereignty, and suggests that greater clarity could be achieved in discussions of political theory if we focused directly on these ideals rather than on the notion of sovereignty. He argues, moreover, that the doctrine that the people are, or ought to be, sovereign is misleading in potentially dangerous ways—ways that are conducive to a misunderstanding of the nature of politics, governance, and social order. He concludes that we would do well to come to grips with the errors of this doctrine, and that our understandings and justifications of democracy should dispense with the notion of popular sovereignty.

Popular rule has been viewed by some theorists as incompatible with the strong protection of individual rights. Josiah Ober challenges the view that democracy fails to foster constitutional liberalism and negative rights in his essay "Quasi-Rights: Participatory Citizenship and Negative Liberties in Democratic Athens." Ober maintains that democracy in ancient Athens promoted forms of law, social practice, and cultural expression that were relatively liberal. Moreover, he argues that the extension of democratic participation rights in Athens to an economically diverse body of free, adult, native males led to the extension of negative liberties, in the form of specific legal immunities, to slaves, children, non-natives, and women. Greek opponents of democracy, as Ober points out, frequently complained that the Athenians allowed too much freedom and equality to slaves, foreigners, and women, and specifically associated those tendencies with democracy. Nevertheless, the liberties and immunities held by Athenians were not rights in the modern sense. Ober suggests that the Athenian citizen's access to political institutions and the noncitizen's legal immunities might best be called "quasi-rights," because they were not regarded by the Athenians as inherent or inalienable, but as the contingent artifacts of established patterns of social behavior. The law, in and of itself, was recognized as being without force in the absence of the consistent, pragmatic willingness of citizen-volunteers to act (as prosecutors and jurors) according to its provisions and on its behalf. In spite of these qualifications, Ober concludes that the example of ancient Athens offers evidence that democracy can support constitutional liberalism.

The importance of democratic participation and the influence citizens may have on the political process are themes that run through the next four essays in this volume. In "Is There a Duty to Vote?" Loren E. Lomasky and Geoffrey Brennan ask whether a case can be made that voting in democratic elections is morally superior to abstaining. Lomasky and Brennan sketch and critique a range of arguments that are commonly thought to support a moral duty to vote. They examine prudential arguments that link voting with one's own self-interest, and act-consequentialist views that take into account the effects on all citizens of one's decision to vote or to abstain. They also consider generalization arguments, which make a case for voting based on the presumed ill-effects of widespread abstention, and they explore arguments that take voting to be an act of political expression—an act which can have value even if one's vote has only a tiny chance of affecting the outcome. Lomasky and Brennan believe that the expressivist approach is the most promising, but they argue that, in the end, all four of these approaches fail to support the idea that voting is morally meritorious. They conclude with a discussion of why people typically believe that voting is a praiseworthy act, focusing on three possible explanations: the belief in a duty to vote may hark back to an earlier time, when activist citizens played a larger role than they do today; or the belief may promote the self-esteem of voters; or the belief may be propagated by those who have the greatest stake in the electoral system—political candidates, officeholders, and members of the media.

As Lomasky and Brennan note, political acts such as voting can have an expressive function, and the same is true of the passage of laws. In "Postmodern Liberalism and the Expressive Function of Law," N. Scott Arnold offers a critique of the practice of using laws and public policies to make statements and to express support for values, ideals, and norms. Arnold notes that many elements of the modern welfare state—such as antidiscrimination laws or social insurance programs—are supported by expressive considerations: they signify a society's opposition to unfair practices or its commitment to shared values. Nevertheless, he argues that expressive considerations are not good reasons either for or against the passage of a law, policy, or program. Apart from certain special cases, acts of expression are best left to individuals and associations acting voluntarily within the private sector. In order to make his case for this claim, Arnold presents a comparative analysis of law (on the one hand) and nongovernmental organizations (on the other) as expressive vehicles and as vehicles for changing norms and values. He argues that, because of their flexibility and their voluntary nature, nongovernmental organizations are superior to laws and state action in terms of their ability to shape norms and express people's values. In light of this, he concludes, laws and policies should not be instituted on the basis of expressive considerations, except perhaps in the case of laws that protect fundamental rights by prohibiting certain kinds of action by the state: such laws may be uniquely suited to expressing a society's commitment to these rights.

Russell Hardin's essay "Democratic Epistemology and Accountability" explores the kind of knowledge that people can have about political issues and about the actions of their elected representatives, and asks whether it makes sense to hold government officials accountable for serving the interests of the people. Hardin begins by observing that the knowledge that people have about politics is not different in kind from the knowledge they have about anything else: much of it is accepted on the authority of others; little of it is verified first-hand, since such verification can be quite costly in terms of time and resources. Thus, the quality of knowledge that people have about politics will depend, as it does in other areas, on the incentives they have to acquire it and on the costs of obtaining it. Given this, Hardin argues that the very notion of holding elected officials accountable is suspect. It might make sense to hold officials responsible if they could reliably know what their constituents' interests were, and could demonstrate credible commitments to serving those interests, and if citizens could accurately judge whether their representatives were acting responsibly. Yet these conditions generally are not met. Hardin concludes that, given the incentives involved, it will typically be rational for people to forgo the considerable costs associated with gathering the extensive knowledge that they would need to judge the performance of their representatives, and that this is the normal state of affairs in modern democratic polities.

The issue of whether citizens should have equal influence in the political process is the subject of David Estlund's contribution to this volume, "Political Quality." Estlund challenges normative democratic theories that assume or argue that democracies should strive to equalize the opportunities that their citizens have to influence political outcomes. He contends that an insistence on equality of political input is unwarranted, since it would preclude even modest inequalities that would increase input for everyone. Under favorable conditions, Estlund argues, a greater quantity of input improves the expected quality of political decisions; thus, we need a good reason if we are to stand in the way of increased input. Considering potential objections to his position, Estlund acknowledges that it would be perfectly proper to object to inequality of influence if it were based on invidious comparisons among citizens—for example, on the view that some citizens are more knowledgeable or worthy than others and, therefore, should exercise greater influence. He also acknowledges that high levels of inequality of influence are very likely to harm the expected quality of political outcomes. Nevertheless, Estlund argues that modest inequalities—if they are designed to significantly increase input for all—may be capable of improving the tendency of political decisions to be substantively just and proper in a way that it would be unreasonable to deny. To illustrate his point, he describes a system of "Progressive Vouchers" under which citizens would be free, within limits, to purchase extra political influence (in the form of vouchers that could be used to make campaign contributions). The proceeds from these vouchers would be distributed in a way that would increase (albeit modestly) the ability of all citizens to influence the political process (by allowing them to increase their own level of contribution to political campaigns). Estlund believes that a voucher scheme such as this, while deviating from strict equality of influence, could provide a practical device for increasing the quality of political outcomes and policies overall.

The next four essays deal with various aspects of radical or deliberative democracy. Amy Gutmann and Dennis Thompson defend a conception of deliberative democracy in their contribution to this volume, "Why Deliberative Democracy Is Different." They begin by noting that all democratic theorists must confront the fundamental problem of finding a morally justifiable way of making binding collective decisions in the face of continuing disagreement. Most theorists, Gutmann and Thompson contend, propose solutions that make the problem seem more tractable than it is, because they discount much of the disagreement that gives rise to the problem in the first place. Gutmann and Thompson argue that a deliberative theory of democracy provides a different, and more defensible, approach to this problem, because it leaves open the possibility that the moral values expressed by a wide range of theories may be justifiable. The fundamental principle of their deliberative theory is that citizens owe one another justifications for the laws they collectively impose on one another. On this view, citizens or their accountable representatives must offer reasons to one another in an ongoing process of mutual justification. The distinctive feature of this process, Gutmann and Thompson maintain, is that the principles that guide it are morally and politically provisional, and thus allow for the persistence of moral disagreement about laws, policies, and institutions; at the same time, these principles allow for the possibility of moral agreement about those laws, policies, and institutions that are mutually justifiable.

In "The Institutions of Deliberative Democracy," William Nelson argues that the theory of deliberative democracy has little to tell us about the issue of institutional design. Deliberative theory, Nelson notes, involves two ideas: first, an abstract ideal of social and political life in which people live under rules they would construct if they were to deliberate reasonably; and second, a set of prescriptions concerning the exercise of whatever institutional rights they have. Nelson maintains that neither of these ideas is of much use in resolving disagreements between theorists who defend more thoroughly majoritarian institutions or more "direct" democracy, and those who favor more restrictions on majorities and greater power for the judiciary to overturn policies or programs established through a democratic process. Self-styled democrats, he observes, often defend greater reliance on majoritarianism or heightened democratic participation, and such democrats see liberals as defending judicial oversight and restrictions on majorities. Yet Nelson contends that, in the abstract, the deliberative ideal is hardly distinguishable from liberal contractualism—the idea that institutions must be justifiable to all who are to be bound by them. What's more, he concludes, liberal contractualism yields a more direct argument for (suitably constrained) majoritarian institutions than does deliberative democratic theory.

Kenneth Minogue offers a critique of deliberative democracy and other forms of radical democratic theory in his essay "Democracy as a *Telos*."

Minogue compares the radical democratic program to other programs aiming at social transformation, such as communitarianism or socialism. Like these movements, radical democracy seeks to realize a certain ideal which involves the pursuit of greater equality in three areas: political life, social and economic life, and family life. While radical democracy arises out of a noble impulse—the desire to move away from power and toward justice in social relations—it results in an increase in government interference in people's lives. This increased interference, Minogue argues, undermines the private sphere, replaces personal judgment with collective decision-making, and imposes a kind of paternalism that undermines individual initiative. In the course of his essay, Minogue touches upon a range of issues, including the nature of democratic representation, the politics of inclusion and exclusion, and the problem of identifying the will of the people. He concludes that the radical democratic project ultimately fails because it attempts to derive our complex political institutions from a single concept: radical democrats should recognize that democracy, like justice, freedom, and community, is only part of the ideal structure of what we call the modern state.

Theorists of radical democracy often contend that there is a close connection between participation in political self-government and the enhancement of personal freedom and autonomy; this alleged connection is the subject of Steven Wall's essay "Radical Democracy, Personal Freedom, and the Transformative Potential of Politics." Wall begins by examining two important themes that underlie the radical democrats' claim: the idea that political discussion leads to greater autonomy, as individuals critically reflect upon their own commitments, beliefs, and needs; and the idea that freedom is enhanced when citizens collectively identify with the authorization of political power in their society. He goes on to contrast the radical democrats' discursive conception of autonomy—which involves the adoption of an inward-looking and self-critical attitude toward one's interests, commitments, and projects—with the liberal pluralist conception—which holds that individuals are autonomous when they have access to a range of options, are relatively free from coercion, and have the mental capacities necessary for self-directed action. Wall argues that radical democrats fail to make the case that political participation does more to enhance personal freedom and autonomy than do other kinds of social interaction. He concludes that there is only a weak connection, if any, between personal freedom and democratic participation, and that the liberal pluralist view of politics (as a forum for bargaining and the aggregation of individual preferences) offers a more adequate account than the radical democratic view.

Pluralism and its role in political theory is also the subject of William A. Galston's contribution to this volume, "Democracy and Value Pluralism." Galston sets out a view of value pluralism which holds that what we value in our lives turns out to be multiple, heterogeneous, not reducible to a common measure, and not ordered hierarchically. On such a view, there is no single dominant value or set of values binding on all individuals in all circumstances. He then argues that we should bring this view of value to bear on political theory, and that when we do, it has important consequences for our understanding of democracy. If value pluralism is true, Galston contends, then the scope of legitimate democratic political authority is restricted in a number of ways. Democratic processes should not determine the course of scientific inquiry, for example, nor should they override fundamental liberties such as freedom of religion or the right to a fair trial. What's more, Galston believes, value pluralism implies that there are legitimate alternatives to democracy within the political sphere—for example, within juries, where unanimity is required for a binding decision; or in cases where decisions are best left to experts who are not subject to political pressures; or in cases where appeals to the common good can sometimes justify overriding democratic norms. Galston concludes by arguing that an acceptance of value pluralism can shape our understanding of democratic processes; it can lead us to the belief that democratic deliberation and decision-making should be guided by mutual acceptance and the quest for inclusive rather than exclusive policies.

The final essay, "The Problem of Russian Democracy: Can Russia Rise Again?" by Dmitry Shlapentokh, moves from the realm of theory explored in the earlier essays to the "real world." Shlapentokh's concern is with the dim prospects for democracy in post-communist Russia. Shlapentokh notes that Western theorists generally assume that democracy is the best form of government and is universally applicable, yet he argues that in the case of non-Western societies, the demise of a strong leader almost invariably leads not to a democratic society but to a deterioration of society and a degeneration toward anarchy. Shlapentokh illustrates his thesis with an extensive discussion of events in Russia at the end of the czarist regime in 1917 and at the end of the Soviet regime in 1991. He goes on to claim that while non-Western societies can quickly crumble when they lack a strong ruler, they can also be easily reassembled once a strong ruler again takes power. As an example of this phenomenon, he offers the collapse of imperial Russia in 1917, which was followed in a short time by the reestablishment of a powerful state under strong Bolshevik leadership. Shlapentokh suggests that a similar reemergence could take place in today's Russia, if a strong leader should emerge. Ultimately, however, only time will tell whether Russia reemerges as a global power or continues on a path of economic and political decline.

The form that democratic institutions should take and the limits of democratic rule are central issues in political theory. The essays in this volume offer valuable contributions to ongoing discussions of the nature of popular sovereignty, the place of deliberation in collective decision-making, and the proper relationship between citizens and the state.

ACKNOWLEDGMENTS

The editors wish to acknowledge several individuals at the Social Philosophy and Policy Center, Bowling Green State University, who provided invaluable assistance in the preparation of this volume. They include Mary Dilsaver, Terrie Weaver, and Carrie-Ann Biondi.

The editors would like to extend special thanks to Executive Manager Kory Swanson, for offering invaluable administrative support; to Publication Specialist Tamara Sharp, for attending to innumerable day-to-day details of the book's preparation; and to Managing Editors Harry Dolan and Matthew Buckley, for providing dedicated assistance throughout the editorial and production process.

CONTRIBUTORS

Christopher W. Morris is Professor of Philosophy at Bowling Green State University. He is the author of *An Essay on the Modern State* (1998) and the editor of two recent collections, *The Social Contract Theorists: Critical Essays on Hobbes, Locke, and Rousseau* (1999) and *Rational Commitment and Social Justice: Essays for Gregory Kavka* (1998), the latter coedited with Jules Coleman. His current research is for the most part on moral conventionalism and questions of justice in international affairs.

Josiah Ober is the David Magie Professor of Ancient History at Princeton University, where he is Chairman of the Classics Department and holds a joint appointment in the University Center for Human Values. His work centers on the theory and practice of classical Greek democracy and on its relevance for the critical assessment of contemporary political arrangements and social values. He is the author of several books, including *Mass and Elite in Democratic Athens* (1989), *The Athenian Revolution* (1996), and *Political Dissent in Democratic Athens* (1999), all published by Princeton University Press.

Loren E. Lomasky is Professor of Philosophy at Bowling Green State University. He previously taught for and chaired the Philosophy Department at the University of Minnesota, Duluth, and has held visiting positions at Virginia Polytechnic Institute, Australian National University, and the Australian Defence Force Academy. He is the author of *Persons, Rights, and the Moral Community* (1987), for which he was awarded the 1990 Matchette Prize for the best philosophy book published during the preceding two years by an author under age forty. His most recent book, coauthored with Geoffrey Brennan, is *Democracy and Decision: The Pure Theory of Electoral Preference* (1993), and he also coedited with Brennan a collection entitled *Politics and Process: New Essays in Democratic Theory* (1989).

Geoffrey Brennan is Professor of Economics in the Social and Political Theory Group, Research School of Social Sciences, Australian National University. He is currently completing a book with Alan Hamlin entitled *Democratic Devices and Desires*, to be published by Cambridge University Press. His earlier works include *The Power to Tax* (1980) and *The Reason of Rules* (1985), both coauthored with James Buchanan, and *Democracy and Decision* (1993), coauthored with Loren E. Lomasky.

N. Scott Arnold is Professor of Philosophy at the University of Alabama at Birmingham. He is the author of *The Philosophy and Economics of Market Socialism* (1994) and *Marx's Radical Critique of Capitalist Society* (1990). He has been a visiting scholar at the Hoover Institution at Stanford University and at the Social Philosophy and Policy Center at Bowling Green State University.

Russell Hardin is Professor of Politics at New York University. He is the author of *Liberalism, Constitutionalism, and Democracy* (1999), *One for All* (1995), *Morality within the Limits of Reason* (1988), and *Collective Action* (1982). He was for many years the editor of *Ethics*. He is currently at work on a book on problems of the rationality and epistemology of ordinary mortals.

David Estlund is Associate Professor of Philosophy at Brown University, and has taught previously at the University of California, Irvine. He has received fellowships from the American Council of Learned Societies, the Harvard Program in Ethics and the Professions, and the National Endowment for the Humanities. His publications, mainly on normative issues relating to liberalism and democratic legitimacy, include articles in the *Journal of Philosophy*, *Philosophical Review*, and *Ethics*.

Amy Gutmann is Laurance S. Rockefeller University Professor of Politics at Princeton University. She is also the Founding Director of Princeton's University Center for Human Values. Among her books are *Liberal Equality* (1980); *Democratic Education* (1987); *Democracy and Disagreement* (1996), coauthored with Dennis Thompson, which *Choice* named as one of the "outstanding political science books for 1997"; and *Color Conscious: The Political Morality of Race* (1986), coauthored with Anthony Appiah, which won the American Political Science Association's Ralph J. Bunche Award "for the best scholarly work in political science that explores the phenomenon of ethnic and cultural pluralism." She has also edited many books, most recently *Freedom of Association* (1998), and has published many articles in moral and political philosophy, education and multiculturalism, and ethics and public affairs.

Dennis Thompson is the Alfred North Whitehead Professor of Political Philosophy at Harvard University, and the Founding Director of Harvard's Program in Ethics and the Professions. In addition to *Democracy and Disagreement* (1996), coauthored with Amy Gutmann, he is the author of *The Democratic Citizen: Social Science and Democratic Theory in the Twentieth Century* (1970), *John Stuart Mill and Representative Government* (1976), *Ethics in Congress: From Individual to Institutional Corruption* (1995), *Political Ethics and Public Office* (1987), and numerous articles on democratic theory and political ethics.

William Nelson is Professor of Philosophy and Chair of the Department of Philosophy at the University of Houston. He is the author of *On Justifying Democracy* (1980) and *Morality: What's in It for Me?* (1991), as well as a number of essays in moral, political, and legal philosophy. He is currently working on issues concerning moral and legal rights.

Kenneth Minogue is Emeritus Professor of Political Science at the London School of Economics. He was born in New Zealand, was educated in Australia, and is the author of *The Liberal Mind* (1963), *Nationalism* (1967), *The Concept of a University* (1974), *Alien Powers: The Pure Theory of Ideology* (1985), and *Politics: A Very Short Introduction* (1995). He has coedited (with Anthony de Crespigny) *Contemporary Political Philosophers* (1976) and (with Michael Biddis) *Thatcherism: Personality and Politics* (1987). In 1996, he edited *Conservative Realism: New Essays*, and he has also edited and introduced the Everyman edition of Hobbes's *Leviathan*. As Senior Research Fellow at the Social Affairs Unit in London, he wrote *The Silencing of Society: The True Cost of the Lust for News* (1997), and he has written *Waitangi, Morality and Reality* (1998), a study of Maori-Pakeha relations in New Zealand, for the New Zealand Business Roundtable.

Steven Wall is Assistant Professor of Philosophy at Kansas State University. He has taught previously at the University of Virginia and at Baruch College, City University of New York. He is the author of *Liberalism, Perfectionism, and Restraint* (1998), and is currently working on a study on the value of democratic political participation.

William A. Galston is Professor at the School of Public Affairs, University of Maryland, and Director of the Institute for Philosophy and Public Policy. His publications include *Kant and the Problem of History* (1975), *Justice and the Human Good* (1980), *Liberal Purposes: Goods, Virtues, and Diversity in the Liberal State* (1991), and *Virtue* (coedited with John W. Chapman, 1992). He has also served as Deputy Assistant to President Clinton for Domestic Policy (1993–1995) and Executive Director of the National Commission on Civic Renewal (1996–1998).

Dmitry Shlapentokh is Associate Professor of History at Indiana University, South Bend. He was born and educated in the former Soviet Union, and received his Ph.D. in Russian/European history from the University of Chicago. He has held research appointments at various institutions, including Harvard University, Columbia University, and the Hoover Institution at Stanford University. Among his many publications are *The Counter-Revolution in Revolution* (1999), *The French Revolution and the Russian Anti-Democratic Tradition* (1997), and *The French Revolution in Russian Intellectual Life* (1996).

THE VERY IDEA OF POPULAR SOVEREIGNTY: "WE THE PEOPLE" RECONSIDERED*

By Christopher W. Morris

The sovereignty of the people, it is widely said, is the foundation of modern democracy. The truth of this claim depends on the plausibility of attributing sovereignty to "the people" in the first place, and I shall express skepticism about this possibility. I shall suggest as well that the notion of popular sovereignty is complex, and that appeals to the notion may be best understood as expressing several different ideas and ideals. This essay distinguishes many of these and suggests that greater clarity at least would be obtained by focusing directly on these notions and ideals and eschewing that of sovereignty. My claim, however, will not merely be that the notion is multifaceted and complex. I shall argue as well that the doctrine that the people are, or ought to be, sovereign is misleading in potentially dangerous ways, and is conducive to a misunderstanding of the nature of politics, governance, and social order. It would be well to do without the doctrine, but it may be equally important to understand its errors. Our understandings and justifications of democracy, certainly, should dispense with popular sovereignty.

I. Sovereignty

I shall start with an explication of the notion of sovereignty. The analysis I offer is complex and cannot be fully defended here.[1] While I would contend that this account captures the essential elements of modern notions of sovereignty, it may appear to beg the question against popular sovereignty. For it will be hard to see how the people *could* be sovereign on my analysis. Still, it will be useful to begin with an explication of the concepts relevant to this question.

* Versions of this essay have been presented to audiences at the University of Illinois, Urbana, the University of Toronto, York University, New York University Law School, the conference on "Democracy, Pluralism, and Citizenship" held in Montréal in the fall of 1996, and to my graduate seminar on "Constitutionalism and the Rule of Law." I am grateful to many people for questions and comments, in particular to David Copp, John Ferejohn, and Pasquale Pasquino. Comments and suggestions from Ellen Frankel Paul, and from the other contributors to this volume, were also very helpful.
[1] See my book *An Essay on the Modern State* (Cambridge: Cambridge University Press, 1998), ch. 7.

1

Sovereignty is not a simple idea. As one should expect with a notion that has a long and controversial history, it is rather complicated. To understand the different elements of the notion of sovereignty, it is important to keep in mind certain aspects of the history of the emergence of the modern state in the sixteenth and seventeenth centuries. Medieval rule was, broadly speaking, feudal, imperial, and/or theocratic. The early modern competitors of the state were city-states and leagues of cities, as well as empires, the Church, and various remnants of feudalism. Two features of modern governance were relatively absent in all of these earlier forms of rule: exclusivity of rule (a "closed" system of governance) and territoriality. The (modern) state only emerges when its claim (or that of its head, the monarch) to govern alone, exclusively, is recognized. And a determinate realm, with relatively unambiguous geographical boundaries, is a prerequisite of the (modern) state and is largely missing in early forms of political organization. A "sovereign" is the unique ruler of a realm, whose sphere of authority encompasses the whole realm without overlapping that of any other ruler. It—initially the monarch, later the state, then "the people" (of a state)—rules without superiors. As the historian F. H. Hinsley claims, "at the beginning, the idea of sovereignty was the idea that there is a final and absolute political authority in the political community . . . *and no final and absolute authority exists elsewhere.*"[2] The last clause alone suggests that the notion is new. With the development of the concept of sovereignty, we have the main elements of what is called the state system: independent states and "international relations" (and "international law").

Let me present my analysis. The core notion of sovereignty I shall express thus: *To be sovereign is to be the ultimate source of political power within a realm.* This I take to be the core of the modern notion of sovereignty that is developed by Jean Bodin, Thomas Hobbes, Jean-Jacques Rousseau, and other modern political thinkers.[3] I shall explicate, in turn, the different elements of this general characterization.

Sovereignty pertains, first of all, to political power *within a realm.* The notion of sovereignty is characteristically modern. The realms in question are, for the most part, modern states, territorially defined. The jurisdiction of the rulers is a well-defined territory.[4]

---

[2] F. H. Hinsley, *Sovereignty,* 2d ed. (Cambridge: Cambridge University Press, 1986), 25–26.

[3] See Jean Bodin, *Les Six livres de la république* [1576], translated as *The Six Bookes of a Commonweale,* trans. R. Knolles, ed. K. D. McRae (Cambridge, MA: Harvard University Press, 1962); Thomas Hobbes, *Leviathan* [1651], ed. R. Tuck (Cambridge: Cambridge University Press, 1991); and Jean-Jacques Rousseau, *Du Contrat social (On the Social Contract)* [1762], in *Oeuvres complètes,* vol. 3, ed. B. Gagnebin and M. Raymond (Paris: Editions Gallimard, 1964). See my *Essay on the Modern State,* ch. 7, for an analysis of sovereignty and additional references.

[4] While Christendom, with its ambiguous and indeterminate boundaries, could be a suitable realm for a "sovereign" (i.e., an emperor or a monarch), in modern times the notion of sovereignty is typically connected to territories with well-defined borders. The modern notion does, of course, borrow from Roman law, but the boundaries of the Roman Empire were ambiguous. See my *Essay on the Modern State,* chs. 2, 7, and esp. 8.

A *political power* in these contexts is a political *authority*. Something is an authority, in the sense relevant here, only if its directives are (and are intended to be) action-guiding. The law, for instance, forbids us from doing certain things, and it intends these prohibitions to guide our behavior; specifically, these prohibitions are reason-providing. Authorities, then, guide behavior by providing reasons for action to their subjects. This is, for instance, Hobbes's view of the law: "Law in generall, is not Counsell, but Command ... addressed to one formerly obliged to obey him [who commands]," where command is "where a man saith, *Doe this*, or *Doe not this*, without expecting other reason than the Will of him that sayeth it."[5] On this view, political authority is not to be understood simply as justified force. Something is a genuine authority only insofar as its directives are reasons for action.[6]

It is possible for something to have authority in this sense without possessing any (non-normative) power or without being able to impose sanctions for disobedience. However, it may be that *political* authority cannot be *justified* if it is not, to some extent, effective, and effectiveness for most political regimes may require some capacity for imposing sanctions. On this view, justified political authority requires political *power*, understood as a *de facto* or causal ability to influence or control events (e.g., by imposing sanctions).[7]

---

[5] Hobbes, *Leviathan*, ch. 26, 183, and ch. 25, 176. It is, of course, controversial whether Hobbes had the theoretical resources to defend this account of the normativity of law. Influenced by Joseph Raz's account of exclusionary reasons, H. L. A. Hart interprets Hobbes's account of a command to mean that

> the commander characteristically intends his hearer to take the commander's will instead of his own as a guide to action and so to take it in place of any deliberation or reasoning of his own: the expression of a commander's will that an act be done is intended to preclude or cut off any independent deliberation by the hearer of the merits pro and con of doing the act.

See H. L. A. Hart, "Commands and Authoritative Legal Reasons," in *Essays on Bentham* (Oxford: Clarendon Press, 1982), 253.

[6] My analysis follows Joseph Raz; see Raz, *The Authority of Law: Essays on Law and Morality* (Oxford: Clarendon Press, 1979), chs. 1–2; and Raz, *The Morality of Freedom* (Oxford: Clarendon Press, 1986), chs. 2–3. See also Raz, *Practical Reason and Norms* [1975], 2d ed. (Princeton: Princeton University Press, 1990); and Leslie Green, *The Authority of the State* (Oxford: Clarendon Press, 1988).

[7] This thesis is substantive, for it depends on the reasons for which political authorities are desirable (e.g., resolving assurance problems, providing collective goods, securing justice, redistributing wealth). See my *Essay on the Modern State*, ch. 7. Raz holds that effectiveness is a condition of something's being a legitimate political authority; see Raz, *The Authority of Law*, 8–9; and *The Morality of Freedom*, 75–76.

Note that when I speak here and elsewhere of *justified* authority or power, I do not mean "regarded as or thought to be justified." It is possible that some theorists believe that a power is justified if it is widely believed to be so (but this sort of view always raises the question of what it means to believe that something is justified). Rather, I speak of justification *simpliciter*, without distinguishing between moral, rational, and other kinds. A lengthier discussion can be found in my *Essay on the Modern State*, chs. 4–6.

Sovereignty is the ultimate source of *political* authority/power within a realm. What is the scope of 'political' here? Clearly, the law is included. Sovereignty is the source of (positive) law within a realm. Does it also include morality? By this, one might mean that sovereignty could be a source of moral authority in the sense that it could determine (i.e., constitute) what is morally right or wrong. One might read Hobbes and Rousseau in this way, but it would not be a very plausible view of morality, even for moral conventionalists.[8] So I shall not understand sovereignty to be a source of moral authority in this way.[9] A consequence of this interpretation is the possibility of being (politically or legally) obligated to do something that is morally wrong.

What is it for a source of authority to be *ultimate*? In this as well as other contexts, this word can have several meanings. An authority may be ultimate if it is the *highest* authority. In this sense, sovereignty requires a *hierarchy* of authorities, such that one (or more) can be at the summit, as it were. A distinguishing characteristic of modern governance is that it is *direct*, by contrast with the indirect rule characteristic of medieval Europe. Rule is *direct* if there are no intermediaries with independent authority. The highest authority in a chain of direct rule, then, has authority over all levels of the hierarchy. An ultimate authority in this sense is the highest element of a continuous chain of direct governance (a strict ordering). Directness in this sense is one of the distinguishing features of *modern* rule, characteristic of contemporary states.[10]

Secondly, an ultimate authority is also *final*. There is no further appeal after it has spoken; it has, as it were, "the last word." Finality in this sense does not mean that moral appeals are excluded.[11] It merely means that no further appeals are possible within the system.

Lastly, an ultimate authority may be one which is *supreme*. 'Supreme' is sometimes just a synonym for 'ultimate'; but the sense I wish to isolate is special: an authority which is supreme (in a realm) can regulate all other sources of authority (in that realm). If the state claims supremacy in this sense, then it claims authority over all other authorities (e.g., corporate,

---

[8] But see David Gauthier's recent work on "public reason": for instance, "Public Reason," *Social Philosophy and Policy* 12, no. 1 (Winter 1995): 19–42.

[9] There is another sense in which we might speak of the political here as including the moral. It may be that political (and legal) authority *override* or *preempt* morality. I discuss this below when I explain the meaning of 'ultimate'.

[10] See Charles Tilly, *Coercion, Capital, and European States* (Oxford: Basil Blackwell, 1990), 24–25, 103–6, 144–46; and my *Essay on the Modern State*, ch. 2. See also Quentin Skinner, "The State," in *Political Innovation and Conceptual Change*, ed. T. Ball, J. Farr, and R. L. Hanson (Cambridge: Cambridge University Press, 1989), 90–131.

[11] Consider the U.S. constitutional system, which incorporates moral rights into the law through the Ninth Amendment ("The enumeration in the Constitution of certain rights shall not be construed to deny or disparage others retained by the people"). See my "Droits originaires et Etats limités: Quelques leçons de la république américaine," *Science(s) politique(s)* 4 (December 1993), 105–15.

syndicate, church, conscience).[12] The state's authority, then, is supposed to "preempt" all competing authorities. Hobbes and many classical theorists of the modern state so understand the state's authority: it overrides all competing sources of authority, even that of morality (and especially that of religious authorities and of conscience).

Summarizing, then, *sovereignty is the highest, final, and supreme political and legal authority (and power) within the territorially defined domain of a system of direct rule.*

The classical modern theorists—e.g., Hobbes and Rousseau—understood sovereignty also to be absolute, indivisible, and inalienable. Sovereignty is *absolute* if it is unconstrained or unlimited.[13] Sovereignty is *indivisible* if it is unique and cannot be divided. And it is *inalienable* if it cannot be delegated or "represented." This conception of sovereignty, which I attribute to Hobbes (and Rousseau), I shall refer to as "the classical view":[14] the sovereign is the ultimate source of absolute, indivisible, inalienable political authority within a realm.

The doctrine that states are sovereign in the classical sense proved to be enormously influential. William Blackstone's views are not unrepresentative. He thought that "there is and must be in all of [the several forms of government] a supreme, irresistible, absolute, uncontrolled authority, in which the *jura summi imperii*, or the rights of sovereignty, reside." While recognizing that the sovereignty of Parliament is constrained by natural law, he held that

> [i]t hath sovereign and uncontrollable authority in making, enlarging, restraining, abrogating, repealing, reviving and expounding of laws, concerning matters of all possible denominations, ecclesiastical, or temporal, civil, military, maritime or criminal; this being the place where that absolute despotic power, which must in all governments reside somewhere, is entrusted by the constitution of these kingdoms. All mischiefs and grievances, operations and remedies, that transcend the ordinary course of the laws, are within the reach of this extraordinary tribunal. It can regulate or new model the succession of the crown. . . . It can alter the established religion of the land. . . . It can change and create afresh even the constitution of the

---

[12] This is Raz's account of supremacy in these contexts (*Practical Reason and Norms*, 150–52). Certainly, this is what Hobbes and many modern theorists also claim for the state's authority.

[13] "For Power Unlimited, is absolute Soveraignty" (Hobbes, *Leviathan*, ch. 22, 155). Rousseau appears to agree; see his *Social Contract*, Book IV, ch. 4, 374–75, and ch. 5, 376. See also Robert Derathé, *Jean-Jacques Rousseau et la science politique de son temps* [1950], 2d ed. (Paris: Vrin, 1988), ch. 5, esp. 332ff.

[14] Even though Bodin's account antedates it. For Rousseau, sovereignty is also indivisible and inalienable (*Social Contract*, Book II, ch. 2, 369–70; Book II, ch. 1, 368). Additionally, the sovereign cannot bind itself to itself or to others (Book I, ch. 7, 362–63).

kingdom and of parliaments themselves. . . . It can, in short, do every
thing that is not naturally impossible. . . .[15]

Classical sovereignty is no longer as popular as it once was. It is now
widely thought that sovereignty can (and should) be limited. It is often
thought as well that one of the most effective institutional means of
limiting the authority and power of states is to divide sovereignty among
a plurality of agents or institutions; there need be no single authority.
Contra Hobbes and others, republican and democratic theory has stressed
the value and importance of divisions of power within states. Thus, in-
divisibility is no longer assumed to be essential to sovereignty. Our notion
tends to be one of limited sovereignty.[16]

II. The Sovereignty of the People

In early modern times, European monarchs fought the limits imposed
on them by imperial and papal authorities and sought as well to overcome the independent powers of feudal lords, self-governing towns, and
autonomous guilds. The struggles that ensued, as well as the ferocity of
religious conflicts, suggested to many the need for unitary absolute power,
and the modern notion of sovereignty was born.[17]
Sovereignty was initially attributed to, or claimed by, monarchs.[18] In
Britain it became customary to attribute sovereignty to the trinity of "the
King in Parliament" (i.e., the monarch and the two houses of Parliament).
On the Continent, sovereignty was usually understood to be a defining
attribute of *states* (as opposed to governments). Rousseau and some of

---

[15] William Blackstone, *The Sovereignty of the Law, Selections from Blackstone's Commentaries on the Laws of England*, ed. Gareth Jones (Toronto: University of Toronto Press, 1973), 36, 71. On the influence of Blackstone's views, Gordon Wood writes:

> By the early 1770's, particularly with the introduction of Blackstone's *Commentaries* into the colonies, the doctrine that there must be in every form of government "a supreme, irresistible, absolute, uncontrolled authority, in which the *jura summi imperii*, or rights of sovereignty, reside" had gained such overwhelming currency that its "truth," many Americans were compelled to admit, could no longer "be contested."

Gordon Wood, *The Creation of the American Republic, 1776–1787* (New York: Norton, 1969), 350; see also 345, 362, 382–83.
[16] While theorists of what I have called the classical view of sovereignty tend to be indifferent or hostile to division of power, and checks and balances, these institutional devices may serve to limit sovereignty. Hence, partisans of limited sovereignty may also support divided powers. While the issues are more complex than I have implied, it should be kept in mind that sovereignty pertains first of all to the nature of political authority, and that questions about division of powers concern the design of institutions.
[17] Hinsley claims that "[s]overeignty has been the 'constitutional' justification of absolute political power. Historically, it has been formulated only when the locus of supreme power was in dispute. . . . It is the justification of absolute authority that can arise and exist only when a final power is considered necessary in a body politic . . ." (*Sovereignty*, 277).
[18] Unless we understand the Deity's authority and power as a type of sovereignty.

the founders of the American system attributed sovereignty to the people, and the French *Déclaration des droits de l'homme et du citoyen* of 1789 claims sovereignty for the "nation."

Many, if not most, modern theorists shared Blackstone's view that "there is and must be in all of [the several forms of government] a supreme, irresistible, absolute, uncontrolled authority, in which the *jura summi imperii*, or the rights of sovereignty, reside." These theorists understood states to be forms of political organization with considerable authority over all internal persons and entities ("internal sovereignty") and independence from all external powers ("external sovereignty"). This authority was to be exerted over the residents of well-defined territories, the boundaries of which must be recognized and respected by all alike. This dual concern with internal and external authority reflected the historical context of classical conceptions of sovereignty.

States are still thought by many to possess sovereignty, especially in their ("external") relations to other states. But it is also widely thought today that *peoples* are the rightful bearers of sovereignty. The doctrine of *popular sovereignty* is especially influential in the American and French political traditions, and it may be a central feature of the dominant conceptions of political power of these political cultures.

Who are the holders of sovereignty, then, according to this influential doctrine? We need immediately to distinguish 'the people' from 'a people'. The two notions need to be sharply distinguished. 'The People'—hereafter with a capital—in its modern sense, is a term that originally designated the members of the nonaristocratic (and nonclerical) classes of society. The radical idea of the French Revolution was that these classes (or their representatives) had the right to rule, *contra* the claim of all of the European aristocracies. Gradually 'the People' comes to be more inclusive, covering at least all members of the polity and sometimes all those subject to its governance (including, e.g., nonmember residents). The old connotations of the term remain—"he is a man of the people"—but, generally, it is now to be understood in these contexts to include almost every inhabitant of a state. This notion of "the People" echoes classical Roman ideas, as does its associated notion of citizenship.[19]

'A people', by contrast, designates a collective entity whose unity is social and not primarily political. The notion of a people, then, is similar to that of a nation or national group; it is of a group of humans united by ties of history, culture, or "blood." Many think that groups of this sort are entitled "to assume among the powers of the earth the separate & equal

---

[19] Even in its extensive sense, 'the People' is ambiguous with regard to the inclusion of many subjects who are not full members—e.g., foreign legal residents, tourists, immigrants, and, in Western Europe, citizens of other countries of the European Union. I shall return later to this point.

station to which the laws of nature . . . entitle them."[20] But few theorists today attribute sovereignty to peoples in this sense.[21] Nationalists, contemporary and classical, are properly better interpreted as seeking statehood or another political status for peoples.[22] Popular sovereignty is the attribution of sovereignty to the People (which need not be *a* people).

The claims of states (and monarchs) to sovereignty—classical or limited— may be found wanting, or so I argue elsewhere.[23] We might query whether transferring sovereignty to the People may be more plausible. Given my characterization, however, it is most unlikely that the People could be sovereign. It is hard to imagine how the People's rule could be direct in the manner characteristic of modern states, much less how its authority could constitute a hierarchy of authorities. In all democracies, insofar as the People may be said to rule, they do so through intermediaries. Additionally, it is difficult to see how the People could be a source of law, except occasionally through referenda and the like. Law in modern states is determined by legislatures and courts, and only occasionally through direct popular consultation.[24] The sense in which the sovereign People is a source of legal authority would be a rather weak one. Certainly, it would not be what we ordinarily mean when talking about sources of the law.

The classical and contemporary problems about aggregation of the "general will" also create difficulties for this interpretation of popular sovereignty. The People cannot speak until they are given the means to express themselves. There are numerous such means (e.g., voting procedures, polling methods, systems of representation), and it is hard to see how the choice among them could be made by the People in the requisite manner. Additionally, it may often turn out that the People talk in circles, so to speak, or have nothing to say.[25]

[20] The opening paragraph of Jefferson's Declaration of Independence attributes certain entitlements to peoples, in this sense. (Proto-nationalist ideas are present, but not usually noticed, throughout Jefferson's document: "a distant people," "our British brethren," "the voice of justice and consanguinity," "to send over not only souldiers of our common blood, but Scotch & foreign mercenaries . . . these unfeeling brethren.") I quote from the version of the Declaration of Independence printed in *The Portable Thomas Jefferson*, ed. M. Peterson (Harmondsworth, Middlesex: Penguin, 1975), 236–41.

[21] The attribution of sovereignty to the "nation" in the French *Déclaration* of 1789 is probably best understood as designating the People as the source of political authority.

[22] For instance, were the province of Québec to secede from Canada, all current residents of Québec, not merely French nationals, would presumably share sovereignty (of some sort).

[23] See my *Essay on the Modern State*, ch. 7.

[24] This claim about the "sources" of law should be taken loosely, since I do not want to rule out theories, for instance, that understand the law to be the best interpretation of the practices of a country or legal culture.

[25] That is, we should acknowledge the possibility of preference cycles or empty choice sets. I make allusion in passing to social choice theory. These sorts of problems seem to me devastating for most doctrines of popular sovereignty, though I shall not belabor the point. See, for instance, Russell Hardin, "Public Choice versus Democracy" [1990], in *The Idea of Democracy*, ed. David Copp, Jean Hampton, and John Roemer (Cambridge: Cambridge University Press, 1993), 157–72.

There are additional problems in attributing sovereignty to the People. The matter of determining what is a People only starts with the distinction between *"a* people" and *"the* People." The individuation of Peoples (with the definite article) is considerably more problematic than may have been noticed. What is surprising perhaps is the casualness with which political thinkers have assumed that Peoples are readily identifiable. Certainly, prior to modern states, it is hard to identify Peoples in our general or inclusive sense.[26] With the advent of the state, the People becomes identified with the bulk of the subjects or residents (of the state). This may be inadequate for many of the concerns that now trouble us.[27] Still, it is an initial answer. Defenders of popular sovereignty, however, cannot say that *states* determine who constitutes a People. For it is "We the People" who are supposed to be constituting the state in the first place! If states are prior, then their constitution by the People becomes impossible.[28] A constitution can, coherently, create a new body and then empower it. But the People cannot be understood to possess sovereignty in the ways claimed by their supporters if the People's powers are granted it by a constitution and not merely "retained."[29]

We could try to individuate Peoples by identifying them with *peoples* (with the indefinite article). Thomas Jefferson is famous for his assertion (in the Declaration of Independence) of "the right of the people to alter or abolish [government destructive of the ends of life, liberty, and the pursuit of happiness], and to institute new government." This right is evidently a right of the People (in our sense). Jefferson also seems to believe that peoples (with the indefinite article) have claims. His famous opening paragraph asserts that the laws of nature entitle "one people . . . to assume among the powers of the earth [a] separate and equal station." Many later passages, some excised by the Continental Congress, clearly make reference to peoples in the sense of a socially determined set of individuals. Both notions of "people" are evidently present in Jefferson's

[26] The exceptions are those forms of political organization—for instance, Rome—that explicitly identified the People. But ancient Peoples never included the total population of a realm.

[27] For instance, the rights of illegal immigrants (and of their children), and the rights of noncitizen (legal) residents to vote in local elections.

[28] In a number of places, Akhil Amar says things that imply that the American People are or were constituted by the state or the Constitution. See Amar, "Of Sovereignty and Federalism," *Yale Law Journal* 96, no. 7 (June 1987): 1463 n. 163, where Amar writes that "the most important thing that the Constitution constitutes is neither the national government, nor even the supreme law, but one sovereign national People, who may alter their government or supreme law at will"; and Amar, "The Consent of the Governed: Constitutional Amendment Outside Article V," *Columbia Law Review* 94 (March 1994): 489, where Amar writes that "the Constitution formed previously separate state peoples into one continental people—American!—by substituting a true (and self-described) Constitution for a true (and self-described) league. . . ."

[29] Many of the arguments about the People's "retention" of various powers require their existence prior to and independently of the state. Some make use of classical claims about inalienability, which would be unintelligible without this priority and independence.

Declaration, whether or not he himself was aware of this. Whatever is to be decided about the interpretation of Jefferson's thought, one could try to individuate Peoples by identifying them with peoples; the People, thus, is constituted by a people. There are a few plausible cases for the claims of peoples or national groups to independence. But they tend to impose a number of conditions and constraints on the rights of peoples (or "encompassing groups"), and these make it impossible to generalize the identification of peoples and Peoples.[30] In the American context, we might just note that the identification of the People with the "one people" referred to in Jefferson's Declaration would exclude Africans, native peoples, and some European immigrants from citizenship.[31]

We could simply identify the People with "the governed," but this is also problematic. The governed consist of subjects and citizens, the latter being a proper subset of the former. The notion of "a subject" here is not, of course, the classical one of someone who is *subjugated* to another; a subject in this formal sense is merely someone *subject to* the laws of a state or polity. Foreigners, whether residing or just passing through, are subjects but not citizens. Normally, one might identify the People with the set of full members, that is, citizens. But this is not always plausible. Certainly, it would not have been prior to "universal suffrage." In the case of states or empires which have colonies or which govern "subjected peoples," many subjects would not have the status of membership. In some other states, there may be many more nonmember residents than citizens. Independently of what we think of the justice of the case, identifying the People with the set of citizens yields rather nonpopulist implications in the instance of Kuwait, Monaco, Israel (including the West Bank and Gaza), Germany, or classical democratic Athens. Additionally, especially in an increasingly interdependent world, there are third parties, neither citizens nor subjects, whose lives are affected in important ways by the decisions of states. Simply excluding them by fiat, by identifying the People with citizens or subjects, is question-begging.

Political theorists often appear to assume that individuating Peoples or even societies is not problematic. John Rawls, for instance, assumes that societies are easily individuated.[32] But what exactly is the justification for attributing unity to sets or networks of people interacting in a particular

[30] See Avishai Margalit and Joseph Raz, "National Self-Determination," *Journal of Philosophy* 87, no. 9 (September 1990): 439–61.

[31] Recall Jefferson's cry against "these unfeeling brethren," deaf to "the voice of justice and consanguinity," who sent over "not only souldiers of our common blood, but Scotch & foreign mercenaries." Scotch and German, presumably, were alien and could not easily join the "one people" Jefferson is thinking of.

[32] Recently Rawls has characterized the basic structure of a society as "a society's main political, social, and economic institutions, and how they fit together into one unified system of social cooperation from one generation to the next." Rawls, *Political Liberalism* (New York: Columbia University Press, 1993), 11. In *A Theory of Justice*, Rawls restricts his attentions to a society "conceived for the time being as a closed system isolated from other societies," and he assumes that "the boundaries of these schemes are given by the notion of a self-contained

geographical space? In most cases, where the geographical setting is not saliently one and distinct—where it is not, for example, an island—or where the individuals do not evidently constitute a single people or nation, the attribution of unity to "the society" seems question-begging.[33] We need to be careful here lest we transfer to societies (or to particular sets of individuals) some of the features that are characteristic of modern states. It is interesting to notice that when we talk of "a society" there is implicit individuation in the designation. The U.S. or Italy, for instance, are supposed to be societies in this sense, but Europe or North America are not. But what makes a society *one*, a unified social entity? The unity that we tend to attribute to societies or to Peoples may be genuine; but when it is, it may be *political* and a consequence and artifact of the political form of organization, namely, its state. The examples of Italy and the U.S., just cited, are cases in point.[34]

I have argued that it is hard to see how the People could be sovereign, at least on my account of sovereignty. Additionally, it is difficult to see how Peoples are to be individuated independently of states. If their identification is not prior to and independent of the existence of their states, then the People's sovereignty cannot be constitutive of states. The sense in which the People, or the subjects of a realm, may be sovereign must be some other than the notion I have analyzed. Determining the sovereignty of the People seems to be considerably more complex than determining the sovereignty of states. What I shall suggest is that many different theses are expressed, usually misleadingly, by appeals to popular sovereignty. Disentangling and evaluating these, however, is a rather complicated affair.

III. "We the People" Reconsidered

Appeals to the People's sovereignty, I shall suggest, may express half a dozen or more claims. All may be expressed or articulated in other ways, without making use of the notion of sovereignty. Only some of these claims are plausible. However, my primary efforts will be analytical—namely, to distinguish and clarify these different claims. I shall suggest

---

national community." See Rawls, *A Theory of Justice* (Cambridge, MA: Harvard University Press, 1971), 8, 457.

[33] Even with islands, attributing unity may not be warranted (e.g., Ireland or England).

[34] Michael Mann's comparative and historical sociology is based on the assumption that *societies* are not unitary. He urges us to think of them instead "as confederal, overlapping, intersecting networks"; they are "constituted of multiple overlapping and intersecting sociospatial networks of power." Mann, *The Sources of Social Power*, vol. 1 (Cambridge: Cambridge University Press, 1986), 16, 1 (italics omitted). David Copp offers an account of society which allows societies to overlap considerably and to be nested within one another; see his *Morality, Normativity, and Society* (New York: Oxford University Press, 1995), ch. 7. While his account makes societies less unitary than most, it still seems to apply most problematically to medieval Europe.

that popular sovereignty may express a number of different ideas or ideals, some more closely related than others.

The first idea expressed by popular sovereignty is simple and, today, commonplace. It is the idea that the ends of a polity should be determined by the interests or desires of its members.[35] It is assumed as well that membership should be accorded to the great majority of permanent inhabitants of the realm. Calls for popular sovereignty in France in the late eighteenth century may be understood as demands that full membership (i.e., citizenship) be accorded all (male) inhabitants and that the interests of all citizens be considered in determining the ends of the polity.

The legitimate scope allowed citizens in determining the ends of the polity may not be as great as many have thought; I consider this question below. The question here is the narrow one of whether policy is to be determined by considering the interests of the ruling class or the interests of all. Classical "sovereigns" (i.e., monarchs) and governing elites considered the realm *theirs*—the king's "estate"[36]—and thus would not have thought of including the interests of all, except instrumentally, in the ends of the polity. This (and full membership) is precisely the demand of the spokesmen of the People toward the end of the eighteenth century.

The proposal to include the interests of all of the members of the polity has not been contested for a long time. Even tyrannical regimes that rarely or never consult the People attempt to justify their rule by populist claims. The view that the interests of all should determine the ends of the state is commonplace today. We forget that it was once a radical and controversial proposal.

This idea, that state policy be governed by the interests of all, is tied to various ideas about popular involvement in government, the scope of the People's authority, and the conditions for the determination or aggregation of the public interest to which I briefly alluded. These we shall consider later. The second idea that I wish to discuss is the model of political *authorization* that is implicit in popular sovereignty. It is a "bottom-up" conception of authorization. Government has authority (i.e., is permitted or has the right) to act only insofar as it is so authorized, and this authorization must come from the People governed. In earlier times, authority or the right to rule came from above, as it were; rulers in Christendom often were thought to derive their (just) powers from God. The station and duties of the governed were similarly determined. This model of authorization is "top-down." Note that both conceptions are hierarchical; they differ simply in reversing the direction of authorization:

---

[35] I shall not, for the most part, distinguish between 'interests', 'desires', 'preferences', and their cognates. But I should warn that a more complete treatment of these issues requires such distinctions.

[36] "L'État c'est à moi" ("The state is mine"), as Louis XIV might have said. See Herbert H. Rowen, "'L'État c'est à Moi': Louis XIV and the State," *French Historical Studies* 2, no. 1 (Spring 1961): 83–98.

Top-Down	Bottom-Up
Ruler(s)	Ruler(s)
⇓	⇑
People	People

The "bottom-up" model of authorization emerges at the same time as skepticism about the idea that some are "born to rule," entitled to rule by nature. This claim, often associated with the aristocratic classes, ceases to be plausible. The assertions of human equality in the writings of, say, Hobbes, Locke, and Jefferson must be understood (primarily) as denials of these classical claims of aristocracies to rule by virtue of their birth.[37] The thesis of human equality, so understood, is a negative claim, and it effectively sets a condition for acceptable accounts of political authority: rulers must obtain their right to rule from the governed. As sympathetic as Hobbes was to the cause of monarchs and absolute sovereigns, he is one with most modern theorists on this point; for him the governed must authorize their ruler.[38]

With the realization that no one is entitled by birth to rule, it is very natural to come to think of rulers as *agents* of the ruled. Much of modern political theory is an attempt to explicate the appropriate agency relations, as well as to address the age-old problems of "agent and principal." The bottom-up model may suggest an agency conception of political authority.[39] Locke understands the relation to be one of *trust*, establishing a fiduciary relationship.[40] We take such ideas for granted today, as few contest them. Our complacency here should not lead us to forget that they are part of what early proponents of popular sovereignty struggled to express.

The thesis that the interests or wishes of all should determine the ends of the polity (constrained by justice), and the bottom-up model of autho-

---

[37] Locke is especially clear that this is his point. See his *Second Treatise of Government* [1690], in his *Two Treatises of Government*, ed. Peter Laslett (Cambridge: Cambridge University Press, 1988), sections 4, 54.

[38] It was the limits of the sovereign's power, apparently inherent, as required by this bottom-up model of authorization, which led Bishop Bramhall to understand *Leviathan* as "a Rebell's Catechism." See Jean Hampton's interesting discussion in *Hobbes and the Social Contract Tradition* (Cambridge: Cambridge University Press, 1986), 197–207.

[39] See Hampton, *Hobbes and the Social Contract Tradition*, chs. 8–9; and Hampton, *Political Philosophy* (Boulder, CO: Westview Press, 1996), chs. 2–3. "The service conception" of political authorities is what Raz calls the view that "their role and primary normal function is to serve the governed"; see Raz, *The Morality of Freedom*, 55–67.

[40] Locke, *Second Treatise of Government*, sections 149, 156, 221, 240. A trust sets an *end* to be pursued, e.g., the preservation of members (their life, liberty, and property) (section 171), establishes a *responsibility* of the trustee, giving the latter certain discretion (sections 159–68). Unlike a contract, however, the trust need not benefit, the trust is revokable without injury to the trustee, and the settlor (the creator of the trust) may be the sole judge (section 240). See A. John Simmons, *On the Edge of Anarchy: Locke, Consent, and the Limits of Society* (Princeton: Princeton University Press, 1993), 68–72.

rization, are ideas worth retaining. I do not wish to challenge them, even if the precision with which I have expressed them leaves much to be desired and more to be said. These two elements of popular sovereignty seem worth retaining. The same may not be true of the remaining ideas or theses expressed by appeals to popular sovereignty.

Jefferson famously asserts that to secure our rights "governments are instituted among men, deriving their just powers from the consent of the governed." Part of what he undoubtedly expressed thereby was the idea of bottom-up authorization that I have just discussed. He is often interpreted as putting forward another thesis as well, one commonly associated with Locke: the thesis of *political consensualism*, which holds that the consent of the governed is necessary for legitimate rule. This is the third thesis that I associate with the assertion of popular sovereignty.

If, in the past, we may have been rather casual with the notion of consent and of related ideas of agreement, it is harder to do so today. The contemporary literature makes evident a number of distinctions that are required for clarity on these issues. Genuine consent is an engagement of the will. It must involve a deliberate and effective communication of an intention to bring about a change in one's normative status (one's rights or obligations).[41] There are varieties of consent, the most important in this context being *express* (direct and explicit) and *tacit* or *implied* (indirect).[42] Political consensualism would thus express the thesis that express or tacit consent is required for legitimate authority. The "will" of the People is a condition of legitimate rule.

Political consensualism today has many rivals. It is not a commonplace, at least once we make the distinctions mentioned and understand it correctly. While virtually no one today claims that someone's rule is legitimated by his or her birth, many claim that the *nature* and *quality* of rule may legitimate it: good government may be self-legitimating. Some utilitarian and, more generally, consequentialist theories may hold that political authorities are legitimated by the beneficial consequences of their

[41] My formulation is a paraphrase of Simmons's characterization; see his *On the Edge of Anarchy*, 69–70. See also Raz, *The Morality of Freedom*, 80–94. These distinctions are not clear in Hobbes's work, since his account of the will is eliminativist, reducing intention to the desires that immediately precede action (see *Leviathan*, ch. 6).

[42] Hypothetical consent is not, however, a type of consent. This point must be stressed, as it is not always recognized. See Raz, *Morality of Freedom*, 81n. ("Theories of hypothetical consent discuss not consent but cognitive agreement"); Christopher Morris, "The Relation of Self-Interest and Justice in Contractarian Ethics," *Social Philosophy and Policy* 5, no. 2 (Spring 1988): 121–22; Morris, "A Contractarian Account of Moral Justification," in *Moral Knowledge? New Readings in Moral Epistemology*, ed. W. Sinnott-Armstrong and M. Timmons (New York: Oxford University Press, 1996), 219–20; Gerald F. Gaus, *Value and Justification* (New York: Cambridge University Press, 1990), 19, 328; and Simmons, *On the Edge of Anarchy*, 78–79, where Simmons writes that hypothetical contract theory bases "our duties or obligations not on anyone's actual choices, but on whether our governments (states, laws) are sufficiently just, good, useful, or responsive to secure the hypothetical support of ideal choosers. . . . [T]he 'contract' in hypothetical contractarianism is simply a device that permits us to analyze in a certain way quality of government. . . ."

rule. Similarly, other accounts may determine legitimate authority by the level and distribution of benefits. Certain contractarian or conventionalist theories may accord legitimacy to political arrangements that are mutually beneficial in certain ways. For none of these accounts is consent necessary, and on some it may not be sufficient either. Consensualism, in this sense, is merely one of many ways of developing the bottom-up conception of authorization.[43]

This is not the occasion to evaluate political consensualism, since the issues, especially in moral theory, are very complex.[44] I do not, in fact, endorse it, so I should not want to counsel acceptance of this thesis of popular sovereignty. At the least, it would assist clarity not to express consensualist theses by using the notion of popular sovereignty. I am not sure that classical partisans of the People were very clear about these issues. I note in this respect an emerging consensus in the literature that political consensualism can only with great difficulty, if at all, escape "philosophical anarchism," the thesis that no political authority in fact is justified.[45] Certainly this was not intended by early proponents of popular sovereignty.

Proponents of "participatory democracy," who think that democracy requires active citizen participation in governance, as well as many republicans, who worry about the corrupting influence of commerce, might deny the *sufficiency* of consent for legitimacy. And some such theorists have understood claims of popular sovereignty (e.g., by Rousseau) to imply an activist or participatory conception of governance.[46] The second element of "government of the people, by the people, and for the people" may be understood to require something more than mere consent. Democracy, it may be argued, is *self-rule*, and only the active involvement of citizens can ensure this. The fourth claim to be associated with popular sovereignty might then be these familiar calls for activist or participatory governance.

[43] The works cited by Leslie Green (in note 6) and John Simmons (in notes 40 and 45) are representative of contemporary consensualism; see also Robert Nozick, *Anarchy, State, and Utopia* (New York: Basic Books, 1974). Utilitarian or more generally consequentialist positions are commonplace. The best examples of mutual-advantage contractarian and conventionalist accounts, respectively, are probably the classical theories of Hobbes and Hume. Some very useful distinctions are drawn by David Schmidtz in his essay "Justifying the State," *Ethics* 101, no. 1 (October 1990): 89–102.

[44] For instance, do our basic or fundamental (moral) rights protect *choices* or *interests*?

[45] Philosophical anarchism, it should be noted, seems to be the dominant position in the contemporary literature. For those not familiar with recent discussions, I might note that the position is compatible with the view that most people, most of the time, have reason to obey just laws (but not necessarily the sorts of reasons the law claims). See, for instance, A. John Simmons, *Moral Principles and Political Obligations* (Princeton: Princeton University Press, 1979), ch. 8; and Green, *The Authority of the State*, chs. 8–9. I think as well that some states can be legitimate even if their claimed authority is not justified and their subjects' obligations are considerably less extensive than they assert (see my *Essay on the Modern State*, chs. 7 and 10).

[46] If sovereignty is inalienable, then popular sovereignty may require, as Rousseau argued, participation in governance.

Recall my substantive claim earlier that while it is possible for something to have authority without possessing any (non-normative) power or without being able to impose sanctions for disobedience, it may be that *political* authority cannot be *justified* if it is not, to some extent, effective. Effectiveness, for most political regimes, may require some capacity for imposing sanctions. On this view, justified political authority requires political *power*, understood as a *de facto* ability to influence or to control events (e.g., by imposing sanctions). I mentioned earlier that this thesis is substantive, for it depends on the reasons for which political authorities are desirable. Now if we retain this substantive thesis and want to make the People the ultimate source of political authority, then some sort of activist or participatory conception of popular rule may be required. For authority will be popular only if power is to a considerable degree popular. But I am skeptical that the requisite institutional forms for the required efficacy of *popular* rule can be established, at least in large, anonymous societies such as the U.S. It may not be possible even to establish the institutions necessary for effective *state* rule.[47]

Now one should not understand the rejection of activist or participatory popular rule to imply a denial of a right to rebel against tyranny or to overthrow illegitimate government. In fact, the medieval doctrines of popular resistance against tyrants, to which modern partisans of popular sovereignty appealed, defended something like a right to rebel.[48] The modern doctrine may be associated with medieval opposition to the Pauline prescription of non-resistance to tyrants. Now we can perfectly well accept the (moral) right of rebellion while denying that a more active participation in government is required. In medieval and early modern times, some argued that subjects *always* had an obligation not to rebel against their rulers.[49] Some today interpret popular sovereignty as nothing more than the denial of the thesis that it is never right to rebel.[50] But if all that is expressed by popular sovereignty is the right to overthrow tyrants, then not much is claimed. It is unclear why we need to make use of an important and complex classical notion in order to express this; it would be better simply to say what we mean.

[47] This is a complicated, and possibly controversial, matter. See my *Essay on the Modern State*, ch. 7.

[48] See Quentin Skinner, *The Foundations of Modern Political Thought*, 2 vols. (Cambridge: Cambridge University Press, 1978).

[49] I formulate the thesis in terms of an obligation not to rebel, rather than a right to rebel, for several reasons. First, the right to rebel cannot, without great difficulty, be a legal right. (What is rebellion? If it is the overthrow of the constitutional order, *that* order cannot authorize it. Cf. Kant's problems with a right to revolution in "On the Common Saying: 'This May Be True in Theory, but It Does Not Apply in Practice'" [1793], and in *The Metaphysical Elements of the Theory of Right* [1797], both in Immanuel Kant, *Political Writings*, 2d ed., ed. H. Reiss [Cambridge: Cambridge University Press, 1991], esp. 81–83, 143–47.) Secondly, someone like Hobbes could not make sense of a claim-right to rebel, though he could make room for the dissolution of the obligation not to rebel.

[50] See Charles Beitz, "Sovereignty and Morality in International Affairs," in *Political Theory Today*, ed. David Held (Stanford: Stanford University Press, 1991), 236n.

These participatory and activist claims are familiar to anyone acquainted with contemporary political theory. They merit serious study and reflection. I should like to suggest only that one need not be committed to them by acceptance of the first two elements of popular sovereignty—the inclusive understanding of the public interest and the bottom-up view of authorization. An activist or participatory understanding of popular rule may have much to be said for it, but it cannot plausibly be claimed to be entailed by the first two theses associated with popular sovereignty. Additionally, one might want to argue that republican and participatory ideals of self-rule, however admirable, may not be particularly well-suited for contemporary societies and temperaments. It is not clear why political activism must be an aim of all or even most adults in our large impersonal societies; in normal times, many politically inactive ends may be more fulfilling for most individuals. For now let me merely assert that this activist or participatory thesis is not necessarily part of popular sovereignty. As I said, however, there is much more to be said about the (more important) question of the merits of this view.

The claim to popular sovereignty may merely assert the People's right to intervene occasionally in governance (e.g., through popular referenda). Aside from extraordinary powers of *constituting* a state and its government,[51] the People may retain extraordinary powers, as Locke believed, to alter the state and its constitution. The latter is the thesis recently defended regarding the American system by the legal scholar Akhil Amar. He argues that the fifth article of the U.S. Constitution (governing the amendment process) should be read as permitting popular revision:

> My proposition is that We the People of the United States—more specifically, a majority of voters—retain an unenumerated, constitutional right to alter our Government and revise our Constitution in a way not explicitly set out in Article V. Specifically, I believe that Congress would be obliged to call a convention to propose revisions if a majority of American voters so petition; and that an amendment or new Constitution could be lawfully ratified by a simple majority of the American electorate.[52]

I take no stand on the question of the interpretation of the U.S. Constitution and the matter of its amendment. I agree with Amar and others that one cannot understand the origins of the American constitutional order without reference to late-eighteenth-century debates about sover-

[51] As Jefferson famously asserted in the Declaration: "[W]henever any form of government becomes destructive of these ends, it is the right of the people to alter or abolish it. . . ." See also Locke, *Second Treatise of Government*, sections 149, 212–16, 220, 221, and 240.

[52] Amar, "The Consent of the Governed," 459. See also Amar, "Of Sovereignty and Federalism."

eignty.[53] But I have three worries about this sort of view. The first is that many of the arguments for popular sovereignty in the early American context were poor. Invariably they depended on assuming that "there is and must be in all of [the several forms of government]" a sovereign, that relations of authority had to form a continuous hierarchy (or strict ordering), or that sovereignty had to be indivisible.[54] But all of these assumptions are mistaken. It is not the case that a sovereign (of the sort envisaged) is in fact necessary—American political society is a case in point—and sovereignty can be divided.[55]

My second worry is that this sort of understanding of popular sovereignty makes it into a kind of *occasionalism*: the People intervene only occasionally in governance. At the very least, it is odd to express this sort of view in terms of a notion like that of sovereignty. Consider the following theological analogy: when eighteenth-century natural philosophers suggested that the Deity intervened in the natural order only to set the whole mechanism going, most believers considered this a diminution of his powers (and considered the suggestion heretical). Sovereignty is diminished considerably, I should have thought, if the body that holds it can exercise it only occasionally.[56] And this is related to my third worry:

---

[53] I rely on Wood's account here:

> Confrontation with the Blackstonian concept of legal sovereignty had forced American theorists to relocate it in the people-at-large, a transference that was comprehensible only because of the peculiar experience of American politics. . . . Only a proper understanding of this vital principle of the sovereignty of the people could make federalism intelligible. . . .

See Wood, *The Creation of the American Republic*, 599–600 (see also 545–47, and earlier references). A more thorough treatment of these questions would have to address Bruce Ackerman's account of the American tradition; see his *We the People: Foundations* (Cambridge, MA: Harvard University Press, 1991), and his *We the People: Transformations* (Cambridge, MA: Harvard University Press, 1998).

[54] Consider James Wilson's argument at the Pennsylvania ratifying convention:

> There necessarily exists, in every government, a power from which there is no appeal, and which, for that reason, may be termed supreme, absolute, and uncontrollable. . . . The truth is, that, in our governments, the supreme, absolute, and uncontrollable power *remains* in the people. As our constitutions are superior to our legislatures, so the people are superior to our constitutions. . . .

Quoted by Amar, "The Consent of the Governed," 474. Garry Wills claims that Wilson was strongly influenced by Rousseau's *Social Contract*; see Wills, "James Wilson's New Meaning for Sovereignty," in *Conceptual Change and the Constitution*, ed. Terence Ball and J. G. A. Pocock (Lawrence: University of Kansas Press, 1988), 100.

[55] Or so I argue elsewhere; see my *Essay on the Modern State*, ch. 7.

[56] An (or the) "ultimate" power may also mean something like "determining in special circumstances." For instance, Carl Schmitt famously attributes sovereignty to whomever decides in exceptional circumstances ("*Souverän ist, wer über den Ausnahmezustand entschneidet*"); see Schmitt, *Théologie politique* [1922], trans. Jean-Louis Schlegel (Paris: Gallimard, 1988), 15. This is, to borrow Karl Löwith's term, a species of "occasional decisionism"; see ch. 2 of his *Martin Heidegger and European Nihilism* [1984], ed. Richard Wolin (New York: Columbia University Press, 1995).

It is not obvious that the body that has the greatest say in special circumstances has sovereignty. For it need not be that the body that determines what happens, for instance, occasionalism, if expressed in the language of sovereignty and "ultimate" authority, suggests a very misleading conception of politics, social order, and political authority. There is considerable fluidity and indeterminacy in political life, even in stable, well-ordered polities. And the very features that allow for accommodation and conciliation are threatened by the hierarchical conception of authority and power (implicitly) defended by fans of sovereignty. I shall say more about this in Section IV.

What I called political consensualism—the thesis that political authority is legitimate only if based on consent—should be distinguished from what may be called *political voluntarism*. This view understands political authority to be *will-based*. What unites theorists like Hobbes, Rousseau, and many members of the German idealist tradition is an understanding of political authority as emanating from a will.[57] Political voluntarism is the counterpart for political authority and may be understood as another thesis, the fifth, implicit in many claims of popular sovereignty.

Political voluntarism is not the same as what I called political consensualism, the view that the consent of the governed is necessary for legitimate rule. The latter is an account of the legitimate authority of a state or polity, whereas the former concerns the nature and "sources" of (authoritative) law. Voluntarism requires that genuine law emanate from the will of some individual or collective; the law's normative status requires that it be determined by a decision or choice. While many political consensualists are also political voluntarists, they need not be. One could require consent for the legitimacy of a political order that determined law in some will-independent manner (e.g., natural law). Just as acceptance of a bottom-up model of authorization does not commit one to consensualism, so the latter does not commit one to what I have called political voluntarism.

We are familiar with will-based accounts of morality (e.g., divine-will theories, Kant). Such accounts of the right have long had to face the Euthyphro problem (is something good or obligatory because it is willed, or is it so willed because it is good or obligatory?). One answer divine-will theorists can give stresses God's goodness; he could but would not choose to will what would be bad for us.[58] Rousseau's account similarly

---

when social order breaks down is the same one that decides matters in other circumstances. It is as if 'ultimate' here means something like "when all else fails," and this is thought to secure some reduction ("it all comes down to . . .").

[57] As I said earlier, Hobbes's view of the will reduces it to desire. Rousseau's general will may be best interpreted as both moral and political; morality consequently, at least in the *Social Contract*, is will-based. For the German idealist tradition, see G. W. F. Hegel, *Elements of the Philosophy of Right* [1820], ed. Allen W. Wood, trans. H. B. Nisbet (Cambridge: Cambridge University Press, 1991); and Bernard Bosanquet, *The Philosophical Theory of the State* [1923], 4th ed. (London: Macmillan, 1965).

[58] See Robert Merrihew Adams, "A Modified Divine Command Theory of Ethical Wrongness" [1973], in *Divine Commands and Morality*, ed. Paul Helm (New York: Oxford University Press, 1981), 83–108.

solves the problem of the sovereign willing what is not in our interests.[59] But will-based systems of right without formal or material constraints are dangerous. At the least, it is hard to see how they could be made to sustain the law's claims on us.

It is worth considering here Leibniz's criticism of Hobbes's theory. On Hobbes's unusual (but not surprising) account of God's authority, it would be God's "irresistible power" that is the source of his rule over us.[60] Rejecting "gunmen" accounts of law and obligation, we may be more inclined to recognize God's sovereignty by considering his competence and benevolence. Criticizing Hobbes, Leibniz concludes that "Hobbesian empires"

> exist neither among civilized peoples nor among barbarians, and I consider them neither possible nor desirable, unless those who must have supreme power are gifted with angelic virtues. For men will choose to follow their own will, and will consult their own welfare as seems best to them, as long as they are not persuaded of the supreme wisdom and capability of their rulers, which things are necessary for perfect resignation of the will. So Hobbes' demonstrations have a place only in that state whose king is God, whom alone one can trust in all things.[61]

Leviathan, "that *Mortall God*," lacking God's competence and benevolence, will not possess authority over us. Classical sovereignty effectively demands "perfect resignation of the will," and Leibniz saw clearly that Hobbes's story is credible "only in that state whose king is God, whom *alone* one can trust in all things" (emphasis added). Only a being with God's competence and benevolence could command that sort of authority. Similarly, the People's will, lacking the Deity's competence and benevolence, and possibly even less well informed than the will of Hobbes's Mortall God, could not plausibly possess the authority attributed to it by fans of popular sovereignty, at least in the absence of the (genuine) consent of all.[62]

---

[59] Rousseau, *Social Contract*, Book II, ch. 3, 371 ("*la volonté générale est toujours droite et tend toujours à l'utilité publique*").

[60] "The right of Nature, whereby God reigneth over men, and punisheth those that break his Lawes, is to be derived, not from his Creating them as if he required obedience, as of Gratitude for his benefits; but from his *Irresistible Power*." Hobbes, *Leviathan*, ch. 31, 246.

[61] G. W. Leibniz, *Caesarinus Fürstenerius (De Suprematu Principum Germaniae)* [1677], in *The Political Writings of Leibniz*, 2d ed., ed. Patrick Riley (Cambridge: Cambridge University Press, 1988), 120.

[62] James Wilson and others may well have wanted to apply Rousseau's account of popular sovereignty to the American federal state, but this is likely to be a doomed undertaking. The conditions for the existence of a general will are very unlikely to obtain in large or pluralistic polities. The choice set for large contemporary states is likely, on this interpretation, to be empty.

I shall say no more about political voluntarism as such. It is a very controversial position, and one could not do justice to it in a short space. But, again, if this is the core of popular sovereignty, then clarity would be better served by abandoning talk of sovereignty and using another term.

The sixth thesis that may be associated with popular sovereignty has to do with the unlimited or relatively unconstrained nature of (legitimate) political authority. It is this thesis that may be the most interesting and the most controversial. It has been claimed by many, especially in modern times, that political authority is unlimited. Just as Hobbes sought absolute authority for monarchs, so Blackstone attributed the same to the trinitarian British "King in Parliament" ("It can, in short, do every thing that is not naturally impossible . . ."). Allowances being made for excesses of rhetoric, we may read Blackstone's statement as endorsing a conception of sovereignty as unlimited, unconstrained by law and perhaps by justice itself.[63] Such an account is hostile to most constitutional government, at least of the American sort, where lawmakers are constrained by law, both procedurally and substantively.

Some contemporary theorists of the left seem to want to attribute similarly unlimited powers to the People. Adam Przeworski and Michael Wallerstein, for instance, seem to endorse some such view:

> People, by whom we mean individuals acting on the bases of their current preferences, are collectively sovereign only if the alternatives open to them as a collectivity are constrained only by conditions independent of anyone's will. Specifically, people are sovereign to the extent that they can alter the existing institutions, including the state and property, and if they can allocate available resources to all feasible uses.[64]

At the very least, Przeworski and Wallerstein seem to be endorsing a view of sovereignty as unlimited or at least as unconstrained, say, by natural or prior rights (especially to private property).

These claims about the unlimited nature of popular authority can easily be confused with a thesis about the *comprehensive* nature of legal authority. The law, Joseph Raz thinks, claims comprehensive authority in claiming authority to regulate any type of behavior. Something's claim to authority is *comprehensive*, in this sense, when there are no limits to the

---

[63] Gareth Jones, the editor of the edition of Blackstone's *Commentaries* I have cited (in note 15), notes that it is "impossible to reconcile Blackstone's ideas about natural (absolute) rights which no human law could contradict, with his conception of a sovereign" (xxxviii).

[64] Adam Przeworski and Michael Wallerstein, "Popular Sovereignty, State Autonomy, and Private Property," *Archives européennes de sociologie* 27 (1986): 215.

range of actions which it claims to regulate.[65] The comprehensiveness of political authority is a claim concerning its *scope*, concerning the *range of actions* which it claims authority to regulate. To claim that political authority is comprehensive is to assert a normative thesis. The same is true of the thesis of the supremacy of political authority. A political authority is *supreme* in this sense if it (rightly) claims the right to regulate all other normative systems of rules within its realm.[66] There are several senses, then, in which a political authority may be held to be "unlimited." It may be unlimited with regard to the range of actions which it claims authority to regulate, and with regard to competing sources of authority. It may also be unlimited, in a different sense, regarding the type of reasons it claims to issue.

I said earlier that authority is a reason-giving relation. What sorts of reasons do authorities claim to issue? These reasons are supposed to preempt, in a special sense, all other authorities. We may, following Raz and others, understand the reasons provided by authoritative directives to be *preemptive* in a special sense: they are meant to exclude and to take the place of some other reasons. Such reasons are *content-independent*; they provide reasons by virtue of being authoritative directives, not by virtue of what they direct people to do.[67]

The supremacy of a political authority and the preemptive nature of its reasons need not be understood to mean that it is *absolute* in another sense. We can say that a reason is *absolute* in this sense if and only if there cannot be another reason which would override it. An authoritative directive would be absolute in this sense if and only if there could be no reason which would override it. This might be yet another sense in which a political authority might be unlimited.[68]

Constitutional states, as well as others, usually understand their authority to be limited or not absolute in the above sense.[69] But the supremacy of the state's authority is compatible with its being limited. The state's authority may have limits, constitutional and customary, but these limits are those recognized by the state; that is, all but only those limits recog-

---

[65] Raz, *Practical Reason and Norms*, 150–51; Green, *The Authority of the State*, 83–84. If sovereignty is unlimited, then it is unconstrained legally (and morally?). This will entail that it is *comprehensive* in Raz's sense: it claims authority to regulate any type of behavior (in addition to the above, see Raz, *The Morality of Freedom*, 76–77, where most states are said to claim unlimited authority). Note that a state may be limited (or non-absolute) and yet retain the claim to comprehensive authority.

[66] Raz claims that this feature of legal systems is entailed by their comprehensive natures; see his *Practical Reason and Norms*, 151–52.

[67] Moral reasons are supposed to be preemptive but not, presumably, content-independent.

[68] Although Hobbes sometimes suggests that the monarch's authority is absolute in this sense, even he is probably not best interpreted as endorsing this consequence. For reason may sometimes advise against obeying a sovereign—for example, when the latter is threatening one's life. While Hobbes may deny us natural claim-rights, he does think we retain an inalienable (Hohfeldian) liberty.

[69] The mere fact of being a system may impose limits on the law. See, for instance, Raz, *The Authority of Law*, 111–15.

nized by the state are held to be legitimate. Its authoritative directives may be overridden, so they are not absolute; but the only considerations that may override them are those determined by the state.[70]

Just as it is implausible to think that the *state's* authority might be comprehensive and supreme—much less unlimited or absolute—so it is not plausible to think the same of the People's *authority*. If the People's authority is supreme in our sense, then it has the right to determine the authoritativeness of conscience and—to return to old debates—the Church (or churches). It would have, as well, the right to regulate the authority of the community and of national groups to which individuals might belong. External sources of authority, such as the European Union, would have authority only insofar as the People were to recognize them. Is that really plausible? Note that the People's authority in states such as the U.S. is constrained by law and by the fundamental rights of individuals. The former refers to the *legal* constraints imposed on the People's right to remove their leaders or change the Constitution, the latter to the rights of the American Bill of Rights.[71] Given these implications, many will not find the People's claim to supreme authority here credible. And modern moralists who understand the scope of justice to be universal to all humans or all persons should also find this claim hard to accept.[72]

The problem with the People's claim to comprehensive authority is similar. In both cases, too much is claimed. The People's authority, like that of the state, is limited in ways that neither wishes to admit. Their authority, in fact, is piecemeal and contextual. And this conflicts with their self-image.[73]

IV. CONCLUDING REMARKS ON POLITICAL POWER AND GOVERNANCE

The idea of the People's sovereignty turns out to be, at best, a rather complex notion. Debates about the notion are quite muddled. Part of the problem is that sovereignty turns out to be a cluster-concept, made of several elements, some of them easily confused. (Consider only the ambiguities of terms like 'ultimate' or 'absolute'.) Disambiguating these elements and distinguishing different theses can alleviate much of the confusion. But I think that many partisans of popular sovereignty may be

[70] Ibid., 30–31; Raz, *The Morality of Freedom*, 77; Green, *The Authority of the State*, 83.

[71] Amar would recognize that only majorities can commit the People to a constitutional change or a change of leadership, but perhaps this constraint is not specifically a legal one.

[72] Even contractarians and moral conventionalists who deny the universality of justice may find these claims made on behalf of Peoples implausible.

[73] Perhaps appeals to popular sovereignty are intended to express merely that the state is, in some sense, *ours*. A more thorough treatment of the topic would consider an interesting thesis put forward by Jean Hampton: "What is distinctive about modern democracies is that their structure explicitly recognizes that political power and authority are the people's creation." See Hampton, *Political Philosophy* (Boulder, CO: Westview Press, 1997), 105.

attracted to certain classical ideals of order and authority, and these may be unrealizable. The conditions for *anything's* sovereignty, classical or limited, are hard to realize in any social setting. The essential problem is that the conditions for a sovereign—a highest, final, and supreme political and legal authority (and power)—are unlikely to obtain, at least in any large society or state.[74] Attributing sovereignty to Peoples does not alleviate the problem in the slightest way.

The persisting thought that sovereignty must rest *somewhere* may motivate many who think it must be attributed to Peoples. This thought often betrays a certain pyramidal picture of political authority and power which is very misleading. The relations of political authority in most societies are unlikely to constitute a hierarchy of direct rule. Typically, political order is not the product of the sort of determinate, hierarchical system presupposed by various notions of sovereignty. Rather, it is usually the result of a combination of many different things: force, fear, hope, acquiescence, habit, adjustment, agreement, loyalty, coordination, and the like. Stable social orders are those where most people, most of the time, have reasons to act in ways that support and maintain the system. But the variety and combinations of reasons that support a stable system can be large. One should not think, as so many political thinkers have, that social order depends on all, or even most, people acting on particular kinds of reasons—for instance, authoritative directives.

Consider the pluralism and diversity of many contemporary societies, where significant numbers of people differ on a significant number of important political or social issues. Many contemporary American philosophers hold out the hope that it may be possible to forge agreement on certain fundamental principles, even in the absence of a consensus on so-called "conceptions of the good" or "comprehensive doctrines." But it is not even clear that these very distinctions—between conceptions of the good and principles of justice or conceptions of political authority—as well as related distinctions between "public" and "private" concerns, can elicit agreement. Alternatively, consider what I think we characteristically do when faced with seemingly intractable differences or disagreements. Usually, we avoid or fudge the question as long as possible (e.g., assisted suicide, abortion in the U.S. before *Roe*). The doctrine that what the state (or the law) or the People determine is in fact authoritative is not credible here, even in legalistic political cultures such as the U.S. or statist ones such as France. And this may be just as well. We can often get by, and do quite well, without the state or the People "determining once and for all" what ought to be done on certain matters. Sometimes it is better to avoid confronting an issue, especially if the main alternative is to fight.

People not infrequently use force and attempt to impose their will on others, as we all know. Equally important, however, they also compro-

---

[74] See my *Essay on the Modern State*, ch. 7.

mise and accommodate. Social order is maintained in each of these ways, and the commanding picture of society as a smooth hierarchy of authority and power relations is very misleading. In the conditions of the modern world, we may very well need states and governments. But they do not conform to their self-images ("there is and must be in all of [the several forms of government] a supreme, irresistible, absolute, uncontrolled authority"). It turns out we can do without the state's sovereignty.[75] I believe that the sovereignty of the People is not needed either.

The confusions about actual authority and power implicit in most doctrines of sovereignty are misleading and potentially dangerous. They are especially dangerous if they are conjoined with *majoritarianism*. The latter is, very roughly, the view that policy and law ought to be determined by *simple* majorities. Contrary to what once might have been believed by some contemporary partisans of popular sovereignty, majoritarianism is not self-evident.[76] Certainly, the mathematical properties of simple majority decision principles do not translate easily into a plausible defense of majoritarianism.[77] There is the argument that other voting rules allow for minority veto and thus are wrong or unjust; but this, in most discussions, simply begs the question. Additionally, such a view would threaten all basic or fundamental rights, for these are vetoes of sorts.[78]

We may think instead of majoritarianism as the view that *permissible* collective choices—i.e., those not unjust or forbidden for other reasons— ought to be determined by simple majorities. On this view majorities determine policy or law when, for instance, basic or fundamental rights are not at stake. I am skeptical that issues of justice (e.g., rights) and other questions of policy and law can be neatly distinguished in the manner required for this conception of majoritarianism. There may be some issues (e.g., pure coordination problems) where justice leaves matters completely undetermined, but there cannot be many, or so one might think.[79]

[75] A central theme of my *Essay on the Modern State*.

[76] Amar, "The Consent of the Governed," 460 and elsewhere. One does not know what to make of these eighteenth-century views, however self-evident they may have appeared to their proponents. (In fact, 'self-evidence' is somewhat of a special term in these contexts. I employ it in a less technical sense.) On these views, what was meant by a 'simple majority' was usually a plurality, and none of the standard considerations in favor of the former justified the latter. Were defenders of majoritarianism just confused?

[77] It is somewhat misleading to suppose that certain theorems from social choice theory show that simple majority "is the only workable voting rule that treats all voters and all policies equally" (Amar, "The Consent of the Governed," 503).

[78] Amar does, in fact, say that "[i]n the end, individual rights in our system are, and should be, the products of ultimately majoritarian processes" ("The Consent of the Governed," 503). The factual claim is, I think, unlikely to survive careful unpacking of the terms 'in the end' and 'ultimately'. More importantly, the normative claim ought to be challenged.

[79] Even if majoritarianism fails, we might still have good reason, most of the time, to accord special status to collective decisions endorsed by majorities or even pluralities. It is just that the reasons are not the sort claimed by partisans of the People. The issues about majoritarianism, however, are more complex than my brief remarks may suggest. There may

We need not dwell, at least at present, on the dangers of majoritarianism. But it may be noted how odd it is for defenders of the People to want simple majorities to determine policy and law. The classical theorists—for instance, Locke and Rousseau—required unanimity initially.[80] Members of the People can be oppressed just as well by simple majorities as they can by minorities. Giving individuals the power to block certain laws—for example, through supermajoritarian voting rules, or through basic rights—need not result in some others being oppressed.

Many contemporary theorists and political actors appeal to the notion of popular sovereignty and seem to think that it must play a central role in democratic thought and practice. I have argued that, to the contrary, the notion should not be made central to our theory, largely because the People are not to be accorded the sweeping political authority associated with sovereignty. I have suggested that infatuation with popular sovereignty often betrays a mistaken hierarchical view of political society and of governance.

Philosophy, Bowling Green State University

---

be situations where it is preferable, for instance, to have majorities of citizens interpret fundamental law than to have courts or officials do so.

[80] For Locke, constituting a "Body Politick" requires the assent of all who are to be full members; they are bound by simple majority rule only after they join (*Second Treatise of Government*, ch. 8, section 95). The interpretation of Rousseau's controversial introduction of majority voting is more complicated; on one reading, it is introduced only in an epistemic context. The unanimity rule occupies a privileged position in James Buchanan and Gordon Tullock, *The Calculus of Consent* (Ann Arbor: University of Michigan Press, 1962).

QUASI-RIGHTS: PARTICIPATORY CITIZENSHIP AND NEGATIVE LIBERTIES IN DEMOCRATIC ATHENS

By Josiah Ober

I. Introduction: Democracy versus Liberalism?

The relationship between participatory democracy (the rule of and by a socially diverse citizenry) and constitutional liberalism (a regime predicated on the protection of individual liberties and the rule of law) is a famously troubled one. The purpose of this essay is to suggest that, at least under certain historical conditions, participatory democracy will indeed support the establishment of constitutional liberalism. That is to say, the development of institutions, behavioral habits, and social values centered on the active participation of free and equal citizens in democratic politics can lead to the extension of legally enforced immunities from coercion to citizens and noncitizens alike. Such immunities, here called "quasi-rights," are at least preconditions for the personal autonomy and liberty in respect to choice-making that are enshrined as the "rights of the moderns." This essay, which centers on one ancient society, does not seek to develop a formal model proving that democracy will necessarily promote liberal constitutionalism.[1] However, by explaining why a premodern democratic citizenry of free, adult, native males—who sought to defend their own interests and were unaffected by Enlightenment or post-Enlightenment ideals of inherent human worth—chose to extend certain formal protections to slaves, women, and children, it may point toward the development of a model for deriving liberalism from democratic participation. Development of such a model could have considerable bearing on current policy debates.

The notion that democracy has any meaningful relationship to liberalism is often denied. Fareed Zakaria, for example, argues for a sharp distinction between democracy and "constitutional liberalism." For Zakaria, democratic citizenship has no intrinsic value and democracy should be valued only if it were shown to be an efficient instrument for obtaining

---

[1] Barry R. Weingast, "The Political Foundations of Democracy and the Rule of Law," *American Political Science Review* 91, no. 2 (June 1997): 245–63, develops the game-theoretic basis for a rational choice model along these lines. Although my argument here focuses on social practices and values rather than on rational choice, it is compatible with Weingast's model. I received very helpful comments on earlier versions of this paper delivered at New York University, the University of California at Santa Cruz, Stanford University, and Princeton University's Center for Human Values. Special thanks to Barry Strauss and Phillip Mitsis, for discussions that led to the writing of this paper, and to Emily Mackil for editorial assistance and substantive comments.

27

the desirable end of constitutional liberalism—for protecting what are sometimes known as the "rights of the moderns." Other political means for obtaining this same desired end would, for Zakaria, be equally acceptable and, indeed, preferable if those means proved more efficient. Although he is unable to point to a contemporary example of liberal constitutional autocracy, Zakaria sees no principled reason to prefer democracy to a hypothetical autocratic alternative. Zakaria therefore suggests that the makers of American foreign policy should reorient their priorities—away from encouraging the growth of democracy abroad, in favor of fostering the growth of liberal constitutionalism—even if that means supporting autocracy.[2]

If we suppose, with Zakaria, that democracy is nothing more than an instrument for gaining the higher end of protecting the rights of individuals and minority groups, there seems no innate reason to prefer being a "democratic citizen" to being a "rights-holding subject" of a benevolent nondemocratic sovereign. Thus, the only reason to prefer democracy to autocracy is the presumption that democracy is more likely than autocracy to foster the growth of liberal ideals and constitutional governmental structures. But Zakaria claims that this is not the case. His quick survey of modern European history and contemporary developments in the Third World leads to a simple conclusion: "Constitutional liberalism has led to democracy but democracy does not seem to bring constitutional liberalism."[3] Leaving aside various other problems with Zakaria's argument (e.g., his tendency to conflate "constitutionalism" *simpliciter* with the special form of "*liberal* constitutionalism"), this essay attempts to use the example of classical Athens to rethink the relationship between (first) the core values that constitute the primary commitments of contemporary liberalism, (next) the constitutional "rule of law," and (finally) participatory democracy, with its focus on the duties and privileges of the citizen.

Zakaria's primary focus is foreign policy, but the claim that democracy has nothing to do with the desired end of achieving constitutional liberalism has much wider policy implications. If Zakaria is correct, then there is (for example) no reason for liberals to worry about "democratic citizenship" per se or "the education of citizens." Rather, the proper concern

---

[2] Fareed Zakaria, "The Rise of Illiberal Democracy," *Foreign Affairs* 76, no. 6 (November/December 1997): 23–43. For a good discussion of the traditional conflict between the liberal "rights of the moderns" (religious liberty; liberty of conscience, thought, and expression; rights of person and property) and the democratic "rights of the ancients" (freedom of political speech, and participation rights), and an argument that these can be conjoined within a conception of deliberative democracy based on reasonable plurality, see Joshua Cohen, "Procedure and Substance in Deliberative Democracy," in *Democracy and Difference*, ed. Seyla Benhabib (Princeton: Princeton University Press, 1996), 94–119.

[3] Zakaria, "Rise of Illiberal Democracy," 28. Zakaria's examples of constitutional liberalism leading to democracy include nineteenth-century Britain, Hong Kong, and contemporary "semi-democratic" East Asian regimes. His examples of democracy failing to bring about constitutional liberalism include sub-Saharan Africa, Haiti, Central Asia, and "the Islamic world" (ibid., 26–29).

would seem to be with the liberal education of a few elite leaders capable of guaranteeing that a constitutional apparatus is properly established and maintained. Assuming that constitutional liberalism is the only desired end and that democracy is a dispensable instrument will therefore lead to a preference for an educational system with some of the same general goals (if not any of the specific features) of the educational system designed to produce Guardians in Plato's *Republic*. But if democracy does foster liberal values and the rule of law, then a very different sort of civic education would seem to be in order.

Dragging ancient Greece into the debate over democracy and constitutional liberalism is not idiosyncratic. Zakaria acknowledges that the modern emphasis on individual liberty "draws on a philosophical strain, beginning with the Greeks."[4] But his position on the relative importance, and ultimate separability, of democracy and liberalism builds on Isaiah Berlin's celebrated elaboration of Benjamin Constant's distinction between "positive liberty" (i.e., participatory political community-building, or political shareholding, which Constant specifically identified with Greco-Roman antiquity) and "negative liberty" (i.e., the distinctively modern individual freedom from interference by others in the processes of personal choice-making). For Berlin, the "classical republican" notion that participatory politics undertaken by "citizens" was a precondition to the secure maintenance of individual rights was incoherent, since he supposed that negative liberties could just as well be ensured by a sovereign for his subjects. Zakaria's argument builds on Berlin's claims that negative liberty "is not incompatible with some kinds of autocracy, or at any rate with the absence of self-government," and that it is a mistake to suppose that there is any "necessary connexion between individual liberty and democratic rule."[5]

While it is obviously impossible to prove the existence of a *"necessary connexion"* between democracy and liberal values by reference to a single historical case study (or, indeed, by reference to multiple historical cases), I will argue that in ancient Athens something resembling modern liberal values did in fact emerge—for the first time in recorded human history— quite directly from the development and experience of democratic political processes. Thus, whether or not one supposes that participatory democracy is a good in itself (for the record, I do), there is some reason to suppose that a democracy may indeed foster the values, institutions, and

---

[4] Ibid., 26.
[5] Benjamin Constant, "The Liberty of the Ancients Compared with That of the Moderns," in Benjamin Constant, *Political Writings*, ed. and trans. Biancamaria Fontana (Cambridge: Cambridge University Press, 1988), 307–28; Isaiah Berlin, "Two Concepts of Liberty," in *Four Essays on Liberty* (Oxford: Oxford University Press, 1969), 163ff., esp. 164f. On Berlin's conception of negative liberty and his debt to Constant, see John Gray, *Isaiah Berlin* (Princeton: Princeton University Press, 1996), 5–37, esp. 20. The Berlin quotes in this paragraph are drawn from "Two Concepts of Liberty," 14, 56, cited by Quentin Skinner, *Liberty before Liberalism* (Cambridge and New York: Cambridge University Press, 1998), 115.

behavioral practices conducive to the development and maintenance of "constitutional liberalism." This is still a long way from a straightforward causal argument: I am not claiming that "democracy" is a necessary and sufficient condition for either constitutionalism or liberalism. But I do think that a case can be made that the habits associated with the practice of democracy have a lot better chance of leading in those desirable directions than do the habits associated with autocracy.

I will argue, then, that the answer to the question "Is the practice of democracy conducive to the development of negative liberties?" is at least a qualified "Yes." The answer is qualified, first, because classical Athenian democracy never evolved into a fully liberal regime—never extended participation rights to all those residents who would be regarded as appropriate rights-holders under any twentieth-century regime claiming the title "liberal" or "democratic." And it is further qualified because the rights which were guaranteed by the Athenian regime never had the ontological status of "inherent or universal human rights." In Athens, individual rights were acknowledged as performative and contingent rather than being regarded as natural, innate, and inalienable. I have dubbed them "quasi-rights" because the Athenians never supposed—as modern rights theorists sometimes do—that rights had a universal or metaphysical existence, that they were either God-given or naturally occurring. Rather, for the Athenians, rights were to be enjoyed by those who demonstrably deserved them, and—this is the key point—only for so long as other rights-holders were willing to acknowledge them and willing voluntarily to act consistently and collectively in their defense. The Athenians were, in a sense, "rights pragmatists."

The Athenians developed a detailed, and emphatically procedural, code of law. They recognized, however, that absent appropriate political behavior, the law code was meaningless, mere written words without substance or authority. In this they were highly realistic. Laws, even in the most mature of liberal and constitutional regimes, remain in force only for as long as the behavior of the powerful generally conforms to them. Law codes will survive the challenge of serious misbehavior by the strong only when society is willing to respond with superior strength in defense of the law. Modern constitutional regimes depend, of course, on government agents to enforce the law. Thus, when these agents misbehave, the only viable response is a multiplication of government agencies charged with investigating and prosecuting other agents of the government. That process can continue, as recent U.S. history suggests, ad nauseam, if not ad infinitum. The result is a growth of political cynicism on the part of the populus. Government, politics, and the rule of law itself, come to be seen as a sideshow, occasionally entertaining but generally irritating and largely irrelevant. By contrast, the Athenian citizens depended directly and immediately upon one another to enforce laws and to reify, in action, the values on which laws were predicated. Democracy meant, for the Athenians, that the collective strength of the individually weak "many" was available for deployment against the capacity for coercion possessed by powerful individuals and syndicates. Although they were indeed concerned to prevent the misuse of governmental authority, Athenians never forgot that threats to human dignity are just as likely to emanate from private individuals capable of monopolizing social power.

My second main argument concerns democratic ideology and the legal consequences of political sociology. The democratic Athenians included within the privileged category of "free and equal citizens" many persons normatively regarded by the traditional Greek "social mentality" as incapable of being citizens on the grounds of their putative dependence and moral inferiority (i.e., day-laborers, small-scale traders, and craftsmen possessing little or no real property). I will suggest that this inclusiveness led to the development of what I am calling quasi-rights. Moreover, it soon opened the way (in legal practice as well as in political theory) for the extension of legal immunities in the form of "negative liberties" to other Athenians regarded as dependent and inferior: children, women, slaves, and resident foreigners. I will *not* argue that this "liberalizing" tendency to extend immunities beyond the boundary of the citizen body was the conscious or stated intention of the Athenian democratic regime or anyone associated with it. Rather, it was an unintended effect of ideological complexity. But the fact that the Athenian citizenry did not *intend* to foster extra-citizen liberalism only strengthens the argument that (at least under the conditions existing in classical Athens) the practice of participatory democracy itself can foster liberal practices and values and can, moreover, extend those practices and values into new and unexpected social contexts.

II. DEMOCRACY IN THE ATHENIAN STYLE

The primary body of Athenian rights-holders-and-defenders was the citizen body: the *dêmos*. This large (ca. 30,000 persons) and socioeconomically diverse group was defined by age, gender, and (ordinarily) by birth: typically, the Athenian citizen (*politês*) was a male over eighteen years of age, legitimately born of an Athenian father and Athenian mother, whose neighbors had formally (by voting in the local assembly) accepted him as such, and whose name had been inscribed in his ancestral township or neighborhood (deme) citizen-list.[6] The citizen body was thus homogeneous in terms of gender and ethnicity (or imaginary ethnicity: some citizens were naturalized foreigners); but it remained highly stratified in terms of wealth and income. Economic distinctions

---

[6] See David Whitehead, *The Demes of Attica 508/7–ca. 250 B.C.: A Political and Social Study* (Princeton: Princeton University Press, 1986), 67.

had been specifically linked to constitutional participation-rights in the early sixth-century B.C. (predemocratic) governmental system established by the reformer-lawgiver, Solon. Each of the four Solonian census classes enjoyed specific participation-rights, based on a sliding scale of annual income measured in terms of agricultural produce. These census classes were never abolished, but by the fourth century B.C., if not before, they were ignored in political practice (Aristotle, *Athênaiôn Politeia* 7.4). Rich and poor Athenian citizens were political and legal equals: each citizen was an equal voter (*isopsêphos*), enjoyed an equal right to public speech (*isêgoria*), and an equal standing before the law (*isonomia*).[7]

By classical Greek (and pre-twentieth-century Western) standards, the most remarkable feature of Athenian citizenship is an absence: despite the range of wealth classes within the citizen body, there was no property qualification for the active exercise of citizenship: the landless Athenian day-laborer was in meaningful institutional terms the political and legal equal of the largest landowner. For Aristotle (and other ancient theorists), it was precisely the absence of property qualifications for citizenship that distinguished democracy from oligarchy.[8] By instituting democracy, the Athenians had agreed, in effect, to extend the frontier of citizenship (and its associated protections) wide enough to enclose the entire native adult male population—to extend the border of political belonging remarkably far (by contemporary Greek standards), but (in principle) no further.

Despite having defined the citizenry as a body of politically equal shareholders, Athenian citizens remained intensely aware that wealth inequality translated easily and inevitably into inequalities in social power. And they were well aware of the manifold humiliating and painful ways in which the misuse of the superior power of those who were rich, well connected, well educated, and consequently strong could play out in the lives and on the bodies of the poor, isolated, relatively ill-educated, and weak. Among the primary ethical goals of the Athenian *dêmos* was to limit the practical effects of social-power inequality by political and legal means. The story of the development and manifestation of quasi-rights in democratic Athens can be told in terms of the concurrent development of a strong civic identity among the members of the *dêmos*, the elaboration of a popular and political ideology to explain that identity, the creation of governmental and legal institutions to defend that ideology, and the evolution of self-conscious habits of employing democratic ideological and institutional powers (including judicial authority). In Athenian popular ideology and elite political theory alike, these concurrent developments

---

[7] For a general discussion of Athenian democratic equality, see Kurt A. Raaflaub, "Equalities and Inequalities in Athenian Democracy," in *Demokratia: A Conversation on Democracies, Ancient and Modern*, ed. Josiah Ober and Charles Hedrick (Princeton: Princeton University Press, 1996), 139–74.

[8] Aristotle, *Politics* 1291b3–34.

were achieved and maintained by the day-to-day actions of numerous
"poor" Athenian citizens (*penêtes*: i.e., those who had to work for a
living—in actuality, an economically diverse group that included middling landowners and day-laborers). The "poor" employed their collective political and legal power to counter the social power of a much
smaller body of leisure-class (*plousioi*) elite citizens (again, an internally
diverse group, ranging from the marginally leisured to the extremely
wealthy).[9]

It was by institutionalizing what Robert Dahl has called "The Strong
Principle of Equality" (the assumption that all persons within the relevant
group are competent to participate in decision making and that no one
individual or junta can or should be counted upon to make better decisions about the best interests of the group or its individual members than
they could make for themselves) that the Athenians instantiated and
maintained a direct and participatory form of democratic self-governance.
Democracy worked in practice because the Athenians assured, through
public speech, daily behavior, and legal procedure, that structures of
patronage (and other forms of socioeconomic domination with overtly
political effects) were strictly limited in practice. The quasi-rights enjoyed
by Athenian citizens were predicated upon the conviction that each citizen and the citizen body as a whole would and should be committed to
the defense—notably, although not exclusively, through the enactment
and vigorous implementation of a code of laws and legal procedures—of
each citizen's freedom of speech, association, and action (*eleutheria*), political and legal equality (*isotês*), and personal security from degradation
or assault (*sôtêria*). Within the boundaries of the citizenry, the citizens
themselves would police one another's behavior on a day-to-day basis.
When necessary, they would employ social and legal sanctions to ensure
conformity to a standard of behavior that limited the material and psychic
effects of socioeconomic inequality.[10]

This sort of policing may seem to be exactly the sort of social control
opposed by the sort of liberalism advocated by J. S. Mill in *On Liberty*. But
Mill, and his fellow British liberals, were (I think rightly) impressed with
the defense of the relative openness of Athenian society praised by Thu-

---

[9] The story of how the *dêmos* came to be defined in terms of "non-leisured" Athenians (or,
conversely, all native adult males) rather than in terms of the elite is important and inter-
esting, but is not my main focus here: cf. Josiah Ober, *The Athenian Revolution: Essays on
Ancient Greek Democracy and Political Theory* (Princeton: Princeton University Press, 1996),
esp. ch. 6; Victor D. Hanson, "Hoplites into Democrats: The Changing Ideology of Athenian
Infantry," in *Demokratia*, ed. Ober and Hedrick, 289–312; Barry S. Strauss, "The Athenian
Trireme, School of Democracy," in ibid., 313–26; and my exchange with Kurt Raaflaub in
Democracy 2500? Questions and Challenges, ed. K. Raaflaub and I. Morris, Archaeological
Institute of America, Colloquia and Conference Papers 2 (Dubuque, Iowa: Kendall/Hunt,
1998), 67–85.

[10] See Virginia J. Hunter, *Policing Athens: Social Control in the Attic Lawsuits, 420–320 B.C.*
(Princeton: Princeton University Press, 1994); and David Cohen, *Law, Sexuality, and Society:
The Enforcement of Morals in Classical Athens* (Cambridge: Cambridge University Press, 1991).

cydides' Pericles in the Funeral Oration: "Our public life is conducted in a free way, and in our private intercourse we are not suspicious of one another, nor angry with our neighbor if he does what he likes; we do not put on sour looks at him which, though harmless, are not pleasant."[11] Pericles' point is that in comparison to the obsessive concern with all aspects of public and private behavior manifested by aristocratic/oligarchic Sparta, the Athenians took little notice of one another's private lives and affairs. Pericles' comments point to a distinction that will be important to my argument: the contrast between the concerns of the democratic *polis* and those manifested by the normative (idealized standard) aristocratic *polis*. One serious problem with some recent political-theoretical discussions of ancient Greece is a tendency to reify "the *polis*" as a single analytic category by conflating Athens, Sparta, Plato's Kallipolis (described in the *Republic*), and the "*polis* of our prayers" of Aristotle's *Politics*.

If it was remarkably extensive by contemporary Greek standards, the Athenian definition of the citizen as a native adult male is, of course, highly exclusivist by twentieth-century standards: children, and, much more problematically, women and non-native residents (including numerous slaves) were excluded from the ranks of the *dêmos*.[12] The Athenian political-legal order has, therefore, been regarded by some scholars as predicated on an ideology grounded in a stark distinction between "citizens" and "others." Moreover, it has been argued that the exclusion of "others" from the participation-rights associated with political standing was not an unfortunate blindspot of an otherwise admirable system, but a foundational premise of the system itself. On this reasoning, the Athenians were only able to maintain the standards of non-exploitative behavior within the "citizenship boundary" by emphasizing the distinction between the microcosmic, internal civic realm of "*polis* as state (or citizen-estate)" and the macrocosmic, external realm of "*polis* as whole society."[13] Because, it is argued, the Athenian citizen body was officially defined in the naturalizing terms of gender and ethnicity, its ideological underpinnings were not only exclusivist but essentialist, and Athenian political essentialism is, on this view, best understood as forthright misogyny and racism.[14] Viewed in this harsh light, Athenian democracy would seem to be not only contingently, but irremediably illiberal, a graphic illustration

[11] Thucydides, *The Peloponnesian War*, ed. and trans. Benjamin Jowett (Oxford: Clarendon Press, 1881), with revisions of Simon Hornblower, *A Commentary on Thucydides* (Oxford: Clarendon Press, 1991), 2.37.2.

[12] On Athenian demographics, see Mogens H. Hansen, *Demography and Democracy: The Number of Athenian Citizens in the Fourth Century B.C.* (Herning, Denmark: Systime, 1985). The number of foreign residents and slaves was large, but cannot be accurately estimated. In any event, citizens cannot have been more than about one-fifth of the total population at any time during the democracy.

[13] On this distinction, see Ober, *Athenian Revolution*, ch. 11, and the literature cited therein.

[14] On the bipolarity of Athenians and others, see Paul Cartledge, *The Greeks: A Portrait of Self and Others* (Oxford: Oxford University Press, 1993); on the link between this bipolarity and democracy, see Jennifer Tolbert Roberts, "Athenian Equality: A Constant Surrounded by

of Zakaria's argument that democracy in and of itself has nothing necessarily to do with the values espoused by constitutional liberalism.

III. Ideology and Subversion

Although I am very aware of the illiberality of Athenian democracy—
when it is viewed at any particular moment in its history, and when it is
contrasted to contemporary liberal ideals[15]—I suggest that focusing exclusively on the binary opposition between "citizen" and "other" elides
too much of the ideological complexity central to Athenian politics and
society. "Ideology" is defined here as including the logic of common
practices as well as commonly held ideas and normative values.[16] It has
no metaphysical existence outside of ongoing lived experience. Like a
river, ideologies must be continuously replenished from multiple sources;
while rivers and ideologies may appear to exist in a steady state, no river
and no ideology can stand still. Yet very unlike the waters of a natural
river, the raw material of ideology is willful human activity: thought,
speech, and action. Ideology is necessarily pragmatic and performative,
in the sense of being a living set of beliefs, norms, protocols, and responses. Ideology is not, therefore, just a fixed and given part of people's
mental furniture, but it is publicly "performed" through thinking, saying,
doing, and writing by self-conscious, choice-making human agents. Although a dominant ideology may close off some avenues of choice (and
seek to close off others), no ideology (and a fortiori no democratic ideology) has the totalizing capacity to reduce human interactions to a pre-
determined set of rote behaviors.[17]

Moreover, although every ideology, by definition, is held by more than
one person, not even the most dominant ideology will be perfectly stan-
dardized or can function as a seamless whole within a group of persons
manifesting any meaningful degree of social diversity. A highly robust
ideology will be eagerly embraced and more or less accurately performed
by a lot of people, frequently, and in many and various contexts—but
never by all of the people, all of the time, and everywhere. The performance of culture is not limited to "authorized personnel." Performances
by different-minded or inappropriate persons, or under peculiar circumstances, may result in challenges to the dominant ideology, and as a
consequence culture sometimes changes. The dissonance between official
performances and "alternative" performances will necessarily affect atti-

---

Flux," in *Demokratia*, ed. Ober and Hedrick, 187–202; on racism and misogyny, see Ian
Morris, *Archaeology as Cultural History* (Cambridge: Cambridge University Press, forthcoming).

[15] See Ober, *Athenian Revolution*, ch. 11.

[16] The distinctions between what people say and what they do, and between what people
say in official circumstances and what they say among intimates, is relevant here, but hard
to specify.

[17] See, for example, Ober, *Athenian Revolution*, ch. 5, on the inevitability of criticism.

tudes and force questioning of established norms, and thus may lead (sooner or later) to substantive revisions of the ideological context itself and of those social identities that depend upon it.[18]

Furthermore, ideology not only informs history, it exists within history. Political ideology, as one part of social context, is responsive to other context shifts (e.g., demographic change); the social and political order inevitably changes over time in reaction to events (broadly construed).[19] In response to internal factors (alternative performance) and external factors (events), every given ideology will evolve and perhaps may occasionally be rapidly and radically transformed through the diachronic processes affecting social and cultural reproduction: even with the best (or worst) will in the world, no human group (or dominant subgroup) can maintain a genuinely stable ideology or political culture indefinitely. Yet it is not necessary to suppose that all aspects of an ideology will change at the same rate: some elements may prove to be much more durable than others.

In some recent discussions of ancient Greek social attitudes a useful contrast is drawn between long-term and relatively stable "mentality" and the shorter-term, more variable and responsive "ideology."[20] Following recent work by Ian Morris and Leslie Kurke, I would suggest that by the sixth century B.C., a fairly cohesive and deeply engrained "mentality" had developed among an important subset of the native adult male (hereafter NAM) population of the Greek city-states. This mentality emphasized values characteristic of what is sometimes called the hoplite or "middling" class—i.e., those NAMs who owned enough land (or equivalent wealth) to feed their families, may have owned one or more slaves, and fought in the ranks of the heavy infantry. The middling sensibility privileged a common, public, inward-looking, and political center (*to meson, to koinon*) over the individualized, sometimes foreign-oriented, and diverse private realm (*to idion*). It privileged the values of the relatively large (perhaps 40 percent of the NAM population) "moderate and middling" ranks of society (*hoi metrioi, hoi mesoi*: generally associated with the heavy-infantry hoplites rather than the elite cavalry). It tended to reject the values of the small (perhaps 5 to 10 percent of NAMs) leisure-class, luxurious, and cosmopolitan elite. And by the same token, it excluded from consideration all NAMs with inadequate property, those incapable of arming themselves as hoplites.

---

[18] Judith Butler, *Excitable Speech: A Politics of the Performative* (New York: Routledge, 1997), offers one account of the relationship between performance and culture; my thanks to Susan Lape for clarifying for me how Butler's work can be applied to Athens. My own understanding of how dominant ideologies are challenged by alternative performances is sketched in *Athenian Revolution*, 148–54.

[19] See Morris, *Archaeology as Cultural History*.

[20] Ibid., ch. 4. In my own work, I have tended to use the term "ideology" to cover aspects of both thought and practice, and it is important to keep in mind that there is no practical way to segregate "mentality" from "ideology" in the thought of any given person at any given time.

The middling mentality emphasized moderation, self-control, self-sufficiency, self-sacrifice in the common interest, and the high intrinsic value of citizenship itself. By the same token, it rejected any celebration of luxurious living, ostentatious public displays of wealth, or fascination with extra-*polis* (and especially extra-Greek) relations. The middling mentality honored freedom (qua lack of dependency) and equality (among the ranks of the *mesoi*). It placed the hard-working (on his own land), hard-fighting (in common with his fellow infantryman), male, warrior-landowner at the center of the social and political universe, and counterpoised that central figure with the marginal categories of women, foreigners, and the unfree generally. The unfree included chattel slaves (or, in the case of Sparta, serf/helots) but also those NAMs who lacked the material resources necessary for inclusion among the ranks of the *mesoi*.[21] By about 500 B.C., many Greek *poleis* were dominated by a republican political order defined by the middling mentality—in these regimes, which Aristotle would variously define as aristocracies, as "polities," or as moderate forms of oligarchy, propertyless men were denied citizenship, but property qualifications were low enough that it was the *mesoi* who ruled.[22]

IV. The Historical Development of Athenian Democracy

The historical development of Athenian democratic citizenship is a large topic, fruitfully and recently reexamined by Brook Manville.[23] In Athens, the victory of the middling mentality was signaled by the constitutional reforms of Solon (594 B.C.) and paradoxically confirmed during the relatively benevolent (and generally anti-aristocratic) reign of the tyrant Pisistratus (546–528 B.C.). The major step from the republican conception of the "rule of those in the middle rank" to a more radical form of democracy which enfranchised even propertyless laborers was taken in 508/7 B.C., in the aftermath of a popular uprising against a Spartan-sponsored attempt to install a narrow oligarchy as the government of Athens. This Athenian Revolution, and the constitutional order that emerged from it, set the stamp on Athenian civic identity and laid the groundwork for the developed democratic order of the fifth and fourth

---

[21] Chattel slaves, either Greek prisoners of war or (more often) non-Greeks imported specifically to serve as slaves, could be bought and sold as ordinary property. Helots and other unfree "serfs" were tied to the land; they could not be bought or sold, but otherwise lacked liberties and immunities.

[22] See Ian Morris, "The Strong Principle of Equality and the Archaic Origins of Greek Democracy," in *Demokratia*, ed. Ober and Hedrick, 19–48; Leslie Kurke, "The Politics of *Habrosunê* in Archaic Greece," *Classical Antiquity* 11 (1992): 91–120; and (believing the *metrios* ideal to be a reality rather than an ideology) Hanson, "Hoplites into Democrats."

[23] Philip Brook Manville, *The Origins of Citizenship in Ancient Athens* (Princeton: Princeton University Press, 1990).

centuries B.C.[24] From this time on, it would be the *dêmos*, qua the body of NAMs, who ran Athens according to their own conceptions of the best interests of the *dêmos* and the *polis*. This meant that democratic Athenian political ideology was, in an important sense, and from the beginning of the democracy itself, in conflict with the less capacious "middling mentality."

Within the middling mentality, the core values of freedom and equality were linked to sufficient property-holding. Thus the marginal penumbra of "unfree/dependent, unequal/inferior, politically useless noncitizens" included all those NAMs (perhaps 50 percent of the total) who were regarded as inadequate in terms of wealth. By extending the border of political inclusiveness so as to include even genuinely destitute NAMs as actively participatory citizens, the Athenians counterpoised their political practice and an emerging democratic political ideology to the norms fostered by the well-established (although never uncontested) middling mentality. Just as archaic Greek culture had been defined by a fierce contest between an ideology favorable to luxuriousness (*habrosunê*) and the eventually and generally victorious middling (*metrios*) mentality,[25] much of the drama of Athenian culture may be sketched in terms of the tension between the middling mentality (especially as it was reformulated in the work of critical intellectuals) and an increasingly self-confident and coherent popular democratic ideology. In democratic Athens, the core *metrios* values of freedom and equality among citizens were maintained, but redefined by being stripped of any strong association with property-holding. And with that radical redefinition came the possibility that, in practice and over time, the values of freedom, equality, and security of the person might prove robust enough to survive their application in even more unexpected contexts and to persons outside the ranks of the NAMs.

In the democratic Athenian case, given the forthrightly pragmatic orientation of democratic government and the prominence of political life in the organization of society as a whole,[26] we may expect political ideology

---

[24] Ober, *Athenian Revolution*, ch. 4.

[25] For the struggle between the *habrosunê* mentality and the *metrios* mentality, see Morris, "Strong Principle of Equality"; Kurke, "Politics of *Habrosunê*"; and Kurke, *The Politics of Meaning in Archaic Greece: Coinage, Bodies, Games, and Gold* (Princeton: Princeton University Press, 2000).

[26] On the centrality of politics, see Pierre Lévêque and Pierre Vidal-Naquet, *Cleisthenes the Athenian: An Essay on the Representation of Space and Time in Greek Political Thought from the End of the Sixth Century to the Death of Plato*, ed. and trans. David Ames Curtis (Atlantic Highlands, NJ: Humanities Press, 1996); Christian Meier, *The Greek Discovery of Politics*, trans. David McLintock (Cambridge, MA: Harvard University Press, 1990); and Jean-Pierre Vernant, *The Origins of Greek Thought* (Ithaca, NY: Cornell University Press, 1982). My argument does not embrace extreme claims about the "primacy of politics" in Greek culture (see, e.g., Paul A. Rahe, *Republics Ancient and Modern: Classical Republicanism and the American Revolution* [Chapel Hill: University of North Carolina Press, 1992]), but it likewise rejects the attempt to read Athens as primarily family- and cult-centered (see, e.g., Cynthia Patterson, *The Family in Greek History* [Cambridge, MA: Harvard University Press, 1998]).

to be especially responsive to public performance and misperformance. And so, as I have argued in detail elsewhere, it was.[27] In the citizen assembly and people's courts and in the pubic square—but also on the streets, in the fields, in workshops, and in mercantile and service establishments—citizens gathered, conversed, persuaded or failed to persuade, and chose courses of action accordingly. They behaved toward one another conventionally or innovatively, were noticed or ignored, and were rewarded and punished accordingly. They took note of all of this activity, forming opinions, thereby confirming or challenging their presuppositions, and resolving or changing their minds. In so doing, they reproduced political culture and reconstituted social structures by their variously accurate and subversive performances of popular ideology.

Considerable traces survive of some public Athenian discussions— most especially the preserved (as inscribed stone *stêlai*) records of Assembly decisions and (in the literary record) speeches of prosecution and defense written by or for litigants in the people's courts. Because these epigraphic and forensic corpora can be analyzed, in the aggregate, for their ideological content, it is possible to speak with some confidence about the content of Athenian political ideology.[28] It is important to keep in mind, however, that these inscriptions and speeches, as records of the most overtly political and most highly public of Athenian discussions, are at once descriptive and normative: they employ the speaker's suppositions about the actual experienced reality of Athenian social life and the attitudes of the *dêmos*, but they also refer to social relations and attitudes that the speaker supposes (and supposes his audience to believe) *should* pertain in the democratic city.

Our records thereby point to the matrix of convictions about actuality and normativity that constituted Athenian democratic ideology—or at least the part of that ideology suited to public assertion. Because our surviving records tend to concern relations between citizens, and because the judges (Assemblymen and jurors) of the speech contests recorded in our surviving documents were Athenian citizens, sitting in a specifically "citizenly" politico-juridical capacity, these records are a particularly good indication of the ideological "party line" of the Athenian *dêmos* qua exclusive corporation of political shareholders. It is probably safe to say that these documents quite accurately define a good part of the ideological spectrum but fail to reproduce the entire spectrum: they portray Athenian political ideology as more unitary, coherent, and stable, and less liable to subversion by outside (i.e., noncitizen) pressures, than we may suppose it was in the experience of Athenian social life "in the round." The frac-

---

[27] See Josiah Ober, *Mass and Elite in Democratic Athens* (Princeton: Princeton University Press, 1989); and Ober, *Athenian Revolution*.

[28] On inscriptions, see David Whitehead, "Cardinal Virtues: The Language of Public Approbation in Democratic Athens," *Classica et Mediaevalia* 34 (1983): 55–74. On speeches, see Ober, *Mass and Elite*.

tion of Athenian ideology to which we have relatively easy access is highly relevant to the question of the relationship between democracy and liberal values: I will suggest that maintaining this public ideology in intra-citizenry contexts was essential if the Athenian "citizen many" were to retain the functional capacity to restrain, by political and legal means, the social power of the wealthy few. And that capacity was essential to the survival of both democracy and the liberalizing tendency exemplified in the expansion of quasi-rights.

We are much less well informed about how citizens talked with one another in less obviously public fora. Moreover, outside the works of Athenian dramatists, pamphleteers, and philosophers, we have only scant traces of day-to-day interactions between citizens and noncitizens, or among noncitizens. In order to assess the extension of "quasi-rights" within the wider Athenian society, I have looked at two sorts of evidence, and have attempted to read them against each other. First, there is the relatively official record of public forensic speeches, which include descriptions of legal and quotidian practices and make normative claims. Second, I have looked at the ways in which philosophical and dramatic texts critically expose the extension of protections within both Athenian society and utopian (or dystopian) imaginary societies. My claim will be that certain quasi-rights were applied to noncitizens more often and in more diverse contexts than could be predicted by an interpretive model that emphasizes binary opposition between citizens and others as the primary principle of Athenian sociopolitical organization. The extension of negative liberties is due to a variety of factors, and these probably cannot be isolated. They must, however, include conscious attempts at subversion on the part of noncitizens. There is, furthermore, the citizens' recognition (whether fully conscious or not) of contradictions between the three spheres discussed above: the relatively exclusivist claims of the traditional *metrios* mentality, the more capacious democratic political ideology, and the complex lived experience of social life. Both subversive activity and the capacity to recognize contradictions should, I suppose, have something to do with the historical development and subsequent complexity of Athenian ideology. They should also help us to understand Athenian ideology's insistence on juxtaposing political (and legal) authority to nonpolitical (especially economic) forms of social power.[29]

I would not claim that it is possible, by employing the approach sketched above, to give a historically satisfactory account of Athenian social life.

[29] The contrast, among republics, is with societies like that of ancient Rome, in which religious, social, economic, and political power were concentrated in the hands of an aristocratic oligarchy. I know much less about monarchical societies (e.g., classical China), but I suppose that they might manifest an even more fully developed isomorphism between various sorts of power, and consequently fewer obvious contradictions or opportunities for ideological confusion.

But that is not my goal here: I hope only to show that there is reason to assume considerable discontinuity between what we might call the "official intention" of the *dêmos*—the distribution of positive and negative rights exclusively *within* the closed context of the society of Athenian citizens (the "politico-*polis*")—and the functional distribution of negative liberties within the more open and fluid society comprising the entire population of the residents of the local Athenian territory of Attica (the "geo-*polis*"). The general point I hope to make is that Athens was, at least in this respect, from the beginning of the democratic era, considerably more liberal than certain of its own premises allowed. The trend toward liberality was particularly noteworthy in the fourth century B.C.—the age of Plato and Aristotle. As noted above, Athens never evolved into a society that could fairly be described as "essentially liberal" in modern terms. The liberalizing trend was perhaps slowed, or even reversed, in the aftermath of the Athenian loss of formal independence to the autocratic Macedonians after 322 B.C.[30] How liberal Athens might have become had its independence been maintained remains entirely conjectural.

V. PSEUDO-XENOPHON AND ARISTOTLE: CITIZENSHIP AND ITS DISCONTENTS

The fascinating late-fifth-century polemical pamphlet by an anonymous malcontent sometimes called "the Old Oligarch" (Pseudo-Xenophon, *Constitution of the Athenians*)[31] seeks to teach its reader that Athenian democracy is the efficient and rationally self-interested rule of the "bad" (because poor and uneducated) many (*hoi polloi*, *to plêthos*, or *ho dêmos*) over the "good" (wealthy and cultured) few. The pamphlet seems initially to encourage hopes for an antidemocratic coup d'état, but it ends on a decidedly discouraging note: the last paragraph of the text begins *in medias res*: "But someone might interject that no one has been unjustly disenfranchised at Athens" (3.12). The implied context here is the potential for oligarchic opponents of the democracy to foment a civil war. In the classical Greek *polis*, the ordinary stake in a civil conflict was enfranchisement—membership in the citizenship qua political community of the *polis*. The end result of successful revolutionary action would be a change in the composition of the citizen body.[32] Thus, the probable

---

[30] On democracy in post-classical Athens, see Christian Habicht, *Athens from Alexander to Antony* (Cambridge, MA: Harvard University Press, 1997). On the ways in which post-classical Athenian political culture may have resorted to essentializing ideological tactics, see Susan Lape, "Community and Politics in Menander," Ph.D. dissertation, Princeton University, 1998.

[31] Pseudo-Xenophon, *Constitution of the Athenians*, ed. G. W. Bowersock (Cambridge, MA: Harvard University Press, 1971).

[32] On this passage of Pseudo-Xenophon, cf. Arnold W. Gomme, "The Old Oligarch," in Gomme, *More Essays in Greek History and Literature*, ed. David A. Campbell (Oxford: Basil Blackwell, 1962), 61–62, 67–68; originally published in *Athenian Studies Presented to W. S.*

supporters of a revolutionary movement were those who were currently disenfranchised—and especially those who regarded their disenfranchisement as unjust. Pseudo-Xenophon replies to his hypothetical interlocutor that although a few men had in fact been unjustly expelled from the community of citizens by the Athenians for official malfeasance of one sort or another, the number was very small indeed, "but to attack the democracy at Athens not a few (*oligoi*) are required." Successful revolution apparently requires "many" (*polloi*) who, because they believe themselves to be unjustly disenfranchised, will support a change in regime. At this point in the essay, Pseudo-Xenophon's tendency to use *"dêmos"* as a synonym for "the unleisured many" (*hoi polloi*) rather than "the citizenry" *tout court* pays out. With the *dêmos/polloi* securely in control, it is impossible to suppose that "many" will be disenfranchised, and thus revolution is shown to be impossible on the original sociological premises of the argument. Pseudo-Xenophon concludes his tract and his practical lesson: at Athens, where it was the members of the *dêmos* who held the magistracies, how would anyone suppose that "the many" (*hoi polloi*) would ever be disenfranchised? And so, "in view of these considerations, one must not think that there is any danger at Athens from the disenfranchised" (3.13).

Pseudo-Xenophon's somewhat cryptic argument is elucidated by a text written just a century later: Aristotle's *Politics*. Like the Old Oligarch, Aristotle was deeply concerned with the relationship between citizenship and civil unrest. Among Aristotle's goals in the *Politics* is the elucidation of the sources of civil conflict and the discovery of ways in which civil war might be prevented via preemptive and meliorative constitutional adjustments. Aristotle is at one with Pseudo-Xenophon in seeing the goal of civil war as the enfranchisement of those who regarded themselves as worthy of the status of citizen (or the disenfranchisement of those who were thought to be unworthy of citizenship). The prime cause of civil unrest was, consequently, the discontent of those who were unjustly (as they supposed) disenfranchised. Although Aristotle has many suggestions for minor constitutional tinkering that might serve to reduce tensions, it is clear from his account that he thinks the most straightforward way to solve the problem of citizenship and political unrest would be for the citizen body of the *polis* to be coextensive with the body of those who both desired and deserved the status of citizen. If there were no body of noncitizens within the *polis* who wanted to be citizens, there would be no reason for a civil war aimed at revising the criteria for citizenship.

It is this concern with citizenship and its discontents that unites the "practical" discussion of the middle books (according to the traditional arrangement) of the *Politics* with Books 1 and 7. Book 7, the account of the *"polis*

Ferguson: *Harvard Studies in Classical Philology*, supplementary vol. 1 (1940), 211–45. The association of revolutionary change in the *politeia* with a change in the dominant element in the citizen body (*politeuma*) is a key issue for Aristotle in the *Politics*; see below.

of our prayers," presents a hypothetical *polis* in which the felicitous situation sketched in the previous paragraph obtains in practice—the body of "potential citizens" is coextensive with the body of "actual citizens," and thus the *polis* not only manifests a high degree of happiness, but also is optimally stable. With the right sort of attention given to the processes of social reproduction (especially formal education, sketched in the fragmentary Book 8), the "*polis* of our prayers" should not be subject to the subversive misperformances that led other (real) *poleis* into a seemingly never-ending series of constitutional/sociological changes (*metabolai*: cf. Aristotle, *Athênaiôn Politeia* 41.2, for an account of the twelve major Athenian *metabolai*). In order to arrive at this happy end, however, Aristotle must necessarily decide what the appropriate criteria for citizenship actually should be. This work is undertaken in Book 1 of the *Politics*, where Aristotle sketches the hypothetical origin of the fully developed *polis* from first principles.

In briefest summary, Aristotle suggests that the *polis* is the natural context for human flourishing, indeed the only context in which humans can hope consistently to achieve their highest ends. The *polis* is imagined as growing up organically from the conjunction of men and women into families (*oikoi*) for purposes of biological reproduction, then families into villages and clans for the purpose of security, and then villages and clans into the *polis* for the purpose of achieving justice and autarky.[33] Given the evolution of the *polis* via the conglomeration of families, which are (in Aristotle's view) properly composed of husband, wife, children, and slaves, the society of the ideal-standard *polis* itself was made up of native adult men, native women, their children, and their slaves. The activities of each of these categories of persons was necessary for the existence and maintenance of a proper *polis*, but not all of these persons were considered to "have a share" (*metechein*) in the *polis*. Indeed, as in Athenian ideology, only NAMs were regarded by Aristotle as potential citizens/shareholders. Aristotle explained the exclusion from shareholding of non-NAM residents by reference to their innate psychologies: due to specific defects in their deliberative capacity (*to bouleutikon*), women, slaves, and children simply could not function as citizens. Male children were only temporarily impaired; they were expected to have developed appropriate deliberative capacities upon achieving adulthood. Women and slaves, however, although manifesting somewhat different psychologies, were permanently and irremediably impaired. Aristotle gives his reader no reason to suppose that a woman or a (natural) slave would ever (justly) desire any of the attributes or protections of citizenship, at least so long as she or he were treated justly by her or his husband/master (*kurios*).

There is a serious practical problem with this naturalizing scenario, one that would be clear enough to any classical Greek, and Aristotle faces it

---

[33] For a fuller account, see Ober, *Athenian Revolution*, ch. 11.

quite squarely (if chillingly): Some Greek-owned slaves were Greek citizens of other *poleis*, men who had been captured in war and sold into slavery. These persons remained "psychological citizens." As such, they were necessarily unhappy in their status as slaves and thus a likely source of ideological/constitutional subversion. Aristotle's solution is a sketchy doctrine of "natural slavery" which posits the existence of persons who are "slaves by nature." He tentatively identifies most barbarians, and especially those of Asia, as likely natural slaves. The best *polis* will abjure enslaving those who are not slaves by nature, but may actively seek out opportunities to acquire natural slaves by imperialistic warfare.[34]

With the development of the doctrine of natural slavery, Aristotle's "natural *polis*" is complete. At first glance it appears to be a democracy on something like the Athenian model: all NAMs seem, on the psychological premises of the argument, to meet the criteria for "shareholding citizens." Yet in the last chapter of Book 1 (1.13), Aristotle introduces a further complexity that mandates a good deal of further discussion of citizenship: those persons (including many NAMs) who worked for others, and received directions from them, were in some important sense assimilated into the category of slaves. Such persons are summed up under the related categories of *banausoi* (craftsmen) and *thêtes* (laborers). These quasi-slaves did not enjoy the leisure that Aristotle reminds us (the point was made in the *Nicomachean Ethics*) is necessary to the development of political virtue. Moreover, it seems that the labors of *banausoi* and *thêtes* could, in and of themselves, be regarded as having corrupted any genuine and innate political capacity. It was precisely in their approach to the political standing of "sub-*metrios* NAMs" that Athenian democrats differed from those who advocated more restricted criteria for the active exercise of citizenship. Thus, by equating *banausoi* and *thêtes* with slaves in his treatment of normative citizenship, Aristotle diverges from democratic definitions of citizenship, and leans toward the thinking of earlier and more overtly oligarchic political theorists, like Pseudo-Xenophon.

Elsewhere in the *Politics*, however, Aristotle treats democracy as the best of the "commonly existing" regimes (the alternatives being oligarchy and tyranny). Aristotle's recognition of the (contingent, if not absolute) justice of democratic practice on the grounds of what might be called "natural citizenship" (for Aristotle: lack of innate psychological impairment), and his simultaneous methodological acknowledgment of the validity of settled sociological judgments of his elite interlocutors who regarded many NAMs as quasi-slaves, is the source of considerable tension in the argument of the *Politics*. The seriousness with which Aristotle treats certain of the claims underpinning democratic government (for

---

[34] For Aristotle's doctrine of natural slavery, see Aristotle, *Politics* 1252a24–1256b40, and the discussion of Peter Garnsey, *Ideas of Slavery from Aristotle to Augustine* (Cambridge: Cambridge University Press, 1996), and the literature cited therein.

example, the "summation argument" in support of the potential validity of collective decision-making) is among the most interesting and (for a modern democrat at least) most attractive features of his text. For our current purposes, however, the important point is that Aristotle's philosophical/psychological/naturalizing premises take the place of Athenian popular ideology in the project of explaining the basis of shareholding and social justice in the *polis*.

Like Aristotle, the Athenian *dêmos* was very concerned with the issue of justice. But unlike Aristotle's "*polis* of our prayers," in which all potential citizens were both actual citizens *and* members of the leisure class, and where all productive labor was to be the province of natural slaves, the Athenian democracy had to reconcile the concerns of a socially and economically diverse citizen body with the concerns and interests of other residents of the "geo-*polis*" without reference to a well-developed naturalized teleology. Unlike Aristotelian political theory, Athenian civic ideology had no well-articulated psychological premises with which to explain why citizenship (and its attendant privileges and protections) should be restricted to NAMs and denied to women and slaves—or for that matter, to resident foreigners (metics: a large category of persons, to which Aristotle himself belonged, but one of very limited analytic importance within the argument of the *Politics*). Although the Athenians did attempt (with varying degrees of success) to naturalize political distinctions based on gender, there is reason to suppose that Athenian NAMs regarded slaves and metics as psychologically similar, or even identical, to themselves.

Pseudo-Xenophon makes special note of the startlingly uppity behavior (*akolasia*) of Athenian slaves and metics, and he relates this phenomenon to the culture encouraged by democracy and to its material bases: he points out that in Athens "you" are not permitted (*oute . . . exestin*) to hit slaves and foreigners at will, nor will a slave stand aside for you. Pseudo-Xenophon's own explanation for this disturbing (to his implied reader) state of affairs is that the lower-class individuals constituting the Athenian *dêmos* were not recognizable as citizens: they were no better dressed nor any more handsome than individual slaves and metics. Hence, if an elite gentleman were allowed free license to strike slaves at will, he might well strike an Athenian citizen, mistaking him for a slave (1.10). And so, Pseudo-Xenophon claims, it was in order to ensure their own physical security that the *dêmos* forbade the casual beating of slaves. Moreover, he suggests that the Athenians' willingness to grant equality in regard to speech (*isêgoria*) to metics and slaves, and to allow slaves to become rich, and their tendency to manumit slaves were all quite rational (*eikotes*: 1.11–12). He claims that the explanatory key is the material importance to the lower-class Athenians of Athenian naval power—like Aristotle (*Politics* 1327a40–b16), Pseudo-Xenophon relates naval might directly to the social conditions that fostered democracy (1.2; 1.11–12). The navy required the availability of considerable free capital (*chrêmata*) and a variety of specialized trades (*technai*). He argues that metics provided the necessary skills, while money was acquired by taking a portion of the earnings of slaves. If, as was the case at (oligarchic) Sparta, your slave feared me, he might simply give up making money so as not to be at risk on account of his possession of wealth. Pseudo-Xenophon implies that this would not be a problem for the Spartans, whose land-based military organization did not demand the accumulation of capital; whereas for the Athenians the drying-up of the capital resources now gained by extracting the surplus value generated by the willing labor of profit-motivated slaves (who were presumably saving up to buy their manumission) would impair the operations of the navy.

For Pseudo-Xenophon the underlying premise is self-interest. The Athenian *dêmos* protected slaves and metics from physical mistreatment first because they feared being mistaken for slaves or metics. Athenians next protected the property rights of slaves and metics because they believed they could profit from the willing labor of slaves and metics who would work productively only if they were secure in their possession of property and some part of the fruits of their labor.[35] The Old Oligarch's highly tendentious explanation for Athenian liberality in respect to slaves and resident foreigners is reiterated by Plato and other ancient critics of democracy. Their point is that when compared with more restrictive citizen regimes (like that of Sparta), democracy was perversely (yet rationally) unwilling to patrol the boundaries between citizens and noncitizens. The Athenians allowed noncitizens access to protections that should (in aristocratic thought) "properly" be restricted to citizens alone. This perversity was explained by democracy's critics in terms of political sociology: the presence of poor ("ill-dressed, ugly") laborers and craftsmen within the Athenian citizen body. It was because the ordinary citizens (*hoi polloi*) themselves were "slave-like" when compared to the "good and beautiful" (*kaloi k'agathoi*) elite that they extended certain protections to slaves.

While rejecting the Old Oligarch's premises about the natural inferiority of the poor, I would suggest that he is right to link the extension of privileges to the sociological diversity of the Athenian *dêmos*. Once the "natural" association between participation rights and high social standing had been breached, there was a strong tendency for certain negative liberties to be extended beyond the citizen body itself.

---

[35] The Greek text is partially corrupt here; see Gerald Bechtle, "A Note on Pseudo-Xenophon, *The Constitution of the Athenians* 1.11," *Classical Quarterly* 46, no. 2 (1996): 564–66, where Bechtle discusses the difficulties and offers a sensible solution. The point, for Pseudo-Xenophon, is that because the Athenians enter into legally binding financial agreements with their slaves, under the terms of which the slaves are eventually able to manumit themselves, the free Athenians are not able to do whatever they wish with respect to slaves and are therefore "slaves to slaves."

VI. Demosthenes' *Against Meidias*: Quasi-Rights and the Law on *Hubris*

It is hard to say how closely Pseudo-Xenophon's (undoubtedly polemical) claims about Athenian treatment of metics and slaves reflects the lived experience of most real persons in classical Athens. But his statement about Athenian unwillingness to tolerate overt public violence against non-NAMs is supported by an important Athenian legal statute: the law (*nomos*) dealing with acts of *hubris*. As N. R. E. Fisher has exhaustively demonstrated, *hubris* refers to the propensity for and the act of deliberately seeking to disrespect or dishonor another person through outrageous speech (gross verbal insult) or action (physical violence).[36] Aristotle (*Rhetoric* 2.2.1378b23–31) usefully associates the tendency to commit *hubris* with the possession of wealth (especially new wealth) and other elite attributes. But our best single source for the Athenian law on *hubris* is the politician/orator Demosthenes' prosecution speech, *Against Meidias*, composed in 346 B.C. The speech is especially relevant to my current purposes, because in the course of exposing the extent and illegitimate application of his opponent Meidias's wealth-power via acts of *hubris*, Demosthenes explores in detail the existence and function of the quasi-rights of personal (as well as communal) liberty, equality, and security within the citizen body.[37]

Demosthenes argues that, in the face of potentially destabilizing economic inequalities among the citizens, the maintenance of liberty (qua the right to do what one wishes and especially to speak out in public), equality (of opportunity and political voice), and individual personal security (living without fear of being constrained by the actions of stronger persons within one's own society) are functionally essential components of democratic Athenian culture. For him, the maintenance of these quasi-rights was among the primary purposes of democracy; without them, the powerful would rule the state in their own interests, and democracy would cease to exist. The possibility of "benevolent" oligarchs, who would recognize the justice of granting negative liberties to the weaker many, is as foreign to Demosthenes' thought as the possibility of "enlightened" democrats, who accept the moral superiority of aristocrats, is to the thought of Pseudo-Xenophon.

Demosthenes' prosecution speech offers a particularly eloquent defense of the notion that the maintenance of quasi-right protections is predicated *not* on any natural or divine dispensation, or on the contractual delegation of powers to an abstract sovereign, but upon political participation: the willed activity of the concerned individual citizen

---

[36] N. R. E. Fisher, *Hybris: A Study in the Values of Honour and Shame in Ancient Greece* (Warminster: Aris and Phillips, 1992).

[37] See note 38 for a modern edition of Demosthenes' speech. I offer a detailed analysis of the speech in *Athenian Revolution*, ch. 7.

and of the collective citizenry in the defense of the outraged individual. Demosthenes (21.223–225) explicitly reminds his audience of jurors that Athenian laws have no independent existence or agency; it is only the willingness of the citizens actively to work the machinery of the law (as voluntary public prosecutors and jurors) that gives the law substance and force. The modern reader is forcefully reminded that there was no meaningful distinction in Athens between "citizenry" and "government." In Athens it was the aberrant powerful individual or syndicate, rather than "the government," that threatened the freedom, equal standing, and fundamental dignity of the ordinary (non-elite) citizens. Demosthenes' speech is a testament to the assumed determination and capacity of the *dêmos* to restrain the hubristic individual. At the same time, it offers ample evidence for the very considerable scope of action and opportunity of the wealthy elite, and the relative security of their property rights.

In the midst of his demonstration that Meidias (by punching Demosthenes in the theater of Dionysos, while Demosthenes was serving as chorus producer for his tribe) was guilty of the worst sort of *hubris*, Demosthenes pauses to quote the (typically highly procedural) Athenian law forbidding acts of *hubris*:

> If anyone treats with *hubris* any person, either child or woman or man, free or slave, or does anything unlawful (*paranomon*) against any of these, let anyone who so wishes, of those Athenians who are entitled (*exestin*), submit a *graphê* (written complaint) to the *thesmothetai* (legal magistrates). Let the *thesmothetai* bring the case to the *Heliaia* (people's court) within thirty days of the submission of the *graphê*, if no public business prevents it, or otherwise as soon as possible. Whoever the *Heliaia* finds guilty, let it immediately assess whatever penalty it thinks right for him to suffer or pay. Of those who submit *graphai* according to the law, if anyone does not proceed, or when proceeding does not get one-fifth of the votes, let him pay one thousand drachmas to the public treasury. If he (the accused) is assessed to pay money for his *hubris*, let him be imprisoned, if the *hubris* is against a free person, until he pays it. (Demosthenes 21.47, trans. MacDowell, adapted)[38]

Having cited the law in full, Demosthenes then points to its remarkable scope: "[Y]ou hear the generous consideration (*philanthrôpia*) of the law, men of Athens: it does not even allow acts of *hubris* against slaves. Well by the very gods!" Demosthenes then proposes a sort of thought experiment: What if someone were to transport a copy of this law to "the

---

[38] Douglas M. MacDowell, *Demosthenes, Against Meidias (Oration 21)* (Oxford: Clarendon Press, 1990), 21.47.

barbarians from whom slaves are imported to Greece," and were to praise the Athenians by pointing out that despite the many wrongs they have suffered at the hands of barbarians (a reference primarily to the Persian wars of 490–478 B.C.) and their consequent natural enmity, "nevertheless [the Athenians] don't think it right to treat insolently even the slaves whom they acquire by paying a price for them, but have publicly made this law to prevent it, and have before now imposed the death penalty on many who transgressed it." Demosthenes suggests that in these circumstances, the grateful barbarians would immediately appoint "all of you" to the honorific position of *proxenoi*: "local consuls" who look after the interests of persons from some specific foreign locale (21.48–50). Demosthenes' explication of the *hubris* law is constructed in the form of an *a fortiori* argument, to show how spectacularly wrongful was Meidias's behavior in punching a fellow citizen who was performing a public liturgy. And Demosthenes himself, with his "by the very gods!" seems a bit startled by the results of his own explication of the law's scope and by the law's failure to distinguish between citizens and noncitizens as protected persons.

A few other aspects of the law on *hubris* (which cannot, unfortunately, be dated or securely assigned to a specific lawmaker) merit our attention here. First, its provisions are remarkably broad: not only does it proscribe *hubris* against all categories of residents of Athenian territory, it prohibits the commission of any action that was *paranomon*—which can be translated either as "unlawful" or "against what is customarily regarded as proper"—against the same extensive list of persons. Since neither *hubris* nor *paranomon* is specifically defined by the law, it was up to the voluntary prosecutor to convince his audience of jurors that a given action was, when viewed in context and judged by prevailing community standards, "hubristic" or "legally/customarily improper." We can now see why Pseudo-Xenophon would have regarded it as prudent for a visitor to Athens, evidently used to freely asserting his superiority at home, to refrain from engaging in behavior toward anyone that might be regarded by Athenians as demeaning or otherwise offensive.

The *hubris* law points to an important distinction between positive (participation) rights and negative liberties. Although citizens have no special standing among those protected by the law, it is only "Athenians who are entitled" (i.e., citizens not suffering from full or partial disenfranchisement: *atimia*) who are empowered to initiate a prosecution under the anti-*hubris* law. As in the case of other Athenian criminal actions, if a voluntary prosecutor were to initiate a legal action, but fail to pursue it in court, he himself would suffer *atimia*. Moreover, if the prosecutor failed to convince one-fifth of the jurors of the justice of his claims (the votes of jurors—generally five hundred for this category of offense—were counted after the carefully timed speeches of prosecutor and defendant were complete), then he must pay a stiff fine (roughly three years' wages for a skilled craftsman). Clearly, the Athenians were concerned to prevent frivolous prosecutions, and they backed up their concern by putting the voluntary prosecutor, as well as the defendant, at risk. The exercise of positive rights can entail serious consequences, but it is the exercise of positive rights by "the enfranchised" which defends the negative liberties of the entire resident population.

Finally, the law draws a distinction between the potential punishment of a person convicted of *hubris* against free persons as opposed to *hubris* against slaves: the man convicted of the latter will not face prison, even if he is unable to pay an assessed fine. It is worth noting, however, that a monetary fine was only one of the possible penalties that might be suggested by a successful prosecutor and accepted by the jury. Demosthenes appears to claim (the syntax allows some vagueness) that "many" persons had in fact been executed for committing *hubris* against slaves. Demosthenes may, of course, be engaging in hyperbole. We do not know how often (if ever) Athenian citizens actually were prosecuted for *hubris* against non-NAMs, nor, if they were prosecuted, what the rate of conviction or the seriousness of the assessed punishment might have been. It seems, on the face of it, unlikely that a man would be prosecuted for *hubris* against members of his own household, whether slave or free. But then it also might seem, on the face of it, unlikely that the Athenian citizens would pass or keep on the books a law that is so little concerned with citizens as a specially protected category. The law on *hubris* confirms Pseudo-Xenophon's claim that metics and slaves could not be struck with impunity at Athens, but it shows that the scope of protection was (in the letter of the law, anyway) even broader: children and women were granted identical protections.

VII. METICS AND SLAVES

Before turning to gender roles, we should pause to consider briefly other evidence for the formal or informal application of negative liberties to metics and slaves. Although ownership of real property ordinarily remained a monopoly of Athenian citizens, the Athenians sometimes granted metics the right to own real estate (*enktêsis*); others were granted remission of the head-tax ordinarily paid by resident foreigners (*isoteleia*). A detailed forthcoming study by Edward E. Cohen amply demonstrates that Pseudo-Xenophon was right that metics and even slaves could and did accumulate considerable private fortunes and that their property rights were as secure as any Athenian citizen's.[39] Cohen also argues that in certain sorts of civil lawsuits (*dikai*) concerning property, metics

---

[39] On *enktêsis* and *isoteleia*, see David Whitehead, *The Ideology of the Athenian Metic* (Cambridge: Cambridge Philological Society, 1977). On wealthy metics and slaves, see Edward E. Cohen, *Athenian Nation* (Princeton: Princeton University Press, forthcoming).

and even slaves could represent themselves rather than depending on legal representation by an Athenian citizen, and by the same token they could initiate prosecutions, even against citizens.[40] Metics and slaves enjoyed as much religious freedom as anyone in Athens; they were treated as functional equals in the context of certain important Athenian cults and rituals, notably the state-sponsored and state-protected Eleusinian Mysteries.[41]

But given that citizenship, with its specific participation-rights, remained centrally important, what of naturalization? An Athenian law dating to the mid-fifth century predicated citizenship on birthright, mandating double native descent—an Athenian father and an Athenian mother—for those persons accepted as citizens by the demes (townships). This restriction was ideologically buttressed by resort to the myth that Athenians were autochthonous—originally born of the earth of Attica. Public speakers could claim that with autochthony came a common inborn patriotism.[42] Yet naturalization was in fact possible, for individuals and even for groups of persons, by special decree of the citizen Assembly. Some metics, and even former slaves, were enfranchised in this way. In the best-known case (because the family's complex legal affairs are well documented in the corpus of Demosthenes' forensic speeches), the family of the extremely wealthy former-slave and bank-owner Pasion, became prominent members of Athenian society. Pasion's son, Apollodorus, went on to become a well-known Athenian politician and public speaker. In several preserved forensic speeches, Apollodorus speaks openly of his ancestry. Although he allows that he and his relatives owed a special debt to the Athenians for the gift of citizenship, he claims that this indebtedness is a source of his own intense patriotism and his dedication to the good of his adopted *polis*.[43]

[40] See Edward E. Cohen, *Ancient Athenian Maritime Courts* (Princeton: Princeton University Press, 1973); and Cohen, *Athenian Nation*.

[41] On the question of religious freedom and the law against impiety, see Robert Parker, *Athenian Religion: A History* (Oxford: Clarendon Press, 1996), 207–11, 214–15. On metics and slaves in Athenian religious life, see Cohen, *Athenian Nation*. The Eleusinian Mysteries were celebrated each year with a grand procession from Athens to the deme of Eleusis, where initiates were shown and told secret things that led them to have hopes for the afterlife.

[42] On Periclean citizenship law, see Alan L. Boegehold, "Perikles' Citizenship Law of 451/0 B.C.," in *Athenian Identity and Civic Ideology*, ed. Alan L. Boegehold and Adele C. Scafuro (Baltimore and London: Johns Hopkins University Press, 1994), 57–66, and the literature cited therein. On the move from autochthony to patriotism, see Ober, *Mass and Elite*, 261–66. In *Athenian Nation*, Cohen discusses the evidence for naturalization in detail. He also argues that the citizenship law potentially allows any individual to be legally accepted as a citizen so long as he was born of two long-term noncitizen residents of Attica, but I do not believe that the evidence he cites supports the sharp legal distinction between the terms *astos* and *politês* upon which his argument depends.

[43] On the procedure for enfranchisement and its relative rarity, see M. J. Osborne, *Naturalization in Athens* (Brussels: AWLSK, Klasse der Lettern, Jaargang 43, Nr. 98, 1981). On the house of Pasion and Apollodorus, see Ober, *Mass and Elite*, 212–14. See also Jeremy Trevett, *Apollodoros the Son of Pasion* (Oxford: Clarendon Press, 1992).

Metics (regularly) and slaves (more often than is generally acknowledged) served in the Athenian armed forces.[44] Their faithful service led,
on several occasions, to formal proposals in the citizen Assembly for mass
manumission of slaves and mass enfranchisement of metics. Although in
each case the Athenians eventually balked (sometimes after the decree
had been successfully challenged in the people's courts), there was clearly,
from time to time at least, considerable sympathy (and potential, if not
fully realized, ideological space) for the inclusion within the Athenian
citizen body of many persons who were obviously not "autochthonous."
Indeed, even the standard story of Athenians as a pure "earthborn" race
was counterbalanced by the equally well-known and celebrated story of
Athenian receptiveness to foreign immigrants in mythological times.

In practice, it is certain that many "non-ethnic" Athenians slipped into
the ranks of "the Athenians" without being approved by special decree of
the Assembly. This was perhaps especially common in periods of revolutionary political change (Aeschines 1.77; Demosthenes 57.26: *diapsêphis-
mos*). But it also occurred on a more casual and endemic level at the level
of the deme (township) registration procedure: the deme assemblies voted
to accept as citizens any number of men who fell short of the double-
descent requirement. The periodic calls for "cleansing of the deme lists"
(e.g., in the 340s B.C.) are evidence for Athenian concern for maintaining
the fiction of the citizen body as a closed corporation, but they also point
to the fact that it was indeed a fiction, and that many persons undoubtedly were registered as "Athenians" because their neighbors had, for
whatever reason, chosen to ignore actual ethnicity in regarding them as
worthy of that distinction.[45]

VIII. CONTROLLING WOMEN (AND CHILDREN)

Pseudo-Xenophon limits his criticism of Athenian laxness in the matter
of treatment of non-NAMs to metics and slaves. But in the *Republic*, Plato
(562b–563d) seems to pick up where the Old Oligarch had left off, noting
that the freedom and equality characteristic of democratic regimes lead
not only to metics becoming equal to citizens, but to the young becoming
equal to the aged, and to women becoming equal to men. Plato's Socrates
had advocated a sort of cross-gender role equality within the closed and
carefully educated ranks of Kallipolis's Guardian class (on the analogy of
the similarity of the nature of male and female dogs, to which the Guardians are frequently compared). But Plato clearly regards the putative
equalization of gender relations within the real world of the democratic

---

[44] On metic service in Athenian armed forces, see Whitehead, *Ideology of the Athenian
Metic*, 82–86. On slaves in military service, see Peter Hunt, *Slaves, Warfare, and Ideology in the
Greek Historians* (Cambridge: Cambridge University Press, 1998).

[45] Cohen, in *Athenian Nation*, discusses the evidence in detail.

polis to be among its most grievous faults. Plato's claim here (like Pseudo-Xenophon's, above) is part of a critical project and cannot be taken as a simple description of Athenian reality. However, in light of the specific inclusion of women in the Athenian law against *hubris*, and the frequent assertion by modern scholars that women in democratic Athens were actually much less free and less equal to men than they were in aristocratic societies (e.g., among archaic *poleis* and in classical Sparta),[46] it is worth asking whether there might be some real-world basis to Plato's complaint that democracy encouraged the extension of inappropriate privileges across gender lines—just as it did across the lines of metic versus citizen and slave versus free.

In the context of a discussion in the *Politics* about what sorts of institutional arrangements are suited to each type of regime, Aristotle makes a suggestion that has considerable bearing on the general topic of women's standing in democratic and nondemocratic *poleis*:

> The controller of children (*paidonomos*) and the controller of women (*gunaikonomos*), and any other office that has authority of this sort of superintendence (*epimeleia*) is aristocratic, and certainly not democratic. For how is it possible to prevent the wives of poor men (*aporoi*) from going out [of the house]? Nor is it oligarchic, for the wives of oligarchs live luxuriously. (1300a4–8)

Later, Aristotle notes that

> peculiar to those *poleis* which enjoy greater leisure and are more prosperous, and which in addition take thought for orderliness (*eukosmia*), are the offices of guardian of women, guardian of the laws, guardian of children, and gymnasiarch, and, in addition to these, the superintendence of gymnastic games and the Dionysian festival contests, and any other spectacles that there may be. Of these sorts of offices, some are clearly not democratic, such as that of guardianship of women (*gunaikonomia*) or guardianship of children (*paidonomia*), since poor men (*aporoi*) necessarily use their wives and children as subsidiary workers (*akolouthoi*) due to their lack of slaves. (1322b37–1323a6)

These two comments directly link the sorts of behavior that could reasonably be enforced by agents of the government with the sociologically determined propensities of the sort of citizens definitive of various regime-types: that which was suitable for leisured aristocrats was simply imprac-

---

[46] For the claim that women in democratic Athens were actually less free than in aristocratic *poleis*, couched in negative terms, see Roberts, "Athenian Equality."

ticable in a democracy, dominated as it was by people constrained to work for their living.

The office of the *paidonomos* is otherwise unattested, but *gunaikonomoi* did exist in some *poleis*—including post-democratic Athens.[47] Aristotle's explanations for women's behavior under different regimes (and his silence on the matter of children's behavior) suggests that he was more interested in *gunaikonomoi* than in *paidonomoi*. He supposed that, were a *gunaikonomos* appointed, the wives of citizens would be prevented (or officially discouraged) from "going out" and from living luxuriously. In the case of oligarchy, in which citizenship was defined specifically by reference to wealth alone, Aristotle assumes that oligarchs' wives lived luxurious lives with the tacit approval (or even open encouragement) of their husbands. Display and enjoyment of wealth is assumed to be central to the oligarchic identity, and, that being the case, there was no reason for an oligarchic regime to seek the appointment of an official whose duty would be to restrain luxurious behavior.

The case of democracy is more complex, and Aristotle's commentary is fuller: he assumes it is simply impossible (even if it were, in principle, regarded as desirable) to prevent the wives of working men from leaving their homes. His reasoning in the first passage is clarified by the second: the "poor" household lacked slaves, and therefore depended on the productive labor of all of its members (including women). Some part of this labor was typically carried out, we must suppose, in extra-household contexts. Once again, as with Pseudo-Xenophon on the lenient treatment of slaves, the association between what sort of behavior is allowed and the socioeconomic basis of democracy is brought to the fore: for Aristotle, it is specifically because in a democracy the citizenry included slaveless "poor men," who were constrained to act (and to allow other members of their households to act) in certain ways due to their lack of material resources, that the "aristocratic" office of "controller of women" is particularly unsuited to a democracy.

There is nothing wrong with Aristotle's reasoning in these passages: he allows us to suppose that Greek men (including democrats) would, on the whole, prefer that their women stayed at home and out of sight.[48] A regime which restricted citizenship to those men financially able to keep women at home, and one concerned with ensuring "good order" via

---

[47] On *gunaikonomoi* at Athens and elsewhere, see B. J. Garland, "Gynaikonomoi: An Investigation of Greek Censors of Women," Ph.D. dissertation, Johns Hopkins University, 1981. See David Cohen, *Law, Sexuality, and Society: The Enforcement of Morals in Classical Athens* (Cambridge and New York: Cambridge University Press, 1991), on the myth of seclusion of women at Athens.

[48] Cf. Thucydides 2.45.2: "If I may speak also about the women who will now be widows, I shall define it all in a brief admonition. For great is the glory for you not to be worse than your existing nature, and not to be talked about for good or evil among men" (trans. J. S. Rusten, *Thucydides, The Peloponnesian War, Book II* [Cambridge: Cambridge University Press, 1989], with adaptations suggested by Hornblower, *A Commentary on Thucydides*).

"supervision"—i.e., an aristocracy—would be likely to appoint a magistrate with the duty of assuring that this norm was enforced in practice. As we have seen, in Aristotle's view oligarchs lacked the will to prevent private luxuriousness among women. But under a democracy, whatever the normative preference of the NAMs, there was, practically speaking, no way for the regime to survive unless women went out of the home to work. If the women of the poor could not work, the poor would starve, and thus material necessity trumped whatever normative preference for the seclusion of the wives and daughters of citizens might have existed among the Athenian NAMs. Thus, we might begin to develop a context for taking seriously Plato's comment about the tendency of democracy to promote relatively greater practical equality of women and (citizen) men without invoking a self-conscious liberalism among the NAM population.

It is impossible to determine whether or not Athenian women valued the lack of legal restrictions on their freedom of movement and association as a substantive liberty. Yet if we regard the creation of a formal government officer "in charge of controlling women" as a move specifically designed to place limits on women's life-choices, then we might want to question the scholarly habit of correlating Greek democracy with oppression of women, and aristocracy with inter-gender liberality. We are, however, still a long way from making an argument for a *positive* correlation between democracy and (relatively) liberal gender-role relations or attitudes. If we accept that it was quite common for Athenian citizens' wives and daughters to work outside the home, and that this material necessity was recognized (at least in negative terms) in Athenian institutional arrangements, do we have any warrant to go further? Do we have reason to suppose that the lived and performed Athenian experience of gender roles was otherwise more liberal than the "official" normative line? Or that Athenian ideology responded over time to the fact that women's labor was essential to the survival of democratic culture?

The best source of evidence for the last question, at least, is Athenian drama: at Athens, tragedy and comedy were officially sponsored by the democratic state and famously depicted strong, willful, even overtly "political" women. When watching Aristophanes' *Ecclesiazusae* (ca. 393 B.C.), Athenian citizens were confronted with a comic scenario in which women are made citizens by decree of the Assembly and subsequently undertake a radical reorganization of the *polis* along social lines that are hyper-egalitarian (among the free population).[49] I suppose that comedy (I am deliberately leaving tragedy to one side) had an institutionalized critical function. The Athenians intended for comic poets to present on stage culturally subversive material, to make visible the ideological contradictions and evasions by which the Athenians ordinarily lived their personal

---

[49] See also Josiah Ober, *Political Dissent in Democratic Athens: Intellectual Critics of Popular Rule* (Princeton: Princeton University Press, 1998), 122–55.

and (especially) their political lives. And I suppose that the democracy challenged itself in this way because of an implicit recognition of the dangers inherent in ideological ossification, and a recognition of the essential role that sharp and profound internal criticism plays in the continued flourishing of a democratic political order.[50] In the terms employed above, we might suggest that drama very literally "alternatively performed" aspects of Athenian ideology and thereby stimulated the democratic imagination and opened the way for other (imitative, reactive, creative) alternative performances outside the Theater of Dionysos. A reconsideration of the Athenian law on *hubris* may help us to think about the relationship between drama, Athenian democratic ideology, and the wider Greek context.

I would suggest that the *hubris* law might be read as a (non-intentional) democratic counterpart and rejoinder to aristocratic laws establishing "controllers of women" and perhaps similar, less well attested, offices for control of other categories of noncitizens.[51] We may suppose that both democratic Athens and the normative aristocratic *polis* passed their laws primarily intending to protect the standing of the citizen body. In both cases, there was a deep concern with behavior, especially in public (although perhaps also in private) that might be contrary to, and thus threatening to, the established rules (i.e., *paranomon*), thereby manifesting the potential to destroy the regime that was maintained by adherence to those rules. The general Greek assumption that lawcode and regime are intertwined, fragile, and thus incapable in practice of surviving serious breaches is familiar from Aristotle's *Politics* and is interestingly reconfigured by Plato's *Crito*—a text that has caused liberal readers considerable anguish.[52] In this conviction, then, Athenian democrats were at one with the aristocratic upholders (at whatever remove) of the *metrios* ideal.

The contrast between Athens and the normative aristocratic regime arises in where the threat to "laws and regime" was perceived to *originate*, how it was *manifested*, and how it was *answered*. The aristocratic ideology that eventuated in *gunaikonomia* legislation saw a prime need for behavioral control to be exerted upon those noncitizens most intimately connected to citizens: children and (especially) "citizens' women." If we take Aristotle's *Politics* as our source, the threat was thought to be manifested

---

[50] The argument here is made in more detail in Ober, "How to Criticize Democracy in Late Fifth- and Fourth-Century Athens," in *Athenian Revolution*.

[51] Although Aristotle's concept of aristocracy is a complicated philosophical contrivance, the fact that some nondemocratic *poleis* did indeed have "controllers of women" allows us to use the term "aristocracy" rather more broadly than Aristotle (sometimes) did. Some scholars have supposed (although it is not provable) that the *hubris* law was enacted by Solon, to whom are also attributed laws restricting the behavior of Athenian women at funerals (Plutarch, *Solon* 21.5). But the point here concerns what laws are enforced under the democratic regime.

[52] On Plato's *Crito*, see Richard Kraut, *Socrates and the State* (Princeton: Princeton University Press, 1984).

by the inappropriate public appearance of those who should remain invisible, and by the enjoyment of luxury by those who should not live in a luxurious manner. Although presumably children were also potentially sources of dangerous behavioral deviance, in Aristotle's account it is wives and adult daughters of citizens who are the primary objects of concern: Evidently the women of aristocrats manifested some tendency to "go out in public"—that is, to imitate the very public-oriented lives of their husbands, brothers, and fathers. And/or they tended to want to live over-luxuriously in private—that is, to conform to the behavioral norms typical of the archaic *habrosunê* ideology, an ideology which had conflicted with the *metrios* ideal normatively embraced by classical aristocrats (at least those of the Aristotelian sort). Because manifestations of these tendencies were affronts to the *metrios* ideal, the preservation of "good order" required scrutiny of women and official suppression of their subversive practices. The potential threat was answered by the creation of a formal government office: a bureaucracy (in effect) that was assigned formal responsibility for rooting out women's misbehavior and chastising any breaches uncovered. The rest of the citizen-aristocrats were, by implication, left to pursue other matters, public and private.

By contrast, the Athenian democratic ideology construed the threat to public order, the prime suspect of "paranomic" activity, as the hubristic individual—he who was strong enough and arrogant enough to seek to establish preeminence via the humiliation of others within the *polis*. By combining the language of the *hubris* law itself and Demosthenes' normative language in explicating that law,[53] we may say that Athenians saw women, children, slaves, and (presumably) foreigners, along with the weaker of the citizens (i.e., those commanding few resources), as the potential objects of illegitimate activity, rather than the willful originators of threats to the public order. The powerful hubristic individual was imagined as seeking to establish hierarchical relations within the *polis* on his own terms by demonstrating his capacity to humiliate, by outrageously insulting weaker persons by speech or deed (especially sexual violation), and by seeking to do so with impunity. And if he (or the class of powerful persons he represented) were successful in establishing a secure "personal" social hierarchy within the *polis*, a social space free from the legal authority of the democratic state, it would clearly mean the end of the effective rule of the *dêmos*: this is why a successfully perpetrated, unchastised act of *hubris* could be characterized as signifying "the overthrow of the democracy."[54]

---

[53] This would be a problematic procedure if the primary concern was the intention of the original lawmaker, but since that is unknowable and undatable (per note 51 above), I am concerned here with the way the law was used and understood in fourth-century practice.

[54] On the phrase *kataluein ton dêmon* (or similar phrases) and its association with *hubris*, see Aristophanes, *Ecclesiazusae* 453; and Thucydides, *The Peloponnesian War* 3.81.4 (civil war on Corcyra).

Equally distinctive is the Athenian notion of how to respond to the threat of *hubris*: not by the establishment of a formal office, a hypothetical "controller of hubristic persons," but rather by the willful intervention of "whoever among the enfranchised Athenians so wishes." The voluntary prosecutor (NAM in good standing) took it upon himself to initiate a legal action before a large body of citizens and at considerable legal (as well as, we must assume, in some cases, less formal but very real) risk to himself.[55] The maintenance of "good order" in Athens was consequently dependent upon the presence of individuals willing to serve as voluntary prosecutors—whether out of a concern for the public good, a desire for personal revenge, a desire for self-aggrandizement via public display, or (most likely) some combination of these. Unlike the normative aristocratic *polis*, which assigned the responsibility for investigation and chastisement to an appointed individual and (potentially and in principle) left the rest of the citizens out of it, in democratic Athens the entire citizen body was (potentially and in principle) involved in the maintenance of public order through the prosecution of the deviant individual.[56]

How should we read the Athenian legal conflation of women, slaves, and weaker citizens as potential objects, rather than originators, of subversive behavior? In light of the strong women depicted in Attic drama, it seems illegitimate to read the *hubris* law as proof that Athenians saw women as fundamentally "apolitical" or incapable of agency. The women of Aristophanes' *Ecclesiazusae*, for example, seem to manifest all the characteristics of Aristotle's "natural citizens." Their stated motivation in seeking to seize control of the government is the communal project of "saving the *polis*." Led by the attractively portrayed character Praxagora, the women-citizens of the play seek to reconcile various aspects of *metrios* mentality and democratic ideology. Their program of collectivization would end in freeing all Athenian NAMs from the necessity of labor and in equalizing opportunity for the enjoyment of such pleasures (especially food and sex) as the society had to offer.

Notably, Praxagora is not portrayed as an elite woman: she is the wife of Blepyros, a citizen who owns but a single cloak and depends in part upon his Assembly pay for the sustenance of his family (cf. Aristotle, *Politics* 1300a1–4). Praxagora "goes out in public" when necessary, without prior approval of her husband, and not only to engage in economically productive work. She excuses a nocturnal absence by claiming that she was called out to aid a friend undergoing childbirth (*Ecclesiazusae*

---

[55] Demosthenes' description of the various bad things done to him in private life by Meidias and his cronies illustrates the potential harms that could arise from challenging the powerful, even in Athens.

[56] The Athenians annually appointed many magistrates (by election or, more often, by lot) to undertake various aspects of public business; see Mogens H. Hansen, *The Athenian Democracy in the Age of Demosthenes* (Oxford: Basil Blackwell, 1991), 225–45. But the work of magistrates was subordinate to the popular Assemblies and lawcourts, and did not include moral policing.

526–34). Her excuse points to an Athenian world of female friendship, association, and mutual aid—a world that would presumably be restricted in an aristocratic regime characterized by the presence of a *gunaikonomos*. Praxagora had no slave attendant and therefore ventured out all alone—she explains that she donned Blepyros's male clothing in order to appear more formidable to potential cloak-thieves. We are reminded of Aristotle's comment that among the poor, women (and children) perform the sorts of tasks (in this case, defense of property) that the wealthy delegated to slaves. The point, once again, is the problematic (from the perspective of the *metrios* mentality) inclusion of poor men among the active-citizen body, which leaves open the possibility of the (situationally contingent and partial) assimilation of the women (and other non-NAMs) into the category of citizens.

It is not easy (maybe not possible or even desirable) to sustain a claim that any given drama guides its audience to a simply positive or negative evaluation of that possibility. It seems highly likely, however, that drama was at once informed by the complexity of democratic ideology, and contributed in some measure to how Athenians thought about the evolving matrix of social and political values with which and by which they lived their lives.

IX. Conclusions: Ancient Politics and Modern Theory

I have suggested that in classical Athens the practice of participatory democracy led to the development of a regime that was at once constitutional and fostered something like modern liberal values. Democracy promoted the development of both positive participation-rights and negative liberties. Whereas participation-rights were limited to NAMs, certain negative liberties were (at least in legal principle) extended to all residents of Athenian territory. If we regard the NAM body as a collective sovereign, the Athenian case might (ironically) be taken as proof of Isaiah Berlin's contention that subjects of an autocrat may enjoy negative liberties. But the sociologically diverse Athenian *dêmos* is very different from Berlin's imagined unitary sovereign, and I have argued that the *ideological* complexities associated with the *social* diversity of the citizenry provide the key to understanding the development of what I have been calling "quasi-rights." The Athenian constitutional order developed from and was sustained by a complex and contradictory ideology. The contradictions of the ideology were exposed by both "external" critics like Plato and by institutionalized critics, notably the comic poets. The experience of regularly being confronted with contradictions between social norms and the implications of political practices was an important aspect of the education of the democratic citizen. It encouraged habits of public deliberation, cut against the binary opposition between "citizens and Others," and so promoted a distribution of relations of justice that was considerably wider than the majoritarian logic of participatory democracy would otherwise have demanded.

The more general question of what Greek democracy might mean for contemporary politics and political thought has been asked, overtly and implicitly, in much recent work by both political theorists and classicists.[57] I conclude by reiterating three reasons that the study of the Athenian experience of democracy seems to me useful to modern political theorists.

First, the Athenian example highlights the potential interpretive leverage gained by assessing a variety of text genres (here: historiography, comedy, forensic oratory, and partisan pamphlets, as well as political philosophy), and by juxtaposing practices, law, ideological assumptions, normative statements, and formal philosophical claims. The modern academic tendency (which is, happily, far from universal) of subdividing the study of politics such that political theorists and philosophers deal with "ideas" while the analysis of political practices and ideologies is delegated to historians, leaves too much out of any given picture. The establishment of sharp dichotomies between the "rational discourse" of intellectuals and the ideological assumptions common to ordinary people tends to obscure how indebted intellectual thought may be to ordinary political discourse and ideological presuppositions. Athenian political texts discourage this sort of dichotomous thinking, in part because they were written in a "pre-disciplinary" era.

The second reason that the study of the Athenian experience seems useful is the overt Greek concern with the practical and ideological effects of social-power inequality, especially that produced by wealth inequality. The Greeks approached the issue of wealth-power from a perspective very different from that generally assumed by modern writers, who find it difficult to approach issues of wealth and class outside the interpretive framework defined (in schematic terms) by Adam Smith (and his advocates and critics) on the one hand, and by Karl Marx (with his advocates and critics) on the other. Whereas it would be very foolish to suppose that the ancient approach to "social life and politics" is inherently superior to modern discussions, it is, I think, potentially valuable in offering a pre-capitalist, pre-Marxist viewpoint.

The third reason, and for me the most important, is the unambiguous classical Athenian focus on the pragmatic and performed status of political privileges and legal immunities. Lacking any clear distinction between citizenship and government, or any metaphysical basis for the assertion of rights claims, the Athenians saw that establishing and maintaining individual dignity and democratic public authority was predi-

---

[57] A good deal of recent work is summed up in Peter Euben, *Corrupting Youth: Political Education, Democratic Culture, and Political Theory* (Princeton: Princeton University Press, 1997); and *Demokratia*, ed. Ober and Hedrick; and the bibliographies of both books point to more.

cated on the actions of society's members. If rights were not consistently and accurately reperformed by most of the people most of the time, they would simply cease to exist. This understanding might offer some purchase on the failure of traditional forms of liberal universalism to come fully to grips with assertions of "group rights" predicated on the establishment and maintenance of a specific group identity.[58] Moreover, the Athenian democrats' willingness to trust "voluntarism," and their general reluctance to delegate important authority to specific governmental agents, may offer an alternative to the modern tendency to associate the maintenance of rights with the strength of the formal institutions established by a powerful (if potentially threatening) central government.

Of course, no *polis*—not even democratic Athens at its best and understood in the best possible light—is an appropriate model for the establishment of a modern social or political regime. My point is not that we should take Athens as a paradigm, but that the history of the democratic *polis* is "good to think with." It offers us, as moderns, a perspective on the possible spectrum of relationships between democratic politics, political sociology, and moral values that is at once strikingly familiar and radically alien. As such, Athens may present a therapeutic challenge, not only to those who would deny any connection between participatory democracy and the extension of negative liberties, but to a complacent "end of history" tone that sometimes seems to affect even the best work by contemporary liberal thinkers.

Classics, Princeton University

---

[58] See, for example, Charles Taylor et al., *Multiculturalism: Examining the Politics of Recognition*, ed. Amy Gutmann (Princeton: Princeton University Press, 1994).

IS THERE A DUTY TO VOTE?*

By Loren E. Lomasky and Geoffrey Brennan

I. Introduction

The genre of public service advertisements that appear with two- and four-year cyclical regularity is familiar. Cameras pan across scenes of marines hoisting the flag on Iwo Jima, a bald eagle soaring in splendid flight, rows of grave markers at Arlington. The somber-voiced announcer remonstrates: "*They* did their part; now *you* do yours." Once again it is the season to fulfill one's civic duty, to vote.

Good citizenship in the final decade of the twentieth century does not seem to require much of the individual beyond simple law-abidingness. We have traveled a far distance from the Athenian agora. However, there exists a remarkable degree of consensus that voting is requisite, that one who fails to exercise the franchise is thereby derelict. Candidates for the nation's highest office publicly proclaim that duty; so do one's neighbors and associates—perhaps with some asperity in their voices—when informed that you chose to absent yourself from the polls that they took the trouble to visit. We call that consensus remarkable because, as will become evident, it is exceedingly difficult to develop a persuasive rationale for the existence of a duty to vote. Often that duty is simply taken for granted. Where arguments are given, they typically invoke either fallacious reasoning or dubious empirical premises. A cautious surmise is that the assurance with which the duty to vote is affirmed is not matched by equivalent cogency of justification. But we wish to advance a bolder conclusion: There is no satisfactory rationale for a duty to vote. Contra the popular wisdom, an individual who chooses not to exercise the franchise does not thereby fall short with regard to any responsibility entailed by citizenship.

The argument that follows does not trade on any ambiguity or delicate nuance in the term 'duty'. Thus, some may concede that there is, in the strict sense, no *duty* to vote, yet affirm that omitting to vote is nonetheless morally subpar.[1] Our claim is stronger. We argue that, under standard

* Previous versions of this essay have been presented at the University of Minnesota, Australian National University, the Australasian Association of Philosophy annual meeting, and various public establishments catering to thirsts philosophical and otherwise. We are grateful to the vigorous interlocutors we encountered at these venues who challenged us to clarify and sharpen these arguments.

[1] We are in sympathy with this distinction, believing that the Kantian equation of moral worth with adherence to duty is seriously deficient. That theme will not, however, be pressed in what follows.

circumstances, voting is not morally superior to abstention. One does not do morally better to vote than, say, to spend the time playing golf instead. That is not to maintain that individuals have no reason to vote. Some do, some don't. The same is true for golfing: if voting/golfing affords one enjoyment or otherwise contributes to leading one's preferred mode of life,[2] then one has reason to vote/play golf; otherwise one does not.

We know of no way to generate a general nonexistence proof of the duty to vote. Instead, this essay follows a strategy of enumeration. Section II specifies the range of voting scenarios over which the discussion is meant to apply. The succeeding four sections take up, in turn, various families of arguments that have been offered in support of the existence of a citizen's duty to vote. Section III examines the prudential case for a duty to vote. It is most often encountered in public service propaganda: "Your vote matters!" "Only by voting can *you* be heard!" But these hardly amount to even an embryonic justificatory argument. Indeed, we are unaware of any important *normative* theory of democracy that locates the duty to vote in the enlightened pursuit of self-interest. Mainstream *positive* theories of voting behavior do, however, routinely hypothesize that individuals decide both whether to vote and how to vote as a prudentially motivated investment in political outcomes. By explaining why voting cannot reasonably be construed as that sort of straightforward advancement of self-interest, we sharpen the difficulties that will be faced by the other normative theories to be investigated. Section IV examines the act-consequentialist case for a duty to vote; Section V examines that duty's putative derivation as the conclusion of a generalization argument. Section VI addresses the case for voting grounded on an "expressive ethics," one we have elsewhere developed at some length and found to supply the most persuasive rationale for the moral superiority of voting over abstention.[3] Each of these, even the last, ultimately fails to support a general duty to vote. We therefore conclude that no such case can be made. There remains the puzzle of why, given the insufficiencies of the supporting arguments, there obtains a strong and widely held intuition that voting is meritorious. Section VII offers some speculations concerning why this might be so.

II. The Argument Delimited

Sometimes one does wrong not to vote. An impaneled juror who declines to cast a ballot concerning the guilt or innocence of the defendant

---

[2] For example, one may establish valuable business contacts while on the links; one can appease querulous folk who do believe in the existence of a duty to vote by putting in an appearance at the polls.

[3] See Geoffrey Brennan and Loren E. Lomasky, *Democracy and Decision: The Pure Theory of Electoral Preference* (New York: Cambridge University Press, 1993), ch. 7.

fails to fulfill one of the duties attached to that office. Similarly, a university faculty member who absents herself from a departmental decision concerning a junior colleague's tenure and promotion case is, exceptional considerations aside, derelict. In both instances the duty to vote is consequent on the individual's occupying a special office or role, the satisfactory performance of which requires, but is not confined to, casting a vote. (It is also part of the officeholder's duty that the vote be well-considered, based on admissible evidence, and so on.) To infer from these special cases a citizen's duty to vote in general elections would, of course, be invalid.

One may, in virtue of special circumstances, be morally obligated to vote in a general election. If, for example, Jones has promised her spouse that she will cast a ballot in the upcoming presidential election, then she stands under an obligation to do so as an entailment of the duty to keep promises one has made. If Smith is an active member of a political party who has aligned himself with others in the task of securing its victory at the polls, then he may be guilty of bad faith, of letting the side down, if he chooses to spend election day sharpening his short iron play. The former explicitly, and the latter implicitly, voluntarily took on a commitment that created an obligation to vote which, in the absence of that undertaking, would not have obtained.

A further qualification concerns the nature of the venue in which the general elections take place. Abercrombie lives in a small community in which all adult residents routinely enlist themselves in public business. Among its traditions are that individuals serve on various committees, attend town meetings, publicly announce their views, and periodically make themselves available to hold down the community's elective offices. It is plausible to maintain that Abercrombie and all his co-residents have a duty to vote. They are the beneficiaries of practices of widespread political involvement in which each citizen plays a roughly equal and complementary part with all others. One who declines to vote or in some other manner opts out can be seen as free-riding on the exertions of others.[4] If Abercrombie has chosen to live in the community in order to secure advantages arising from patterns of citizen involvement, then the existence of the duty seems manifest; if Abercrombie is the inadvertent recipient of benefits not deliberately sought, the existence of a strict duty derived from considerations of fairness is more questionable.[5] Even in the latter case, however, voting would seem to be more morally meritorious than abstention.

In Australia it is a legal requirement, backed up by a $50 fine, that all adult citizens vote. That law may or may not be well-conceived. But if

---

[4] Why this does not generalize to more usual democratic polities is discussed in Section V.
[5] See Robert Nozick's discussion in his *Anarchy, State, and Utopia* (New York: Basic Books, 1974), 90–95.

there is a moral duty to obey the laws of a reasonably just society, then Australians have a moral duty to vote. The latter duty is entirely derivative from the former.

The subsequent discussion of the duty to vote is not meant to apply to cases like these. We explicitly restrict our discussion to voting in general elections by people who are under no special obligation to exercise the franchise and who are not required by law to do so. We further confine our attention to the kinds of elections that characteristically occur in modern nation-states and their substantial political subunits in which populations number in the hundreds of thousands or millions and in which, for most individuals, political activity is only an occasional, part-time pursuit. When there is reference in what follows to a *citizen's duty to vote*, that is the context we have in mind.

III. The Argument from Prudence

How things go with a person can be substantially affected by collective determinations. "Your vote makes a difference," the pre-election propaganda intones. If that is so, then prudent individuals will vote in order to augment the probability that electoral outcomes will favor their interests. If prudence is a duty (or, if not a duty in the strict sense, then a virtue), then one ought to vote.

Whether individuals owe duties to themselves, including a duty of prudence, is debatable. That question can, though, be set to one side here, because the key premise of the prudential argument is defective. In any election with a large number of voters, the chance that my vote will make a difference to the outcome is small. On most electoral occasions it will be infinitesimal. Therefore, one aiming to maximize her own utility may have many alternative paths for doing so, but almost surely one of the least efficacious will be to bestir herself to cast a ballot in order to influence electoral outcomes. That will be so even if much hangs on the results of the election.[6]

Consider an election between candidates/policies A and B in which there are 2n other voters (in addition to Voter I).[7] Voter I will bring about the victory of A if the other voters array themselves such that there are exactly n ballots cast for A and n for B. In such a circumstance we describe the ith voter (Voter I) as being *decisive*. Otherwise, a vote for A will not affect the electoral outcome. Thus, we can represent the expected return to a vote for A insofar as it bears on electoral outcomes as:

---

[6] We argue below that political rhetoric routinely overstates the magnitude of the electoral stakes.

[7] The assumption of an odd-number electorate simplifies the analysis by allowing us to ignore the possibility of ties and rules for handling them. It does not modify the conclusion regarding the relative inconsequentiality of an individual vote.

(1) $U_i = p[V_i(A) - V_i(B)]$
  where
  U_i = Utility to a vote for A by Voter I
  p   = Probability of being decisive
  $V_i(A)$ = Return to Voter I of A's being victorious
  $V_i(B)$ = Return to Voter I of B's being victorious

We can, in turn, represent the likelihood of being decisive as:

(2) $p = f(E, m)$
  where
  E = Total number of those casting votes
  m = Anticipated proportional majority

More explicitly, holding other factors constant, the larger the number of voters, the lower the probability of being decisive. Among these other factors, the most significant for purposes of this analysis is the expected closeness of the result. Closeness here is usually conceived in terms of the probability that an individual voter selected at random casts a ballot for A rather than B; the nearer that probability is to .5, the smaller m will be.

The direction of these relationships is intuitive. Less so are the relative magnitudes. It can be demonstrated that p is a slowly decreasing function of E but a very quickly decreasing function of m. To pass quickly over calculational complications which we address at length elsewhere,[8] in a large-number electorate the size of a U.S. congressional district, a voter who would benefit a great deal from the victory of A over B (measuring the benefit in monetary terms, suppose the voter would gain $1,000) has an expected return to a vote for A of a few pennies if m is zero. If, though, the anticipated proportional majority is as small as .01 (i.e., the probability that a randomly selected voter will vote for A is 50.5 percent), then for U_i to be valued as high as one cent, the ith voter must value A's victory in excess of $1 million. But an anticipated majority of .01 represents what we would normally think of as an exceedingly close election, one the pollsters dub "too close to call." The formal model generates a conclusion in accord with most people's intuitions: the chance that one's vote will be decisive in a national or large subnational election ranges between vanishingly small and infinitesimal.

Voting is costly in the opportunity sense. The time and effort and perhaps other resources that go into casting a ballot have alternative employments. These costs will vary from individual to individual, but for virtually everyone these will be orders of magnitude greater than the expected return to a vote as expressed in (1). Therefore, a rationally self-

---

[8] See Brennan and Lomasky, *Democracy and Decision*, esp. ch. 4, "The Analytics of Decisiveness," 54–73.

interested individual will vote neither for A nor for B, but will instead refrain from voting. At least that will be so if voting is exclusively an investment in electoral outcomes. If, however, there are direct returns to a vote—avoiding a fine if one is an Australian, securing a pleasant warm glow if one simply enjoys the act of voting, and so on—then self-interest may indeed prompt one to vote. We can restate the individual's utility calculation as:

(3) $U_i = p[V_i(A) - V_i(B)] + S - C$
where
S = Direct return to I of a vote for A
C = Cost to I of voting

For reasons adduced above, in virtually all large-number elections the probabilistic impact on electoral outcomes is nil, and thus the ith voter's utility is approximated very closely by:

(4) $U_i = S - C$

In other words, a prudent individual votes if and only if the direct return to casting a ballot exceeds the cost. Note that voting so understood is a consumption good among other consumption goods, rather than an investment in political outcomes. I may indeed have self-interested reasons to vote, but these reasons have virtually nothing to do with the advantages that would accrue to me from the victory of the more favored candidate. Casting a ballot, then, is similar to bowling or tending petunias or listening to a "Metallica's Greatest Hits" tape: if one appreciates that sort of activity, then one has reason to engage in it; otherwise one does not. From the perspective of prudence there is nothing intrinsically commendable or inadvisable about any of these activities.

IV. THE ARGUMENT FROM ACT-CONSEQUENTIALISM

The result of the preceding section is not likely to prove upsetting to many exponents of a citizen's duty to vote. Few will have conceived it to be primarily a self-regarding duty. To the contrary: even if the act of voting involves some measure of personal sacrifice it is meritorious because of the benefits thereby conferred on the population at large. That is precisely the point of speaking of it as a *citizen's* duty.

Nonetheless, a shift of perspective from prudence to the well-being of the entire community does not remove the sting of the preceding section's analysis. If the inconsequentiality of voting renders it unimportant with regard to one's own self-interest whether one bothers to cast a ballot, then that inconsequentiality also infects the claim that one is producing some public good through exercising the franchise. It seems on first blush, then, that only a slightly modified version of the argument from prudence is needed to dispose of the argument from act-consequentialism. Why should minute probabilities draw one to the polls in the latter case if they do not in the former?

The answer the consequentialist will give is: because the stakes are disproportionate. When appraising voting prudentially, only *one's own* utility enters into the picture, but when thinking about how a vote can bear on the political community's well-being, *everyone's* utility counts. Moving from the micro to the macro dimension effects a change in degree which, because it is so great, becomes a difference in kind as well. Derek Parfit offers an analogy:

> It may be objected that it is *irrational* to consider very tiny chances. When our acts cannot affect more than a few people, this may be so. But this is because the stakes are here comparatively low. Consider the risks of causing accidental death. It may be irrational to give any thought to a one-in-a million chance of killing one person. But if I was a nuclear engineer, would I be irrational to give any thought to the same chance of killing a million people? This is what most of us believe. . . . When the stakes are very high, no chance, however small, should be ignored.[9]

Some hyperbole in the concluding sentence aside, Parfit's point seems undeniable: even very small probabilities that bear heavily on the well-being of a multitude ought to be incorporated in the deliberations preceding one's decision on how to act. Brian Barry interprets this as a generally applicable utilitarian rationale for voting:

> If an act-utilitarian really gives full weight to the consequences for *everyone* that he expects will be affected, this will normally provide an adequate reason for voting. If I think that one party will increase the GNP by 1/4 per cent over five years more than the other party, that for a utilitarian is a big aggregate difference. Are there *really* so many more beneficial things one could do with fifteen minutes?[10]

Do these observations indicate, then, that if we extend the scope of our concern from one solitary individual to many, there is a directly consequentialist rationale for a duty to vote despite the minuscule likelihood of altering the outcome? In a word, no. We have no quarrel with the other sides of the respective analogies: it is, indeed, for almost all people almost

---

[9] Derek Parfit, *Reasons and Persons* (Oxford: Oxford University Press, 1984), 74–75 (emphasis in the original).

[10] Brian Barry, "Comment," in *Political Participation*, ed. Stanley Benn (Canberra: Australian National University Press, 1978), 39 (emphases in the original).

all of the time, a worthwhile moral bargain to expend fifteen minutes to avert a one-in-a-million chance of a nuclear power plant meltdown or to bring about a one-quarter percent increase in GNP over five years. What we deny is the relevance of these analogies to voting.

There is no question that a nuclear accident costing a million lives is a terrifically bad outcome. Somewhat less spectacularly, it is also uncontroversial that, all else equal, an increase in the national wealth amounting to several billions of dollars is welcome news indeed.[11] A terrible disaster or its nonoccurrence; a noteworthy augmentation of the citizenry's wealth or its absence—who doubts where the balance of good lies or whether it is large enough to make a valid claim on one's attention and effort? But alternatives faced in electoral competitions are not of that sort. We do not see Party B campaigning on the platform, "We commit ourselves to doing everything that Party A promises and in exactly the way that Party A promises to do it—except that in addition we propose to sabotage a nuclear power plant at the expected cost of a million lives"; or "We pledge to run the economy much as Party A does—but one-quarter percent less efficiently." In hotly contested elections there is never anything approaching consensus concerning which candidates or which set of policies will best secure the common good. Each side identifies some ends as valuable and proposes various political means to secure them. The competing sides typically will concur to a considerable extent concerning which items are to be valued and which disvalued (both are pro-liberty; both favor prosperity) but will assign different weights to the various goods and bads, thereby differing in the trade-offs that they will countenance (for example: "Shall the liberty of workers to strike be limited so as to secure greater prosperity?"). Or they will differ concerning factual propositions ("We are/are not in the midst of a period of global warming"). Or they will advance opposed judgments concerning the instrumental merits of different policies advocated to secure the ends they value ("Capital punishment will/will not decrease the homicide rate"). Or they will dispute the competence or commitment of would-be executors of policy, or enter into subtle semantic debates (Is affirmative action best described as setting "goals" or "quotas"?). And so on. When each side has its fervent partisans, its roster of so-called experts, its loquacious evangelists, assurance concerning where the common good lies is apt to be elusive.

This is not to deny that during the course of an election campaign there will be numerous affirmations of unshakeable conviction concerning the manifest merits of Party A and the gross deficiencies of the candidates and policies put forward by Party B. It is, though, to note that their epistemic clout is tainted by outpourings of equally confident testimony

---

[11] But all else is quite certainly not equal; see below.

issuing from the other side. There is, of course, nothing surprising in the existence of this phenomenon. Political operatives are in the business of winning adherents to their cause, the more zealous and unshakeable the better. To the extent that a candidate or party succeeds in persuading citizens—for most of whom political involvement is a very occasional avocation—that momentous matters are indeed at stake and that here is the side of Truth and Goodness, the opponent's side that of Disaster and Despair, citizens are thereby provided with an incentive to make their way to the polls on election day and to cast a ballot in the desired direction. Ratcheting up emotional fever makes for loyal party supporters in the political arena, much as it makes for loyal fans in sporting arenas. An important difference between the two brands of enthusiasm is that probably not even the die-hard fans themselves are inclined to correlate the lustiness of the cheers that ring around them with epistemic warrant. Citizens embroiled in political campaigns do, however, mistake their own depth of conviction for evidentiary weight. They should not set an example for theorists who conduct their analyses from a safe emotional distance.

By way of contrast to the Parfit/Barry analogies, a more recognizable (although still greatly simplified) rendering of the voter's scenario might go something like this. Party A proposes a set of economic policies that have some hard-to-quantify but non-negligible likelihood of generating a higher national product over the next five years than those of Party B: a best rough estimate is something on the order of one-quarter percent per year. Party B's economic program, however, seems likely to yield somewhat less inflation over the course of those five years. Complicating matters further are conflicting estimates concerning the economic policies' respective merits with regard to effects on capital investment, unemployment, the trade balance, and measures of economic equality. All that one can be reasonably confident of is that A's policies will do better with regard to some of these, and B's policies will do better with regard to others. And beyond the parties' economic programs there are another two dozen or so major areas of dispute—over defense, civil rights, education, housing, environmental policy, etc. With regard to each, a greater or lesser degree of murkiness obtains; different trade-offs are on offer; both sides swear fealty to the common good. What is the conscientious act-utilitarian now to do? Does it still seem so apparent that spending fifteen minutes to cast a ballot is one of the most socially beneficial things one can do with one's time—especially if one has not previously invested for each of those minutes several dozen hours devoted to securing and assessing relevant political information?

The utilitarian rationale for voting can be expressed by a variant of expression (1):

$$(1')\quad U = p[V(A) - V(B)]$$

In this variant, relativization to the self-interest of the individual voter is replaced by a representation of overall effects on well-being. When the affected population is large, U may be substantial even for very small p values. But what the preceding discussion suggests is that (1') stands in need of modification. It would be adequate as it stands if we could estimate with assurance the [V(A) − V(B)] term. Since we cannot, however, the value of U must be discounted not only by the probability of being decisive but, additionally, by the probability that one has overestimated or even reversed the respective merits of A and B. Call this the *epistemic discount rate*.

Although the appropriate rate of epistemic discounting will vary from election to election and, of course, from voter to voter, in virtually all real-world election scenarios and for the vast majority of voters, it will be large enough to bring the U term very close to zero. That is because political uncertainties are not all of one species but several, and they compound each other. First, as suggested above, one has to discount for mistakes in assigning comparative weights to the various competing goods (or, more rarely, for having identified as a good something that is a bad, or vice versa). Second, one has to discount for the fallibility inherent in empirical assessments concerning matters of fact and causal judgments concerning the instrumental effects of alternative policy options.

Third, one must then discount by the likelihood that the platform on which the party is running is indicative of the actions that it will indeed undertake should it gain office. That is, even if one knew with certainty that giving effect to the A platform would be superior to realizing the B platform, the return to a vote for A has to be discounted by the probability that A will defect from its own standard. It is not only inordinate cynicism about politicians and their campaign promises that might induce one to attach substantial weight to this factor; political history is full of spectacular and momentous turnarounds. To take just twentieth-century United States presidential elections as examples, in 1916 Woodrow Wilson ran for reelection on the slogan "He kept us out of war!" He was duly reelected and then didn't. In 1964, Lyndon Johnson alleged that if the wrong candidate was elected the U.S. would find itself mired in an unwinnable land war in Asia. So it proved. And of course there is the whimsically delightful insouciance of George Bush's "Read my lips; no new taxes!"

Fourth, one must discount for historical accidents and inadvertencies. Unpredictable wars, assassinations, stock market crashes, famine, or incapacity of the officeholder might turn what had *ex ante* seemed to be a good bet into an *ex post* loser. Fifth and finally, one must discount all of the above by a measure of one's own judiciousness or lack of same as a political evaluator, asking: How well-attested is the data on which I rely? How adequate are my technical capabilities in economics, international affairs, defense studies, social policy, etc. for supporting the instrumental analyses I bring to competing policy proposals? Is my judgment liable to be affected by any hidden biases or blind spots? How successfully have I managed to detach myself from evanescent enthusiasms so as to preserve a cool objectivity? And the like.

If, after all the discounts are appropriately assigned, it still seems manifest that A is the better party/candidate, then one may have some utilitarian reason to cast a ballot for A. But even then, perhaps not. If knowledge of the superiority of A is not confined to some esoteric coterie but rather is possessed by me because it is readily available to the citizenry at large, and if members of that citizenry for the most part will vote against a palpably inferior candidate should they bother to vote at all, then employing one's fifteen minutes to vote may, on utilitarian grounds, be inadvisable. Recall that the value of p is a rapidly diminishing function of m, the expected proportional majority. If, say, for any representative voter in an electorate in which one million individuals cast ballots, it is .6 likely that she will recognize B to be inferior and thus vote in opposition, then the likelihood of one's own vote being decisive is so indescribably small as to be entirely negligible. (If the question is, "Should we bestir ourselves to avert nuclear meltdowns?", how likely is it that my vote will be needed to tip the balance?) To oversimplify a bit, on those occasions when one's vote is most likely to make the sort of difference that stirs the hearts of act-consequentialists, there will rarely be any firm indication concerning for whom it ought to be cast; and when there is unmistakable evidence concerning which is the better candidate or policy, it is almost inconceivable that one's vote will be needed.

Suppose, for the sake of argument, that all the preceding cautions could be met by an exceptional public-spirited citizen confident of her ability to evaluate the issues, judge the fitness of the candidates, and cast a well-directed ballot. That would still not support a general duty to vote. Rather, it would at most show that there are consequentialist reasons for *someone who is good at voting* to do so—and consequentialist reasons for someone who is bad at voting to abstain. If, for example, despite my best efforts I am more likely than not to be a sucker for an inferior candidate (this is my track record; past attempts to mend my ways have met with no success; etc.), then I confer on the citizenry a benefit by staying at home on election day. It follows that there cannot be a completely general citizen's duty to vote, because *I* am a citizen and it does not include me.

One does not, however, need so strong an assumption of political ineptitude to support a rationale for not voting. That is because the relevant measure of facility as a voter is comparative. To see that this is so, consider a radically simplified electorate of three individuals, voters X, Y, and Z. X and Y have demonstrated an aptitude of .6 for identifying which of two candidates is the better one. Z is yet more skilled, with a success rate of 90 percent. When they all vote in an election contested by candidates A and B, they select the better candidate—let us assume it is A—whenever either X and Y, X and Z, Y and Z, or all three of them vote for A. That sums to a success rate of 79 percent. But if X and Y should abstain, the likelihood of selecting the better candidate soars to 90 percent.

Whether those with lower voter-facility scores increase the likelihood of a favorable electoral determination by abstaining will depend on the actual distribution of scores. So, for example, if X and Y each had a .8 aptitude, the expected value of the outcome would be diminished rather than enhanced by their abstention. But although no universal generalization is at hand, over a wide range of distributions it will be the case that those who are considerably below the median level of voter facility will improve electoral outcomes by abstaining. That will raise the median level of the remaining voter population, thereby making it incumbent on those citizens in the new bottom group to abstain. Again the median has been raised, and again a new crop of abstainers sprouts, the process iterating until only a small number of extraordinarily acute political evaluators remains in the voting pool. Something has gone awry, but piquantly so. For on the way to providing a utilitarian argument for a citizen's duty to vote, Parfit and Barry have (re)invented—the regime of Philosopher-Kings!

It could be argued in response that not everyone is a utilitarian. There will be lots of people casting ballots predicated on some incentive other than concern for the greatest happiness of the greatest number. Predictably, many will vote self-interestedly; others will cast ballots expressive of malice; some will just grab the lever closest to their dominant hand. Some always vote for the Democrat, some never do, and others are as irregular as a quantum particle dance. In virtue of such diverse political phenomena, it is by no means out of the question that the consequentialist stakes are indeed large and that your estimate of their size and direction is substantially better than average. Under such circumstances, the utilitarian objects, there may well be a morally compelling reason for you to vote.

We need not look too deeply into the particulars of the sort of case hereby envisioned to observe that all such scenarios are intrinsically incapable of supporting a generalized duty to vote. If they carry any moral entailments, it is not to a duty to vote *simpliciter* but rather to a citizen's duty to *vote right*. That is, assuming that A is the better of the two candidates,

$$V_A > \text{Not voting} > V_B$$

where V_A represents voting for candidate A and V_B represents voting for candidate B. But this is not how a duty to vote is supposed to work. Rather, when it is said that voting is morally meritorious, what normally is meant is that the goodness of rousing oneself to visit the polls is independent of the subsequent choice of which candidate will receive one's vote. (There may be additional moral merit in ascertaining who is the best candidate and then voting for that person, but this is in addition to that which attaches to the voting act as such.) On an act-consequentialist analysis, however, it is the direction of the vote that is crucial; any of those B voters would have done better with regard to his duty as a citizen had he instead spent his fifteen minutes in the pub.[12]

There is a further reason why the consequentialist case for a duty to vote is strained. The argument hinges on there being matters of huge moment at stake so as to offset the tiny likelihood of one's own vote tipping the balance. However, there are good reasons in general to think that this will not often be the case—at least if democracy is working tolerably well. It is a well-established proposition in the formal literature on electoral competition that parties/candidates will be constrained to offer policy platforms that lie not too far from that which the median voter prefers. In two-party electoral races of the familiar kind, political equilibrium, if it exists, will be characterized by the parties/ candidates locating themselves in near-proximity to each other, and this co-location result is quite robust to assumptions about voter motivation. One does not have to take these formal models too literally to recognize the force of the simple reasoning at stake—namely, that competition tends to restrict the policies that parties will offer, to the extent that those parties are interested in maximizing their chances of being elected. Such centripetal forces depend on the threat that voters will vote against things they do not like—but if that threat has been effective, then it is not necessary for citizens actually to exercise the franchise! In the limit, when rival candidates offer virtually identical policies, it seems inordinately precious to insist that we should all turn out because of some putative democratic duty. At least that is so within an act-consequentialist scheme.

We conclude that on every front the argument from act-consequentialism fails. It cannot support a duty to vote except when the stakes are very high, a circumstance which we have given reason to believe is rarer than is commonly made out. Even then, act-consequentialism does not support a duty to vote but rather a duty to vote *right*. Thus, it is not a duty of the citizenry at large, but only of the political cognoscenti. Even for political junkies, a healthy dose of confidence that one is in fact voting right is rarely justified; and the more likely it is that such confidence is justified, the less likely it is that one's vote will be needed to tip the balance. Conclusion: On any list of the top thousand or so ways an ordinary citizen can usefully augment social well-being, casting a ballot on election day will either rank low or not be present at all.

---

[12] We omit here complications arising from the voter's *beliefs* concerning the merits of the candidates, the *intentions* that inform the act of voting, and the *motivation* for exercising the franchise rather than abstaining. Different consequentialists attach different moral implications to these, and their resolution is, in any event, peripheral to an alleged duty to vote.

V. The Argument from Generalization

But what if everyone were to stay home and not vote? The results would be disastrous! Therefore, I (you/she) should vote.

Some version of the preceding is, by our casual tally, the most commonly adduced justification for a duty to vote. It can be presented as a reflection on the utility ramifications of a general practice of nonvoting, or it can take on a more Kantian wrapping in which willing the universalized form of the maxim "Vote only if it involves no sacrifice of one's own interests" is shown to embody an inconsistency. Often, of course, it is neither, but merely the inchoate apprehension on the part of the thoroughly nontheoretical man that he is doing wrong by abstaining from an activity that he would not wish most of his compatriots to omit. Although there are significant differences among various generalization strategies, the following analysis abstracts from those differences. Instead, we attempt to identify certain features that regularly separate persuasive from less persuasive generalization arguments. We then show that the generalization argument for a duty to vote falls among the latter.

To begin, we note in passing that the claim that it would be disastrous if no one voted is far from evident.[13] That is because the scenario under which abstention becomes universal has not been specified. There are an indefinite number of possible worlds in which no one votes. In some there is no voting because there are no elections; in others there is no voting because there are no people. For purposes of a generalization argument, some of these possible worlds are more relevant than others. Presumably, what is intended is a scenario in which there are eligible voters, there are contested elections in which they are at liberty to cast ballots, but all refrain from doing so in order to pursue their various private ends. That is a possible world sufficiently close to the actual world to have some purchase.

Even so, the indicated conclusion is ambiguous. To limn the details of this possible world, we might suppose that people abstain from voting because political determinations are largely irrelevant to their interests: Collective action beyond that in which people voluntarily engage is almost never required to secure any appreciable good, and when it is required, one candidate for office is as likely as any other to do a creditable job in orchestrating it. So no one bothers to vote. Is this a woeful world in which to find oneself? To our eyes it has more the aspects of a paradise! Alternatively, for the sake of theological balance we may speculate that no

---

[13] Compare Anthony Downs in his classic *An Economic Theory of Democracy* (New York: Harper and Row, 1957), 269: "Since the consequences of universal failure to vote are both obvious and disastrous, and since the cost of voting is small, at least some men can rationally be motivated to vote even when their personal gains in the short run are outweighed by their personal costs."

one bothers to vote in Hell because the totals invariably are corrupted. Splitting the difference leaves one agnostic concerning the putative badness of universal abstention.

Such qualms duly noted, let it be granted for the sake of argument that generalized nonvoting would indeed be undesirable. Still, the indicated conclusion ("Therefore I/you/she ought to vote") does not automatically follow. It is notoriously easy to produce arguments that display the same surface form as the generalized-failure-to-vote argument, yet yield preposterous conclusions. For example, suppose that Dalrymple is considering leaving the farm to pursue a career as a dentist. The question is put to her, "What if no one grew fruits and vegetables?" The result, Dalrymple admits, would be disastrous. Therefore, it is urged, she would do wrong to abandon farming for dentistry. Against this suffices the retort, "But *not everyone will* give up farming!"

By way of contrast, Throckmorton is about to take a shortcut across the newly seeded lawn and is brought up by the reproof, "Well, what if everyone were to walk across the lawn? All the grass would be killed!" The reply, "But not everyone will cut across the lawn; most people take more heed of signs than I do," carries distinctly less conviction. The two cases display the same surface form, yet one intuitively is weak and the other strong. What accounts for the difference?

We cannot here attempt to offer a comprehensive theory of soundness in generalization arguments, especially as we are abstracting from different underlying approaches to generalization. There are, though, certain more or less readily identifiable features which attach to those generalization arguments that intuitively persuade and which are notably absent from those that do not.

Sometimes by doing or refraining from some action one thereby perpetrates an *unfairness*. This will be so when one benefits from or otherwise assigns positive value to the opposite type of performance on the part of others. By not doing as others do, one takes a free ride on their compliance. When Throckmorton ignores the "Keep Off the Grass!" sign and cuts across the newly seeded lawn, he thereby secures a quicker route to his destination; when others comply with the directive, they get to enjoy a flourishing green lawn—but so too does Throckmorton. The individual who picks out an apple from the orchard saying, "One won't be missed," may be entirely correct, but he is thereby presuming that the disappearance of this particular apple will not be followed by the like disappearance of bushels more; that is, he is presuming that others are more firmly bound than he is himself by norms of property ownership.[14] And simi-

---

[14] Here the benefit secured by others' compliance extends primarily to the orchard owner but can be understood derivatively as a public good, the obtaining of a higher level of obedience to law, enjoyed equally by those who contribute to the production of that good and those who do not.

larly for the casual litterer, the tax evader, the illicit occupier of "Handi-capped Only" parking spots, and their numerous kin.

In many though not all cases of such free-riding behavior, initial de-fection by one or a small number of persons tends to promote further defections. In the extreme case the equilibrium outcome is universal de-fection. Suppose that one individual backs out of paying her share of the cost required to produce some public good. That single act of defection increases the per-person cost of the good to the remainder of the group, which may, in turn, induce others to back out, and so on, until production is no longer sustainable and the free-riding behavior becomes self-annihilating. This is one (not very Kantian) way of reconstructing Kant's demonstration in the *Grundlegung* of the inconsistency generated by ap-plication of the Categorical Imperative to a practice of borrowing money in the expectation that one will not be able to pay back the loan when it comes due.

In cases such as these, generalization is useful, if only as a heuristic device. It simultaneously levels the playing field and puts the tendency of an individual's action under a moral microscope through which the wrong-ness of the conduct is rendered evident. Free-riding, when generalized, is shown to be no more viable than the village in which everyone made a living by taking in others' washing. Strictly speaking, what makes an ungeneralizable action wrong is not that it fails the generalization test. Rather, it fails the generalization test because of underlying unfairness, and it is the unfairness that accounts for the action's wrongness. Passing a generalization test is secondary; fairness or the lack of same is what is primary.

That is why some arguments that exhibit disastrous results of a certain generalized practice fail to persuade. They are examples in which the universal practice of S would indeed be unfortunate, but not because of any unfairness embedded in an individual instance of S. Such is the case with the decision to abandon farming in order to take up dentistry. When Dalrymple ceases to farm she does not thereby perpetrate any unfairness on those who remain in farming. Rather, each remaining farmer is, all else equal, rendered better off at the margin in virtue of the lower level of competition. In a large economy the effect may be so small as to be entirely unnoticeable, but the key point is its direction, not the magnitude. Moreover, as one person or several people leave farming, there is no tendency to set up a spiral of further departures; just the reverse. The process is self-stabilizing, with inducements to remain (or, once having left, to return) growing progressively greater the more who withdraw. The equilibrium that emerges is morally satisfactory; there will be both dentists and farmers, and neither reaps unfair advantage at the expense of the other.

Abstaining from voting is more like choosing a profession of dentistry than it is like cutting across a newly seeded lawn or failing to pay one's share of taxes. Individuals who choose to vote do so because, as modeled in expression (3), the benefits they secure from voting exceed the costs. Those benefits are the sum of direct returns to a vote—for example, "having my say!"[15]—and the return constituted by raising the probability of the desired electoral outcome taking place. When an eligible voter abstains, thereby lowering E, the total size of the electorate, the probability p of one's own vote proving decisive increases. That is, each remaining voter is rendered better off by the lower level of electoral competition. In a large electorate, as with a large economy, the effect of one person's withdrawal may be so small as to be entirely unnoticeable, but the key point is its direction, not the magnitude. Therefore, as in the preceding example, the process tends to be self-stabilizing. An equilibrium emerges that does not have any evident morally unsatisfactory properties.

Some will respond by objecting that this equilibrium may be substantially less than full citizen participation, perhaps well under 50 percent of the eligible population,[16] and therefore is objectionable for being less democratic than full participation. We are unmoved by this response because we are unsure what it means to be "more/less democratic" and why in this context being more democratic should be deemed better than being less democratic. If "more democratic" simply *means* displaying greater levels of citizen participation, then of course it is true that high rates of voting are more democratic than lower ones, but it would be begging the question to take that definitional circumstance as a reason for preferring greater participation. If what is meant is that democratic institutions do better with greater levels of participation, then we would need to have a specification of the normative criteria for "doing better" and empirical grounds for maintaining that these criteria are more fully realized with increased participation. It is not obvious to us that democratic ideals would be better served if, instead of two major parties, there were twenty, or if the size of Congress were enlarged by a factor of a hundred, or if elections were held on a fortnightly basis. Against each of these envisioned "reforms," the status quo does not seem obviously inferior. Similarly, we do not find it obvious that election outcomes would be "better" or political institutions more "legitimate" (in whatever nontrivial senses of these words might be supplied) if voting were to take place at

[15] For a model of voting behavior that takes electoral activity to be primarily motivated by expressive concerns, see Brennan and Lomasky, *Democracy and Decision*, especially ch. 3, "The Nature of Expressive Returns," 32–53.

[16] During recent decades, turnout for American presidential elections has tended to be near the 50 percent mark of the eligible population, turnout for off-year elections well under 50 percent. For example, in 1996 and 1992 (presidential election years), voters constituted 49.1 percent and 55.1 percent respectively, while the figures for 1994 and 1990 were 38.8 percent and 36.5 percent respectively. Note that approximately one-quarter of the eligible population is not registered to vote. Statistics on voter turnout are available on the Infoplease.com website (http://www.infoplease.com/ipa/A0763629.html).

90 percent rather than 50 percent or even 5 percent participation levels. And even if more did mean better, it would still require further argument to show that this establishes a duty to vote. Wishing not to prejudge such complex questions, we conclude this section by observing that no such duty emerges straightforwardly from a generalization argument.[17]

VI. Expressive Ethics and Voting

Not all that uncommonly during classroom discussions of the ethics of democratic participation which we have superintended over the years, some student would rouse himself to a greater than customary pitch of moral seriousness and exclaim, "If you don't bother to vote, then you don't have any right to complain afterwards about what the government does!" Often this rebuke elicits a buzz of approval from the other students.

It is not difficult to find any number of reasons to dismiss this declaration as more passionate than cogent. In no actually legislated bill of rights or credible theory of free expression is a right to complain about the activities of government contingent on one's prior electoral participation. And if there were such a theory, what would it look like? Would someone who has voted for A over B have no right to complain about anything the government subsequently does should A in fact defeat B? If one wished to be sure of retaining the right to complain, would it not be prudent to vote for some obscure third-party candidate in order to assure that one is not muffled by one's prior electoral support? Doesn't the plausibility of this entire series of speculations presume that one had—and then, by abstaining, irresponsibly squandered—some realistic opportunity through one's vote to make a difference with regard to political outcomes, a proposition examined and rejected in Section III? If no voter or no nonvoter is individually responsible for the outcome that emerged, why should one more than the other be consigned by shame or compunction or opprobrium to silence? It may seem appropriate, in short, to conclude that this line of thought is the sort of sophomoric effusion not uncommon in a classroom of sophomores.

---

[17] Sometimes the case for a duty to vote is offered as a quasi-generalization argument based on the observation that, in real-world politics, abstention is not uniform across groups or classes. We might, for example, observe that the frequency of voting by poor black single mothers is less than that of well-to-do white male retirees. Then, on the assumption of reasonably systematic interest-based voting, the results that can be predicted to emerge if everyone votes can be compared with those that actually prevail: the difference becomes a measure of the *democratic deficit* which one might be thought to have a duty to overcome. But even if this constitutes a rationale for voting by the electorally underrepresented, it just as strongly argues for abstention by the overrepresented. (And since all of us are members of an indefinitely large number of classes—single mothers, left-handed philatelists, Albanian Buick-owning Rosicrucians—it will be hard to come up with an unambiguous criterion for determining whether one's proper home is among the under- or overrepresented.) Unsurprisingly, if a generalization argument is directed at specific groups, it cannot really function as a generalization argument.

The dismissal is too quick. (Take the preceding paragraph as a pedagogical confession.) The student's response is, to be sure, naive, but it conceals a promising insight that has largely been banished from more sophisticated ethical theories. Interpreted charitably, the response maintains that alongside, and to a considerable extent independent of, direct or indirect consequential considerations there exist *norms of expression*. Through one's spoken utterances and other expressive activity, one aligns oneself with certain values and opposes others. To the extent that it is inherently and not simply instrumentally good to identify—and to identify oneself with—that which is good (and evil to align oneself with that which is evil), an ethics of expression is not reducible to even a sophisticated consequentialism.[18]

The universe of value is enormous, and no one can stand for everything that is intrinsically worthy. Each of us, though, is situated by circumstance or by our own prior choices in proximity to certain morally trenchant items. One's stance with regard to them goes a long way toward defining one's character as an acting being. That stance incorporates both consequentialist and nonconsequentialist aspects. No more than the passionate sophomore are we able to offer an in-depth account of their interworkings, but we would be surprised if most readers do not acknowledge in their own moral lives expressive as well as outcome-directed imperatives. In particular, we expect considerable concurrence with the assessment that one is obliged on suitable occasions to express support for certain practices and institutions if one is to be entitled to play any significant part within them. Some examples:

To be a fan of the New York Yankees is more than to have a "pro" attitude toward the Yankees' winning ball games and pennants. It additionally involves a disposition to engage in activity that expresses support of the team. A true-blue fan may never actually attend a game, but if she does she will cheer as the Yankees load the bases, and will commiserate with other fans as the rally is snuffed out by a double play. Fans will scream and contort themselves even in front of unresponsive TV screens. To observe that these antics do no good with regard to the team's win-loss statistics is to miss the point; the practice of being a fan has very little to do with undertaking consequentially fruitful activity on behalf of the object of one's passions and very much to do with expressing support.

Friendship is in some ways similar, in some ways different. Friends do act to procure goods for each other. One not only expresses a wish that the friend's life go well but endeavors to make that be so. Sometimes, however, there is nothing one can do for one's friend. He is gravely ill; the doctors will either find some way to save him or they will not; it is entirely out of one's own hands. But one who can do

---

[18] Nor is it in any obvious way a corollary of Kantian ethics, but this is a matter that could bear further examination.

nothing for the recovery will nonetheless expressively support that eventuality.[19] To do otherwise is literally to render oneself a "fair-weather friend"—that is, not a genuine friend at all. The practice of friendship carries both consequential and expressive elements, with neither reducible to the other.

Numerous related instances can be adduced. The momentousness of particular items of our experience is regularly underscored via symbolic acts that express our respect, regret, appreciation, devotion, implacable opposition, or other intentional stances. One who insists on representing all rational activity as directed toward the production of consequences will be unable satisfactorily to account for the retrospective dimension of our activity. For example, sacramental or commemorative activities will be systematically misunderstood as essentially forward-looking—that is, as other than they represent themselves as being—if not indeed as embodying some harebrained confusion about the temporal direction of causality.

Not only in private life do expressive considerations come to the fore. It is in the nature of democratic politics that matters presented and widely acknowledged as items of momentous concern to all members of the polity are held up to examination, debated, and eventually put to popular determination through elections. Even in the age of the professionally packaged candidate and the ten-second sound bite, a certain measure of pomp and ceremony still attaches to the electoral process, thereby emphasizing that it is indeed serious business. The individual in her capacity as *citizen* has an assigned role in this process. Outsiders may be affected by the polity's electoral determinations, but the citizen is, additionally, an *agent* of those determinations. Through appearing at the polls and casting a ballot, she expresses her engagement with the concerns and undertakings of her compatriots and displays her assent to the legitimacy of the public enterprise through which she and they are bound together as partners within civil society.

Conversely, it can be argued, someone who chooses to be absent from the polls thereby expresses detachment from the enterprise, if not indeed active disdain. The doings of the polity are not his affair, he proclaims through his absence. It can go on without him—and he very well without it. That which is a matter of profound significance to his neighbors does not merit the allocation of even a few minutes of token symbolic support. It is for this reason that one who fails to vote imperils any right sub-

---

[19] It is a piece of conspicuous consequentialist obtuseness to attempt to find the rationale for all such expressive activity in the effects that such messages of support will have on the stricken individual's medical prognosis or emotional state. Is it necessary to explain to anyone who is not deep in the caverns of utilitarianism that, for example, one does not automatically score high marks as a friend if, instead of displaying a long face before the bedridden individual, thereby adding misery to misery, one eschews the hospital visit in favor of an evening's carousing at the pub?

sequently to complain about the government—not in the technical sense of being legally barred from doing so, but as an implication of common decency. One ought not bother others by raising matters that are none of one's business, and insofar as one who is eligible to vote declines to do so, one is expressing a disinclination to acknowledge the business of the *res publica* as one's own. To complain after the fact may be within the law, but it is base. It is like fulsomely bemoaning at the end of the season the also-ran finish of the Yankees after making no prior effort to take in a game, to apprise oneself of the team's fortunes, or even to cheer from a distance. It is anomalous in the same way as gnashing one's teeth and weeping bitter tears at the passing of someone of whom, in life, one was oblivious. It is, we might say, an exercise of bad faith and is to be condemned as such. That is the fleshed-out rendering of the student's exclamation.

Abstention by itself is not bad faith. It is, though, arguably discreditable. The office of citizen is no mean one, and to fail to display adequate regard for the station can be categorized as inherently condemnable. Not voting, so construed, is akin to declining to stand at the playing of the national anthem or trampling on the flag. Each is an expressively laden action that aligns one with certain political values and against others. Therefore, they are properly subject to praise or blame in virtue of what they *mean*, not simply because of what they *bring about*. The expressive argument for a duty to vote maintains that one evinces a minimally decent level of regard for the political weal by periodic appearances at the polls; to do less is to do too little.

Of all the rationales for a duty to vote, we find the expressive account strongest, if only by default. At one time we pronounced ourselves half-persuaded that the case it makes is sound,[20] but that now seems to be an overestimation. The chief inadequacies of the expressive case for a duty to vote are internal: the mere act of showing up at the polls every several years and grabbing some levers is palpably inadequate to qualify as a significant act of political expression.

Is exercise of the franchise to be construed as the expression of fidelity to the country's democratic institutions? Day-by-day residence within its borders and adherence to its laws and customs attests more explicitly and continuously to one's allegiance. Should the act of voting instead be construed as expressing some appreciation of the significance to the polity of the particular issues and debates that are spotlighted by the current election campaign? That is to read rather a lot into the act of voting. As exponents of a duty to vote often remark, for most people voting is a low-cost activity. No political literacy test must be passed before one is allowed to matriculate at the polls. Because the ballot is secret, the direction of one's vote is not subject to scrutiny and thus lacks the expressive

[20] See Brennan and Lomasky, *Democracy and Decision*, 186–89.

dimensions of a genuinely public performance.[21] A vote cast from habitual allegiance to one party or TV-ad-induced prejudice or whimsy counts as much as one that is the product of diligent pre-election scrutiny of the candidates and issues. To presume that the act of voting expresses significant psychic involvement in the political affairs of the nation is like inferring from someone's sporadic church attendance an abiding concern with the theological ramifications of the Augsburg Confession.

This is not to deny the expressive salience of political activity. We are among the millions of people worldwide who were transfixed by the televised image of the anonymous man in Tiananmen Square who time and again defiantly interposed his body before the advancing tanks. We admired his heroism for reasons quite apart from any speculations concerning its likely effect on the decision making of the autocratic Beijing gerontocracy. Similarly, we acknowledge the expressive richness that was inherent in political participation by free citizens of the Greek *polis*, Roman republic, or Renaissance city-states. For them, political involvement gave shape to large swatches of a life in its public aspect. For some people today, it still does. But no such elevated status can be claimed for a desultory visit to the polls every few years. We do not deny that the rush of events can sometimes impose on citizens certain expressive obligations; it may be culpably shameless during times of great civic unrest or national mourning to present oneself to one's compatriots as uninvolved and unconcerned. And we acknowledge the coherence, if not the persuasiveness, of a republicanism that promotes vigorous citizen involvement in public affairs. There is, however, no sense in attaching to a perfunctory political performance more expressive weight than it can bear.[22]

Finally, there is the simple point that refraining from voting can be no less expressive than voting. One may wish to record one's total contempt for all the candidates, or one's conscientious objection to some policy that is a feature of all the major candidates' platforms, or one's belief that the entire enterprise is a fraud and a delusion. Turning one's back on the entire business, refusing to be implicated—these may not be the most extreme forms of civic rebellion, but they are ones that the democratic form

[21] See Geoffrey Brennan and Philip Pettit, "Unveiling the Vote," *British Journal of Political Science* 20 (1990): 311–33.

[22] In the mid-1970s, when soaring inflation was ravaging the economy, President Gerald Ford commandeered the nation's television screens to display to the American people WIN ("Whip Inflation Now") buttons that they were bidden to wear as a signal of their determination to overcome the blight. At the time, some critics lampooned the buttons as an ineffective instrument for combating ratcheting price levels. That was unfair. What rendered the WIN button ludicrous was not lack of causal efficacy but rather its bathetic expressive quality. It was of a piece with Ford's errant golf shots and occasional airport tarmac pratfalls.

Much contemporary passion directed toward collecting newspapers and bottles in recycling bins has about as much effect on the level of depletion of natural resources as WIN buttons did on the level of inflation. However, recycling activity has an inner complexity adequate to render it expressively articulate with regard to the ends thereby endorsed. Recycling's wisdom may be disputed, but the practice is not inherently laughable.

characteristically admits. And compared to rushing to the barricades or joining the Michigan Militia, they have the added merit of civic gentleness. We
might disagree in particular cases concerning the moral advisability of expressive abstention, but it is certainly not an incoherent practice.

VII. BELIEF IN A DUTY TO VOTE

One question raised by the foregoing is why, if grounding for a duty to
vote is so distinctly shaky, belief in its existence should be widespread
and insistent. Although popular sentiment is not decisive in these matters, one might reasonably locate the onus of proof on those who would
call into question a venerable piece of folk wisdom. We believe that this
onus has been successfully borne in the earlier sections. Since the argument has proceeded by enumeration, however, suspicion may remain
that popular sentiment rests on some significant line of support that has
been left unexamined. There is no way to put such a suspicion entirely to
rest, but it is rendered less acute if the prevalence of the belief can be
explained by factors other than those that would constitute its justification. Three factors suggest themselves.

First, in some political environments ancestral to that of contemporary
representative liberal democracy, the persona of the activist citizen was central in a way it need not and cannot be today. In republics where free adult
males possessing affluence sufficient to allow attention to affairs of state
were a small minority of a small population, the demand that all who were
entitled to participate should do so enjoyed considerable cogency. We are
heirs to the political tradition of Aristotle's *Politics*, Renaissance human-
ism, the *Federalist Papers*. It is not surprising that we remain partially in
thrall to ideals that were informed by very different conditions.[23] Civic republicanism is an ideology crafted by and for political elites. Its classical
formulations have nothing to say about vast mega-states, universal enfranchisement, widely shared economic affluence, far-advanced division of political labor with concomitant specialization of function, neutral public
bureaucracies, moderated party competition, and a host of other shifts in
circumstance that separate us from our republican forebears. It is no longer
possible, let alone desirable, that all free citizens devote themselves inten-
sively to public concerns. Insofar, though, as traces of that superannuated
republicanism linger, they support an ethos of universal participation, the
lowest common denominator of which is periodic appearance at the polls.

Second, belief in a duty to vote promotes the self-esteem of voters. The
public rhetoric of democracies is redolent with invocations of the dignity
of active citizenship; it is fully one-third of government of the people, by
the people, and for the people. Yet most individuals find themselves, in

---

[23] Compare the transition from eighteenth-century ideals of a citizen's militia to the
variety of contemporary enthusiasms for a right to keep and bear arms.

their daily affairs, distant from the precincts in which governance is exercised. The gulf of separation between one's democratic faith and predominant patterns of private activity can engender a sort of cognitive dissonance. That dissonance will be eased if one can establish for oneself solid lines of association with "the people" who are supposed to be sovereign within a democracy. The act of voting constitutes such a connection. One who votes can say, "Well, I did *something*." If that something can, additionally, be characterized as the discharge of a solemn civic trust, there is comfort to be taken in its fulfillment, no matter how meager the demands thereby placed on one's wit and energies, the irrelevance of one's vote to the emergence of political outcomes, and the paucity of expressive potential in casting a ballot. Cheap grace is, after all, still grace.

Third, we ask, *Cui bono*? Who are the major beneficiaries of the myth of a duty to vote? Well, we can begin with those who do vote, since they can bask in the satisfaction of duty done. However, since the logical foundations of that supposed duty are rickety, its survival stands in need of some external nurturing. The opening sentence of this essay observed that such nurturing is periodically provided by public service announcements in the media; it is also provided by earnest declarations from political plenipotentiaries that yes, each citizen's vote is heard—that they, the people, are the true masters and candidates for office only their would-be servants. These sonorous harmonies are, to be sure, balm for democratic anxieties, but we might speculate that the benefits accruing to those who hum the tune are yet more substantial. Unlike the general run of citizens for whom political activity is an occasional thing, for a minority it is the primary business. Its rewards include position, prominence, power, and financial prosperity, and the fact that there is never a shortage of aspirants willing to enter the fray is some evidence that the magnitude of those rewards is substantial.

For the circle that thrives on the practice of politics it is, therefore, a matter of no small significance that those who foot the bill remain, if not eager to do so, then at least complaisant. If citizens come to believe that their abbreviated appearances at the polls suffice to render them crucial contributors to democratic affairs, respected and heeded by those who bid for their votes, then they are more likely to feel satisfied with the rules of the game as it is actually played rather than grump about the shortness of their end of the stick. From the perspective of political elites, widespread belief in a duty to vote passes the Goldilocks test: it is not too small, it is not too big; it is just right. If citizens were to believe that political activity had no moral claim on them at all, then they might feel alienated from its practice, especially as the costs they must bear to sustain democratic forms are not negligible. If, on the other hand, citizens believed that they were morally obligated to understand the issues, scrutinize carefully the performances of officeholders, investigate gaps between promised benefits and realized outcomes, and organize independent campaigns whenever they determined that the current political establishment was lax in its attention to the public weal, they would make terrible pests of themselves. The mean between these defective states is just enough participation to make ordinary citizens feel importantly implicated in the process and no more. Belief that voting is necessary and sufficient to enjoy the status *good citizen* is the perfect moral underpinning for that mean. No wonder, then, that it receives such enthusiastic support from political elites. Belief in a duty to vote is the opiate of democratic masses.

VIII. CONCLUSION

We have argued that a duty to vote cannot be sustained on prudential grounds, nor can it be justified through act-consequentialistic, generalization, or expressive reasoning. There are, though, several plausible explanations of why such a belief, though groundless, can be expected to enjoy wide currency among citizens of contemporary democracies.

That is not, of course, to argue that voting by citizens is morally wrong. Nor is it to call into question the supreme importance of the right to vote enjoyed by citizens of a democracy; on that matter we chant in unison with the civics textbooks and profess ourselves well-pleased to live in jurisdictions in which suffrage is universal and elections vigorously contested rather than, say, Burma or Cuba.[24] It is not even to argue against legally compulsory voting.[25] This much should be clear. But we know based on responses to prior versions of this essay that some people will take us to be saying that voting is irrational, "a waste of time." Not so. There are numerous good and sufficient reasons why someone might decide to vote. The point is merely that the belief that there is a general citizen's duty to do so is not among them. Through voting I can "get it off my chest"; I can evince solidarity with some cause or candidate; I can occupy a walk-on role within the ongoing kaleidoscopic civil drama; or I can simply take comfort from being in step with my neighbors.[26] In short, voting is like playing golf or being a member of a choral group or piecing together patchwork quilts: if it is the sort of thing in which one enjoys participating then there is a reason to do so, but morality does not nudge, one way or the other, except in special cases. And special cases do not make for a general duty.

Philosophy, Bowling Green State University
Economics, Research School of Social Sciences, Australian National University

[24] Nonvoting no more undermines the foundations of the right to vote than does remaining a bachelor undermine a right to marry.

[25] Consider a parallel case: A law requiring two witnesses for a will to be valid is not shown to be undesirable by a proof that there is no antecedent moral duty in the state of nature to have one's testament doubly witnessed.

[26] Some of these reasons might explain why some people choose to bear modest tariffs by dialing a special number that constitutes a vote in a telephone poll that elects nobody and brings about no outcome.

POSTMODERN LIBERALISM AND THE EXPRESSIVE FUNCTION OF LAW*

By N. Scott Arnold

I. Introduction

In 1992, the city of Boulder, Colorado, passed an ordinance forbidding discrimination against homosexuals in employment and housing.[1] Two years later, voters in the state of Colorado passed a constitutional amendment forbidding the passage of local ordinances prohibiting this form of discrimination. The constitutional amendment did not mandate discrimination against homosexuals; it merely nullified ordinances such as Boulder's.[2] The amendment was later struck down by the U.S. Supreme Court as unconstitutional.[3]

On the face of it, the controversy surrounding the ordinance and the constitutional amendment was a tempest in a teapot. Boulder, the home of the University of Colorado, enjoys a reputation as a tolerant city. Discrimination against homosexuals in employment and housing did not appear to be a significant problem in the city. To be sure, victims of this form of discrimination did not see it that way, but even if such discrimination is wrong, it does not follow that there should be a city ordinance against it. The law cannot right all wrongs, and discrimination ordinances of this sort are generally relatively easy to evade. So what is the point?

Similarly, at the state level, the need for the constitutional amendment was not evident. Although Aspen and Denver had similar ordinances, there was no evidence that other municipalities were about to pass some form of the Boulder initiative. Why should the citizens of Colorado care about city ordinances such as these? Even if other municipalities were about to pass them, it is hard to see what benefits might flow from this amendment. It is difficult to believe that laws prohibiting discrimination against homosexuals would have an adverse effect on the moral fiber of Coloradans, even if one supposes that homosexual lifestyles are morally dubious. So what was the point? Why did passions run so high?

A plausible answer to these puzzles can be found in the fact that the law can have an *expressive* dimension or function. Typically, laws try to

* For helpful comments and suggestions, I would like to thank Ellen Frankel Paul and the other contributors to this volume.

[1] Boulder, Colorado, Code, Title 12 (1981; amended in 1992).
[2] Ned Zeman, "No 'Special' Rights for Gays," *Newsweek*, November 23, 1992, 32.
[3] *Romer v. Evans*, 517 U.S. 620 (1996).

change behavior by attaching criminal or civil sanctions to disfavored behaviors or patterns of behavior. Effective laws are ones which are relatively easy to enforce and which attach sanctions sufficient to deter the undesired behavior. Ineffective laws are those which are easy to evade or which have weak sanctions attached to them. Independent of the effectiveness or ineffectiveness of the law, however, is the fact that the law can be used to say something. What developed in Colorado was a situation in which the city council of Boulder wanted to make a statement in favor of tolerance, acceptance, or validation of homosexual orientation and/or gay lifestyles. The citizens of Colorado, led by the Christian Right, wanted to make an opposite statement—a statement of intolerance, rejection, or invalidation of homosexuality as an acceptable lifestyle. The statement-making function of the law is separate from the more direct effects of the law's sanctions. The Colorado case brings this out rather nicely, since the practical effect of the city's ordinance is probably negligible. The effects of the amendment to Colorado's constitution, had it withstood constitutional challenge, would likely have been even less significant. Those who are blind to the expressive dimension of law might have advised the Boulder city council that the ordinance should not be passed because it would be likely to have little positive impact, would stir up opposition to homosexuals at the local and state level, and would just make government more intrusive and meddlesome. The citizens of Colorado might have been given similar advice about the proposed constitutional amendment.

This essay is about the expressive function or dimension of the law. Specifically, I want to defend a kind of blindness to this expressive element. Citizens and their legislative bodies will perhaps always pass laws to make statements, but I am interested in the normative question of whether they should do this. One way of framing the issue is in terms of what counts in a public forum as a good reason for passing a law.[4] Simply put, I shall argue that expressive considerations are not good reasons. Although this argument is framed in terms of reasons for changing the law, it applies equally to reasons for not changing the law. For example, in the debate about the legalization of recreational drugs, those who favor the status quo (continued criminalization) often do so on the grounds that legalization would "send the wrong message." If the argument of this essay succeeds, this is not a good reason for the continued criminalization of recreational drugs, though, of course, there may be other reasons in favor of the existing policy.

This essay begins with a discussion of how actions in general, and laws in particular, can be used to make statements. Following this discussion

---

[4] Throughout this essay, I operate with an intuitive understanding of what counts as a public justification. For a subtle and nuanced account of public justification that is consistent with the understanding adopted here, see Gerald Gaus, *Justificatory Liberalism* (Cambridge: Cambridge University Press, 1995).

will be an articulation and evaluation of the case for taking the expressive dimension of law seriously as a reason for or against a given law. I claim that this evaluation must be a comparative one. That is, one must evaluate the efficacy of using government and the law as expressive vehicles in comparison to the private sector and its actions, that is, nongovernmental organizations and their actions. I shall argue that in general the latter are better situated to give expression to the values and ideals for which people are inclined to use the law. Before proceeding, however, I need to more carefully delineate the scope of this argument and to identify the larger issue this topic engages.

At the outset, I shall stipulate that the scope of this argument excludes expressive arguments for laws that secure fundamental rights. The latter include basic human rights (e.g., the right to life, the right to physical security), and basic political rights (e.g., the right to vote, the right to freedom of expression). What makes these rights fundamental is that they enjoy constitutional protection: that is, they are immune from majoritarian repeal or revision. In a justification for fundamental legal rights, it might be claimed that the latter are uniquely suited to express the importance of certain widely shared values. For example, a fundamental legal right to life might be the most appropriate expression of the importance of innocent human life; a legal right to freedom of expression might be the most appropriate expression of the importance of free speech in a democratic society, etc. Without passing judgment on whether or not expressive arguments like this are ultimately successful, the scope of the main argument of this essay excludes them. The reason for this exclusion is that the case against countenancing the expressive function of law developed in this essay appeals to nongovernmental institutions as more appropriate expressive vehicles. Because fundamental rights involve prohibiting the state from acting in certain ways, it is hard to see how nongovernmental institutions could do this, at least under ordinary circumstances.[5] Generally speaking, the most effective way to ensure that the state does not overstep its bounds is through a system of rights that is relatively immune from majoritarian repeal or revision.

The scope of this essay is nevertheless vast. It includes many of the most important arguments offered for regulatory laws, laws creating and sustaining numerous government programs, and even elements of the tax code. All have been supported by expressive considerations. For example, antidiscrimination law is supposed to express a commitment to social

---

[5] For an example of circumstances under which nongovernmental institutions could play a leading role in securing fundamental rights, consider the case of Poland in the 1980s. It is arguable that what most effectively constrained the Polish state in the 1980s in the area of human rights—to the extent that it was constrained—were the actions and policies of the Roman Catholic Church. Constitutional rights in communist societies were not worth the paper they weren't written on. This exception noted, nongovernmental organizations have obvious weaknesses in confronting the state, and it is only in unusual circumstances that they can effectively constrain the latter.

equality; laws establishing entitlements to welfare or old-age insurance are supposed to express communitarian values of shared intergenerational responsibility; and an increase in the income-tax deduction for dependent children is intended to express a (stronger) commitment to families and family values. Any such law, policy, or provision might be justified on a variety of grounds; this essay is about only one class of arguments that has been or might be offered.

Despite the fact that this essay is concerned only with arguments and not with the laws or policies themselves, the question of the legitimacy of the expressive function of law has important implications for the larger issue of the legitimate scope of governmental activity. Specifically, how this question is answered has an important bearing on the debate between classical liberals and modern liberals about the proper role of government. Classical liberals believe that the legitimate functions of government are limited to protecting people's fundamental rights, providing public goods, and dealing with externalities.[6] For classical liberals, making statements, even if the statements are politically correct from their perspective, is not a proper function of the state or its laws. This, in part, explains classical-liberal opposition to large portions of regulatory law, a wide array of government programs, and the manipulation of the tax code for various social purposes. By contrast, modern liberals—who might more aptly be called 'postmodern liberals' because of their belief in the importance and legitimacy of the expressive function of law—tend to favor all these things, often on expressive grounds, though not exclusively on those grounds.[7] Contemporary conservatives, on the other hand, straddle the fence on the expressive function of law. One species of contemporary American conservatives—the Christian Right—sometimes favors using the law to make statements. For example, they were behind the proposed constitutional amendment in Colorado. On the other hand, conservatives of various stripes often oppose government regulation and state-run social welfare programs on the grounds that government would exceed, or has exceeded, its proper scope and function (that is, on what

[6] Implicit in this observation is another reason why a discussion of expressive arguments for fundamental rights can be bypassed. Liberals of all stripes tend to agree that it is the job of the state to promulgate and enforce such rights, so whether or not such arguments succeed in the case of fundamental rights will have no bearing on the larger issue of the proper scope of government. There is, of course, disagreement among liberals about the nature, source, and implications of these rights, but not all policy disputes among liberals are disputes about rights, and those that are tend to be peculiarly inconclusive. My interest in this essay is in narrowing the grounds on which policy debates among liberals should take place.

[7] Inventing a term such as 'postmodern liberal' ordinarily calls for a discussion of conceptual geography in which postmodern liberalism is distinguished from other varieties of liberalism. For the purposes of this essay, however, a rough characterization will do. Postmodern liberalism is just the liberalism of the political left in the twentieth century, which means it does not include elements of the far left that have rejected liberalism's commitment to democracy, human rights, and the more or less free market.

are essentially classical-liberal grounds). Perhaps the way to distinguish postmodern liberals from conservatives on the expressive function of law is by reference to the content of the messages being sent. However their differences are to be sorted out, this essay defends a classical-liberal position on the expressive dimension of law, in part by way of a critical evaluation of the arguments of postmodern liberals.[8] The argument has sufficient generality to apply to conservatives who favor using the law to make statements, but the focus will be on postmodern liberals for the simple reason that they have more fully articulated the case for countenancing the expressive dimension of law as a reason for passing laws and inaugurating government programs. If the argument of this essay succeeds, the kinds of considerations that can legitimately be offered in support of government involvement in civil society will have been narrowed.[9] This would represent progress in the debate between classical liberals and their postmodern counterparts on the central question of the legitimate scope of governmental activity.

II. Social Meanings

Actions, whether we intend it or not, sometimes have meanings. We signal things to others by what we do. Driving a certain kind of automobile or joining a certain club may be ways of making a statement. If a teenage girl dyes her hair purple and paints her fingernails black, she is making a statement rejecting some of the dominant values of her culture. Those who write on this topic sometimes seem to believe that social meanings are mysterious miasmas enveloping social life. However, there is a more mundane way of understanding them. Social meanings are nothing more than intentional states (e.g., beliefs, modes of valuation, affective states) expressed by the agent and apprehended by others. For example, if a teenage male wears gang colors in a certain part of a big city, the social meaning of his action is that he is (and is proud to be) a member

---

[8] Perhaps the most articulate defender of the legitimacy of the expressive function of law is Cass Sunstein. See especially Cass Sunstein, "On the Expressive Function of Law," *University of Pennsylvania Law Review* 144 (1996): 2021; Sunstein, "Social Norms and Social Roles," in *Free Markets and Social Justice* (New York: Oxford University Press, 1997), 32–69; and Sunstein, "Incommensurability and Valuation in Law," in ibid., 70–107. See also Lawrence Lessig, "The Regulation of Social Meaning," *University of Chicago Law Review* 62 (1995): 943; and Elizabeth Anderson, *Value in Ethics and Economics* (Cambridge, MA: Harvard University Press, 1993).

[9] It is for this reason that the scope of the argument that follows should also be taken to exclude laws that do not impose sanctions or restrict people's freedom. For example, proclamations honoring individuals or groups (e.g., veterans) might be justifiable on purely expressive grounds, as might resolutions condemning individuals or groups (e.g., terrorists). Even proclamations establishing national holidays might be justifiable on expressive grounds, so long as they do not restrict freedom (e.g., by requiring businesses to grant a new paid holiday). There is no need for classical liberals to be so stiff-necked as to oppose proclamations, resolutions, and national holidays.

of the gang. Not just any beliefs and affective states count as social mean-ings; at the very least, they must be widely shared. Otherwise, they would not be *social* meanings. However, the social meaning of an action, as it is apprehended by members of the community, may not be the intended meaning of the person or persons who perform the action. The potential for miscommunication always exists. For example, it used to be a com-mon practice for white fans of the University of Mississippi to wave the Confederate battle flag at football games. The intended meaning was an expression of pride in, and a connectedness with, their Southern heritage. Many African Americans took this as an expression of racism and nos-talgia for the days when whites dominated blacks. White protestations that waving this flag was not an endorsement of slavery, racism, or white domination were often (though perhaps not always) sincere and genu-ine—as sincere and genuine as the offense that blacks took at the display of this symbol.

As this example illustrates, it is misleading to talk about *the* social meaning of an action, since there may be more than one such meaning, especially if the action is done in a setting in which there are members of different groups, cultures, or societies. In addition, sometimes an action may have no particular meaning in one culture, but it may be fraught with meaning in another culture. For example, in Budapest, Hungary, passengers often ride in the front seat of taxicabs. If an American pas-senger buckles his seat belt, he may not intend to make any statement at all; he may simply want the added safety that a secured seat belt pro-vides. To the Hungarian taxidriver, however, the meaning of his action is distrust and fear, and it is taken as an insult.[10] In light of these observa-tions, it is useful to distinguish the *intended* social meaning of an action from what might be called the *apprehended* social meaning of an action. An action is *ambiguous* when the intended meaning diverges from the appre-hended meaning or when there is more than one apprehended meaning, as is often the case when different groups "take" the same action differently.

Let us return to intended meanings. Why do people make statements with their actions? Sometimes they are literally making a statement in the sense that they intend to convey some proposition to the rest of the world. The teenage boy wearing gang colors is, in part, saying that he is a member of a particular gang, a statement from which further inferences may be drawn. But usually more is going on than just the transmission of information. Often, people are also expressing (the importance of) certain values by which they live their lives. If an animal rights activist throws red paint on a woman wearing a fur coat, he is not merely expressing the proposition that making furs involves shedding blood. He is also indi-cating strong moral disapproval of the woman and the fashion industry. Many people who perform symbolic acts of political protest seem to find

---

[10] This example comes from Lessig, "The Regulation of Social Meaning," 960.

value in the act of protest itself, apart from any consequences it might have in righting some wrong. In other words, making the statement is intrinsically valuable. This is not the only reason people engage in protest, of course. Protesters may want to change norms, that is, rules prescribing or proscribing a range of behaviors, and the attendant attitudes and values that go with these rules. For example, the black students who sat in at segregated lunch counters in the South in the 1960s were trying to change existing norms about segregation. Prior to that time, blacks and whites eating together at a lunch counter "was just not done." The student protesters wanted to change that norm and the associated practice. When norms change, the social meaning of actions change. Today, the act of a black person sitting down next to a white person at a lunch counter has no social meaning in most places in the South, unlike the situation prior to the early 1960s. The causal story of changes in norms and the associated social meanings is, of course, complex, and many factors are usually responsible; but sometimes expressive actions, as they might be called, are an important part of the story. That seems to have been the case in the changes in norms and social meanings relating to the integration of public accommodations in the South. The activities of the civil rights protesters were undoubtedly a factor in bringing about these changes.

Another consequence of a change in norms is a change or redefinition of social roles. Social roles such as teacher, student, judge, employee, wife, consumer, citizen, etc., are, in part, defined by a set of expectations about how those who occupy the roles will behave in certain circumstances. These expectations have a positive and a normative dimension. The positive dimension consists in the fact that people have reasonable expectations about how role-occupiers will behave in certain circumstances. For example, it is reasonable to believe that a licensed physician will correctly diagnose most common ailments. This is simply a prediction about how physicians will behave. There is, in addition, a normative dimension to expectations surrounding social roles. If a teacher does not evaluate students on the basis of the quality of their work, she has violated (normatively) legitimate expectations of her students and her superiors and is a proper object of moral censure. The relevance of these observations to expressive actions is that people often try to use the latter to alter social roles and the relevant behavior by altering the norms associated with those roles. For example, a woman may violate norms governing who does the housework as a way of forcing a change in her role in the home.

To summarize, expressive actions can be a causal factor in changing norms and the associated social roles and social meanings. These consequences are to be distinguished from the purely expressive properties of actions themselves. An action may be a perfect vehicle for expressing values—notably moral outrage—and yet have no effect whatever on the targeted practice and the surrounding norms, social roles, and social meanings. Furthermore, the expressive properties of an action may play little or no role in changing the targeted behavior even if that behavior does in fact change—as, for example, when the latter changes entirely in response to the incentive effects of the sanctions associated with a new law or in response to broader social forces.

III. The Expressive Function of Law

Why might someone favor using the law to make statements? The state is an important form of human community, and a citizen or legislator may believe that it is important for a leading, and in some ways the dominant, community in a society to make a statement. As in the case of other actions, the statement a law makes is not limited to propositions. Values are also expressed, and if someone thinks the values expressed are important enough, then for that person the expression of those values might be a sufficient reason to pass the law. In the mind of a supporter, the values expressed by the law are so important that she is willing to use coercion to change behavior. Indeed, typically, those who support state action on expressive grounds believe that the willingness to use coercion to change behavior should be part of the message the law is sending.

Some people seem to value the expressive function of a law so highly that they would support the law even if it had (on balance) negative consequences by other criteria. For example, a number of years ago, the U.S. Supreme Court ruled that burning the American flag was a form of speech protected by the First Amendment. In response, some conservatives supported a constitutional amendment outlawing flag-burning. It is reasonable to suppose that had such an amendment passed, it would have led to more instances of flag-burning than would occur in the absence of this amendment. Supporters did not seem to care; it was so important to them that the law make a statement about the importance and sacredness of the national symbol that they seemed to be willing to countenance more acts of flag desecration than would have occurred without the passage of the amendment.[11] Let us call people who have this sort of attitude 'Pure Expressivists'.

In their blindness to the further consequences of the law under consideration, Pure Expressivists seem irrational, and indeed it is difficult to find clear examples of purely expressive arguments for laws or policies. The only class of exceptions are proclamations or resolutions, which recognize achievements or contributions or, alternatively, condemn someone or some group for some vile deed or attitude. In these cases, the sole purpose is expressive, and the further consequences of the action are negligible. As indicated earlier,[12] the scope of the current discussion does

---

[11] They would also take pleasure in seeing flag-burners jailed, but this is not the sort of consideration that anyone could offer as a serious (i.e., public) reason for making flag-burning illegal.

[12] See note 9.

not include proclamations or resolutions, since the latter do not attach penalties to noncompliance or otherwise restrict people's freedom. They are, therefore, irrelevant to the larger issue of the proper role of government in civil society. Having noted this class of exceptions, it seems reasonable to say that most people are not Pure Expressivists about the laws they support. Typically, those who care about what statements are, or are not, being made by the law also claim that further good (or bad) consequences will follow from implementing the law. For example, early in 1998, the U.S. Department of Health and Human Services was considering a clean-needle exchange program for drug addicts. Senator John Ashcroft opposed this program on expressive grounds, but he offered other reasons as well:

> Federal funds should never be used to encourage illegal drug use, according to U.S. Sen. John Ashcroft. Ashcroft today called on the Administration to continue the ban on federal funding for clean-needles programs, contending that needle-exchange programs amount to a stamp of approval from the federal government for illegal drug use.
> "The nation's leaders have a fundamental responsibility to call Americans to their highest and best," Ashcroft said. "Giving clean needles to drug addicts is like giving bullet proof vests to bank robbers. This proposal would hurt kids, tear apart families, and damage the culture. It is accommodating us at our lowest and least. Such a policy would tell vulnerable youngsters that it is OK to use drugs— 'If it's not OK, then why are they handing out free needles?' many teens would ask. America deserves better. We must set a higher standard than providing clean needles for drug users."[13]

Whether or not such dire consequences would indeed occur, Senator Ashcroft seemed to feel compelled to argue that they would. While making the "right" statement (or not making the "wrong" statement) might have considerable intrinsic value, those who advance such arguments seem to realize that other considerations need to be brought to bear in a public forum. Perhaps they see that they cannot simply assume that others will share their values—at least to the point where they would support a law as a way of giving expression to those values. Further dire consequences must be predicted to get others onboard. The apparent dearth of such consequences might explain why the proposal for a constitutional amendment to ban flag-burning has made no headway, despite the fact that it expresses values shared by the vast majority of Americans.

[13] Press release issued by U.S. Senator John Ashcroft. Source: *U.S. Newswire*, March 31, 1998.

The debate about the Civil Rights Act of 1964 provides a richer and more attractive picture of how expressive considerations might fit into a comprehensive public justification for a law. The act prohibited discrimination on the basis of race in employment and public accommodations. It was and is a way of stating the importance of social equality among the races. Independently of this expressive function, however, the law had more direct effects, namely, those attributable to its sanctions against those who engage in discrimination. Some discriminatory acts do not take place which would have occurred had the law not been in effect. Of course, passage of the law did not eliminate discrimination, but it raised the costs of discriminatory behavior and lowered the costs of equal treatment. Prior to the passage of the act, businesses bore some costs for discriminatory behavior: lost business from blacks and a smaller labor pool, to name the most obvious. However, there were also benefits, notably the ability to satisfy the preferences of their customers, some of their employees, and themselves for treating black people as second-class citizens. Passage of the act made discriminators vulnerable to lawsuits, thereby raising the costs of discriminatory behavior. It also lowered the costs of equal treatment, primarily by making the social meaning of equal treatment ambiguous. Businessmen who treated blacks equally had often been ostracized by the white community as "nigger lovers." After the act's passage, they could plausibly claim that giving equal treatment was simply a question of obeying the law. Everyone knew that, and thus the social meaning of equal treatment changed or at least became ambiguous.[14] Finally, it was argued that the act would have indirect effects on norms governing the treatment of blacks by whites. One intended result was to alter a variety of social roles occupied by both blacks and whites. Thus, the intended effects of the law included not only an improvement in the socioeconomic status of blacks (more and better jobs, better services from businesses) but also beneficial changes in norms, social meanings, and social roles.

Whether or not this argument, suitably fleshed out, does in fact justify that law, it illustrates the kind of argument that can be made in support of a law that puts expressive considerations at the center of a public justification of that law. The argument, however, does not appeal only to the fact that the law gives expression to widely shared values; it also appeals to changes in behavior directly traceable to the incentives provided by the law's sanctions and to collateral effects on norms, social meanings, and social roles. Cass Sunstein calls efforts to bring about these collateral effects 'norm management'.[15] That is, in addition to the pro-

---

[14] This observation about the change in social meaning comes from Lessig, "The Regulation of Social Meaning," 966–67.

[15] Sunstein, "On the Expressive Function of Law," 2023–28; Sunstein, "Social Norms and Social Roles," 61–64; and Sunstein, "Incommensurability and Valuation in Law," 91–93. See also Lessig, "The Regulation of Social Meaning," 966–67, 1016. As Sunstein uses the term,

posed law's purely expressive value, and apart from its direct effect on human behavior via the sanctions it imposes, Sunstein and others argue that by making the appropriate statement, the law can change norms and values. Changes of this sort are desirable because internalized norms and values more reliably produce changes in behavior than do threats of legal sanctions alone. Moreover, if norms change, then the social roles that norms define also change, as do the social meanings of an array of actions. For example, as indicated above, part of the case for the Civil Rights Act of 1964 was that it would be an important factor in changing white Americans' norms, the associated social roles of whites and blacks, and the social meanings of many actions. The self-image of blacks would also change, it was argued, in part because of a change in white attitudes and behavior, and in part because of the effect of the law's "statement" on the norms and values of black people. In other words, by using the law to make a statement in favor of racial equality, blacks would be better treated by whites and would be more inclined to demand the respect and equal treatment that was their due.

The proposition that the state can and should engage in norm management captures an important element of postmodern liberalism. Liberals of all varieties used to maintain that government should stay out of people's private lives (which includes their personal values and norms). The philosophical version of this view is that the state should be neutral between different conceptions of the good life. Postmodern liberals have rejected these ideas as myths. Although they continue to maintain that rights restrict the legitimate scope of governmental activity, they also believe that government is inevitably involved in shaping the values and norms by which people lead their lives and thus that it cannot remain neutral with regard to different conceptions of the good life. The only questions that remain concern which values and norms the government should try to inculcate and how it should carry out this task.

IV. The Law as a Vehicle for Expressing Values and Managing Norms

To evaluate the case sketched above for taking into account the expressive function of law, a comparative analysis is called for, since any successful consequentialist argument for a law or policy must show that the latter achieves or realizes the relevant ends or goals better than the next best alternative. Specifically, two questions must be addressed: (i) How effective are laws and government policies as expressive vehicles in com-

'norms' include not only rules prescribing or proscribing behavior but also the associated values and attitudes. For example, the black students who sat in at the department-store lunch counters were trying to change not only the rules that proscribed this behavior but also the associated attitudes that whites and blacks had toward the behavior and ultimately toward each other.

parison to the alternatives? and (ii) How effective is the state as a norm manager in comparison to the alternatives? In both cases, the alternatives would involve letting these tasks (making statements, managing norms) be handled by the private sector—in other words, by nongovernmental organizations (hereafter, 'NGOs'). These include not only, nor even primarily, business organizations, but churches, volunteer organizations, professional associations, and organized interest groups.[16] Organizations are rule-governed domains of human behavior that have some explicitly recognized goal or purpose. They are a proper subset of social institutions, for while all institutions serve some function or other, it is only organizations that have explicit goals or purposes. To meet those goals or purposes, NGOs, and the specific actions or policies they undertake, embody and express certain values and ideals. NGOs also try to change or maintain behavior and an associated set of norms among those whom they affect. For example, churches and charities not only try to change the behavior of sinners and the poor, respectively; they also try to change their hearts. An evaluation of the case for using the law as an expressive vehicle, then, requires a comparative evaluation of the state and NGOs in their roles as expressive vehicles and as norm managers. Let us begin with the former role.

A. NGOs versus the state as expressive vehicles

NGOs are generally superior expressive vehicles for people's values and ideals for at least two reasons. First, except in the case of some criminal organizations, all NGOs are voluntary. People are free to join or support the NGOs which express values that are important to them, and they are free not to join or support NGOs which express values they are indifferent about or deplore. On the other hand, as taxpayers, people are forced to support state organizations and programs whether or not the latter express or embody values they endorse. Simply put, the law—and citizens' tax dollars—are used to make statements with which some citizens disagree, sometimes profoundly. This is an important source of unhappiness and alienation in modern societies. Christian fundamentalists who live in Boulder (both of them!) do not want the city to send a message of tolerance, acceptance, or validation of gay lifestyles. Gay citizens of Colorado do not want the state of Colorado sending a message about the unacceptability of gay lifestyles. It is true that the losses in happiness, satisfaction, or utility that accompany using the law to make statements that citizens disagree with are offset to some degree by the

---

[16] Very often, interest groups believe that the most effective way to promote their goals is by trying to get the state to do something for them. In this capacity, their activities are a component of state action. The focus of the present discussion is on NGOs in their role as private actors.

additional satisfaction that supporters of state action get from the offense caused to others. Supporters of the Colorado constitutional amendment get some additional satisfaction out of offending homosexuals, just as gay rights advocates get some additional satisfaction out of offending Christian fundamentalists by passing gay rights ordinances. However, not only are such considerations out of place as part of a public justification for a law or policy, but supporters of state action can achieve a comparable result through NGOs. If someone wants to express moral condemnation of homosexual lifestyles and anger the gay community, he can join a local fundamentalist church which teaches in a highly public way that homosexuality is an abomination. If someone wants to enrage fundamentalists, she can organize or march in a gay pride parade. (The latter seems to exercise fundamentalists much more than antidiscrimination ordinances.) Because of their voluntary nature and their usually narrower focus, the kind of consensus found in NGOs on important value questions is almost always wider and deeper than whatever consensus might develop in a modern polity. This seems particularly true of issues that people want to make a statement about, which are usually highly contentious or divisive.

A second reason why NGOs are superior expressive vehicles is that they typically allow greater flexibility in the manner of participation. Consider, for example, charitable organizations whose purpose is to help the poor. Someone might join such an organization or contribute to it as a way of expressing compassion toward those less fortunate than himself and his family. A person may give money, goods and services, or time, and may do so in varying degrees. By contrast, state organizations are run by professionals, and very often the only thing they can use from the public is the latter's political support or even their indifference. The level of contribution (i.e., tax dollars) is less likely to match the strength of taxpayers' compassion. This is related to another important difference between NGOs and corresponding state organizations noted above: the former tend to be more narrowly focused and nuanced in their goals. This permits a closer fit between the organization's goals and the expressive needs of its members or supporters. Private religious charities in the nineteenth century made distinctions between the deserving poor and the undeserving poor that were extremely important to the religious worldview of their members.[17] State welfare agencies, even if they were so inclined, could not make such distinctions, in part because they are constrained by equal-protection considerations that do not constrain private organizations and in part because their organizations suffer from perverse incentives that lead them to try to keep or even expand their client base. In addition, government programs or policies often require political trade-offs that violate supporters' deeply held values. An environmen-

---

[17] See Marvin Olasky, *The Tragedy of American Compassion* (Washington, DC: Regnery Gateway, 1992), ch. 6.

talist who values the preservation of wild ecosystems is likely to see her values better expressed through the Nature Conservancy's practice of buying the land on which these ecosystems are located than by a comparable program administered by the Forest Service or the Department of the Interior, since the government program may be conjoined, as either a political or a practical necessity, with other programs that the environmentalist finds deeply objectionable (e.g., timber harvesting by private companies on government lands).

Because of the moral and cognitive weaknesses of human beings, perhaps the most important parameter by which to evaluate organizations and institutions is by reference to their damage-control mechanisms. That is, what happens when things go wrong? What happens when states and NGOs fail to express the values and ideals of their members and supporters? There are a number of ways in which this can happen. A policy—or even an entire organization—can be hijacked by those in positions of power to express values that differ profoundly from the values of the organization's members and supporters. Alternatively, people's values can change so that they become dissatisfied with the norms and values that have been traditionally expressed by the organization and its policies.

The options for dealing with these "value-alignment failures," as they might be called, can be brought under two headings: exit and voice.[18] Let us consider exit first. Suppose the values and ideals expressed by an NGO or its policies no longer coincide with an individual's values and ideals. He or she can leave that organization and join or form a new one. Sunstein considers this possibility but finds it ultimately unsatisfactory. He writes:

> [P]eople who are dissatisfied with prevailing norms can vote with their feet, using the power of "exit" to become members of groups built on especially congenial norms. . . . [But] the existence of norm communities is not a full solution to the problem posed by some social norms. It can be very costly to exit from the norm community in which one finds oneself, and the fact that one has been raised in that community may make other options seem unthinkable or horrific even though they might be much better. . . . [I]t might be better if the community as a whole [i.e., the state] could do something about those norms.[19]

However, the very difficulties with norm communities that Sunstein calls attention to are exacerbated when the community is the state (especially at the national level) and the norms and values at issue are the ones it

---

[18] The terminology comes from A. O. Hirschman, *Exit, Voice, and Loyalty* (Cambridge, MA: Harvard University Press, 1970).

[19] Sunstein, "Social Norms and Social Roles," 41.

sustains and ratifies. For example, if one is dissatisfied with the norms and values sustained and ratified by the contemporary American state (e.g., the commitment to capitalism, rampant governmental paternalism), the costs of exit are quite high. And if one has been raised in a society in which the state permeates most aspects of social life, including especially the schools, one would have to have considerable internal resources—or already belong to a dissident norm community—to question the values and norms the state endorses and sustains. Thus, while Sunstein is right to point out that the exit strategy can be costly for individuals in NGOs, costs tend to be even higher in the case of the state.

The other way to deal with value-alignment failures is through voice, that is, by trying to change the institution in question. It might be thought that NGOs would be easier to change than state organizations because they are smaller and more flexible, but that is not always true. Local governments are relatively small and easily influenced, whereas some NGOs are very large and not easily influenced. The Roman Catholic Church comes to mind as an example of the latter. Not only is it very large, but, at least in the case of its American branch, it has suffered persistent value-alignment failures on a host of issues ranging from contraception, married clergy, and divorce to questions about distributive justice. It may be that the threat of exit is generally more credible in the case of NGOs, but that seems insufficient to establish the proposition that value-alignment failures are more easily corrected through voice in NGOs than in state organizations. On the question of voice, there does not seem to be good reason to prefer NGOs to state organizations; nor is there any good reason for the opposite preference.

It might be admitted that NGOs and their actions generally have some advantages over governments and their actions as expressive vehicles for norms and values. Nevertheless, it might be argued, passing a coercive law or funding a government program are uniquely appropriate ways for a society to signify the importance of social problems and society's commitment to dealing with them.[20]

Although this may be true in some cases, there are good rule-utilitarian grounds for denying the legitimacy of this sort of argument or appeal as part of a public justification for laws and government programs. First, it permits a kind of moral posturing which discourages a hard look at the likely consequences of the law or program. Suppose, for example, a leg-

---

[20] In thinking about this argument, it is important to keep the focus on the expressive dimension of the action as opposed to its more ordinary "extensional" consequences. It is always open to friends of the state to argue that state action will more effectively solve some problem than the private sector. This sort of argument for state action, which might be called an "old-fashioned modern liberal argument," has been used less frequently in recent years because of some spectacular failures by modern welfare states, but it is in principle available. By contrast, the argument under consideration here makes the claim that state action is a superior vehicle for expressing values, a claim that is independent of whether or not state action actually achieves its intended (nonexpressive) result.

islator proposes a program to eliminate asbestos in the nation's schools. Now this may be a worthy program, but it may not be. An alternative government program might be better, or the problem might be better handled by the private sector, or it might even be that any attempt to deal with the problem will only exacerbate it. However, if the debate over the proposed program is framed in expressive terms, that is, in such a way that a vote in favor of it is seen as a way of making a statement about the importance of children's health, then there is a diminished need for advocates to make the case that it is, in fact, a good program. Correspondingly, if a vote against it is seen as a way of making a statement of indifference about children's health, it becomes very difficult to oppose it on what are otherwise legitimate grounds. Serious and fruitful debates about policy proposals require that legislators focus on the merits of a given proposal rather than looking into the motives and intentions of their adversaries; this includes the intended meanings of whatever statement the latter might be making by their support or opposition to the measure in question.[21]

Appeals to the apprehended meaning of legislation are equally unproductive. Not only do such appeals empower—and thereby encourage—the most easily offended groups in a population (or the groups with the most easily offended spokespersons), these invocations typically involve unverifiable and unfalsifiable claims about the "message" that legislative action or inaction would send. Appeals to the statement-making function of law, on either the intended or apprehended side, are almost always an attempt to foreclose honest debate on the merits of the issue. This approach is the postmodern version of the *ad hominem* argument.

Is there *any* reason to favor state organizations and policies over NGOs as expressive vehicles? Perhaps. It was conceded at the outset of this essay that expressive arguments for fundamental legal rights might be legitimate. Such arguments are based on the idea that fundamental legal rights best embody or express the importance of certain widely shared basic values, such as the value of human life in the case of the right to life, or the value of individual autonomy in the case of the right to freedom of expression or freedom of worship. Without passing judgment on the merits of these arguments, it is possible to admit that in principle they might succeed. If in fact there is near unanimity about the importance of the values in question, and if in fact fundamental legal rights best express that importance (perhaps because there is no effective way for NGOs to

---

[21] For an excellent illustration of forbearance about the motives and intentions of one's opponents, see Hubert Humphrey's speeches in the Senate in favor of the Civil Rights Act of 1964. When Southern senators raised concerns about whether or not the bill would lead to hiring by quotas, Humphrey met the challenge head on, instead of denouncing these senators as racists who were unwilling to send the right message and who were raising the specter of hiring by quotas as a pretext for opposing the law. See *Congressional Record*, 88th Cong., 2d sess., 1964: 5864, 6000, 7420.

do it), there may indeed be legitimate expressive arguments for fundamental legal rights.

However, expressive arguments for ordinary laws and government programs are not at all like that. Compare an expressive argument for the Colorado constitutional amendment prohibiting gay rights ordinances with an expressive argument for the prohibition on unreasonable searches and seizures guaranteed by the Fourth Amendment to the U.S. Constitution.[22] First, there is near-unanimity among Americans about the value of being free of warrantless searches and seizures. By contrast, there is deep division in the state of Colorado about the propriety of using the state constitution to say something about homosexual conduct, as there is about the propriety of homosexual conduct itself. Second, it is hard to see how the government can be restrained from warrantless searches and seizures by something other than fundamental legal rights (which might explain the "appropriateness" of legal rights as expressive vehicles in this case). By contrast, and on the other hand, there are a variety of ways to make a strong statement against homosexual lifestyles besides passing a constitutional amendment prohibiting municipalities from passing gay rights ordinances. These observations do not imply that there are no good reasons for the state of Colorado to prohibit gay rights ordinances; it is just that arguments offered as part of a public justification for that prohibition should not include the claim that it is important to make a statement about the immorality of gay lifestyles. Similar considerations apply, *mutatis mutandis*, to expressive arguments in favor of gay rights ordinances as well. Once these arguments are ruled out, the two sides will have to argue about the actual projected consequences of the amendment or the ordinance, respectively. In this particular case, if symbolism were taken off the table, cooler heads—classical liberal heads—would likely prevail, and both sides could find something better to do with their time and energy.

B. NGOs versus the state as norm managers

Postmodern liberals might agree that very often the values expressed by the laws they favor are not widely shared but that those values are, nonetheless, the right ones or the most defensible ones. Moreover, an important part of the justification for passing the law, they might argue, is that it is an effective vehicle for changing norms and values. As noted earlier in this essay, the argument seems to be that since what govern-

---

[22] There are, of course, disputes about the content and extent of fundamental rights, though there is agreement about some core areas as well. It is doubtful, however, that such disputes as there are can be resolved by appeal to the underlying values that the right in question is supposed to give expression to. It is even more doubtful that most of the extant disputes about the proper role of the state are best understood as disputes about fundamental rights.

ments do inevitably affects norms, they might as well do it rationally, that is, according to some plan. This is what Sunstein calls 'norm management'. But can the state actually manage norms?

There are legitimate doubts about this. Management implies intention and foresight, so to say that the government can manage norms is to say that state officials (politicians, bureaucrats) can deliberately change or sustain not only behavior but the internalized values and rules that produce the behavior. It is invalid to infer that governments can manage norms from the proposition that governments affect norms. It might be that government policies reflect norms that have their origins in other social or historical forces. Or perhaps governments can unintentionally alter norms as a by-product of doing something else, but they themselves cannot deliberately change norms or even sustain norms that would otherwise lose their hold on the public's mind. There is an illuminating parallel with the government's relationship to the economy. While it is undeniable that government policies influence the economy, there is no meaningful sense in which the government can be said to control the economy. At most, government policies and procedures can change economic behavior within a relatively narrow range of options and can produce a variety of unintended consequences that are often negative and usually unanticipated. This is one of the major lessons learned from our experience with economic policy in the first two-thirds of the twentieth century.

A comparable lesson may be emerging at the end of the twentieth century in other areas of government policy. When it comes to deliberately changing norms, which is what postmodern liberal reformers are often interested in doing, there are special reasons to be skeptical of the efficacy of state action. Because of the coercion implicit in state action, passing a law may produce a change only in visible and public behavior, while both private behavior and the relevant norms and values remain untouched. Threats of sanctions can change what people do in public, but such threats may not change how they feel. For example, threats of sanctions might be able to get racists to hire and serve African Americans in their business establishments; but making a statement in favor of racial equality by passing a law (even with sanctions attached) may have no effect whatever on their values and how they would treat blacks in the absence of sanctions—or how they do treat blacks when they can get away with violating the law. The problem is that statement-making might be causally impotent in changing norms and values, and to the extent that behavior actually does change, it might be that the threat of sanctions does the real work. Changes in publicly observable behavior, then, obscure the fact that the project of norm management has failed. This is especially likely to happen when the statement made by passing a law is ambiguous because the apprehended meaning is different from the intended meaning. The city council of Boulder passed an antidiscrimination ordinance as a way of making some sort of positive statement about homosexuals. Not surprisingly, those who find homosexual conduct an abomination took the passage of this law as a slap in the face. These individuals—the people most in need of a change in norms from the perspective of the postmodern liberal norm managers—were unlikely to have had their norms changed by the actions of their betters on the Boulder city council.

In other cases, resistance to change may be accompanied by the phenomenon of preference falsification.[23] Very often people do not publicly reveal their preferences and values, or they dissemble about them, when those preferences and values are at variance with official ideology. This is especially true when the official ideology is state-sponsored. It is a plausible hypothesis, supported by evidence from totalitarian systems, that preference falsification tends to be more widespread in societies where states are more actively involved in trying to manage norms. Yet another possibility is that norms may change when a law is passed but not because the law is passed, or not because of the statement the law makes. Both the passage of the law and the change in norms might be the product of deeper social forces, or their causes may be entirely unrelated.

One or more of these possibilities may be realized in the case of race relations in America. There is considerable dispute about the extent to which internalized norms governing race relations have changed, especially in the case of whites. Some on the left believe that racist attitudes and norms among whites remain powerful and virulent, while others believe that there has been a significant change in this regard. Among those who believe that norms and values have changed, there is a dispute about how much of that change is due to antidiscrimination statutes and how much of it is due to other factors. It might be that changes in the law reflect changing sentiments and values and do not cause them. Finally, as Timur Kuran (among others) has argued, preference falsification about race relations in general and affirmative action in particular in American society has been widespread.[24] All of these considerations show that there is good reason to be skeptical of claims that governments can actually manage norms. As an aside, it is worth noting that ongoing attempts by many modern states to manage norms governing relations between the sexes seem to face many of the same problems.

Let us suppose for the sake of argument, however, that governments sometimes can manage norms. How might they do it? There seem to be essentially two ways.[25] First, when the dominant norms are entirely dependent upon false beliefs that the state could expose, norm management

---

[23] This phenomenon has been systematically investigated in Timur Kuran, *Private Truths, Public Lies* (Cambridge, MA: Harvard University Press, 1995).

[24] Ibid., ch. 9.

[25] These two ways are discussed in Sunstein, "On the Expressive Function of Law," 2051–55. See also Sunstein, "Social Norms and Social Roles," 56.

could be effected by exposing these false beliefs. Second, a situation might arise in which the old norms have already been substantially undermined by other forces and factors. While they may still guide behavior, including the expression of public sentiment, allegiance to them might in fact be quite weak. Deliberate state action under either of these circumstances could be enough to start a self-reinforcing process that changes norms, a process that Kuran calls a "norm bandwagon" or a "norm cascade."[26] Now that we have before us scenarios under which norm management could take place, it is appropriate to ask the comparative question: Are NGOs or states more effective in starting successful norm bandwagons or norm cascades?

It seems that NGOs would tend to be more effective than the state for reasons that parallel the superiority of NGOs and their policies as purely expressive vehicles. If norm entrepreneurs, as they might be called, try to form or transform NGOs in an effort to change people's norms, they will tend to get more accurate feedback (positive and negative reinforcement) about their efforts from their members because of the voluntary nature of NGOs. If a norm entrepreneur is taking an NGO in a direction that supporters and members cannot be convinced to go, the new organization or the entrepreneur's leadership in the old organization is doomed. By contrast, politicians and bureaucrats get most of their feedback from two types of constituents: those who feel very strongly about a particular issue, and those who have something to gain or lose financially by the passage of the law or program in question. For this reason, their sources of information about what norm changes people are or would be responsive to tend to be more skewed and less accurate. Environmentalists, anti-abortion activists, advocates for the elderly, etc. have many ideas about how their representatives can exercise leadership on important value questions (i.e., how they can be norm entrepreneurs). By contrast, it is rational for citizens with no particular ax to grind to remain uninformed about the doings of their representatives, and therefore they are less inclined to give them feedback when the latter try to manage norms. Finally, when attempts at norm management go awry, members and supporters of NGOs have more options at their disposal for expressing disapproval and sending a message. They can cut back on their support and/or participation in ways that taxpaying citizens cannot. The latter can withdraw their support through the political process or engage in protest, but that means little, unless they are major contributors or their numbers are great and politicians' failures are egregious. When organizations get out of control, it is so much easier and more effective simply to stop writing checks. Of course, in the case of NGOs, some people write much bigger checks than others, but this hardly distinguishes NGOs from the state.

[26] Kuran, *Private Truths, Public Lies*, 71–74.

There are some additional worries about politicians and bureaucrats as norm managers. Consider norms that are based on false beliefs that the state wishes to change. Actually, the beliefs need not be false; they need only be easily manipulated. If the state is charged with developing information on a particular issue that has an impact on people's norms that the state wants to change, it has an obvious conflict of interest. Consider, for example, the current debate about smoking. In the United States, the federal government has arrogated to itself much of the task of gathering and disseminating information on this issue—an issue on which it has a very definite point of view. Not only has the state taken over the direction of most research in this area, it has engaged in a campaign of vilification against alternative sources of information. The Tobacco Institute, the research arm of the U.S. tobacco industry, may indeed be biased and a worthless source of information, but a prudent person should not believe that proposition based on the pronouncements of government officials in charge of the anti-smoking jihad.

Of course, NGOs are often not much better when it comes to developing and disseminating information on issues in which they have a vested interest. For example, the anti-smoking crusade in America has its private-sector true believers as well, and when they are not putting smokers to the state's sword (e.g., by filing lawsuits or goading legislatures into raising taxes), they are busy inflaming the public with inaccurate and misleading information.[27] However, when norm management is left to the private sector, it is easier for alternative sources of information to develop. All the characteristic consequentialist arguments for free speech can be brought to bear.[28] The expression of diverse opinions is more likely to result in the discovery of the truth or more of the truth; the suppression of alternative points of view (even if the suppression is formally noncoercive) causes the dominant point of view to become a "dead dogma" whose grounds, and ultimately whose meaning, are eventually lost; the suppression of competing opinions amounts to an assumption of infallibility; and so on. When the state undertakes to manage norms by managing the beliefs that underlie them, it runs all these risks—risks that tend to be less significant when all of this is handled by the private sector.

Some of these concerns underlie the current dissatisfaction in America with the heavy hand of the state in regulating the content of primary and secondary education. Though there may be a role for the state in seeing to it that young people are imbued with widely shared values that are

[27] Or at least they are not practicing full disclosure. Most people, smokers and nonsmokers alike, tend to overestimate the risks involved in smoking. See W. Kip Viscusi, *Smoking: Making the Risky Decision* (New York: Oxford University Press, 1992). The latest scaremongering is about the evils of secondhand smoke and the effects of tobacco advertising on young people. Public discussion of these phenomena in no way mirrors the uncertainty and tentativeness of the relevant scientific research.

[28] See John Stuart Mill, *On Liberty*, ed. Elizabeth Rapaport (Indianapolis: Hackett Publishing, 1978), ch. 2.

given expression in the fundamental rights of liberal societies, certainly no adequate public justification has been offered for trying to instill in children other, more contentious values, whether in the area of human sexuality or, more generally, interpersonal relations. Even if attempts in these areas by the schools are clumsy, heavy-handed, and generally unsuccessful, parents have a legitimate complaint about efforts by the state to manage the instilling of these norms in their children.

There is one final reason to oppose the use of state power to manage norms, this time in the case of adults. If state power is used in an attempt to manage norms, it fails to respect citizens' autonomy and treats them paternalistically. Instead of merely providing information and offering citizens reasons why they should adopt certain values and ideals, the state is using its coercive power to try to change people's values directly. The strategy seems to be to use coercion to get people to behave in the proper way in the hope that a change in values will follow. It resembles Pascal's description of how one should come to believe in Christianity: take the holy waters, say the prayers, and eventually one will believe. In addition to—or more often, instead of—rational persuasion, the state uses its coercive power to get people to conform their behavior to the preferred values in the hope that their hearts will follow their behavior, that they too will become believers. This may be a more realistic strategy than mere argumentation, but, as a form of paternalism, it has certain distinctive problems.

Some of the more familiar problems with paternalistic policies were clearly articulated by John Stuart Mill in *On Liberty* over one hundred years ago.[29] First, there is no guarantee, indeed there is no increased likelihood, that norm managers from the state will inculcate the "best" or most defensible norms. Though one can admit the abstract possibility that there are some genuine norm experts, there are no agreed-upon criteria by which they can be identified. This means that there is no reason to think that the state is especially adept at finding them. Indeed (and this is a point not made by Mill), the state will face an adverse selection problem when choosing norm managers. The kind of person who would be attracted to the job would be someone who is full of confidence about what values people ought to live their lives by. Because of the diversity of defensible values and lifestyles in modern liberal societies, these are exactly the sort of people one would not want in a position to use the coercive power of the state to attempt to shape people's norms and values.

Second, to the extent that autonomous choice of values is itself a component of human happiness in modern liberal societies, the attempt to use coercion to preempt that choice, even when it is otherwise in the best interests of the person being threatened, is in and of itself a bad thing that should be avoided unless there are clear benefits that outweigh the costs.

---

[29] Ibid., 81–82.

The fact that there is real doubt about whether the state can effectively manage norms, and whether it can do so in a way that "tracks the truth" about how people ought to live their lives, has important implications. Specifically, it makes it less likely that the losses to human happiness that accompany the denial of autonomy will be counterbalanced by gains achieved by people being shepherded along the right path.

When the state stays out of the norm-management business, that does not mean it is neutral. Whatever laws it has on the books express certain norms and values, and by keeping them on the books and enforcing them, the state expresses approval of those norms and disapproval of contrary norms; that much is unavoidable. The deliberate attempt to manage norms and/or to express other values, however, is another matter and comes up only when someone proposes to change the law. Both those who favor change and those who oppose it may then cite expressive considerations, either as ends in themselves or as vehicles for norm management, in an attempt to provide a public justification for their respective positions. If the argument of this essay succeeds, however, those considerations should be ignored.

Philosophy, University of Alabama at Birmingham

DEMOCRATIC EPISTEMOLOGY AND ACCOUNTABILITY*

By Russell Hardin

I. Street-Level Epistemology

Most of the knowledge of an ordinary person has a very messy structure and cannot meet standard epistemological criteria for its justification. Rather, a street-level epistemology makes sense of ordinary knowledge. Street-level epistemology is a subjective account of knowledge, not a public account. It is not about what counts as knowledge in, say, physics, but deals rather, with your knowledge, my knowledge, the ordinary person's knowledge. I wish not to elaborate this view here, but to apply it to the problems of representative democracy. I will briefly lay out the central implications of a street-level epistemology and then bring it to bear on democratic citizenship, especially on the problem of the citizen's holding elected officials accountable for their actions.

Standard philosophical epistemology is concerned with justification, that is, justification of any claim that some piece of putative knowledge is actually true. Street-level epistemology is economic; it is not generally about justification but about usefulness. It follows John Dewey's "pragmatic rule," which is: In order to discover the meaning of an idea, ask for its consequences.[1] In essence, a street-level epistemology applies this to the idea of knowledge, with consequences broadly defined to include the full costs and benefits of coming to know and using knowledge. Note that the pragmatic or street-level epistemology sounds like an economic theory; but it is not an economic theory that presumes full knowledge, as in rational expectations theory or much of game theory. And it is not merely about the costs of information, as in some economic accounts.

Standard philosophical epistemology focuses on the subject of a belief— for example, on the height of Mont Blanc. It is about truth and the justification of truth claims. An economic theory of knowledge focuses on the individual believer or knower, on the costs and benefits of coming to know, which, of course, vary from person to person. Perhaps the chief

* This paper was substantially provoked by a conference at New York University on accountability. It has benefited from discussions at that conference and, especially, from discussions with Adam Przeworski, Bernard Manin, Pasquale Pasquino, and John Ferejohn, and from the comments of the other contributors to this volume.
[1] John Dewey, *Reconstruction in Philosophy* (Boston: Beacon Press, 1948), 163.

way in which standard epistemologies do not fit much of our ordinary knowledge is that the bulk of our knowledge—perhaps virtually all of it—depends on others in various ways. We take most knowledge on authority from others who presumably are in a position to know it. Indeed, we take it from others who themselves take it from others who themselves take it from others and so forth, *all the way down*. There are finally no foundations, or at best vague and weak foundations, for most of an individual's knowledge.

Philosopher Trudy Govier argues that our knowledge therefore depends on trust.[2] It might be better to say that it depends on the trustworthiness of our authoritative sources, although even this is too much. Very little of our knowledge seems likely to depend on anything vaguely like an ordinary trust relationship. I personally know none of the authoritative sources for much of what I would think is my knowledge in many areas. It is not so much that I take that knowledge on trust as that I have little choice but to take it. If I do not take it, I will be virtually catatonic. I am quite confident that much of what I think I know is false, but still I rely on what I know to get me through life because I have to.

Hence, the knowledge that you or I have is from a vast social system, not from anything we have actually checked out. Much of it can only be generated by a social system. We depend on knowledge by authority because it is efficient and because, without division of labor in generating our knowledge, we would have no time for putting much of it to use. Since what we mainly want is to use it, we take it on authority rather than seeking to justify it. We have to either rely on others or massively restrict our lives. As Ludwig Wittgenstein says, "My life consists in my being willing to accept many things."[3] Henry Sidgwick similarly noted that to live at all is prior to living well, and if we are to live at all we must accept many things that do not have reason as their source.

The central epistemological concern in representative democracy is what the typical citizen knows about the actions of public officials. If we make the effort to know something in large part because it serves our interest to know it, then we cannot generally expect people to know very much about what their representatives do. In the argument of Anthony Downs's economic theory of democracy, a citizen typically does not have very much interest in voting.[4] One vote has a miniscule chance of making a difference, so miniscule that, even when it is multiplied by the value of making a difference and getting one's preferred candidate or policy, the expected value of the vote is miniscule. Hence, if there is any real cost

---

[2] Trudy Govier, *Social Trust and Human Communities* (Montreal: McGill-Queens University Press, 1997), 51–76.

[3] Ludwig Wittgenstein, *On Certainty*, ed. G. E. M. Anscombe and G. H. von Wright (Oxford: Basil Blackwell, 1969), section 170.

[4] Anthony Downs, *An Economic Theory of Democracy* (New York: Harper and Row, 1957).

involved in casting a vote, that cost swamps the expected value, to the voter, of voting.

However, if the citizen has no interest in voting, then the citizen has no interest in making the effort to learn enough to vote well. Something that is not worth doing is not worth doing well. If the problem of knowing enough to judge government officials is already hard, the lack of incentive to correct that problem is devastating. Indeed, the costs of knowing enough about government to be able to vote intelligently in one's own interest surely swamp the modest costs, for most people in the United States, of actually casting a vote. The economic theory of knowledge or street-level epistemology therefore weighs against knowing enough to vote well because the incentives cut against investing in the relevant knowledge. The typical voter will not be able to put the relevant knowledge to beneficial use.

The conclusion that we have no incentive to learn enough to vote well was part of Downs's argument, but most of the subsequent research has focused primarily on the incentive to vote rather than on the incentive to know enough to vote intelligently. I am concerned here only with the knowledge problem rather than with the voting problem, although the former is derivative from the latter, because it is the lack of incentive to vote that makes knowledge of how to vote well virtually useless. Moreover, because many people do vote anyway, despite the absence of a personal benefit from doing so, the knowledge problem may well be the more fundamentally serious issue in democratic theory. Just because my vote has miniscule causal effect on democratically determined outcomes, there is no compelling reason for me to determine how to vote by its causal effect on such outcomes.

II. ACCOUNTABILITY TO INTERESTS

For democratic theory, the force of the argument from street-level epistemology can be made especially clear in the context of holding our representatives accountable for what they do after we elect them. Typically, we can effectively hold them accountable only for things we can reliably think we know. For example, we generally can hold them accountable only for things big enough or overt enough to make it into public awareness. We might do more than this if there is a group or agency or person with a strong identification with some issue. That agency might be able to push a representative's (or candidate's) record into public awareness. In this case, as in the general argument above, we accept the authoritative judgment of another about the qualifications and commitments of officeholders. We may also accept the judgment of the press, although all too often we may suspect that any given media outlet is driven by a partisan concern for making a specific case. And sometimes, we may doubt the media more generally as not adequately reliable even about simple facts.[5]

Much of the focus here will not be on the accountability of a government agent but on the prior problem of the agent's responsiveness. There are two quite different reasons for this. First, I think, in large part for reasons to be argued here, that accountability plays a relatively small part in our actual politics.[6] Electorates have held some governments accountable—as in the U.S. presidencies of Herbert Hoover for the Great Depression and maybe Gerald Ford for his pardon of former president Richard Nixon for his wrongdoings in Watergate. And other political bodies have held many officials accountable for their illegal actions. For example, in the United States there have been Nixon most famously and, more recently, Dan Rostenkowski and Bill Clinton.[7] But these were very unusual cases.

Second, we first have to know whether a government has been responsive before we can think to hold it accountable. This is the central issue of this essay. I wish to argue that there is one central form of responsiveness that we want from our political representatives: *We want them to serve our interests*. I will therefore focus on accountability to our interests, as in the case of Hoover, rather than to our moral concerns, or other concerns. But there are two major problems that we and our representatives face in meeting this concern with our interests: epistemological problems, including problems of causal understanding, and commitment problems. Most of the issues in responsiveness and accountability are about securing interests in the light of these problems. Clinton was evidently seen as serving the interests of a large part of the public, who therefore did not

---

[5] This was the problem at issue in a recent pair of *Boston Globe* reporters' failings. One reporter, the black woman Patricia Smith, made up people and quotes. Another, the white male Mike Barnicle, put forward the jokes of comedian George Carlin as his own thoughts (in his smugly titled column "I was just thinking . . ."). Journalist Howell Raines, whose newspaper (the *New York Times*) owns the *Globe*, supposes the *Globe* was racist and sexist in firing Smith but not Barnicle; but he also supposes that journalism and the credibility of the press in general were harmed by keeping Barnicle on the job ("The High Price of Reprieving Mike Barnicle," *New York Times*, August 13, 1998, editorial page A22). In the end, Barnicle was forced to resign after it was discovered that he had earlier written a story that could not be verified and that did not fit the facts of the time (Felicity Barringer, "Boston Globe Columnist Resigns Over Authenticity of 1995 Story," *New York Times*, August 20, 1998, A1, A16).

[6] See James D. Fearon, "Electoral Accountability and the Control of Politicians: Selecting Good Types versus Sanctioning Poor Performance," in *Democracy, Accountability, and Representation*, ed. Bernard Manin, Adam Przeworski, and Susan Stokes (Cambridge: Cambridge University Press, 1999).

[7] Rostenkowski, a powerful Democratic member of Congress from Illinois who was chairman of the House Ways and Means Committee, was accused of misuse of public funds and defeated for reelection from a normally safe Democratic district in 1994. Hence, he was actually held accountable by the electorate for his abuse of office rather than for his policy positions. He was later convicted and served a brief time in jail. Clinton was held accountable by Republicans in the House of Representatives much more than by the electorate for his sexual indiscretions and his deceitful misstatements about them in court depositions.

choose to hold him accountable for actions that did not affect their interests. The epistemological problems are particularly acute for citizen-voters, and I address them throughout this essay. The problem of forming credible commitments is important for citizens who want to hold office-holders accountable, but it is especially important for candidates for office, and I address it below in Section V.

Partly, I focus on serving our interests—rather than our other kinds of demands, such as any demand for government officials to take certain moral positions or to perform certain actions—for methodological and conceptual reasons. Analysis is more productive if we keep it clean and focused. Then we can more easily tell how much we have explained and when something else is at stake. Partly, however, I focus only on interests because I think it is mostly right to do so. Concerns other than interests matter to electorates, but they matter the way they do in life more generally: they typically do not strongly conflict with interests, although, of course, occasionally they do, and they may even trump interests to some extent. For example, some—but perhaps few—U.S. voters may have had to vote against their own interests to support civil rights legislation, and most did so to support welfare policy. But those who voted morally against the British Raj in India, French control of Algeria, or the U.S. war in Vietnam generally may have voted with their interests, as well as with moral concerns.

The focus on responsiveness to interests suggests that we should keep separate (1) whether government is responsive and (2) whether citizens think it is. Running responsiveness together with citizens' perceptions of it raises two difficult issues that I will not address. First, the alternative to looking to interests—looking to brute public opinion—makes responsiveness entirely a function of subjective preferences of the electorate at given moments. This tends to reduce the notion of responsiveness to that of President George Bush's opportunistic effort to mirror the polls day to day. Part of the competence of government is in showing its electorate that its policies are responsive to their interests when the government is not merely mirroring public opinion. Second, running responsiveness together with citizens' perceptions of it makes it hard to separate "objective" interests from manipulated preferences. A good demagogue is virtually always responsive in this corrupted sense. In this sense, Hitler was responsive, not leading the way; and Stalin was plausibly more responsive than Roosevelt.

III. Accountability and Knowledge

To understand the problem of the accountability of democratic representatives we must, at the very least, understand three pairs of quite different things, on the side of the representative and on the side of the electorate. First, on the side of the representative we must understand how a representative could know what to do to be responsive. And on the side of the electorate we must understand how we can know that our representative has been responsive. These are both epistemological issues: they are about how people know or can know relevant matters. Second, we must understand how candidates could demonstrate responsiveness and how an electorate could commit to holding them accountable. These are commitment issues. They are of concern here insofar as they raise epistemological questions of how an electorate can know that an official or candidate is genuinely committed to some program or interest. Finally, we would also need to understand how a representative could be responsive and how an electorate could hold a representative accountable. These are both causal issues. The causal problem of how we hold a representative accountable is a very difficult one, especially in the world of democratic elections as characterized by Downs and Joseph Schumpeter.[8] The causal problem of how we hold a representative accountable is of interest here primarily as it affects what the electorate is likely to know about responsiveness of representatives and as it affects the commitment or the threat that the electorate will hold anyone accountable. As Schumpeter wrote: "[W]ithout the initiative that comes from immediate responsibility, ignorance will persist in the face of masses of information however complete and correct."[9] I may have reason to acquire knowledge because it gives me pleasure, but not because it will be useful in my causing good public effects through my role as citizen.

Again, at the most general level, we usually want government to serve our interests. We may often also want it to enforce a moral code or a religious principle that we have, and we may want it to act at our expense on behalf of others, for example, with welfare programs or with international aid. On such issues, many of the problems of representation that are discussed here are less acute because we can imagine that officials face a genuine mandate from those who voted for them. They might nevertheless violate their mandate because it conflicts with other goals or because they seek support from people other than those who back their supposed mandate. Because I generally focus on representation of interests rather than of moral views, the role of mandates in the discussion below will be to overcome epistemological problems.

To serve our interests, government must sometimes first discover our interests, when we do not even know them—or, possibly, it must stimulate us to have interests we did not previously have. More commonly, however, government must simply divine what are our interests in a world that has changed since the last election, when we might have given

---

[8] Downs, *An Economic Theory of Democracy*; Joseph Schumpeter, *Capitalism, Socialism, and Democracy*, 3d ed. (New York: Harper, 1950).

[9] Schumpeter, *Capitalism, Socialism, and Democracy*, 262.

some clear indication of our interests in the context of the previous state of the world. Or it must infer our interests from too limited evidence. For example, much of legislation is accomplished through packaging of support across unrelated issues. Indeed, compromise is virtually necessary to achieve much serious legislation. But the electorate has typically revealed no position on the ranking of various compromises. The electorate might have given evidence of its preference for x over not-x and for y over not-y; but there may be no evidence on whether x plus not-y is preferred to not-x plus y, and yet this may be the only available choice for some officeholder.

The most interesting problems for accountability arise from a combination of the latter two problems: changed conditions and too limited evidence. For example, suppose that in a campaign George Bush promised "no new taxes." Had the world remained relatively like that in which he made the promise, he would have had no good reason to expect that his promise was not viewed as binding by much of the electorate who supported him (and even by some of the electorate who voted against him). Suppose, however, that the U.S. had been attacked by a foreign power and had suddenly had to increase expenditures for defense. Then Bush's prior promise would not have been seen as binding by those who strongly favored increased defense spending. Those supporters might well have seen their interest as dependent on increased defense spending and, hence, on new taxes to fund the spending. They might even have considered Bush delinquent if he had refused to spend more for defense merely because he had promised no new taxes. The problem for Bush would have been to infer how preferences stood in the changed conditions. In the case of military attack, presumably, this would have been easy to do.

Short of crises and dramatic changes, however, the problem officeholders face is that they must often choose in a state of ignorance of what the interests of their constituents are. What the interests of an electorate are on some issues is often simply beyond practical knowing. This might especially be true for issues over which individual members of the electorate have never previously faced real decisions. As Vilfredo Pareto noted, a peasant woman who has never seen a diamond cannot be expected to give a meaningful answer to the question of how much she would be willing to pay for a diamond necklace if she had greater wealth.[10] How much should our national government spend on airports, research on disease, fighter planes, foreign aid, and the alleviation of domestic poverty? Most citizens have dismal knowledge of the scale of expenditure on such things, and, yet, legislatures regularly make decisions about them. It is in principle very difficult for the electorate to hold representatives

---

[10] Vilfredo Pareto, *Manual of Political Economy* (New York: Kelley, 1971), ch. 4, section 26, p. 188.

accountable when we cannot even judge whether they have served our interests. Notoriously, according to a recent poll, Americans supposed that 18 percent of the federal budget went to foreign aid, when the actual figure is less than 1 percent.[11]

Yet this seemingly dismal state of affairs is the virtually necessary state of affairs. There are two, perhaps related, reasons citizens should not be expected to understand most issues. First, in general the populace are poor theorists because they do not specialize in theory. (But then, even the theorists may be poor theorists, which is a reason for leaving, say, economic theory out of the Constitution.)[12] People's understanding is often very heavily drawn from rhetorical argument and from experience. Suppose an official abandons a promised policy and adopts a contrary policy—as President Ronald Reagan abandoned his long-held policy against deficit spending. The adopted policy is likely to have noticeable effects on many people, including positive effects on some. Those positively affected might switch allegiance from the originally supported policy to the officeholder who has newly benefited them, as may have happened when some of those who benefited immediately from Reagan's tax cuts became strong Reagan supporters.

Second, citizens rightly do not waste their time and resources learning even more information about all of the issues that might have effects on their lives, indeed, important effects. They rightly choose to leave those decisions vaguely to political officeholders. For this massive range of issues, it would be practically incoherent to suppose that officeholders had any charge other than to serve their electors' interests well. Their main task may be to decide which part of their electorate to serve. Southern California Congressman Robert Dornan plausibly served most of his electorate very well for many years with his hostility to welfare programs and to migrants, but enough migrants eventually gained the vote in his district to defeat him in 1996.

IV. Why Mandates?

Here is the central problem of accountability: The standards of what government must do to be responsive to the citizenry or some part of it depend on what the interests of the citizenry are, not on specific policies considered *a priori* and independently of changing context. Yet this raises a severe problem for a candidate for office. Candidate Bush could not campaign on the claim merely to do "whatever" fit the interests of electors unless he had extraordinary credibility and stature in the eyes of the

[11] Steven Kull, I. M. Destler, and Clay Ramsay, *The Foreign Policy Gap: How Policymakers Misread the Public* (College Park, MD: Center for International and Security Studies at the University of Maryland, 1997).

[12] See Russell Hardin, *Liberalism, Constitutionalism, and Democracy* (Oxford: Oxford University Press, 1999), chs. 3 and 6.

electorate. Few if any candidates have ever had such credibility (George Washington may have been the only one in U.S. history, although Franklin Roosevelt in 1936 may have come close for at least a very large fraction of the electorate).[13] Hence, most candidates must establish their submission to credible constraints such as, for example, specific promises and stands on well-defined policies of "no new taxes" and so forth. Their support for particular policies during an election is a *de facto* proclamation of a mandate to serve the interests of the electors.

Given that accountability is to interests rather than to specific policy positions, responsible leaders must do what would be acceptable *ex post*, which need not be what is thought or even claimed to be acceptable *ex ante*. However, given the epistemological problems of electors, candidates face two problems: establishing credible *commitments to serve* interests and establishing the credibility of their *capacity to judge* interests. Both of these run against the problem of opportunism that takes the form of switching policies to curry support from a group other than those who elected the official.

On many classes of issues, credibility might seem to be relatively easy to establish because the candidate cannot expect to get reelected by a different coalition. Hence, the candidate must serve the interests of the members of the coalition well or lose their support. But the initial coalition might be as trapped into supporting their original candidate at reelection time as the candidate is into relying on that coalition. Ronald Reagan, a balanced-budget Republican, was elected in 1980 on the strong supposition that he would be a fiscal conservative. He then ran by far the largest deficits in peacetime American history. Despite his reneging on his supposed commitments to fiscal conservatism during his first term, in 1984 there was no effective alternative for fiscally conservative Republicans but to vote for their betrayer.

Reagan's switch was interesting because it arguably served the interests of his own supporters. Many of these Republicans could rightly have concluded that, although Reagan did not keep his promise on fiscal policy, he very clearly did serve the financial interests of the wealthy, who prospered beyond expectation from his policies overall. They especially benefited from the massive tax cuts at the high end—it was these tax cuts that fueled both the deficit and the gains of the wealthy. For most of the wealthy in America, the ideology of fiscal conservatism probably could not trump avarice. Indeed, many of the fiscal conservatives who voted for

---

[13] It is not impossible for someone to establish credible commitments to well-defined positions. For example, sometimes it is possible to appoint judges with fairly sure expectations of how they will behave in office, because they might have extensive records of performance on lower courts when there is little reason to think that this performance was opportunistically guided. Nevertheless, there are famous betrayals by judges who have gone on to change their positions after appointment to a higher court, as President Dwight David Eisenhower reputedly thought Chief Justice Earl Warren betrayed his expectations.

Reagan in 1980 may have voted for Bush in 1988 on his fiscally irresponsible pledge of no new taxes.

A. Cross-cutting interests

Consider a more complex case in which the interests in play at the time of election are trumped by other interests that cut across the earlier interests. Conscription during World War I had polarized the francophone community of Canada because most of them did not see the war as their war and they did not wish to participate. They had no great love for the English, whose rule in Canada made them second-class citizens, or for the French, whose abandonment of French Canada had left them to the mercies of the English. Hence, they had no enthusiasm for letting their sons die in defense of England and France.

In 1940, with World War II underway, MacKenzie King was reelected Prime Minister of Canada on a strong promise not to introduce conscription to fight the new European war. His Liberal Party depended on strong support from Quebec. After early German successes in World War II and the consequent rise in national fervor among anglophone Canadians, King reneged on his promise and introduced conscription. First, however, he held a plebiscite on the issue. The issue to be decided was: "Are you in favour of releasing the government from any obligations arising out of any past commitments restricting the methods of raising men for military service?" Of course, the anglophone majority voted for conscription while the francophone minority voted overwhelmingly against (francophone Quebecers voted about 85 percent against releasing the government from its pledge, while the anglophone provinces voted about 80 percent for releasing the government). King answered to the majority interest. But the point of his initial pledge had been to reassure the minority francophones.[14] It was therefore a betrayal to use the majority anglophones to undo his pledge to the francophones.

Politicians who face issues that cut across standard party lines may not be able to serve the interests of their supporters while violating their promises to them. Because of the centrality of the issue of conscription and because of its independence from general party positions, King's francophone support could be broken over that one issue. Indeed, King's betrayal of his Quebec supporters may have contributed to the further growth of francophone hostility to the anglophone majority in Canada, hostility that may eventually divide Canada.

B. Generalized accountability

One might suppose that King chose to be essentially a free agent once the war dominated politics in his time. He might well have decided he

---

[14] For an account of this episode, see Margaret Levi, *Consent, Dissent, and Patriotism* (New York: Cambridge University Press, 1997), 153–60, esp. 154.

was accountable only to history. For example, he could have decided that conscription was right not because it served the interests of certain Canadians but because it was morally right to help defeat Nazism. Similarly, from the moment he decided not to run for reelection in 1968 (if the decision was genuine and not a ploy), President Lyndon Johnson similarly became a free agent. He could then renege on commitments that he did not like; he could act in support of what he thought was the national interest or what was morally right no matter what particular supporters wanted; or he could strive to change his own reputation, to convince historians that he was a statesman committed to just causes and capable of learning.

In the abstract, one might think that some one of these is the best attitude for a national leader: that is, one might think leaders, and politicians in general, should hold themselves accountable to general interests, moral rectitude, or something other than the interests of particular groups who elect them. This is, however, a hard position to defend from within democratic theory. The very idea of democratic theory in a society in which democracy must be representative is for those who are elected to be accountable, to be representative. Perhaps on a very long view we might think that a leader had done the right thing even though we would have voted against her for doing it, and we might therefore think that she had acted in our interests in the long run, that she was responsible to us.

This abstraction is consonant with Edmund Burke's eighteenth-century vision of representation. That vision is often posed as one of the standard alternatives in modern politics. It is, however, arguably a vision that owes its central conception to the prior form of government by monarch. An enlightened monarch, clearly the best kind to have, would rule by taking the long view of his or her subjects' interests. Here, however, the long view entails trading off the interests of some for those of others as though there were some collectively right policy or result. The point of representative democracy is to put these interests in contest to decide policy. There is no supra-citizen who can trade off one group's interests against another's. Burke's legislators, however, would merely be a collection of enlightened monarchs. If they were all equally insightful, they would all make the same choices and there would be no need of representation of any groups. In principle, therefore, there would be no need of representative democracy; there could be a single election of a monarch. The only reason for electing an entire legislature rather than merely a monarch would be to reduce the variance in judgment that would follow from mere mistake. This claim is an analog of the Marquis de Condorcet's jury or truth theorem.[15] According to this theorem, if the average juror is likely to have at least a slightly better than even chance of correctly assessing

[15] Jean Antoine Condorcet, "Essay on the Application of Mathematics to the Theory of Decision-Making" [1795], in *Selected Writings* (Indianapolis, IN: Hackett, 1999).

the truth of the innocence or guilt of an accused person, then a very large jury will approach the certainty of getting it right. This follows from the regression toward the mean of a large sample.

Alternatively, Burke's vision was presumably merely of legislators who are specialized or who are selected from among the "true natural aristocracy," and who are therefore better able to see the electorate's interest than is the electorate. If it is grounded only in the claim that those who specialize in policymaking are apt to be better at it than are most people, this is not an antidemocratic vision. For Burke and for many advocates of Burkean representatives, however, it is more likely that the vision is genuinely antidemocratic and that it is grounded in the sense that some (perhaps an aristocracy, perhaps a meritocracy) are more suited to govern and others are more suited to be governed.[16] Such representatives should be accountable, perhaps, but it is hard to specify what that means beyond the claims that the Burkean representatives themselves would make for what it means: "I'm accountable and I know that I have fulfilled my duty of representation. I'm sorry that I can't make you understand why this is so, but trust me."

The representative who claims expertise merely from specialization could be called a Schumpeterian representative. This representative is better able to judge what serves our interests in some well-defined policy area than we are. How could we know that? Unlike the Burkean elitist representative who is intellectually or otherwise superior to us, there are in-principle ways for us to know that our Schumpeterian representative has been responsive to our interests. However, it is unlikely that we or any significant number of us would make the massive effort to discover whether our representative has been responsive. At best, we might expect organized groups to sponsor specialists to monitor our representative's judgment.

V. COMMITMENT

Superficially, one might think that the relationship of citizens to government could be modeled as a trust relationship in which the parties have an ongoing interaction that gives each of them an incentive to take each other's interests to heart. I think this view is conceptually wrong.[17]

[16] Burke's views appear throughout his works. See, e.g., "Speech to the Electors of Bristol" [1774], in *Representation*, ed. Hanna Pitkin (New York: Atherton, 1969), esp. 174–75; and "Appeal from the New to the Old Whigs" [1791], in *The Works of Edmund Burke* (London: George Bell and Sons, 1901), 3:85–87. For later views, see Michael Oakeshott, *Rationalism in Politics and Other Essays* (New York: Harper Collins, 1962), esp. the essay, "On Being a Conservative."

[17] Russell Hardin, "Do We Want Trust in Government?" in *Democracy and Trust*, ed. Mark Warren (New York: Cambridge University Press, 1999), 22–41; Hardin, "Trust in Government," in *Trust and Governance*, ed. Valerie Braithwaite and Margaret Levi (New York: Russell Sage Foundation, 1998), 9–27.

In fact, what we need are accounts of individual commitment and of group and institutional commitment. For individuals and organizations, the ability to make commitments is the ability to secure ourselves great benefits and to accomplish our purposes. Holding government to account requires commitment from citizens just as responsiveness, or living up to some policy or other promise, requires commitment from government and its agents. Moreover, if our commitments are to motivate action by others, *we need ways to make our commitments known to those who should act on them.*

Individuals are commonly able to commit themselves to actions they would rather avoid in the moment in which they are undertaken. They do so in order to secure themselves longer-run benefits. Although there is an extensive literature on fully internal or psychological commitment, the most successful and credible device for individual commitment in typical contexts is likely to be the use of external devices that change one's incentives in relevant moments. Individuals often accomplish the trick of committing themselves through contracts that make their agreements legally binding, through ongoing exchange relations in which failure to fulfill one's commitments entails costs, or through arrangements to make their failure a matter of public or private embarrassment. For example, I commit myself to repaying your loan by entering a contract that is legally enforceable. Of course, I might not be able to obtain the loan at all if I could not credibly commit myself to repaying it.

These are strategic devices that alter the incentives one faces, to make the incentives support fulfillment of one's commitments at some future time. People with short time horizons—children and others who live by instant gratification—undercut their own capacity to make their futures better. People who can adopt such strategic devices as contracting, setting themselves up for public embarrassment, and relying on ongoing relationships can accomplish many things for themselves that would otherwise be difficult or impossible. Some of these devices simultaneously resolve the problem of communicating the commitment and make it credible, as signing a contract typically does. Some, however, are essentially privately known and can become communicated easily only after a long period of repeated performance that establishes a reputation for living up to supposed commitments.

Many children and perhaps all very young children, people who suffer from narcissistic personality disorders, and many who simply think they are most in control when they keep all options open for themselves to decide when the time comes, are similarly unable to commit themselves to future courses of action and are therefore unable to get others to commit themselves. The losses that result from one's failure to commit may be far greater than the supposed gains from keeping oneself ostensibly in control. It would merely be cute to call it a paradox, but the truth of our general relations with others is that we can control our own lives only by submitting ourselves to control by real commitments. The overriding value of being able to keep commitments is being able to coordinate with others, that is to say, *to get others to do what we want them to do.*

People learn to be reliable in ongoing relationships. An individual who is involved with you repeatedly in various exchanges may finally recognize that the advantages of continuing the relationship in the longer run outweigh the potential for quick gain by cheating in the short run. The relationship of citizens to government is not the analog of this simple two-person iterated interaction even if it is iterated for many years or over many election cycles. The two parties are not simply analogous to individual persons. A candidate or officeholder might be, but the electorate is more nearly analogous to a mob, or even a collection of disparately directed mobs. The mob-electorate cannot commit itself to anything, while individual officeholders can make some commitments strongly enough even to force themselves to keep the commitments under duress. Ideally, members of the electorate would wish to have the government, and not merely a particular officeholder, constrained to act in their interest, because the electorate would generally be concerned with policy *outcomes.* As a rule, individual officeholders have insufficient power over policy to make themselves accountable for policy outcomes. At best, they can typically be accountable for sticking by some *position.*

For example, Senator Alan Dixon could not alone have blocked the appointment of Clarence Thomas to the Supreme Court in 1991 by voting with the large minority of senators opposed to the appointment, but he could still be held accountable by the Illinois electorate, especially women, for voting to confirm the appointment, and they voted him out of office in 1992. There is no comparable sense in which the entire Senate could be held accountable, and even Dixon might not have been held so severely to account if he had not faced reelection soon after the Thomas confirmation.

How can political candidates and officeholders establish credible commitments? Those in relatively rigorous party systems can do it by relying on the reputation and force of their party's discipline. In the very loose party system of the United States, this device has no force, and a more rigorous party system would make no sense of American popular positions, as it increasingly makes little sense in European contexts. Some politicians establish very consistent reputations, and some set themselves up for great embarrassment if they change their positions, as Bush did with his slangy "read my lips" pledge on taxes. But politicians cannot use many of the devices available to ordinary individuals. In particular, they cannot genuinely contract with the electorate, although the beloved metaphor of a social contract is often invoked despite its vacuity. Moreover, they cannot engage in one-on-one iterated interactions that commit them by making the future benefits of the interaction depend on their faithfulness in each reciprocal dealing. Because the electorate comes closer to having the structure (or, more accurately, the lack of structure) of a mob than it does to having the structure of a party or a coherent interest group, candidates can constantly shift their appeals across varied interests, as Canadian Prime Minister MacKenzie King did more dramatically than most.

VI. CONCLUDING REMARKS

Epistemological constraints make it implausible that government is substantially accountable to the electorate. It does not serve the interests of the electorate individually to know what they need to know to hold representatives accountable. Hence, they cannot act collectively to hold them accountable. It would be excessive to say that the authors of the U.S. Constitution understood this point and drafted the Constitution in the light of it. Indeed, constitutional theorists often seem to suppose that accountability is majoritarian, that officials are accountable to majority preferences in just the way that cannot make workable sense in a street-level epistemology. Against this view, the legal scholar Rebecca Brown argues that political accountability has been misunderstood in American constitutional theorizing. Her argument is not that accountability cannot be the servant of majoritarianism for epistemological reasons, but that the majoritarian view is not the view of accountability that is at work in the U.S. Constitution. Rather, accountability as enforced through voting "was designed not as a means for the people to participate in government, but as a means for the people to protect themselves from their own repre-sentative government."[18] This accountability is directed at major abuses, not at day-to-day policymaking. Brown's claim fits much of the immedi-ate prehistory of the American constitutional experience, including, of course, the Declaration of Independence with its litany of abuses.

Ex ante, we can do little more than authorize a government or an individual elected officeholder. We—or rather, the larger society, past and present—can also, of course, erect institutional devices to constrain gov-ernments and officials in fairly general ways.[19] When we authorize, we basically empower governments to make policies as they then see fit. We may choose to authorize a government because we expect it to adopt certain policies, but we commonly cannot force it to do so. Authorization to govern does not determine policies. For the most part, we will sit back and allow our government to govern and to make policies without much attention from us. Indeed, as noted above, poll results suggest that Amer-ican voters are astonishingly ignorant of many important aspects of pol-

---

[18] Rebecca L. Brown, "Accountability, Liberty, and the Constitution," *Columbia Law Review* 98 (April 1998): 531–79.

[19] See Russell Hardin, "Institutional Commitment: Values or Incentives?" in *Economics, Values, and Organization*, ed. Avner Ben-Ner and Louis Putterman (Cambridge: Cambridge University Press, 1998), 419–33.

icy. For example, on average, respondents in the poll cited earlier guessed that expenditures on foreign aid programs were about 18 percent of the total federal budget, whereas they held that the level of foreign aid should be about 8 percent.[20] They therefore commonly rail against foreign aid. In actual fact, foreign aid accounts for less than 1 percent of the federal budget, so most voters should be railing against the paucity of foreign aid. When told the actual level, they revise downward their beliefs of how much aid should be given.

Major actions—significant policies or abuses—can commonly cross the threshold of a citizen's perception without need of any effort on the part of the citizen to find out what is at stake. Such actions become known as though they were forced on us. This is obviously true of such massive actions as going to war, or even of the Cuban Missile Crisis of 1962, or President Clinton's attack on reputed terrorist facilities in Afghanistan and Sudan in 1998; but it is also true of much lesser actions. Most Americans relatively quickly came to believe that Reagan's economic policies were enormously beneficial to the wealthy and the near-wealthy. Even someone who read no newspaper and watched no television news was likely to know very quickly that President Nixon's assistants bugged Democratic Party headquarters. One imagines that hardly any voting Quebecer could have failed to hear that MacKenzie King had violated his pledge not to introduce conscription.

Indeed, even for very trivial matters, if they are explicit and are pushed hard enough, it is difficult to escape being aware of them, as in the case of President Bush's broken pledge of "no new taxes." Bush made the pledge especially memorable by invoking the then-current slang for emphasis: "Read my lips." Candidates would be well advised to make their stands especially memorable only if they are sure they can stay committed to them. Otherwise, they may ruefully say, with Bush, "I did it and I regret it and I regret it. Any time you get hammered on something, I guess you want to redo it."[21]

In a commentary on the seemingly perverse poll results on American attitudes on and knowledge about foreign aid, journalist Michael Kinsley says that not only are Americans scandalously ignorant, but "they seem to believe they have a democratic right to their ignorance." He supposes that citizens should be held "to something approaching the intellectual

---

[20] The median levels were 15 and 5 percent, respectively (Kull, Destler, and Ramsay, *The Foreign Policy Gap*). The initial poll was done in January 1995. (See Steven Greenhouse, "Foreign Aid: Under Siege in the Budget Wars," *New York Times*, April 30, 1995, section 4, p. 4.) Other polls have yielded even more extreme results. Foreign aid does not include military assistance; including such assistance would still put the popular estimate far out of line with the facts. When this clarification was added to a follow-up poll in 1996, however, popular estimates of how much aid went for purely economic assistance and development were higher than in the poll cited here.

[21] David Firestone, "Being a Politician Means Never Having to Say You're Sorry," *New York Times*, August 23, 1998, section 4, p. 2.

standard you would apply to yourself or a friend."[22] Presumably, he means that we should expect our fellow citizens to be very well informed or to hold their political opinions in abeyance until they are. The first half of this expectation is hopelessly implausible. Ordinary knowledge about foreign aid and other important issues of public policy is unlikely to be very good, and for compelling reasons. And, in a sense, the second half also is hopelessly implausible, because democracy virtually demands that people vote and that they vote according to their actual views, even though these are unlikely to be very well formed.

Walter Lippmann wrote that, in their quest for popular approval, democratic politicians follow the ignorant will of the people, and thereby cause the "devitalization of the governing power." He called this the malady of democratic states.[23] His point is partly well taken, but his vocabulary is wrong. If we have a malady, we perform or prosper less well in some respect than we normally should. But the ignorant will of the people that Lippmann deplored is the *normal* state of a large polity. Such ignorance is almost logically deducible from the nature of knowledge and its role in democracy. It is individually healthy not to squander much of one's time learning things that are useless.

Politics, New York University

---

[22] Michael Kinsley, "The Intellectual Free Lunch," *New Yorker*, February 6, 1995, 4–5.
[23] Walter Lippmann, *The Public Philosophy* (Boston: Little, Brown, 1955), 29.

POLITICAL QUALITY*

By David Estlund

I. Introduction

Political equality is in tension with political quality, and quality has recently been neglected. My thesis is that proper attention to the quality of democratic procedures and their outcomes requires that we accept substantive inequalities of political input in the interest of increasing input overall. Mainly, I hope to refute *political egalitarianism*, the view that justice or legitimacy requires substantive political equality, specifically equal availability of power or influence over collective choices that have legal force.[1] I hope to show that political egalitarianism exaggerates individual rights in the conduct of political procedures, and neglects the substantive justice of the decisions made through those procedures. Some unequal distributions of influence may better promote just decisions, and without reliance on any invidious comparisons such as the relative wisdom of the wealthy or the educated.

Put in general terms, the goal is to find an acceptable stopping point between merely formal political equality on the one hand, which places no limits on substantive political inequality, and equal availability of political influence on the other, whose distributive constraints are too severe. The principled basis I offer for such a point is a theory of democratic legitimacy that gives a significant role to the epistemic value of democratic procedures—their tendency to produce decisions that are correct by the appropriate independent moral standards.[2] This approach requires more than merely formal equality, since great substantive inequality in political input will be damaging to the procedure's ability to arrive at just decisions. In this it not only accommodates a traditional criticism of classical liberalism, but makes a closely related point against

* I am grateful for useful discussions of this material with Reed Caster, Joshua Cohen, Norman Daniels, Gary Gates, Andy Hoffman, Andy Levine, Erin Kelly, the department of Political Science at the University of Chicago, and the other contributors to this volume.

[1] Some political egalitarians would not limit the view's scope in this way, but it simplifies matters to consider this narrower view. If it is not correct, then the broader version couldn't be either.

[2] I describe an epistemic approach to democratic legitimacy called *epistemic proceduralism* in my essay "Beyond Fairness and Deliberation: The Epistemic Dimension of Democratic Authority," in *Deliberative Democracy: Essays in Reason and Politics*, ed. James Bohman and William Rehg (Cambridge: MIT Press, 1997). I explain the pertinent idea of an independent standard there, and at greater length in "Making Truth Safe for Democracy," in *The Idea of Democracy*, ed. David Copp, Jean Hampton, and John Roemer (Cambridge: Cambridge University Press, 1993), 71–100.

the political-egalitarian ideal of equal *availability* of political influence, since that too is insensitive to the distribution of *actual* influence, and to the epistemic consequences of that distribution. The epistemic approach, then, seeks to structure politics so as to promote the quality of political decisions, but without relying on invidious comparisons between citizens or groups.[3] I defend the epistemic approach to democracy more fully elsewhere. Here my claim is that epistemic considerations should lead us to reject the goal of substantive equality of (available) influence. I thus draw out an implication of the epistemic view of democratic legitimacy for the issue of political equality.

Briefly, it is worth noting that this argument can be extended beyond the concern with epistemic value, though I will not develop these points in much detail. First, even for theories that accept that there is such a thing as epistemic value for some democratic decisions, it is plausible to hold that for other decisions there is no independent standard but only procedural justice. It may seem that the quantity of deliberation is worthless in those cases and all that matters is fairness. Second, some theorists will make no room for such a thing as independent standards for democratic decisions at all. In both these cases it may seem as if all that matters in democratic procedure is procedural fairness, and that my epistemic arguments for inequality would not apply. Notice, however, that in that case we should be satisfied with some random choice procedure. That we would not be satisfied even in the absence of epistemic considerations stems, I think, from the fact that quantity of deliberation, within certain distributional bounds, has other value even in addition to any tendency it might have to promote the discovery of truth. Some will put it in terms of the rationality of the decision, others in terms of letting participants be better informed about their genuine interests, and so on. My point here is only that tension between equality and quantity of input is not limited to contexts or theories where epistemic value is at stake. However, I will mainly press the point in the epistemic context.

Political egalitarianism requires equalizing opportunity for, or availability of, political influence, not actual political influence. This is because a citizen is in no way mistreated by the inequality resulting from her own free choice not to exercise all her available influence. My criticism is based on the value that more political deliberation has, other things being equal, on the quality of political decisions. But these epistemic consequences, as I call them, stem from facts about the amounts of actual input and participation rather than from facts about the amounts of input that are available. Thus, for some purposes below, the actual/available distinction will be important; but for other purposes it is not important. In much of what follows, I will speak of influence or input without specifying whether

---

[3] My criticism of fair proceduralism in "Beyond Fairness and Deliberation" leaves the question of political egalitarianism open. Here I take it up directly.

it is actual or available, and in those contexts I mean what I say to apply equally to both. When I mean one or the other I will be specific. I explicitly consider the difference at several points below.

Political egalitarianism may seem to be an extreme and implausible view, not requiring great efforts to refute it; but there is a plausible case to be made for it, even though, on reflection, it should be rejected. Here is one way of finding political egalitarianism tempting. Disputes over such things as distributive justice are deep and pervasive. Whatever the correct resolution of those disputes may be, we hope that a political decision about distributive justice can be legitimate, even if not just, on the basis of certain features of the political procedure, and not simply on the basis of whether the decision is morally correct, since the latter issue will be too deeply contested.[4] But now imagine a process in which those who have more money than others have more influence over the process. Such a process can easily seem unfair, depleting it of the moral capacity to render the outcomes of the process legitimate. At least if the process were fair, the outputs could be said to be fair in that procedural sense. A fair procedure, some argue, requires equal availability of input, or at least insulation of influence from things like differential wealth. It is natural to conclude that whether or not justice requires economic equality, legitimacy requires substantive political equality—equal availability of political influence—so as to keep the political process fair. Egalitarianism, then, is held to be the proper stance at least with respect to political input. For reasons that vary among its advocates, political egalitarianism is a popular and formidable normative theory of political legitimacy, one not to be easily dismissed.[5]

---

[4] On the distinction between justice and legitimacy in a liberal theory, see my essay "The Survival of Egalitarian Justice in John Rawls's *Political Liberalism*," *Journal of Political Philosophy* 4, no. 1 (1996): 68–78.

[5] Robert Dahl endorses political egalitarianism in *Democracy and Its Critics* (New Haven: Yale University Press, 1989), 109, 114–15. Joshua Cohen, in "Deliberation and Democratic Legitimacy," reprinted in Bohman and Rehg, eds., *Deliberative Democracy*, sketches an "ideal deliberative procedure" which "is meant to provide a model for institutions to mirror" (73). One feature is that "the participants are substantively equal in that the existing distribution of power and resources does not shape their chances to contribute to deliberation . . ." (74). Cass Sunstein, in "Political Equality and Unintended Consequences," *Columbia Law Review* 94 (1994): 1394, says: "Disparities in wealth ought not lead to disparities in power over government." Thomas Christiano writes: "Justice requires that individuals have political equality, that is, equal resources to influence decisions regarding the collective properties of society" (Christiano, *The Rule of the Many* [Boulder, CO: Westview Press, 1999], 87). Harry Brighouse advocates "equal availability of political influence," which "requires the insulation of the political process from [income and wealth] inequalities" (Brighouse, "Egalitarianism and Equal Availability of Political Influence," *Journal of Political Philosophy* 4, no. 2 [1996]: 120). Jack Knight and James Johnson ("What Sort of Political Equality Does Deliberative Democracy Require?" in Bohman and Rehg, eds., *Deliberative Democracy*) advocate "equal opportunity of access to political influence" (280), including "equality in the resources that any participant be allowed to employ in the deliberative process" (293). In addition, Rawls and Dworkin may be committed to versions of it; see notes 10 and 41, respectively. In criticizing political egalitarianism I do not expect to have fully refuted any of these authors, whose views differ in interesting ways from each other and from the simplified version of political egalitarianism that I discuss.

Put in simplest terms, I will argue that equality of input may come at the cost of quantity, and that both are important to the quality of the process and its outcomes. That is why substantive equality of influence is not a proper goal or constraint for the design of democratic political institutions.

A brief taxonomy of competing approaches may help avoid certain misunderstandings.

In what I shall call *authoritarian* theories of political legitimacy, invidious comparisons between people have often been used to justify unequal political rights and liberties even at the formal legal level, such as unequal legal rights to vote or hold office, ostensibly in the interest of high-quality political rule.[6] Another traditional view makes no invidious comparisons and thus accepts equal formal political rights and liberties, but rejects the goal of equalizing substantive political influence—equal availability of political input, including whatever resource distribution this requires. Call this mixed view the *formalist* view of political equality. Some hold, for example, that substantive political equality (in addition to formal political equality) is not compatible with due respect for an individual's right to property, or to freedom of speech, or, more generally, one's liberty to do as one chooses. This version of the formalist view, which I will call *libertarian*,[7] is not based on any claims about the resulting quality of decisions.

Call the principle requiring both formal and substantive equality of political influence, *political egalitarianism*—a view that I will argue wrongly neglects the quality of political decisions. My purpose is not to oppose formal political equality, much less democracy itself, nor to rely on either invidious comparisons among citizens or on strong rights to property or speech. I defend a formalist view, but not on a libertarian basis. On the other hand, the inequality of influence that I will defend does, like the property-based or liberty-based arguments, tend to allow specifically the wealthy to have more political influence than others (though not as much more as they now have). It shares this feature with libertarian theories, but its basis is entirely different.

Political egalitarianism and formalist views (including libertarian views) are anti-authoritarian, or liberal theories. The view I defend is also liberal, and formalist rather than egalitarian, but on an epistemic rather than a libertarian basis (sharing the epistemic concern with some authoritarian views). Call this view a *liberal epistemic view* of political equality (see Figure 1). The liberal epistemic view is formalist because it accepts formal (but rejects substantive) equality of political influence. But formalist views need not say that distribution of substantive political influence does not

---

[6] For quotations of several epistemic arguments used to disenfranchise the propertyless, blacks, and women, see Daniel Ortiz, "The Democratic Paradox of Campaign Finance Reform," *Stanford Law Review* 50 (February 1998): 906–9.

[7] This label is meant only to name a view of political equality. I leave aside the question of the relation between this view and a more general libertarianism.

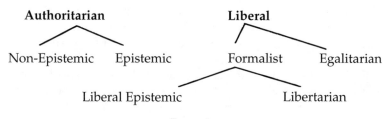

FIGURE 1.

matter at all (we might call that *strict formalism*; some libertarian views take this form). The liberal epistemic view does have the resources to criticize extreme inequality of influence, but rejects *equal* substantive influence as an appropriate goal. It is a *moderate formalism* in rejecting substantive equality, while not assuming that mere formal equality is enough.

My alternative to political egalitarianism diverges from it in approximately the way that John Rawls's difference principle diverges from a strictly egalitarian principle of distributive justice.[8] Rawls's view is often regarded as egalitarian, even though not strictly so. Likewise, the position taken here condemns great substantive (not only formal) political inequalities, but also finds decisive reasons to permit or require unequal influence under certain conditions. It is certainly more egalitarian with respect to substantive political influence than authoritarian or libertarian theories.

While this parallel with Rawls's theory of justice is instructive, the view defended here is also a criticism of a certain Rawlsian argument, and it may be less egalitarian than Rawls's view in one respect. In Rawlsian theory, the liberties to participate in politics must be equal for all. First, they must be formally equal, giving each citizen equal status under the law.[9] But second, they must also be substantively equal (or approximately so) in the sense that people should not have substantially greater opportunity to influence political outcomes as a result of their having a greater share of other primary social goods. While unequal influence would be compatible with formal political equality (formalist views), it is disallowed by a separate provision in Rawls's inviolable principle of equal liberty: each person's political liberties ought to be guaranteed a fair (approximately equal) value in addition to being formally equal under the law. Rawls's political egalitarianism is much stronger than his economic egalitarianism, since the former recognizes no justification for di-

---

[8] The difference principle states that inequalities can be justified if they benefit even the least well-off. See John Rawls, *A Theory of Justice* (Cambridge, MA: Harvard University Press, 1971), 302; and Rawls, *Political Liberalism* (New York: Columbia University Press, 1993), 56.

[9] I will assume that where there is formal equality there is also full compliance.

vergence from the roughly equal value of the political liberties.[10] Specifically, the Pareto-style argument used by Rawls to justify (in principle) economic inequality seems to be denied application to the case of political influence. I begin, shortly, by asking why this is so.

Political egalitarianism neglects the fact that a small and limited discussion is not as valuable a guide to important practical decisions as is fuller, more extensive discussion.[11] There is something to be said for procedural fairness, but also something to be said for applying human intelligence more extensively to political problems. Some writers acknowledge this point,[12] but still avoid the hard question by assuming that equality need not reduce the total quantity of public deliberation. The point I want to urge is that if equal influence can only be achieved at lower levels of input, then the epistemic advantages of a wider discussion might, from any reasonable point of view, outweigh the disadvantages of some degree of unequal influence. This is not just a logical possibility but a real possibility in democratic politics. For this reason, equal political influence, and, more specifically, the complete insulation of political influence from differential wealth, are not appropriate goals in the design of deliberative democratic institutions.

II. Paretianism and Political Input

It is far from clear what equal political influence would mean. It is relatively clear what insulation of influence from differential wealth would mean. But the latter would typically still involve great inequality of influence, since money is not the only route to influence. Social connections, good looks, debating skill, and an eye for good points can all give a person more influence in political discussion than other people. On the other hand, a simple majority vote, without any discussion of the issue at hand, would, if such a thing were even remotely possible, embody pure

---

[10] Rawls stops short of insisting on perfect equality, but mentions approximately equal value of political liberties (*Political Liberalism*, 358). His name for this is "fair," not "equal," value, and this may reflect the view that equality is not the point. The challenge, then, as I see it, is to find a salient standard between merely formal equality and strictly equal substantive influence. It is not clear whether Rawls would include the fair value requirement of the first principle among the requirements of legitimacy, which is generally a lower standard than justice in Rawls's theory. (I discuss this in "The Survival of Egalitarian Justice in John Rawls's *Political Liberalism*.")

[11] I am not making any assumptions about the particular nature of the discussion, or its civility, etc. Some of the literature on deliberative democracy revolves around implausible standards of politeness and reciprocity that I do not want to commit to here. Moreover, the term "discussion" is not meant to exclude nondiscursive contributions to public debate, such as protests or political art. There are important nondiscursive components of any discussion, including public political discussion.

[12] See, e.g., Bruce Ackerman, "Crediting the Voters," *The American Prospect* 13 (Spring 1993): 71–80. I discuss Ackerman's view in more detail in Section V.

equal influence. So would a coin flip to decide among the available alternatives, whether or not discussion had occurred.

Several of the sources of unequal influence mentioned above may well be regrettable. The one that apparently is not regrettable, and not regretted by any democratic theorist I know of, is the extra influence a person has by virtue of offering good reasons in a context where good reasons are appreciated and have influence. That some people are better at this than others is clear from the utter political ignorance or perversity of some people. If they are worse, some are better. How can this unequal influence be allowed or even celebrated by theorists who espouse the theory that equal influence is called for by the principle of equal respect for persons? I do not doubt that extra influence of better reasons is called for, in some way, by equal respect for persons. But I do doubt that the principle that each person is owed equal political influence can cohere with these other ideas. Unequal influence through rational persuasion is one kind of unequal influence. If there are good reasons, deriving from or at least consistent with equal respect, to allow unequal rational influence, then unequal influence does not, in general, violate equal respect. If it does, then unequal rational influence does too.

In what follows, then, I shall interpret the ideal of equal political influence to mean specifically *the insulation of political influence from differential wealth or social rank*. This more familiar and attractive thesis is what I hereafter mean by "political egalitarianism." Still, I think it is mistaken.

I begin with a story some philosophers tell, and which I will criticize, about why opportunities for political influence ought to be equalized among adult citizens. It is true, they grant, that if distributing some good unequally will allow more of that good to be given to everyone, then, at least in many contexts, it would be irrational to insist on an equal distribution. For example, Rawls argues that justice allows distributing primary social goods unequally if and only if doing so benefits all (or at least, for simplicity, the worst off). There might well be a way to do just that if extra social productivity can be induced by giving people incentives for producing more. If more social goods are produced by giving a larger share to the most productive citizens, then perhaps the incentive will still work if some portion of it is channeled to benefit the less well off. If so, who could complain about the productive citizens getting more than the others get, since this benefits everyone?[13] Thus, it is granted that if opportunity for political influence could be improved for everyone by giving some more than others, this would perhaps be justified. But, the argument goes, political influence does not work like that: it is a competitive good. There is no way to increase the quantity available to all by giving some people more than others. So there is no justification for

[13] Rawls, *A Theory of Justice*, 78.

deviating from an equal distribution.[14] I believe this story goes wrong in several ways.

A quick terminological point: One distribution is normally said to be *Pareto-superior* to another just when it is better for some and worse for none. Call a distribution that is better for everyone *strongly Pareto-superior*. Since only the stronger concept concerns us here, I shall use "Pareto-superior" to mean strongly Pareto-superior throughout. I simply do not consider whether weak Pareto-superiority has anything to recommend it in the contexts discussed here.

The first problem with the argument just sketched is that it does not even consider whether any unequal distribution of influence would be *better* for everyone. It asks only whether it could produce more influence for everyone. Even if it could not, though, it might yet be better for everyone, and so perhaps might be justified on that basis. We should distinguish between two ways in which political inequality might be claimed to be Pareto-superior: (a) it might be Pareto-superior with respect to all goods taken together (call this *true Pareto-superiority*); or (b) it might be Pareto-superior specifically with respect to (availability of) political influence or input (call this *political Pareto-superiority*).[15] The argument sketched above inexplicably assumes that political inequality could only be justified by political Pareto-superiority. But why couldn't it be justified by true Pareto-superiority even if this did not satisfy political Pareto-superiority? All might be made better off, even if not all are given more political input or influence. This objection will not be pursued here. I mention it only to introduce the distinction between true and political Pareto-superiority.

Second, the argument supposes that political influence is a competitive good:[16] no one can get more of it without someone getting less. If a person's share of the total quantity of influence exerted is expressed as a fraction of that total, then influence would be a competitive good. But, of course, if one's share of wealth were expressed as a fraction, then wealth too would be a competitive good. We know wealth can be increased for some without decreasing the wealth of others, and thus a person's share can be understood in absolute as well as comparative terms. The same is apparently true of political influence, or if the word "influence" suggests otherwise, it is true of political *input*. Let *input* stand for an individual's

---

[14] See Harry Brighouse, "Political Equality in Justice as Fairness," *Philosophical Studies* 86 (1997): 166–67.

[15] By Pareto-superiority (political or not), I have in mind improvement in all positions in the distribution rather than effects on actual individuals. If two people switched places, so that one was worse off and the other better off, this would not yet count as a change at all from the perspective I want to consider. One distribution is Pareto-superior to the other if their graph lines flowing from lowest holdings to highest never cross, though they may touch (except in the case of strong Pareto-superiority).

[16] One well-known competitive good structure is the "zero-sum game." But that is a special case. Competitive goods need not have a "zero" or fixed sum.

absolute quantity of political participation (measured, for simplicity, in money),[17] and let *influence* stand for a person's fraction of the total political input. If everyone wrote more letters to their congressional representative annually than they now do, the total quantity of input would increase and no person's absolute quantity of input would decrease. Even if influence is a constant sum, the quantity of input is not. The comparative idea of one's share of influence, and the absolute quantity of input, are both important, and the argument below proceeds by taking the latter idea more seriously than usual.

If the total quantity of input can be increased, then we can ask whether there might be any way, beginning from an equal distribution of input, to increase everyone's amount of it by distributing it less equally. Here are two ways it might happen. One way would rely on reasoning familiar from the incentive argument justifying economic inequality on the grounds that it improves everyone's condition. Suppose that the promise of unequally large amounts of political influence for the wealthy increased the desire for wealth and the influence it brings. This, combined with economic incentives for greater social productivity, could be expected to induce more productivity than would exist in the absence of this promise of extra influence. Then perhaps the extra could be taxed or otherwise allocated to subsidize input for those with less influence. Political inequality would be accompanied by political Pareto-superiority. A second way unequal influence might increase everyone's input would be if citizens had to pay a surcharge on each purchased marginal unit of political input, which payment could be used to subsidize increased input for others. I leave aside the details of such a scheme for now, but I will return to the subject later.[18] In principle, this is another way unequal influence could produce more input for all, or political Pareto-superiority. In both of these cases, while everyone's input increases, some will have lost influence (fraction of input) while others will have gained it, and that will have to be figured into our evaluation of the situation. My point here is only that with respect to input, political Pareto-improvement (that is, movement to a Pareto-superior state) is theoretically possible. Later I will argue that it is also really possible, and that it is sometimes justified.

Political inequality and substantive justice

Suppose that unequal input was not mutually beneficial as compared with an equal distribution—that it did not produce more input for all or more social goods for all—but that the unequal scheme did lead more reliably to just decisions. Just decisions will not necessarily benefit everyone, or even anyone, least of all anyone who has so far been benefiting

---

[17] I address this simplification below, in a subsection titled "Input as money."
[18] See the discussion below in Section V.

unjustly. But whether or not it is mutually beneficial, the greater substantive justice of the outcomes of the unequal distribution looks like a powerful reason in its favor. It is a separate standard from either true or political Pareto-superiority.

Can inequality of political influence promote the substantive justice of political decisions? Here is one way it might do so: Suppose that the only way to achieve equal (available) influence is by leveling down—preventing those who would otherwise have the most influence from having any more influence than those who would otherwise have the least influence. If this low level is very low, the reduction in the total volume of deliberation might damage its epistemic value. Think of a choice between two debates and their epistemic value for an onlooker: in one debate the pro side speaks for a total of sixty minutes, and the con side for only fifty. In the alternative debate they are given equal time: two minutes each. The epistemic value of the second debate is probably much lower than the first.[19] Something analogous is theoretically possible in political participation. If equality can only be achieved at a very low level, the epistemic value of the process might be greater under some unequal distribution of political influence. Notice that this reasoning employs no invidious comparisons between participants. And here the Pareto-improvement in input is only indirectly relevant in that it plausibly improves the epistemic value of the procedure.

If we ask what is wrong with equalizing political input at the very lowest level, say at the level of a coin-flip, it is natural to object that political decisions are not likely to be well made by any random choice from among the alternatives. Political decisions are too important to be left to chance. Some procedure that gives citizens the opportunity to influence political decisions will be more likely to lead to wise decisions than would a random choice. This is the epistemic value of a particular arrangement of political influence.[20] By raising the question of an arrangement's epistemic value, we can account for our alarm about the coin-flip method, and thus we can explain why the absolute amount of input is important. Under the right conditions, more input tends to produce more epistemic value.

Epistemic value accounts for a concern about quantity, but can it place any constraints on distribution? If one person has the wisdom it takes to make better decisions than would be made under any more equal distribution of influence, the simple criterion of increasing epistemic value would require empowering this person as the sole political decision-

---

[19] Of course, it would be unfair to formally give the two sides different time limits. But suppose both were allowed sixty minutes, but one side lacked leisure or strength enough to go beyond fifty minutes.

[20] For some purposes, it is useful to distinguish between this general instrumental value, and a specifically epistemic route to it, e.g., via reasoning, knowledge, understanding, etc. This distinction is not important here.

maker. This epistocracy, as I call it, is highly inegalitarian, to say the least. This epistemic approach, then, might seem to be no better at explaining plausible distributive constraints than would a maximizing principle or a Pareto criterion.

The epistemic goal need not be the only relevant consideration, of course. Even granting that some people might be far better at making the morally and technically best political decisions, such invidious comparisons among citizens are bound to be open to reasonable disagreement. I propose to place the following constraint on political justification: that it may not make use of doctrines or principles or assertions that can be rejected even by conscientious, cooperative, reasonable citizens. (In this I follow Rawls's liberal principle of legitimacy.)[21] No test or criterion for distinguishing the better from the worse judges of justice and the common good would be acceptable from all reasonable and conscientious points of view. Since reasonable people can reject invidious comparisons, such comparisons should play no part in political justification.[22] No basic formal or substantive inequality of political influence may be justified on the grounds of the superior skill or wisdom of any individual or group.[23]

Might it not turn out, even without invidious comparisons, that the greatest total quantity of deliberation could only be produced if some citizens had vastly more opportunity for input than others had? If greater total deliberation increases the procedure's epistemic value, then the epistemic approach, even limited by the proscription of invidious comparisons, would not place any limits on permissible inequality of influence. In reality, however, it is doubtful that the epistemic value of a political decision procedure simply increases with the total quantity of input regardless of its distribution. Those with the ability to slant the system in their own favor will often do so, sometimes willfully, sometimes out of ignorance of the legitimate interests of others. As inequality of influence increases, the opportunity for this kind of abuse increases. The epistemic

---

[21] Rawls, *Political Liberalism*, 137.

[22] See my "Making Truth Safe." As William Galston and Steven Wall pointed out to me, citizens who reject the public conception of justice that I hold proper voting to address are very unlikely to promote it through their votes (whatever the value of their political speech), and this could be agreed upon by all reasonable citizens. This is because reasonable citizens all accept the conception. Thus, there is some uncomfortable pressure on my theory to disenfranchise those who reject the conception, or to weight their votes more lightly for legitimate epistemic reasons. There are several lines of reply worth considering, but here I will mention only that if, as I believe, the public conception of justice will consist in rather abstract principles that do not have straightforward practical consequences without interpretation, there may be no method that is beyond reasonable objection for identifying those who reject the conception.

[23] There are complications. Certainly some bureaucratic or representative positions, e.g., entail greater power. The rule against invidious comparisons does not preclude hiring or electing the best-qualified applicants for such positions. But this would not be *basic* inequality so long as the position and its power and the hiring criteria are authorized, at least indirectly, by a legitimate democratic process that relies on no invidious comparisons.

criterion places limits on acceptable inequality all by itself, without any help from the idea that equal influence is intrinsically valuable or required by fairness or equal respect for persons. In the context of political participation, inequality tends to diminish epistemic value even as the total quantity of participation, suitably distributed, promotes it.[24] In light of these countervailing tendencies, the epistemic approach seems bound to steer between a strict political egalitarianism on the one hand, and an utter insensitivity to inequality of influence on the other.

Is there an absolute right to equal influence?

The outlines of my objection to political egalitarianism are now clear. Before going into more detail, it is worth considering whether epistemic considerations are simply irrelevant because they are trumped. Is there a moral right to equal political influence that goes beyond the right not to be the victim of invidious comparisons in political justification? Two arguments for such a right are commonly seen, but both appear to be fallacious.

First, it is often argued that inequality of political influence expresses disrespect for citizens as equals, or expresses the view that some are inferior or less worthy than others in some way.[25] Certainly, unequal political institutions often do express disdain, or condescension. But this is a contingent matter. Inequality does not express disrespect unless it is owed to disrespect. When it is, that is a moral failing of the particular societies involved, not a defect of unequal political influence itself. Unequal influence can, in principle, exist entirely for other reasons.

More to the point, how does the charge of disrespect fare against an argument that advocates inequality of influence only when it will give everyone more input and thereby increase the substantive justice of political decisions? Toward whom does this theory express disdain, condescension, or disrespect? The requirement of equal respect does not directly support a requirement of equal political influence (or its availability) any more than it directly supports the right to an equal income, an equally fulfilling job, or an equally quiet neighborhood.

Second, it is often argued that equality of influence is a requirement of justice because it is fundamentally unjust for some citizens to be deprived of the resources and education required to understand their own authentic values, or to articulate them clearly in public, or to understand the important issues that are at stake in politics.[26] We may grant that such deprivation is unjust; nevertheless, none of these three considerations is

[24] Rawls holds that the fair value of the political liberties "is essential in order to establish just legislation" (*Political Liberalism*, 330).

[25] Brighouse, "Egalitarianism," 123; Thomas Christiano, "The Significance of Public Deliberation," in *Deliberative Democracy*, ed. Bohman and Rehg, 256.

[26] Christiano, "The Significance of Public Deliberation," 341.

a comparative matter, and so none supports equality of influence. No one's self-understanding suffers just because some people understand themselves even better. No one becomes less articulate just because some are more articulate than he or she is. Each of these important considerations supports *improving* cognitive, economic, and other resources. This is precisely the kind of consideration that I think presses *against* a requirement of equal influence, since equality may often mean preventing some from more fully understanding their own values, or from becoming more articulate, if there is no way of getting everyone to a higher equal level. A more frankly egalitarian argument for the egalitarian conclusion would have to say that what is most important is not that people understand their own values, but that each person understand or misunderstand them equally. But that implausible argument has not, to my knowledge, been offered.

Even if unequal opportunity for input does not disrespect those with less, there is still the question of whether it is *unfair*. Political egalitarianism is often presented as required by *fair proceduralism*, the view that democratic outcomes get their legitimacy from the fairness of the political procedure. I have argued against the latter view elsewhere,[27] and have argued here that political egalitarianism is, in any case, unacceptable. And yet, the idea of some citizens having more influence than others can still seem to be unfair to those with less influence. Now if influence were equally available, and those with less had less voluntarily, then the charge could be easily dismissed. But on the liberal epistemic approach defended here, influence would be more readily available to those with more money. How could this be fair?

We need to make several distinctions. First, departures from fairness are not always unfair. Second, there is a difference between a procedure that is internally governed by standards of fairness, and a procedure that (whether fair in the internal sense or not) it is fair to have. Each point requires some elaboration.

Departures from fairness are not always unfair. Consider a decision about which of two people should receive a certain indivisible good. This meager description often inclines us to think that fairness must guide the decision. But if the two people are drowning, and one is my son, fairness is not the operative moral idea. I ought to save my son, and this conclusion cannot be gotten from the idea that my decision process treats the two fairly. I ought to treat my son specially. Doing so is not based on fairness, nor is it unfair. Treating the two fairly would be wrong, though hardly unfair. We can call the right decision fair if all we mean is that it is not unfair, but fairness is still no guide in that case.

Similarly, the liberal epistemic view allows and requires departures from substantive procedural fairness, but this does not make the proce-

---

[27] Estlund, "Beyond Fairness and Deliberation."

dures it recommends unfair. A procedure is unfair only if it *wrongly* departs from fair procedure. Below, in Section III, I defend an "Epistemic Difference Principle" which, I believe, rightly departs from procedural fairness.

Second, a procedure can be thought of as fair to participants[28] in different senses. *Internal procedural fairness* of a decision procedure consists in roughly equal influence. Such a procedure may or may not be the morally right one to use in a given circumstance. A second kind of fairness of a decision procedure is present when the procedure is a fair one to have, whether or not it is internally procedurally fair. A popular way of elaborating this idea says that a procedure is a fair one to have if it is a procedure that would be agreed to in a hypothetical decision procedure in which all affected are represented and treated fairly in the internal procedural sense. This idea is best known from Rawls and Thomas Scanlon, and Charles Beitz analyzes political fairness in just these terms.[29] Beitz argues persuasively that this *external procedural fairness* (my term) may or may not end up endorsing actual internally fair decision procedures. Thus, if external procedural fairness is the proper standard of what procedure we ought to have, internal procedural fairness is of no independent moral significance.

How should authority be distributed in the classroom, or in the economic market? Fairly? We can now see that the issue of fairness applies at two levels. As for internal procedural fairness, it is not an appropriate standard for distributing decision-making authority in a classroom or in the market. This does not mean that departures from a fair distribution are *unfair*, since they do not depart from fairness wrongly. Furthermore, the inegalitarian distributions might be fair in the external procedural sense that they are procedures that it is fair to have if they are beyond reasonable objection suitably understood.

It is not obvious that external fairness is always the appropriate standard for what decision process there ought to be, and I will not consider that question. I will simply assume that this *is* so in the case of decision procedures for electing legislators and making laws for the basic legal structure of a society.

Political egalitarianism, then, calls for an internally fair political decision procedure, but I argue that it is morally mistaken to do so. A fair procedure neglects epistemic considerations and thus could be reasonably rejected in a hypothetical internally fair procedure for choosing actual political procedures. The scheme of Progressive Vouchers discussed

[28] We might distinguish between fairness to participants and fairness to candidates or potential beneficiaries. I am discussing fairness to participants.
[29] Rawls, *A Theory of Justice*; Thomas Scanlon, "Contractualism and Utilitarianism," in *Utilitarianism and Beyond*, ed. Amartya Sen and Bernard Williams (Cambridge: Cambridge University Press, 1982); Charles Beitz, *Political Equality* (Princeton: Princeton University Press, 1989), esp. ch. 5.

below (in Section V) instantiates the liberal epistemic view, and it is not internally fair since extra influence can be bought by those who can afford it. But it is not unfair, and it is a fair procedure to have if the improvement it brings in the epistemic value of the procedure would be acceptable to all in a fair hypothetical choice procedure.

Last, some may hold that social relations must rest on interactions in which wealth or rank bring no extra influence. One might take this simply as basic, or one might be led to this by the thought that only if there is a basic institutional level characterized by equal influence over politics could other inequalities, such as those in the economic realm, ever be justified by their source in those more equal political procedures. It would be a good reply to show that from a suitably formulated hypothetical decision procedure in which influence is pristinely equal, people would accept the inequalities of input required to improve the epistemic value of the political process. I will not attempt any such demonstration here, but I take this point to weaken the objection at hand. Some might have taken it as similarly basic that economic goods ought to be distributed equally, before considering the possibility of inequalities that benefit all. Then it becomes necessary to give some more specific argument about who could legitimately complain. I intend the points about the epistemic value of unequal but more voluminous public political input to raise a similar challenge.

Input as money

For purposes of quantifying input, I will assume it can be measured by money spent on politics. This is most appropriate for the case of a campaign contribution, and more complicated for other kinds of participation whose market value may not be entirely determinate, such as volunteering, writing books, or joining demonstrations or political parties. Money, of course, has only relative value. If the absolute amount of money goes up in a closed economy, its value merely decreases. Money's value depends on the demand for it, just as with any other exchangeable good. So how can the absolute amount of political input go up if it is measured in money? The answer is that we are only looking at one segment of the economy: money spent on politics. When I speak of, say, twice as much being spent on politics, I am assuming that the overall amount of money in the economy has stayed roughly the same. So a dollar has retained its value, and twice as much value is being devoted to politics.

Concentrating on money is a very useful simplifying move, but it has several difficulties. First, *which money* counts as an expenditure on politics? My purposes are at a high enough level of abstraction that my points do not depend on specifying this in much detail. The only problem would be if there were reasons to doubt that any such distinction could usefully be drawn. Certainly there is no sharp line here. The clearest cases would be candidates for office and political parties. Next would be advocacy groups that intentionally and expressly influence officials and voters, such as the American Civil Liberties Union, environmental groups, and so on. What about groups that seek mainly to educate the public about an issue? These are often on the borderline. Public education about the dangers of nuclear deterrence leans, perhaps, in the direction of the political. Perhaps education about how to have safe sex leans away. There will be borderline cases, but I do not see this issue as especially troubling. Numerous doctrines and policies depend on roughly identifying those activities and groups that should count as political for certain purposes, and I readily grant that the present approach would eventually need to rise to that challenge with more specificity.

The second difficulty is the problem of non-money input. It must be asked whether there are so many routes of political influence that cannot be subsumed under the concept of money contributions that the value of the overall model is very limited. Sidney Verba, Kay Lehman Schlozman, and Henry E. Brady, for example, compare contributions of *time* and *money* as different modes of participating in politics.[30] Even this is too simple to capture everything. Those who contribute "time," for example, will have varying degrees of strength, energy, intelligence, experience, and knowledge to contribute in any given period of contributed time. Again, however, this general point does little damage to my argument. It can be put this way: certain important resources employed in politics are such that equalizing their availability might well reduce the epistemic value of the overall process so much as to not be worth it. Money is the paradigmatic example, and is also perhaps the single most significant measure of political resources. Insofar as there are other political resources that do not obey the logic I apply to money, then my conclusions do not apply to them.

Political egalitarianism faces similar challenges, however. Even if it does not concentrate on money, but chooses some probabilistic notion of influence (for example, equal probability of being decisive), its egalitarian principle is impossible to interpret in practice unless more is said about how to measure these probabilities. What gives one person a greater probability of changing the outcome than another? Obviously, we know there are certain things that make such a difference, such as, notably, the amount of money donated to parties and candidates. But if that is a distorting oversimplification, then what are the other important factors, and why can't they be accommodated by the arguments I offer about the epistemic value of quantity, etc.? Answers to these questions may well place qualifications on the conclusions I defend here.

---

[30] Sidney Verba, Kay Lehman Schlozman, and Henry E. Brady, *Voice and Equality* (Cambridge, MA: Harvard University Press, 1995).

III. The Epistemic Value of Equality and Quantity of Input

Epistemic considerations may cast doubt on fair proceduralism, upon which political egalitarianism often rests, but it might be thought that epistemic considerations themselves end up favoring political egalitarianism on other grounds. Fair proceduralism says that outcomes of democratic choice derive their legitimacy from the fairness of the democratic process. But political egalitarianism could instead rest itself on claims about the value of equal political input from an epistemic point of view.[31] It is natural to think that inequality in political input increases opportunities for oppression and discriminatory ignorance, and in these ways decreases the expected quality of democratic outcomes. In this section I want to grant quite a strong epistemic value to equality of input, and to attempt to formulate it in fairly precise terms. The reason is that in the next section I will argue that there are still important cases in which inequality of political input would be justified if there were offsetting increases in the quantity. So, in fact, I will be granting perhaps implausibly much to the epistemic importance of equality of input, but doing so will only strengthen my argument that, nevertheless, political egalitarianism fails.

The assumptions discussed in this section are just that: assumptions. They are not obviously correct, certainly not in all circumstances, nor can their merits be fully discussed here. I attempt to forestall objections but then proceed to show what can be derived from the assumptions. If the results are interesting, this raises the stakes about whether and in what circumstances these assumptions, or something close to them, can ultimately be defended.

I will assume that there is epistemic value to having an equal distribution of input, and that the epistemic value increases with the degree of equality, other things being equal. Thus, the epistemic approach has a place for the value of equality of political input:

Epistemic Value of Equality: Given a quantity of input, a more equal distribution of that input has more epistemic value.[32]

---

[31] Christiano (in "The Significance of Public Deliberation") explores the epistemic basis of political egalitarianism in addition to fair proceduralism. "[E]quality in the process of democratic discussion . . . improves the quality of the outcomes of democratic decision making" (256). Since Christiano advocates equal *access* rather than equal actual input (253), it is not entirely clear how his approach would have epistemic advantages.

[32] By a more equal distribution, I shall mean as measured by the so-called Gini coefficient (a measure of inequality sometimes used by economists). There are various alternative measures, some more appropriate than others for different purposes, but the Gini measure is simple and has no significant disadvantages that I know of for our purposes. The choice between various measures will not matter for my main points, and readers can safely proceed with only an intuitive idea of greater or lesser distributed equality. See Larry S. Temkin, *Inequality* (Oxford: Oxford University Press, 1993), ch. 5, for a critical discussion of several alternative measures of inequality; see esp. p. 129f. for a discussion of the Gini coefficient.

Of course, giving more input to people who are more likely to promote the best decision would be a counterexample. Nevertheless, we are assuming that there is no politically legitimate basis for such invidious comparisons—for holding that some citizens are wiser in this way—since this will always be open to reasonable disagreement. Thus, no distribution of input can be epistemically evaluated by considering *which* citizens are at which levels of input. We proceed for these purposes as if everyone were equally wise, even though none of us need believe that. Under this assumption it is natural and common to hold that inequality of input is harmful to the expected quality of the decision.

Next, it is also natural to assume that under the right conditions more discussion and participation is epistemically better. This is more controversial, and I consider objections shortly.[33] Assume:

> *Epistemic Value of Quantity*: For any given level of equality of input, a greater quantity of input at the same level of equality has more epistemic value.[34]

Note that despite the simplifying name, this does not state that more quantity is always epistemically better. That would be a stronger and less plausible assumption. I assume only that where increases do not increase (or decrease) inequality they promote the expected quality of the decision.

Now each of these two factors, quantity and equality, has some power to compensate for a lack in the other. If increased equality improves quality for any given quantity, then (unless the slightest decrease in the quantity is epistemically catastrophic) there is the possibility of a reduction in the quantity small enough that it could be made up by increased equality of distribution. Likewise, a slightly less equal distribution can be, I will assume, epistemically compensated by a sufficiently great increase in the quantity.

I propose to assume, then:

> *Compensation of Quantity for Inequality*: For an equal distribution E of a given quantity of input, and any degree of inequality *i*, there is

---

[33] See the discussion below in the subsection entitled "Is more better?"

[34] Increased quantity at a constant level of Gini inequality (see note 32 above) may seem to guarantee political Pareto-improvement, but it does not. Here is one category of counterexample: Consider a distribution, call it *Distribution 1*, among ten people. Suppose the bottom person has 0 units of input and the top person has 1,000, and each of the middle eight people has 50. Gini inequality rounds to .58, and the total is 1,400. Now the level of inequality can be maintained even through a Pareto loss, as follows: reduce the middle eight to 48 each (the Pareto loss), but raise the bottom person to 40.8 and the top person to 1,200. This is *Distribution 2*. This also rounds to Gini = .58 (and the remaining difference can be completely expunged by precisely tinkering with the numbers, but I am keeping it simple here). But the total has gone up to 1,424.8. Distribution 2 has a Gini-constant increased quantity, but is not Pareto-superior to Distribution 1.

some (logically possible) arrangement of a greater quantity that has degree of inequality i, and is also epistemically superior to E (unless E was already epistemically infallible, producing the best possible outcome all the time).

We already know that if the inequality were kept the same or decreased (starting from equality, of course, inequality cannot be reduced), then the epistemic value would be increased by raising the quantity. This much follows from the first two principles alone. This third principle says that even if inequality is increased, and no matter how much, the epistemic damage can be offset by a sufficiently increased quantity. This does not follow from the other two principles, since they leave it unsettled how much epistemic value an increased quantity has at very high levels. If this stayed constant at all levels, then the compensation principle would follow. If the marginal epistemic value of quantity of input decreases too fast, then some degrees of inequality might do more epistemic damage than can be offset by increasing the quantity.

Notice that we are forced to accept that the marginal epistemic value of input decreases at least at very high *ex ante* levels of epistemic value, since there is not much road to travel to get to infallibility. For any given degree of epistemic improvement, then, there is some high *ex ante* level of epistemic value that is so close to infallibility that such an improvement is logically impossible. Now perhaps very low levels of *ex ante* epistemic value (or, alternatively, low levels of input) have special features, but let us put that aside and assume that there is, at all levels, decreasing marginal epistemic value of input. Quantity will still always be capable of compensating for inequality so long as the marginal rate does not cause increased quantities to converge on some epistemic value short of infallibility. So long as there is always a quantity great enough to bring epistemic value arbitrarily close to infallibility, then inequality can always be epistemically offset by some increase in quantity. Think of it this way: Begin with an equal distribution of some quantity of input. Now introduce some degree of inequality, thus causing epistemic damage. Now keep the level of inequality constant but increase the total input. There is no logical upper bound on input; thus, if increasing input converges on infallibility (despite a decreasing marginal rate of epistemic value), then it eventually epistemically surpasses the original equal distribution.[35]

---

[35] One very simple way to model the decreasing epistemic value of input is to suppose that, so long as the level of inequality is kept constant, a given extra unit of input produces an epistemic increase that is some constant fraction of the gap between the *ex ante* epistemic value and infallibility. So, for example, each extra unit of input (suppose this is some amount of money spent) might get you 10 percent of the remaining way toward infallibility. The next unit gets you 10 percent of the remaining way, which is less progress than the first unit. Any value for the marginal unit (e.g., $1, $1,000), and any constant setting of this fraction of the

If quantity offsets inequality, there is the question of how much it takes. Consider the epistemic damage done by a given departure from equality. Now, holding that level of inequality constant, how much must the quantity be raised to undo the epistemic damage? More precisely, what must the initial sum be multiplied by to epistemically offset for the inequality? Call this the problem of the *epistemic compensation factor*. If the marginal epistemic value of input were constant rather than diminishing, or at least if we had good reason for fixing on some particular rate of diminution (rather than merely on a family of rates),[36] this would still be a daunting question. Under the circumstances, we cannot hope to arrive at anything like a strong reason for any very precise answer, and I will therefore proceed without one.

Even without knowing how much quantity is required to epistemically offset a level of inequality, we can at least make one assumption that grants more epistemic value to equality for the sake of argument. When inequality is increased by some people gaining input, let us assume that the epistemic damage of the inequality outweighs the epistemic enhancement from the added quantity whenever the increases of those who gain are not shared with all who have less. (There is no reason to suppose that those [if any] with more than the gainers must also gain, since with respect to them alone inequality has been reduced rather than increased. There is no epistemic threat in that segment of the distribution.) Thus, we will assume that:

---

gap (1 percent, 20 percent), will allow increasing quantities to converge on infallibility. I will proceed on the assumption that the marginal epistemic value of input at a given level of inequality has this structure. This says nothing about how fast an extra unit of input increases epistemic value, since this can be set very low or very high consistent with my assumption.

> *Decreasing Marginal Epistemic Value of Input*: Assuming inequality stays the same, then for any quantity, and any epistemic value, there is some constant fraction F, such that a unit of extra input moves the epistemic value of the scheme forward by removing that fraction F of the gap to infallibility.

This assumption is one way of representing the intuitive thought that quantity improves epistemic value, other things being equal. I offer no argument for placing no limit on this improvement short of infallibility, though this seems the simpler position in the absence of any reason to believe there are more severe limits. A weaker claim, placing such limits, would probably be sufficient for practical purposes, but it is difficult to know *which* weaker claim. With this in place, we are entitled to our assumption that quantity compensates inequality.

One odd feature of this model is that it is oblivious to the *ex ante* level of input, but notices only the *ex ante* epistemic value. In one scenario, then, the total input might be $1 million with an epistemic value of .5. Another scenario might find total input at $100 and an epistemic value of .5. If $1,000 moves a distribution 10 percent of the way toward infallibility, it would do this in both cases. This might seem to ignore the apparently greater epistemic value of each unit of input in the latter scenario, which has the same epistemic value as the former but with less input. I leave these complexities aside, but perhaps a more refined model should take account of them.

[36] See note 35.

Gains Must Be Shared Downward: Any less equal distribution is epistemically inferior unless gains are shared downward. (In that case it still depends on whether the inequality is too great.)

Inequality can be produced or increased either by some getting disproportionately more than before, or by some getting disproportionately less, or both. When some get disproportionately more, we have just said that this is epistemically inferior unless the gains are shared downward. If inequality is produced or increased solely by some getting disproportionately less than before, then this both increases inequality and reduces the quantity, so this is always epistemically inferior. Suppose some get less and some get more, with the total quantity and inequality increasing. Here the gains are not shared downward, and therefore the result is epistemically inferior.

These considerations lead to the following notable principle:

Epistemic Difference Principle: No deviation from strict equality is epistemically superior unless everyone gains input.

We can see this as follows: First, no distribution can epistemically top equality unless it is a higher quantity (Epistemic Value of Equality). But from strict equality, any increase in the quantity in which increases are shared downward (as required by the principle that Gains Must Be Shared Downward) must increase the input for all, which gives us the Epistemic Difference Principle.

Since I am criticizing political egalitarianism, it makes sense to let any errors work to the advantage of equality. Again, the Epistemic Difference Principle (and the assumptions from which it follows) may give too much epistemic weight to equality, but this will not harm my eventual conclusion that inequality of input will still often be justified.[37]

Clearly, a defense of inequality on epistemic grounds will rest on the possibility of (strongly) politically Pareto-superior cases, where equality would reduce everyone's absolute level of input. Keep in mind that strongly Pareto-superior options will not be sufficient for epistemic gain, since this

---

[37] If the left-out group is very small, we could increase inequality only a little, increase quantity a lot, and still fail to share downward. Is it plausible to say this does more harm than good? What if only one person out of a million is left out of the increase? Here we should allow that the quantity probably outweighs the inequality. We can avoid this problem if we limit our purview to changes that affect groups that make up a substantial fraction of the whole. Then leaving one group out of an inequality-increasing input increase will raise inequality significantly so long as the quantity is increased significantly. Let us also assume that we mean no more here by social groups than groupings according to amount of political input. So the membership of, for example, the lowest group can change. If two sets of people were to end up with completely exchanged levels of input (set A now has as much input as set B had, and vice versa), the distribution of input would not have changed for present purposes.

depends on the degree of inequality involved and the unknown epistemic compensation factor.

Is more better?

Even theorists who acknowledge the epistemic value of political deliberation often argue that, above a certain quantity of input, there is little or no epistemic value in having more. Ronald Dworkin argues that current levels of political campaign advertising in the U.S. could easily be cut (by stronger contribution or spending limits) in the interest of fairness, without damaging the epistemic quality of the process, since current advertising is often repetitive and negative. "Such limits [would not] seriously risk keeping from the public any argument or information it would otherwise have."[38] Obviously the same could not be said if existing levels of spending were already very low, and thus Dworkin implicitly grants that, up to a point, more campaign speech tends to be epistemically better.

I am granting for the sake of argument that any increase in equality that does not lower everyone's level of input is an epistemic gain (from the Epistemic Difference Principle), but this is a way of assuming an epistemic value of equality strong enough to offset the epistemic damage of the lost speech. Dworkin's argument is different. He doubts that, at current levels, speech that would be lost by limiting spending has any epistemic value in the first place, and so there is little or no loss to offset. If correct, his arguments would call into question my assumption of the Epistemic Value of Quantity: that at a given level of inequality, more input is epistemically better. The arguments, though, are not persuasive.

First, the repetitive and negative nature of campaign discourse (assuming it to be so) by itself hardly damns it as epistemically worthless. The educative power of current campaign advertising is an empirical matter, with a number of studies suggesting that Dworkin's speculation is mistaken and that such advertising adds to the information and understanding of the electorate.[39] Common sense also suggests that repetition of facts, ideas, and reasons can be an important component of learning of all kinds, and that "negative" claims about opponents can be valuable and informative even if some different mix of negative and positive claims would be even better. Simply eliminating some mostly negative ads might very well be an epistemic loss.[40]

[38] Ronald Dworkin, "The Curse of American Politics," *New York Review of Books*, October 17, 1996, 21.

[39] See, for example, Stephen Ansolabehere and Shanto Iyengar, *Going Negative* (New York: Free Press, 1997): "As we have shown in several chapters of this book, television actually fosters the democratic ideals of an informed and reasoning electorate" (145). Their worries about political advertising lie elsewhere.

[40] Ansolabehere and Iyengar also argue (in *Going Negative*) that negative campaigning drives voters away from the polls. This might itself have epistemic disvalue to be weighed against the value of the information provided. But this is not a point specially about high

Second, even if some portion of current speech by big-spending campaigns were epistemically worthless, Dworkin seems to conclude that trimming the big campaigns back to the level of approximate parity with the smallest campaigns would still not entail great epistemic losses. This is certainly less likely to be true, and depends a great deal on how much cutting would be required. Bill Clinton and Bob Dole might produce little epistemic bang for the marginal buck at their high levels of spending; but we cannot conclude, and it seems clearly false, that little would be lost if they were only allowed to spend roughly as much as was available to, say, Ralph Nader. The epistemic cost of equalizing expenditures downward cannot be easily dismissed, though of course this leaves open the possibility that the epistemic value of the increased equality of input might offset the epistemic cost of the lost quantity. Indeed, the Epistemic Difference Principle could probably not condone the present vastly unequal distributions of input that Dworkin is criticizing; but he is too dismissive of the epistemic costs of *equalizing*, and is led to an implausibly strong political egalitarianism.[41]

Finally, it must be acknowledged, if only speculatively, that there are a number of ways that higher levels of input might damage the epistemic value of discussion. Perhaps at high levels of input, campaigning gets negative. Perhaps it gets increasingly repetitive. Perhaps these or other features of discussion at high levels of input drive away voters. Perhaps the more people hear, the more confused they get. Perhaps the more people argue, the more intransigent they get. Even if some of these are true, though, the main conclusions of this essay would continue to apply at quantities of input below these turning points. And even if these effects were known to be genuine in principle, it would often be very difficult to know whether any actual level of input approached the turning point in question. But I must leave the matter here.

In general, the sorry state of present campaign discourse does not support in any simple way the proposition that the quantity could be reduced by imposing spending limits without doing damage to the epistemic value of the process. It may well be that at high levels of spending the epistemic value of the marginal campaign dollar is too low to be epistemically worth the inequality it causes, but that is not our question. The goal at this point is only a defense of the Epistemic Value of Quantity: the claim that at a fixed level of inequality of input, more input is epistemically better. For reasons like Dworkin's, some may doubt that this is

---

levels of campaign spending, unless for some reason high levels of spending increase negativity. And even then, in order to suppose that limits could be imposed without epistemic loss, it would need to be shown that the bad epistemic effects of the marginal speech outweigh the good.

[41] Dworkin is not explicit about how much equality of influence should be sought through campaign finance regulations or other means. But he does say: "Each citizen must have a fair and reasonably equal opportunity . . . to command attention for his own views" (Dworkin, "The Curse of American Politics," 23).

true for the combination of high levels of spending and high levels of inequality. But the doubts are not well founded.

If equality and quantity serve quality in something like the way I have assumed, then some inequality could be justified as a part of an arrangement that promotes quantity and thereby promotes the expected quality of decisions. I turn now, in the next two sections, to whether circumstances favoring inequality on these grounds could actually occur.

IV. An Incentive Argument for Political Inequality

Consider a case where inequality has been introduced but the quantity of input has been increased enough to epistemically offset the inequality. Why distribute the extra quantity unequally? The Epistemic Value of Equality tells us that distributing that same new quantity of input equally would be epistemically even better, so why not do that? If you do not distribute input unequally, you will not need to epistemically compensate for it with quantity, says an important objection.

Under some circumstances, though, a higher quantity is impossible without diverging from equality. Suppose, for example, that input is currently equal, but that no more resources are forthcoming so long as the distribution remains equal. Some citizens are willing to produce more input (say, through money contributions) but only if they get more of this input than others and it is not simply redistributed equally. Thus, the quantity can be increased, but only at the cost of introducing inequality. The higher quantity would indeed produce even more epistemic value if it were distributed equally rather than unequally, but unless it is distributed unequally in a certain way it will not be produced in the first place. One natural explanation would be that those who could produce more input will not do it without special incentives. Let us call this the *incentive argument for unequal input*.

The parallel with disputes about the application of Rawls's difference principle is striking, but limited. Rawls holds that (roughly)[42] economic inequality is not justified unless it benefits the least well-off, and calls this the difference principle. He considers the possibility that certain schemes of inequality might be required to provide incentives for talented people to be more socially productive. If so, and if this extra productivity redounds to the benefit of the least well-off, then the inequality would be justified. Many believe that this is indeed the case and that it justifies wide economic inequalities, though Rawls is noncommittal on this empirical question. This *incentive argument for inequality* and the incentive argument for unequal input are similar.

---

[42] I say "roughly" because he concentrates on primary goods, which are not limited to what is usually understood as economic matters.

There are differences, however. In Rawls's theory, equality and efficiency compete as moral values of a basic social structure. It is not that
inequality causally limits productivity; rather, equality (in the form of the
difference principle) is a moral constraint on productivity. In our case, the
overriding value is the epistemic value of the procedure (in terms that are
beyond reasonable objection). Equality of political input is not placed as
a moral constraint on maximizing epistemic value or increasing the quantity of input. Inequality itself (so we are assuming) damages epistemic
value. Epistemic value is what establishes the tension between quantity and inequality, and not any independent moral value of an equal
distribution.[43]

What is the highest equal level?

The incentive argument shows how it may not be possible to take the
gains from a political Pareto-improvement, and have them distributed so
as to preserve equality of influence. The gains may not be produced but
for the incentives provided by the unequal distribution. For example,
some people might contribute a great deal to the political process only if
the money buys them a certain amount of input that cannot be supplied
to everyone. The highest possible equal level of input might be lower than
the levels that can be provided to all under certain unequal schemes of
distribution. Before illustrating this with an imaginary voucher scheme,
notice that the idea of the highest possible equal level could mean several
different things. It is important to be clear which one is in question when
I claim that there can be political Pareto-improvements over the highest
equal level.

One thing the highest possible equal level might mean is the *de facto*
highest possible level: the highest equal level that is possible given the
attitudes and motives that people actually have, justifiably or not. This
concept will not suit our purposes, since it may only be due to some
people's injustice that some higher equal level cannot be achieved. In that
case, the inequality that is needed in order to surpass that *de facto* highest

---

[43] The similarities between these two incentive arguments for inequality are sufficient,
however, to force us to answer an important objection advanced by G. A. Cohen. Cohen
argues that it is not clear that a proper citizen in a fully just society could have the motives
that the incentive argument assumes. He wonders what would justify a citizen's holding out
for more pay than others when he or she is capable of doing the work without it. Cohen has
developed this criticism in a series of essays, including "Incentives, Inequality, and Community," in *The Tanner Lectures on Human Values*, vol. 13, ed. G. Peterson (Salt Lake City:
University of Utah Press, 1992), 263–329; "The Pareto Argument for Inequality," in *Contemporary Political and Social Philosophy*, ed. Ellen Frankel Paul, Fred D. Miller, Jr., and Jeffrey
Paul (Cambridge: Cambridge University Press, 1995), 160–85; and "Where the Action Is: On
the Site of Distributive Justice," *Philosophy and Public Affairs* 26, no. 1 (Winter 1997): 3–30. I
have defended Rawlsian inequality against Cohen's arguments in "Liberalism, Equality, and
Fraternity in Cohen's Critique of Rawls," *Journal of Political Philosophy* 6, no. 1 (March 1998):
99–112, and those arguments apply fairly directly here as well.

equal level is not entirely just, but represents a capitulation to some unreasonable citizens in order to do the best that can be done under unjust circumstances.

A more appropriate idea of the maximum equal level of input is the highest equal level of input that could be achieved while neither capitulating to any citizen's unjust motives, nor demanding more of citizens than is required by the idea of a fully just society. We might call this the *de jure* equal maximum, but for brevity I will simply call this, the pertinent concept of the equal maximum, *E-max*.

Whatever the epistemic value of E-max, we know that there are logically possible unequal distributions that would be epistemically superior. This is because any given level of inequality, while doing some epistemic damage, can occur at a high enough level of input to have compensating epistemic advantages (see the Epistemic Value of Quantity assumption in Section III). We ought to ask, then, is there a causally possible distribution of input that is unequal but epistemically superior to E-max? If so, we might provisionally suppose that this inequality of input will be at least permitted and perhaps required, keeping in mind that formal political equality is guaranteed.

Next, we will consider a scenario for such epistemic improvements over E-max using an application of the incentive argument for unequal input.

V. How Could Unequal Political Influence Increase Input for All?

Having granted considerable epistemic weight to more equal distributions of input, the fact remains that inequality may yet be called for on epistemic grounds, so long as it is politically Pareto-superior and not too unequal. In this section I argue that this is more than a mere logical possibility.

Suppose a society is supporting elections at the level of E-max[44]— equal available input at the highest level compatible with equality, given citizens' permissible (e.g., not unjust) motives. We know that there are logically possible unequal distributions of input that are epistemically superior to E-max. Some of these may not even require political Pareto-improvements; but to give lots of weight to the epistemic value of equality, for the sake of argument we are assuming that no departure from equal input is epistemically superior unless it is politically Pareto-superior—that is, unless it gives everyone more input. (See the Epistemic Difference Principle discussed above.)

---

[44] For example, suppose Ackerman's Patriot plan (discussed below, in Section V) is already in effect at the maximum equal level.

I want to sketch a simple voucher scheme that represents one way such improvements may actually be induced. My goal here is not to solve the many logistical problems involved in implementing such a scheme but to present a basic causal mechanism that appears to have this potential. It is important to keep in mind that the inequalities introduced may be so great as to cancel the epistemic advantage of the increased quantity. However, we can see that the inequalities might sometimes be very modest, and that this general strategy admits of many variations, some of which might be able to do even better than my examples.

Progressive Vouchers

Assume that a society supports elections at the level of E-max. Now allow additional expenditures through and only through government-supplied vouchers. These have a cash value when contributed to certain political endeavors such as election campaigns, and no value otherwise. Each next or marginal voucher a person buys costs more than the previous, but has only the same value as the last. The cash value of the voucher is then paid, by the administering agency, to the campaign that receives the voucher from a citizen. But the purchase price was more than this, and the extra amount retained by the agency goes into a fund that is used to subsidize the price of vouchers, making them more affordable. This subsidy can be structured in countless ways, and I will sketch only one, which I will call the Singular Voucher version of Progressive Vouchers:[45] suppose the money in the fund is distributed among all those who are happy to receive only their one government-supplied voucher (call this the Singular Voucher). These Singular Vouchers are available for free, or if it seems wise to charge some fee, to avoid frivolous uses, then they are cheap. Their value is determined by the size of the fund and the number of people who want the Singular Voucher. Anyone who wants to contribute more than the Singular Voucher will have to purchase Progressive Vouchers and may not receive a Singular Voucher. This will become clearer with the examples provided below. But first some general points.

If we assume that some citizens would pay more than the cash value for Progressive Vouchers if this were the only way to have additional political input, then this will raise money to pay for Singular Vouchers that are free or very cheap for anyone who wants one. The result would be a politically Pareto-superior distribution of political input. In presenting examples, I will simplify in several ways: (1) I will assume that it is known (say, by experience) how many vouchers will be purchased by how many people. This avoids temporal and strategic complications about

---

[45] The name "Progressive Vouchers" might connote three relevant things: that the voucher plan promotes quantity of input in a politically Pareto-superior way; that it promotes quality of decisions by independent standards of, e.g., justice; and that it involves progressive rates for marginal vouchers.

setting prices and values of the vouchers. (2) I will consider possible purchase patterns in a pretty arbitrary and speculative way without any argumentative support. My purpose is illustrative, and therefore I only need the examples to be plausible enough to warrant further study and refinement by economists, political scientists, and others. (3) I ignore any administrative or transaction costs. (4) I assume that all available input is actually employed.[46]

Consider a community of 200,000 voters, the size of a small city such as Providence, Rhode Island. Suppose that the maximum equal level of contribution would be $5 per voter per election cycle, yielding a total expenditure of $1,000,000. Now suppose we allow vouchers in addition. Let each Progressive Voucher have a value (redeemable by campaigns) of $50, but remember that each one (beyond the first) will cost more than this. To buy one costs $50; to buy a second costs $87.50; a third, $153.13; a fourth, $267.97; and the fifth and final permissible voucher costs $468.95. (The marginal rate of increase is 75 percent, but this can easily be varied for other scenarios.) Alternatively, suppose citizens may buy more vouchers at correspondingly higher prices, but no one does. (This difference matters for First Amendment purposes discussed below.) Each voucher is still worth only $50, but people who can afford it and want to have more political input may well pay more than the cash value; indeed, the cash value has nothing to do with what a voucher will be worth to a citizen. Nevertheless, I will assume in this example that not many citizens will buy many of these increasingly expensive vouchers.[47] Suppose that only 5 percent of voters buy any progressive vouchers: 1 percent buy one; 1 percent buy two; 1 percent buy three; 1 percent buy four; and 1 percent buy all five. Buying all five costs $1,027.55, but a person's input is only $50 times the number of Progressive Vouchers she buys and uses, in this case $250, plus the amount that was already being spent under E-max, or

---

[46] The Progressive Voucher plan suggests that it is possible to epistemically improve upon an equal distribution of actual input. However, political egalitarianism, the egalitarian alternative we are considering, advocates an equal distribution of availability of, or opportunity for, input, not an equal distribution of actual input. Even if Progressive Vouchers can epistemically beat E-max, which involves equal input, can it beat the pattern of actual input that would emerge under equal availability of input?

The epistemic value of democracy under political egalitarianism depends upon the level and distribution of actual input, even though what it seeks to equalize is availability of input. Since Progressive Vouchers can beat the epistemic value of E-max, the highest level of equal actual input, then it would suffice to show that E-max epistemically beats actual patterns of input under political egalitarianism. This is easily shown, and derives from the fact that a scheme of equally available input has no tendency to allow a greater quantity of input than would be present under E-max. In that case, since the distribution of this lower or equal quantity will be a less equal distribution than E-max, which is exactly equal, then by the principle of Epistemic Value of Equality, the epistemic value under political egalitarianism will be less than that under E-max. Therefore, if, as I claim, a Progressive Voucher program can epistemically beat E-max, it can also beat political egalitarianism.

[47] This grants something congenial to opponents of my thesis. If more bought vouchers, it would simply mean that my conclusion would follow more easily.

$5. The total input for the maximum spender under these assumptions is $255. Rounded to the nearest dollar, these purchases build up a fund of $2,628,560. Dividing this into a free or cheap Singular Voucher for every voter who chose not to purchase Progressive Vouchers (95 percent of all voters) yields a Singular Voucher worth about $14. I assume for simplicity that all remaining voters receive and use a Singular Voucher (though if not, these vouchers can be worth more).[48] What is the result of this arrangement?

First, there is a Pareto-superior distribution of political input. Whereas before no voter contributed more than $5 to political campaigns, now no one contributes less than $19 since no one is without the $14 voucher. Second, we have introduced inequality of input. The vast majority are contributing at a value of $19, and a few at a value of $255, and some in between. The input of the highest contributors is about thirteen times that of the lowest; on the other hand, a campaign can get as much by winning over a small coffee meeting of thirteen of the poorest voters as it can by wooing any single fat cat. Third, since the distribution is Pareto-superior, the total contribution is also greater. It has gone from $1,000,000 to $5,128,560—more than quintupled.[49] This greater quantity, we are assuming, has positive consequences for the epistemic value of the process, at least under favorable conditions, and so long as it is not too unequally distributed among participants.

The degree of inequality is certainly minuscule by the standard of actually existing politics in the U.S.,[50] and the increase in the total (with political Pareto-superiority) is enormous by any standard. We have no basis for saying that there is, or is not, a net epistemic gain, but this should be enough to suggest that the general strategy of Progressive Vouchers may offer a way of combining the epistemic values of the quantity of input and of equal distribution in a way that political egalitarianism cannot. Political egalitarianism would have mandated the E-max level of $5 per person for a total of $1,000,000 of input, forgoing the additional $4.1 million of input that could be in-

[48] As Ackerman points out, vouchers can be spent with no opportunity cost, unlike ordinary contributions of money. This fact should vastly increase participation. Still, full spending of the vouchers is an unrealistic assumption made to simplify the model.

[49] This $5,128,560 figure is arrived at by adding to the original $1 million (from E-max) the proceeds from the sale of vouchers. Two thousand voters pay at each of the following five levels: $50 for one voucher, $137.50 ($50 plus $87.50) for two vouchers, $290.63 for three vouchers, $558.60 for four vouchers, and $1,027.55 for five vouchers. Rounding to the nearest dollar, this yields $4,128,560, which, added to the $1 million from E-max, gives us a total of $5,128,560.

[50] Only about 8 percent of eligible voters contribute any money to political campaigns. See Warren E. Miller, and the National Election Studies, *American National Election Studies Cumulative Data File, 1952–1992* (computer file), 6th release (Ann Arbor, MI: University of Michigan, Center for Political Studies [producer], 1994; Ann Arbor, MI: Inter-University Consortium for Political and Social Research [distributor], 1991).

duced if a certain (modest?) amount of inequality (with no invidious comparisons) were acceptable.[51]

Patriot versus Progressive Vouchers

Bruce Ackerman has proposed a different kind of voucher plan to reform campaign financing.[52] Under the Patriot plan each eligible voter would be given a voucher worth, say, $10 which could be spent only on political campaigns, while contributions of regular money would be prohibited. In one stroke this would equalize the availability of a major means of political input. Ackerman, like few others, takes the overall quantity of political speech very seriously. He recognizes that if equality comes at the cost of quantity, it is not an easy choice. However, his proposal fails to face that difficult trade-off. At the $10 level, Ackerman argues that (assuming most or all of the vouchers are spent—a simplification I join him in) aggregate political spending would go up compared to current levels. The more difficult question comes when it is recognized that there must be a maximum level to this equal voucher: maybe it is $5; maybe it is $20. Whatever the equal maximum, or E-max as I have called it, we must ask whether it is worth insisting on equality even if modest inequality could increase aggregate spending dramatically. This is a question Ackerman asks ("Do we really want equality at the cost of shutting down debate?")[53] but does not answer, since he fails to recognize the potential for aggregate increases over the levels provided by his equalized Patriot vouchers.

Ackerman's proposal is apparently to be funded by taxes. We might think about where the highest level of Patriot funding (E-max) lies by considering the following question: Assuming citizens were properly just and public-spirited, how high a tax should they institute in order to pay for Patriot vouchers? (I leave aside the real political challenges under less ideal circumstances.) There is, I assume, no limit to the epistemic value of bigger vouchers (from the principle of Epistemic Value of Quantity), but there must be a limit on how much should be raised for this purpose through taxes. For example, suppose, in a crude model, that there is a limit to how much a citizen should be required to pay in taxes (assume a "progressive" structure of higher rates for wealthier citizens).[54] Add to

---

[51] It might seem useful to know the Gini index for any such set of data. But no single Gini level can be assumed to be epistemically too much or too little. It follows from the Compensation of Quantity for Inequality assumption that higher levels of Gini inequality are epistemically acceptable at sufficiently higher quantities.

[52] Ackerman, "Crediting the Voters."

[53] Ibid., 72.

[54] Note the political problem of the wealthier being required by law to transfer resources to the less wealthy in order to subsidize political activity that may well be antithetical to their interests. But this may be just, and thus so I will not harp on the fact that my Progressive Voucher plan would avoid this political problem.

this all the other important uses for tax money, and Patriot vouchers find themselves with a limited piece of a limited pie, even where the limits are not due to anyone's unjust stinginess or distorted priorities. Ackerman may be right that this would still support aggregate spending that is greater than current levels, though he does not give any argument for that conclusion. In any case, my main point does not depend on challenging that claim. For even if it is correct, there is the question of the potential further aggregate increases that would be allowed by a properly structured incentive scheme such as Progressive Vouchers. If more debate is as important as Ackerman says, then it may be worth accepting some inequality in order to promote it. My aim is to explore under what conditions this might be so.

Free speech implications

This is not the place to fully consider the constitutional questions raised by a scheme like Progressive Vouchers. In the United States, campaign finance reform has recently faced First Amendment obstacles stemming from the important role that campaign contributions and expenditures have in citizens' expression of political views. There remains a wide range of informed opinion about what regulations would be constitutionally permissible. Progressive Vouchers have some advantages in this connection, and I limit myself to briefly laying them out. Comparison with Ackerman's Patriot plan will help illustrate the main points.

The decision in *Buckley v. Valeo* asserted that "the concept that government may restrict the speech of some elements of our society in order to enhance the relative voice of others is wholly foreign to the First Amendment."[55] The Court showed no reservations about public subsidies or "floors." Given the Court's formulation, it is unclear whether its objection was to (a) reduction in the *quantity* of speech, (b) *prohibition* of speech above a certain financial level, (c) a *leveling* motive behind the regulation, or some mix of these. Consider the Progressive Voucher idea in light of these three possible concerns.

First, the Progressive Voucher idea is designed to increase the aggregate quantity of political spending over E-max; thus, if the egalitarian Patriot plan raises the quantity (as compared to current real-world spending), then so do Progressive Vouchers. On this assumption, there is no loss of quantity in either plan. Second, the method of regulation employed by Progressive Vouchers need not be a prohibition of any input at any level of expenditure. Rather, input is made progressively more expensive at higher quantities for a given contributor, but is permissible if paid for. The number of vouchers was limited to five in the earlier example for simplicity. It could equally well be unlimited. Third, it must be confessed that the ar-

[55] *Buckley v. Valeo*, 424 U.S. 1, 48–49 (1976).

gument is partly a leveling one, but not entirely. A separate motive is subsidy of political input. This is a motive that is above constitutional reproach (according to the *Buckley* Court), though that does not mean that it can be pursued in just any manner. The motive is to increase the quantity without too much inequality, and this is achieved without prohibiting speech at any level. If the *Buckley* decision precludes any regulation that has limiting inequality of influence as part of its aim, then Progressive Vouchers would be unconstitutional. But the *Buckley* opinion contains no language that requires that reading. The famous sentence rejecting "restrict[ing] the speech of some elements of our society in order to enhance the relative voice of others" might be meant only to apply to *restricting* speech, which may not include attaching certain taxes or surcharges to it on a viewpoint-neutral basis and without any aim of preventing any particular speech, or any effect of reducing the quantity of speech.

Ackerman's Patriot proposal shares with Progressive Vouchers a leveling motive, but a much more ambitious leveling is involved. In addition, the Patriot plan involves ceilings, outright restrictions prohibiting spending beyond the level of the fixed voucher everyone receives. The Patriot plan may not involve reductions in spending compared with current levels (this depends on what level would or should be supported by taxpayers), but it does forgo the additional quantity of spending that Progressive Vouchers could induce. Ackerman may be right that the Patriot plan is not constitutionally doomed, but from *Buckley*'s point of view Progressive Vouchers have important advantages over the political egalitarian scheme embodied in the Patriot plan. Progressive Vouchers have a stronger claim to promoting quantity of input; they involve no outright restrictions on spending; and their leveling ambition is far more modest and less central to their purpose. Progressive Vouchers are more likely than the Patriot plan to be compatible with the *Buckley* decision.

VI. Final Objections Considered

Why formal equality is preserved

The epistemic argument against political egalitarianism may seem difficult to contain. It is natural to suspect that an argument that places great importance on the epistemic value of the political process is bound, in the end, to recommend what we might call epistocracy: rule by the wise. But this is prevented by the liberal criterion of legitimacy; since the supposedly superior wisdom of any proposed epistocrat will be open to reasonable disagreement, no invidious comparison of that kind is available in a valid political justification. The argument against political egalitarianism permits an epistemic justification for inequality of political influence that does not make any such invidious comparisons.

But if inequality of political influence can be given a noninvidious justification, what is to stop similar arguments from condoning even formal, legal political inequality? In particular, mightn't there be ways of tinkering with the equal political liberties so as to improve the epistemic value of political procedures? If so, the epistemic argument would be led, embarrassingly, to recommend even unequal political rights and liberties under the law.

One way the embarrassment is avoided is by noticing how many possible violations of equal formal political liberties rely on invidious comparisons that are precluded by the liberal principle of legitimacy. Mill suggested that college graduates and certain others be given extra votes;[56] others might propose that Christians, or parents, or pet-owners are specially qualified to have extra influence as a matter of law. But none of these proposals is countenanced by an epistemic approach constrained by the liberal principle of legitimacy.

On the other hand, there are formal political inequalities that make no invidious comparison but, arguably, promote the epistemic value of the political process; but it is no embarrassment to endorse them. For example, members of the U.S. Senate and House of Representatives have more political power, as a matter of formal legal status, than other citizens. They are permitted to vote on momentous matters that you and I are not. One possible justification for the formal inequality involved in representative democracy is epistemic: having a small group of decision makers who can train and accumulate experience, and devote their full time to politics, serves the quality of the outcomes under the right conditions. If so, this is a good epistemic reason for formal political inequality of the most obvious kind, but one that makes no invidious comparison among groups of citizens.[57] No one is given extra political power on the basis of any supposedly greater wisdom or worth. People gain the extra political power of being a representative as a result of election, and the reasons for having a system of elected representatives to serve as legislators nowhere rely on invidious comparisons among citizens.[58]

---

[56] John Stuart Mill, *Representative Government* (New York: E. P. Dutton and Co., 1950), ch. 8.

[57] Political egalitarianism apparently cannot account for this kind of inequality.

[58] For a more difficult case, suppose it could be established beyond reasonable dispute that the quality of political decisions would be enhanced by selecting a small number of voters from the millions who register, and depriving all others of voting privileges. I do not think this has much plausibility, but suppose it were true. Giving only a few adult citizens the right to vote must be reckoned a version of formal political inequality. Now if the voting citizens were selected according to whether they were college-educated, or Christians, or pet-owners, and if this were done on the hypothesis that members of these groups were likely to make better decisions, or more fully deserved the power to vote than others, then the scheme would be utterly illegitimate. But if instead they were chosen randomly, and this still were reliably shown to have advantages for the quality of political decisions, it is no longer clear that the formal political inequality is objectionable. In truth, such a scheme would probably do more epistemic harm than good; but if it had overriding epistemic advantages, implementing it would not express disrespect for anyone.

Thus, the epistemic argument against political egalitarianism can be suitably contained. It is not led to endorse any erosion of formal political equality as it is normally understood.

VII. Conclusion

Insistence on equality of political input would preclude even modest inequalities that increase input for everyone. Under favorable conditions, a greater quantity of input improves the expected quality of political decisions; thus, we need a good reason if we are to stand in its way. It would be perfectly proper to object to inequality of influence if it were based on invidious comparisons among citizens. It may even be illegitimate to base such inequality on putative rights to liberty or property, though I have not considered that question here. But modest inequalities that significantly increase input for all without any implication of disrespect or controversial pre-political rights may be capable of improving the tendency of political decisions to be substantively just and proper in a way that it would be unreasonable to deny. If so, incentive structures such as Progressive Vouchers may be practical devices for pursuing this liberal epistemic conception of political equality.

Philosophy, Brown University

WHY DELIBERATIVE DEMOCRACY IS DIFFERENT

By Amy Gutmann and Dennis Thompson

I. Introduction

In modern pluralist societies, political disagreement often reflects moral disagreement, as citizens with conflicting perspectives on fundamental values debate the laws that govern their public life. Any satisfactory theory of democracy must provide a way of dealing with this moral disagreement. A fundamental problem confronting all democratic theorists is to find a morally justifiable way of making binding collective decisions in the face of continuing moral conflict.

The solutions that most theorists propose make the problem seem more tractable than it is. Because their solutions require the rejection of rival theories, they discount much of the disagreement that gives rise to the problem in the first place. But if, as is the case in pluralist societies and in current theoretical literature, no single theory can reasonably claim to be morally sovereign, the most difficult part of the problem persists: how to deal with the moral conflict that these competing theoretical perspectives express. Furthermore, the problem is not only that the theories conflict with one another, but also that fundamental disagreements arise even within a single theory.

We argue that a deliberative theory of democracy provides a different— and better—approach to this problem because it leaves open the possibility that the moral values expressed by a wide range of theories may be justifiable. Deliberative democracy is a conception of democratic politics in which decisions and policies are justified in a process of discussion among free and equal citizens or their accountable representatives. On our view, a deliberative theory contains a set of principles that prescribe fair terms of cooperation. Its fundamental principle is that citizens owe one another justifications for the laws they collectively impose on one another. The theory is deliberative because the terms of cooperation that it recommends are conceived as reasons that citizens or their accountable representatives give to one another in an ongoing process of mutual justification. The reasons are not merely procedural ("because the majority favors it") or purely substantive ("because it is a human right"). They appeal to moral principles (such as basic liberty or equal opportunity) that citizens who are motivated to find fair terms of cooperation can reasonably accept. Because the range of acceptable reasons is wider than in most theories, the principles of deliberative democracy are, in specific ways we describe below, more open to revision than those of most other theories.

To begin to show why deliberative democracy is different from other theories, and how it can more readily accommodate moral conflict, we need to distinguish between first- and second-order theories of democracy.[1] First-order theories seek to resolve moral disagreement by rejecting alternative theories or principles with which they conflict. They measure their success by whether they resolve the conflict consistently on their own terms. Their aim is to be the single theory that resolves moral disagreement. The familiar substantive views—utilitarianism, libertarianism, liberal egalitarianism, communitarianism—are first-order theories in this sense. Each theory individually claims to resolve moral conflict, or to provide a basis for resolving moral conflict. Each does so in ways that require rejecting the substantive principles of its rivals that conflict with its own. But taken together they are manifestations of the problem of moral disagreement rather than resolutions of it.

Second-order theories deal with moral disagreement by accommodating first-order theories that conflict with one another. They measure their success by the extent to which they can justify their conclusions to everyone who would be bound by them—whether the conclusion resolves the disagreement or shows that it cannot (yet) be morally resolved. These theories are called "second-order" because they are *about* other theories, in the sense that they refer to first-order principles without affirming or denying their ultimate validity. They can be held consistently without rejecting any of a wide range of moral principles expressed by first-order theories. Many procedural theories of democracy usually present themselves as second-order theories, because they purport to be neutral among competing substantive theories. A majoritarian theory, for example, could justify utilitarian, egalitarian, or libertarian legislation, as long as it were adopted by majority rule. But, as we shall indicate, this neutrality is undesirable and unattainable. Each procedural theory individually can produce results that are not morally justifiable. Taken together, these theories reveal substantive moral disagreements among themselves—for example, disagreements between direct and representative, populist and Madisonian, or majoritarian and constitutional theories.

---

[1] Although most substantive theories are first-order theories, and many procedural theories are second-order theories, the substantive/procedural distinction is not the same as the first-order/second-order distinction. The substantive/procedural distinction characterizes theories according to whether they justify political decisions by reference to independent moral principles or entirely by reference to features of the process. The first-order/second-order distinction classifies theories according to whether they affirm the truth of a single consistent set of (substantive or procedural) principles that exclude other such principles, or whether they refer to the principles in a way that is consistent with a range of potentially inconsistent sets (for example, by prescribing certain attitudes or conduct with regard to the principles and the persons who hold them).

Deliberative democracy is also a second-order theory, and therefore (like some procedural theories) makes room for continuing moral conflict that first-order theories seek to eliminate. But it avoids the difficulties of procedural theories by explicitly acknowledging the substantive conflicts underlying procedural theories, and by explicitly affirming substantive principles in its own theory. A full theory of deliberative democracy includes both substantive and procedural principles, denies that either are morally neutral, and judges both from a second-order perspective.

We present an argument for the distinctiveness of deliberative democracy with a particular theory in mind, one that we defend more fully in *Democracy and Disagreement*.[2] That theory aims to develop a second-order theory with both substantive and procedural principles. But regardless of whether that theory is accepted, the problem that the theory addresses poses a challenge that all democratic theories, whether deliberative or not, must confront. So far, none has met it adequately because, in the face of competing first-order moralities, each only reiterates the conflicts that create the problem.

II. DEMOCRATIC RESPONSES TO DISAGREEMENT

In any modern pluralist society in which people are even moderately free, there are persistent disagreements about the principles that justify mutually binding laws and decisions. Utilitarians defend maximizing social welfare, even while disagreeing among themselves about what it means and how it should be done. Should total or average utility be maximized? Does counting each person as one and none for more than one also require, permit, or preclude according equal weight to each person's moral ideals and views about how others should live their lives? Should the common currency be pleasure, preferences, or some other unit of individual satisfaction?

Libertarians defend protecting every individual's freedom from interference, an aim that clearly conflicts with a general principle of maximizing social welfare; but just as clearly, this aim is subject to conflicting interpretations among libertarians themselves. Persons are inviolable; they are not social resources. They own themselves, and are responsible—and should be held responsible—for their own actions and the consequences of their actions. But what institutions, laws, and policies respect these foundational principles of libertarianism? Libertarians themselves reasonably disagree about, for example, questions such as these: To what extent should parents have control over their children's education? Or, to what extent should government provide welfare for persons who may not be capable of providing for themselves?

[2] Amy Gutmann and Dennis Thompson, *Democracy and Disagreement* (Cambridge, MA: Belknap Press of Harvard University Press, 1996).

Libertarians unite, however, in the face of the claims of liberal egalitarians. Most libertarians would agree that the distribution of primary goods in a society need not correct for inequalities in natural endowments, and would therefore reject liberal egalitarian theories that require redistribution to achieve this end. Liberal egalitarians advocate a distribution of primary goods that does not depend on the natural endowments of individuals (they believe it should be "endowment insensitive"), but they still insist that the distribution reflect free choices of individuals as much as possible (they believe it should be "choice sensitive"). Liberal egalitarians respect the capacity of individuals rationally to revise their ends consistently with principles of justice that produce distributions that are endowment insensitive and choice sensitive. The foundational principles of liberal egalitarian theories are at odds with the aims of both maximizing social welfare and protecting every individual's freedom from interference. Liberal egalitarians also reasonably disagree among themselves about some important basic moral issues, including the criteria for endowment insensitivity and choice sensitivity, the priority of protecting liberties over securing opportunities, and the meaning of liberty and opportunity themselves.

Communitarians also disagree among themselves, but most are skeptical about distributive principles that are choice sensitive, whether those principles are utilitarian, libertarian, or liberal egalitarian. Choice-sensitive principles, according to communitarians, presuppose a self that is separable from its constitutive ends. Those constitutive ends are identified with the conception of the good that prevails in a person's community as reflected in the community's language, religion, and other distinctive ways of life. Communitarians therefore give priority to conceptions of the good over conceptions of justice, at least those conceptions of justice that are not grounded in a distinctive conception of the good and therefore might weaken those communal ways of life.

These theoretical disagreements are reflected in many political disputes about public policies. To be sure, most people do not hold the pure forms of these first-order theories, and many disagreements do not explicitly take the form of arguments between first-order principles. Moreover, many people hold combinations of first-order principles from different moral theories. Nevertheless, political disputes often express in various ways theoretical disagreements and deep conflicts among moral principles.

Deep moral differences surface in debates between defenders and opponents of abortion, affirmative action, surrogate parenthood, capital punishment, universal health care, public and private school vouchers, unconditional and work-conditioned welfare, and many other issues of public policy. No doubt some of these disputes arise from misunderstandings, and some are motivated by bad faith and political interests. But legitimate moral differences often remain, differences that cannot be resolved without rejecting the principles of some of the first-order moral theories mentioned above. Yet no theorist has ever managed to find a way of transcending the foundational disagreements that animate many (even if not all) deep disagreements in democratic politics. Insofar as these disagreements reflect differences among first-order theories, or reasonable doubts that any single theory offers all the relevant moral insights, they will not be resolvable by appeals to any such theory.

In the absence of a single theory or set of principles that can resolve these disagreements, a first-order theorist who would apply a theory in politics is faced with two alternatives: impose the theory by undemocratic means, or submit the theory for democratic decision. The first is, of course, not a democratic response at all; and the second abandons any claim to be the sovereign standard for adjudicating moral conflict in politics. On this second alternative, the theory becomes one of many from which citizens may choose, and the process by which they choose must become a central concern of the theory. In this way, first-order substantive theories that seek political authority move toward becoming procedural theories.

A significant attraction of proceduralism for democratic theorists is that it has the potential to avoid the choice between the stark alternatives that confront first-order substantive theories. Procedural theories do not have to claim to be capable of transcending all fundamental moral disagreements. Instead, they can try to offer a way of adjudicating the disagreements in actual politics, without seeming to commit themselves to any particular substantive theory.

But procedural theories take two different approaches here. The first is *pure proceduralism*, which in effect requires the rejection of some substantive theories, and therefore turns out to be a first-order theory itself. Pure procedural theories compete with utilitarianism, libertarianism, liberal egalitarianism, communitarianism, and other first-order moral theories. They do not compete directly by rejecting the first-order theories on moral grounds, but rather indirectly by rejecting their foundations or reasons. The pure procedural form of majoritarianism, for example, presents majority rule as a foundational moral principle that answers the question: On what grounds is this law or public policy justified? Majoritarianism in this form answers this question by substituting the principle of majority rule for principles of utility, liberty, fair opportunity, or a community's conception of the good life as the moral foundation for justifying a decision, and it does so prior to any actual political decision-making. A law or policy is justified for the reason and to the extent that it is adopted by procedures stipulated by the theory.

This kind of proceduralism suffers from the same deficiency as other first-order theories. Because it would replace the justifications or reasons presented by some other first-order theories, it simply reproduces the substantive disagreement that created the problem of disagreement in the first place. Procedural democrats often bring substantive principles in the back door by considering them the conditions of a *fair* democratic process. Procedural democrats try to limit these substantive conditions to those necessary for making the process democratic, such as free speech. But the line between what is and is not necessary is difficult to draw without invoking moral considerations, and in any case some principles (such as free exercise of religion) that any adequate democratic theory must respect do not fit within any plausible definition of necessary conditions. These procedural theories turn out, on closer inspection, not to be purely procedural in any significant sense that would avoid substantive moral disagreement.

Some deliberative democrats may be regarded as pure proceduralists in this sense. The procedure that fully justifies all outcomes is deliberation itself: any law enacted in a deliberative process of reason-giving among free and equal citizens is justified. But like most other pure proceduralists, these deliberative democrats build substantive values into the conditions that define adequate deliberation. On our view, these values, including the value of the practice of deliberation itself, should be made explicit, and subject to deliberative challenge. We (along with some other deliberative democrats) characterize deliberative democracy as not purely procedural.

The other procedural approach—call it *conditional proceduralism*—is more modest than pure proceduralism. It does not seek to replace substantive theories or their justifications. It is, in this respect, a genuine second-order theory. It treats procedures as instrumental to achieving substantive ends, such as stability, legitimacy, or other conditions assumed to be necessary for maintaining democratic order in the particular circumstances, but it is not committed to any ends beyond these minimal conditions. A decision that conforms, for example, to the principle of majority rule is justified, but only conditionally. This kind of proceduralism leaves open the possibility that the decision may be criticized as unjust because it violates substantive moral principles. (A critic might argue, for example, that the injustice of the decision is worse than the gain in legitimacy.) The difficulty with conditional proceduralism is that it lacks the theoretical resources to take advantage of the possibility that it leaves open: it cannot itself support the criticism that a majority decision is unjust. What it lacks is any substantive first-order principles that would ground criticisms of the outcomes of the procedures it prescribes.

Thus, both substantive and procedural responses to the problem of moral disagreement suffer from serious defects. Both fail to come to grips with the problem, either by simply reproducing the disagreement as a first-order conflict, or by resolving the disagreement in a way that violates some important first-order principles. These failures suggest that what is needed is a second-order theory (so that it does not directly reject substantive or pure procedural theories), but one with some substantive content (so that unlike conditional proceduralism it has the capacity to criticize procedurally correct outcomes). Deliberative democracy precisely meets this need: it is a second-order theory with substantive principles.

How is it possible for a theory to include substantive principles and procedural principles while still accommodating a wide range of first-order principles? The key to the answer is that the principles in a theory of deliberative democracy, whether substantive or procedural, have a different status from that of principles in other theories. Deliberative democracy does not seek a foundational principle or set of principles that, in advance of actual political activity, determine whether a procedure or law is justified. Instead, it adopts a dynamic conception of political justification, in which change over time is an essential feature of justifiable principles. The principles of deliberative democracy are distinctive in two significant respects: they are morally provisional (subject to change through further moral argument); and they are politically provisional (subject to change through further political argument). To show how these features distinguish deliberative democracy from other theories, and why they provide a better approach to dealing with the problem of moral disagreement, we first need to explain more fully the substance of the principles that a theory of deliberative democracy might contain.

III. Principles of Deliberative Democracy

The principles of deliberative democracy that we propose in *Democracy and Disagreement* (and that we believe best capture the spirit of an adequate deliberative theory) express, in various forms, the idea of reciprocity. The deliberative principles that flow from reciprocity provide both conditions and content for justifying laws and policies in a democracy. Reciprocity, publicity, and accountability are the chief standards that regulate the conditions of deliberation. Basic liberty, basic opportunity, and fair opportunity are key components of the content of deliberation.

The basic premise of reciprocity is that citizens owe one another justifications for the institutions, laws, and public policies that collectively bind them. Reciprocity suggests the aim of seeking agreement on the basis of principles that can be justified to others who share the aim of reaching reasonable agreement. Some first-order moralities implicitly accept reciprocity, but most do not give it the central role that deliberative democracy does. Deliberative democracy takes reciprocity more seriously than do other theories of democracy, and makes it the core of democratic principles and practice.

Reciprocity is not foundational in deliberative democracy in the way in which principles such as utility or liberty are foundational in first-order theories. Reciprocity is not a principle from which justice is derived, but rather one that governs the ongoing process by which the conditions and content of justice are determined in specific cases. It may be helpful to think of the process as analogous to a feature of scientific inquiry.

Reciprocity is to justice in political ethics what replication is to truth in science. A finding of truth in science requires replicability, which calls for public demonstration. A finding of justice in political ethics requires reciprocity, which calls for public deliberation. Deliberation is not sufficient to establish justice, but deliberation at some point in history is necessary. Just as repeated replication is unnecessary once the truth of a finding (such as the law of gravity) has been amply confirmed, so repeated deliberation is unnecessary once a precept of justice (such as equal protection) has been extensively deliberated.

Guided by reciprocity and its fellow principles, the practice of deliberation is an ongoing activity of mutual reason-giving, punctuated by collectively binding decisions. The decisions may take the form of an electoral verdict, a legislative act, or a judicial opinion, but all are situated in a continuing process of justification. It is a process of seeking, not just any reasons, but mutually justifiable reasons, and reaching a mutually binding decision on the basis of those reasons. It is therefore more than discussion, and it is substantive as well as procedural. Among the substantive reasons that citizens or their representatives consider in this process are some of those expressed in first-order moral theories. This is the source of the instrumental value of deliberation; its tendency to promote mutually justifiable outcomes is part of what justifies the practice itself. Deliberation is valuable in part because it can encourage citizens and their representatives to invoke substantive standards to understand, revise, and resolve moral conflicts in politics. (In this respect, it has epistemic as well as pragmatic value.) But these conflicts may not be and usually are not fully resolved, certainly not always in favor of one substantive theory. A further noninstrumental value of deliberation is therefore also an essential and distinctive part of any justification of deliberation. This further value is to be found in the idea of mutual respect that is part of the meaning of reciprocity. Citizens show respect to one another by recognizing their obligation to justify to one another (in terms that permit reasonable disagreement) the laws and policies that govern their public life.

Mutual respect among those who reasonably disagree is a value in itself; and, in turn, it has further beneficial effects for democratic politics. One of the most important is what we call an *economy of moral disagreement*. When political opponents seek to economize on their disagreements, they continue to search for fair terms of social cooperation even in the face of their fundamental (and often foundational) disagreements. They do so by justifying the policies that they find most morally defensible in a way that minimizes rejection of the reasonable positions that they nonetheless oppose on moral grounds. By practicing an economy of moral disagreement, citizens who disagree on one issue are better able to work together on other causes whose goals they share. Citizens ought to be able to agree, for example, that someone's views on abortion should not affect how she is treated with respect to other public policies. A pro-lifer ought not to favor denying a woman who has had an abortion access to other essential medical care. A pro-choicer should not refuse pro-lifers the right to speak against abortion even in front of an abortion clinic.

Together with reciprocity, two other principles specify the conditions of democratic deliberation. The principle of publicity requires that reason-giving be public in order that it be mutually justifiable. The principle of accountability specifies that officials who make decisions on behalf of other people, whether or not they are electoral constituents, should be accountable to those people. Mutually binding decisions cannot be mu-tually justified if officials are not also accountable to what may be called their moral constituents. The moral constituents of public officials include more than their electoral constituents, and even more than citizens. They include people who are, in effect, bound by the officials' decisions even though they may not have had a voice in making them. People in foreign countries who must live with, for example, the effects of toxic waste exported by our country deserve an accounting from our representatives.

The principles that define the conditions of deliberation resemble some of the principles that procedural theorists put forward. Like some proce-dural theories, deliberative democracy is a second-order theory. Despite these similarities, however, deliberative democracy, as we have already seen, is not a procedural theory. It can therefore claim two important advantages over proceduralism.

First, deliberative democracy has no problem saying that what the majority decides, even after deliberating, need not be right. A majority acts wrongly if it violates basic liberty by requiring a minority to worship as the majority does. Yet through a public and accountable process of fair decision-making, a majority may pass a law requiring all citizens to wor-ship in a way that conforms to the majority's religious beliefs. On a purely procedural conception of democracy, this law would be justified. But it cannot be justified to the minority who do not share the majority's reli-gion and whose personal integrity the law assaults. It would therefore violate the principle of reciprocity (or any ideal of treating every person as a free and equal being).

Second, when procedural theories do accept or reject an outcome fa-vored by a first-order theory, they do so for reasons that are external to the first-order theory. They do not address that theory or its justifications on its own terms, but rather appeal to other considerations such as social stability or fairness. Although these considerations may be moral, they do not engage directly with the moral claims of the positions they reject. They therefore fail to treat their opponents with the moral respect reci-procity requires, and they offer less scope for appreciation of opposing views and for modification of one or more of the opposing views. A procedural theory leaves the competing theories, and their political ad-vocates, in the same moral position in which they began.

Deliberative democracy does not suffer from these difficulties, because it goes beyond proceduralism and explicitly includes substantive first-order principles. But some critics may object that by including substantive principles, the theory creates an even more serious problem for itself. They would object that a substantive principle such as religious freedom should not be part of a democratic theory. The critics would agree that religious freedom is a core part of basic liberty and should be protected; but they would argue that democratic theory should not contain any such principles, however justified the principles are on substantive moral grounds. The argument is not so much substantive as definitional: it is about whether the idea of democracy refers to only procedures.

Is there any reason to define democracy so narrowly that it excludes substantive principles? The reason cannot be because the content of basic liberty or basic opportunity is reasonably contestable—so is the content of principles that are more procedural, such as publicity and accountability. Nor can it be because democratic theory is internally inconsistent if it contains substantive as well as procedural principles. There is no inconsistency in claiming that a defensible democracy must defend the religious freedom and other basic liberties of individuals, their right to vote and to hold their representatives accountable, and that it must also find a way of fairly deciding among competing values when they conflict. Without some substantive principles, deliberative democracy could not provide standards for assessing many political practices, including not only the outcomes of procedures but also the procedures themselves. Moreover, it would be morally incomplete according to its own premise of reciprocity. A democratic constitution that fails to protect, for example, the basic liberty of citizens would not be justifiable to those who are bound by it.

The three principles that provide the content of deliberative democracy—basic liberty, basic opportunity, and fair opportunity—also flow from the basic principle of reciprocity. Laws cannot be mutually justified, as reciprocity requires, if they violate the personal integrity of individuals. The principle of basic liberty therefore calls for protecting the personal integrity of each person, through such protections as freedom of speech, religion, and conscience, and due process and equal protection under the law.

Mutually binding institutions, laws, and policies that deprive individuals of the basic opportunities necessary for making choices among good lives cannot be mutually justified. Those basic opportunities typically include adequate health care, education, security, work, and income. These goods are necessary for living a decent life and having the ability to make choices among good lives. A principle of basic opportunity calls for giving individuals the capacity to make choices among good lives by providing them with the basic opportunities that give them such a capacity.

Reciprocity also prescribes a principle of fair opportunity, which in turn calls for nondiscrimination in the distribution of social resources that are highly valued but may not be essential to living a good life or having a choice among good lives. The principle of fair opportunity rests on the reciprocal claim that discrimination against individuals on morally irrelevant grounds in the distribution of scarce social goods such as professional offices cannot be justified to the individuals who are being discriminated against.

It should not be surprising that these principles resemble those found in many first-order theories. The substantive content of deliberative democracy naturally draws on the same moral sources as other theories, and reflects many of the same conflicts that they generate. Most first-order theories also at least implicitly share the aim of mutual justification. They only appear to reject the aim if they offer justifications for why the demands of reciprocity cannot be met in certain circumstances. If they reject the aim in principle, how can they justify imposing coercive laws and policies on citizens who reject them on moral grounds?

In trying to demonstrate the superiority of their own principles, many democratic theorists tend to emphasize their disagreements with their rivals. In contrast, deliberative democrats at least initially stress agreements. Despite the fundamental conflicts among the theories we have noted, the points of convergence among and within competing first-order theories are substantial. Most theories either directly or indirectly defend the protection of many individual liberties, especially those that are essential to the integrity of persons (the core of the principle of basic liberty). Most theories also claim that if their principles are implemented, all persons will secure the opportunity to live a good life, an ideal that expresses the principle of basic opportunity. Similarly, most theories suggest that their principles support what we term fair opportunity.

These points of convergence provide the initial content for the substantive principles of deliberative democracy. Although other theorists sometimes seek such convergence, deliberative democrats are better situated to achieve it because they do not try to appropriate merely what they, from their own perspective, regard as valuable in rival theories. Although they do not purport to be neutral among all first-order theories, deliberative democrats do not require that competing first-order theories be rejected. The substantive principles of deliberative democracy have a different status in deliberative democracy: they are morally and politically provisional in ways that leave them more open to challenge and therefore more amenable to democratic discretion.

IV. MORALLY PROVISIONAL PRINCIPLES

The principles of deliberative democracy are morally provisional in the sense that they are presented, and only justified when they are so presented, as claims that can be challenged and changed over time in response to new philosophical insights, empirical evidence, or interpretations of both the insights and evidence. Many theories, of course, can and do endorse something like this general outlook—for example, by adopting some form of fallibilism, or more simply by expressing general approval of moral and intellectual open-mindedness. But the provisional stance that deliberative democracy takes toward its own claims is integral to the theory, and supports the means for fundamental change in the content of the theory itself. This capacity of deliberative democracy to subject its own principles as well as other moral principles to critical scrutiny over time is part of what makes it a second-order moral theory. A first-order theory cannot consistently include within itself the possibility for fundamental revision of this kind. When its fundamental principles are substantially changed—say, from utilitarian to egalitarian content—the theory is not just revised, but in effect rejected.

The provisional status of its principles is integral to deliberative democracy because it is implied by the fundamental premise of reciprocity. Citizens who owe one another justifications for the laws that they seek to impose must take seriously the reasons their opponents give. Taking seriously the reasons one's opponents give means that, at least for a certain range of views that one opposes, one must acknowledge the possibility that an opposing view may be shown to be correct in the future.[3] This acknowledgment has implications not only for the way citizens should treat their opponents, but also for the way they regard their own views. It imposes an obligation to continue to test their own views, seeking forums in which the views can be challenged, and keeping open the possibility of their revision or even rejection. This obligation is what makes possible the practice of the economy of moral disagreement described earlier.

How is it possible for deliberative democracy to put forward principles that constitute its own theory and at the same time allow that these principles may be rejected? An important part of the answer consists in taking a dynamic view of the theory, regarding it not as a set of principles fixed at any point in time, but as a set of principles any one of which may be changed over time. Not all principles can be challenged at the same time from within the theory, but any single principle (or even several principles) may be challenged at a particular time by other principles in the theory. The theory in this way contains the means of its own revision. Citizens and accountable officials can revise one principle in a sequential process in which the other principles are held constant. They can alter

---

[3] The range includes what we call "deliberative disagreements," which are those in which citizens continue to differ about basic moral principles even though they seek a resolution that is mutually justifiable. The dispute over abortion is an example of a deliberative disagreement because both sides can justify their views within a reciprocal perspective. A dispute about racial segregation is an example of a nondeliberative disagreement because one side can be reasonably rejected within a reciprocal perspective. See Gutmann and Thompson, *Democracy and Disagreement*, 2–3, 73–79.

their understanding of all the principles by applying them in a different context or at a different time. For example, by understanding the value of basic liberty in protecting personal integrity, citizens begin to judge whether information about a person's private life is legitimately subject to a publicity principle which implies that the politically relevant actions of public officials should be open to public scrutiny. When the person is a public official with a psychiatric history, the values of accountability and personal integrity may conflict. By means of moral reasoning about these conflicting values, the publicity principle may be modified—for example, by restricting its application or by reinterpreting its purpose.

Even the principle of reciprocity provides the means of criticizing its own conclusions. In *Democracy and Disagreement*, we use the principle of reciprocity to defend a federal court decision in a case involving religion and public education. The court denied the claim of some fundamentalist Christian parents who sought exemptions for their children from the standard reading curriculum in a public school in Tennessee because the content of the required textbooks conflicted with their religious convictions.[4] The parents maintained that their children should not be taught to make critical judgments, to use their imaginations, and to exercise choice "in areas where the Bible provides the answer." William Galston takes issue with our criticism of the parents, and invokes the idea of reciprocity itself to defend their claim.[5] Galston imagines the fundamentalist parents saying: "If you believed what I believe . . . you would seek for your child what I am seeking for mine. Moreover, the accommodation I seek is one that I would readily grant, were our positions reversed."[6]

Galston's argument on the parents' behalf, based as it is on reciprocity, is better than any that the parents or their advocates presented in the actual case. Galston and we agree that children, as reciprocity implies, should not be treated either as merely creatures of the state or of their parents. But we disagree about whether a public school may mandate a curriculum that exposes all students to ideas reasonably designed to prepare them for assuming the rights and responsibilities of democratic citizenship if parents of some students believe that those ideas offend their religious beliefs.

Galston's argument has more moral force in a meeting of a school board than it does in a court of law. A school board's discretionary decision can avoid treating children as mere creatures of either their parents or the state. (Since children are also educated in the realms of family and church, public schools per se do not treat children as mere creatures of the

---

[4] *Mozert v. Hawkins County Bd. of Educ.*, 827 F.2d 1058, 1065 (6th Cir. 1987), *cert. denied*, 484 U.S. 1066 (1988). See Gutmann and Thompson, *Democracy and Disagreement*, 63–69.

[5] William Galston, "Diversity, Toleration, and Deliberative Democracy," in *Deliberative Politics: Essays on "Democracy and Disagreement,"* ed. Stephen Macedo (New York and Oxford: Oxford University Press, 1999).

[6] Ibid.

state.) The school board could use its legitimate discretion to search for an alternative way of teaching the children that is mutually acceptable, consistent with the parents' sincere religious beliefs and also with the state's reasonable civic aim of introducing children to ideas such as the dignity of persons, whose justification is not dependent on parental approval. A court's decision to exempt the children, by contrast, would extend the scope of religious freedom so that parents would have the power to exempt their children from any publicly mandated curriculum, even one as basic and reasonable as the reading curriculum mandated by the school board in this case. The dignity of persons was one idea (among several) to which the fundamentalist parents objected to having their children exposed without a statement by the teacher that it is a mistaken idea.

Whether Galston succeeds in his claims on behalf of the fundamentalist parents, his mode of argument shows how even the implications of reciprocity may be subject to revision and reinterpretation by deliberative means. Similarly, deliberative democracy may support critics in an effective challenge to our claim that utilitarianism, when treated as a first-order moral theory, is inconsistent with reciprocity because it does not respect the basic liberty of persons. It may support libertarians in an effective challenge to our arguments, for example, which oppose enforcing some surrogate parenting contracts against the will of the birth mother.[7] And it could support egalitarians who object to our argument that able-bodied citizens should work rather than be entitled to welfare if decent work (and adequate child-care) is available.[8]

It would even be possible for a utilitarian or a libertarian to contest the constitutional principles of deliberative democracy. Any adequate theory of deliberative democracy includes first-order principles (such as the principles of liberty and opportunity we put forward in *Democracy and Disagreement*), and these are subject to challenge no less than the principles of utilitarianism, libertarianism, and egalitarianism. But this challenge must take place in a process that is itself governed by reciprocity. The utilitarian, libertarian, or egalitarian must make moral arguments and appeal to principles that cannot be reasonably rejected by their opponents. The constitution of deliberative democracy is in this way itself partly created and sustained through a process of deliberation.

In a similar way, deliberative democracy can accommodate challenges to the practice of political deliberation. Second-order theories that favor bargaining over deliberation, for example, usually rely on suppressed moral premises. They typically assume that interest-based politics is a morally desirable politics. Their assumptions can be assessed in moral terms and therefore fall within the adjudicative scope of deliberative democracy. Whether political bargaining satisfies the standard of reci-

---

[7] Gutmann and Thompson, *Democracy and Disagreement*, 230–72.
[8] Ibid., 277–82.

procity will depend in part on the actual consequences of political bargaining in a particular social context. If those consequences can be shown to be mutually justifiable to the people who are bound by them, then instituting self-seeking bargaining in place of deliberation can satisfy the principles of deliberative democracy.

A moral defense of political bargaining can be assessed by deliberative principles, even though political bargaining itself does not directly invoke moral terms in its decision-making process. (Deliberative democracy does not imply that moral reasons always must be offered for every political decision or even for most decisions.) A general moral defense of self-seeking bargaining would claim that bargaining generally yields mutually beneficial terms of cooperation. Such a defense would rely on reciprocity to take issue with the argument in *Democracy and Disagreement* that self-seeking bargaining in politics cannot generally be counted on to produce mutually justifiable results. The defense still operates within the realm of deliberative democracy because it relies on the idea of reciprocity.

The practices that deliberative democracy recommends at any given time, like its principles, are therefore provisional in a way that is integral to the theory. Deliberative democracy offers a morally justifiable way of adjudicating reasonable disagreements that arise among people who dispute its first principles, its recommended practices, or both. That justification depends on treating its principles as essentially provisional.

Is there no limit to the disagreements that deliberative democrats can accommodate—no limit to what they treat as provisional? They can encourage reinterpretations of the meaning and implications of reciprocity, but they cannot accommodate the wholesale rejection of the moral justification it requires. They can welcome criticism of any of their principles, but they cannot sanction the general rejection of moral reasoning to justify binding political decisions. To reject the idea of moral reasoning in politics *tout court* is to abandon not only deliberative democracy, but also any form of democracy in which laws must be justified to the citizens who are bound by them.

Deliberative democrats therefore reject, and not just provisionally, any theory that bases politics only on power. They are committed, and not just provisionally, to mutually justifiable ways of judging the distribution of power. Theorists who claim that politics is only about power must reject far more than the moral terms and the adjudicative means of deliberative democracy. They must also reject criticism of any current distribution of power, however unjust it may be, or if they criticize it, they must do so in terms that—on their own view—their fellow citizens have no reason to accept. If they decline to search for political principles and practices that can be mutually justified, who should listen to them? Certainly no one who is motivated to find fair terms of social cooperation. Their audience can be only people who have themselves already given up on finding mutually defensible reasons and arguments. Those who would renounce reciprocal reasons are therefore trying either to persuade the already converted or to reach the unreasonable. In the first case their audience has no need, and in the second case no reason, to listen.[9]

V. Politically Provisional Principles

The principles of deliberative democracy are not only morally but also politically provisional. Deliberative democrats are committed to regarding their principles as subject to revision not only through moral argument by philosophers and other individuals deliberating among themselves, but also through moral argument by citizens and their representatives deliberating together. The justification for this commitment, like the justification for regarding the principles as morally provisional, rests on the value of reciprocity. From the perspective of reciprocity, persons should be treated not merely as objects of legislation, as passive subjects to be ruled, but as autonomous agents who take part in governance, directly or through their representatives, by presenting and responding to reasons that would justify the laws under which they must live together.

This process of reason-giving takes place not in the private homes of citizens or the studies of philosophers but in a public political forum. The laws that bind citizens should actually be justified to them and by them. Deliberative democrats do not consider the hypothetical justifications proposed by some social-contract theories as sufficient. Such justifications may constitute part of the moral reasoning to which citizens appeal, but the reasoning must survive the test of actual deliberation if it is to ground laws that bind citizens. This is not simply a matter of trying to ensure that the law is legitimate, that citizens feel or have good reason to feel that their views were taken into account even though they may disagree with the outcome. Actual political deliberation at some time is required to justify the law for this society at this time. The reason-giving process is necessary (though not sufficient) for declaring a law to be not only legitimate but also just. Otherwise, the principles that justify it may be right in general but not right in the particular case. The justice of a law depends in part on how it is to be interpreted in particular circumstances, and this interpretation, in turn, depends on the reasons that citizens and their representatives give in an actual process of justification.

Like its moral counterpart, political provisionality means that not only the principles of deliberative democracy but also the laws and decisions adopted in a deliberative democracy are essentially revisable. Through actual deliberation, the principles and practices that are justified at any particular time may be revised and replaced by different principles and practices over time, in a way that better accords with the premise of reciprocity. But deliberative democrats are not committed to continual

---

[9] Ibid., 353.

public deliberation, whatever its consequences. Not every single law and decision must be publicly deliberated. There are good reasons of economy and competence—as well as reasons offered by the substantive principles of liberty and opportunity (which are also revisable over time)—that argue against such universal deliberation.

Deliberative democracy should not be confused with civic republicanism. Deliberative democrats may value extensive participation, but not as a primary or universal goal. They do not demand, as Rousseau wished, that citizens continually "fly to the assemblies." Deliberative democracy supports representative government. Public officials who are accountable to citizens may have many good reasons for abridging or omitting deliberation in making some decisions. Deliberative democracy requires only that the decision to abridge or omit deliberation be made publicly and by accountable agents. The circumstances and nature of the policies that are not deliberatively decided should be deliberatively decided. The value of the practice of deliberation itself is provisional; deliberation may be waived or modified if public argument adequately shows that it interferes with the pursuit of substantive ends that are more valuable than deliberation itself would be.

So far we have assumed that the moral and political aspects of the provisional nature of deliberative principles are mutually reinforcing. Through the processes of both moral and political deliberation, citizens assess both the substantive laws and the procedures of deliberative democracy. However, these processes may not always work together harmoniously. A theorist—or any citizen—through personal moral deliberation, may well come to a conclusion that runs counter to the conclusions reached in the (political) process of collective deliberation. The outcome of a deliberative process that deliberative democrats recommend may run contrary to principles of justice that deliberative democrats also favor. This does not seem to be a serious problem for first-order substantive theorists, who would simply declare the outcome unjust. Nor are pure procedural theorists much troubled by it: they would simply accept the outcome as just as long as the procedures satisfy the conditions they specify. We have already indicated why we think that these approaches are not adequate, and why a democratic theory must have principles that are both substantive and procedural in nature. But the inadequacies of other approaches do not dispose of the problem of the potential conflict between moral and political deliberation.

Can deliberative democracy affirm substantive conclusions about politics and still support the value of actual deliberation, which may or may not produce those same conclusions? Political philosophers, including deliberative democrats like us, reach substantive conclusions without engaging in any actual political deliberation. This seems to fly in the face of the commitment to actual rather than hypothetical adjudication of political disagreements. The legal scholar Frederick Schauer presents this as a paradox of deliberative democracy.[10] Schauer argues that if, on the one hand, he accepts the arguments and conclusions of *Democracy and Disagreement*, he need not bother calling for actual political deliberation. The authors give him all the evidence he needs for thinking that sound conclusions can be reached without the aid of actual deliberation. If, on the other hand, he rejects the arguments and conclusions of the book, then he should also reject the deliberation that it recommends. Either way, the theory of deliberative democracy fails to defend the deliberative adjudication of disagreements in democratic politics, and thereby preempts the practice of democratic deliberation.

This objection does not express a genuine paradox. The principles and substantive conclusions that deliberative democrats put forward do not preempt actual deliberation. More than in other theories, the principles and conclusions must be subjected to the rigors of actual deliberation; that is part of what it means to treat them as politically provisional. Deliberative democrats offer their arguments not as philosophical constraints on democratic politics, but as moral contributions to democratic deliberation. The arguments are informed by the basic principles of deliberative democracy, but they are also often based on actual claims already made in actual political debates. These claims are often rooted in the principles of first-order political moralities and fragments of those moralities that are implied by or contained in public debates.

The substantive conclusions that deliberative democrats reach about principles and the policies that they imply should be understood as normative hypotheses. Given certain assumptions about reciprocity, for example, citizens should accept certain principles and practical conclusions. The hypotheses are normative because simply showing that some people, even a majority, in fact reject the principles or conclusions cannot refute them. Welfare for young mothers, for example, may be the best policy even if a majority of American citizens reject it. But a normative hypothesis is still a hypothesis because it may be refuted or refined by showing that there are better arguments for competing principles or conclusions in the same context. Those competing principles or conclusions may be given by a first-order political morality. But whether the normative hypothesis is refuted or refined, this kind of criticism can succeed only by subjecting rival arguments to the rigors of actual deliberation, taking into account the imperfections from which any such process suffers in practice.

When deliberative democrats criticize, for example, the injustice of a welfare policy (as we do in *Democracy and Disagreement*),[11] the criticism does not substitute for actual deliberations. It is intended to capture the most important content of the actual debate, extracting what is valuable from both sides (though without any claim to be neutral or to treat all

---

[10] Frederick Schauer, "Talking as a Decision Procedure," in *Deliberative Politics*, ed. Macedo.
[11] Gutmann and Thompson, *Democracy and Disagreement*, 273–306.

first-order principles equally). Proponents of a "work requirement" as an element of welfare policy, we suggest, are appealing to a principle of personal responsibility, but proponents of relaxing the requirement for mothers with young children are right in recognizing the need to support children, who are not responsible for their own poverty. Such arguments about welfare and many other morally charged issues we present in *Democracy and Disagreement* draw on deliberations that have taken place in American politics, showing how they might be improved, suggesting how deliberation might be extended where it is now neglected. The arguments also try to identify conditions (such as greater inclusion or better information) under which deliberation would come closer to satisfying standards of reciprocity, publicity, and accountability. Furthermore, the general values expressed by these principles, sometimes under different names, are widely accepted, not only by deliberative democrats but also by utilitarians, libertarians, liberal egalitarians, and communitarians, as well as by many ordinary citizens.

At some point, political deliberations come to a conclusion. Typically citizens or their representatives vote, and the collective decision is made—a decision which is binding on all, at least for the present. But what happens before and after the decision is as important as the simple act of voting. The decision is legitimate if it is made according to proper political procedures, but the extent to which it is morally justifiable—how right or just it is—depends substantially on the extent to which it is made and enacted deliberatively. The closer the real conditions that precede the voting, and the conduct that follows it, approximate the ideal conditions of reciprocity, the stronger the moral justification for the policies that are voted into law. Deliberative democrats judge both the process and its outcomes by principles that are both procedural and substantive. Faced with reasonable disagreements, their judgment, like the principles of their second-order theory, are morally and politically provisional.

VI. CONCLUSION

Deliberative democracy is different from other theories because it contains within itself not only the means of its own correction but also the possibility of its own fundamental revision. The provisional status of its own principles allows deliberative democracy to subject to critical scrutiny the content and conditions that it prescribes, as well as principles that other theories propose. Deliberative democracy cannot be dismissed simply by affirming one or another of the moral claims that are the content of first-order moral disagreements. That simply reproduces in its original form the problem of moral disagreement that democratic theory is supposed to transform, if not resolve. But deliberative principles can be appropriately criticized both from within the theory and from without by other first-order theories. And all of deliberative democracy's principles, including reciprocity, could be challenged all at once by proposing an alternative moral basis on which to adjudicate first-order moral disagreements in politics. Although no theory has yet provided such an alternative, deliberative democracy remains open to that possibility, and therefore open even to its own replacement.

At the same time, deliberative democracy remains firmly committed to a central value, reciprocity, which serves as its theoretical and moral compass. Affirming the value of reciprocity is not simply asserting another morality in the way that first-order theorists put forward their principles of justice or utility. Because deliberative democracy adopts a second-order moral perspective on first-order moral disagreements, it can be held consistently with a wide range of first-order principles and positions. With a principle of reciprocity, deliberative democrats offer a way in which citizens who reasonably disagree about first-order moralities can act collectively to shape mutually binding institutions, laws, and policies. To the extent that the principles and practices of deliberative democracy are consistent with reciprocity, the theory provides a justifiable way of dealing with moral disagreements in politics. It is a more generally justifiable way than other democratic theories because, among democratic theories that have resources to criticize existing political principles and practices, it offers the most scope for continuing reasonable moral disagreement among citizens and theorists. Deliberative democracy constructively embraces—without exalting—the moral conflict that underlies so much of contemporary democratic politics.

Politics and University Center for Human Values, Princeton University
Government, Harvard University

THE INSTITUTIONS OF DELIBERATIVE DEMOCRACY*

By William Nelson

I. Introduction

A theory of democratic institutions should provide us with a coherent combination of definition and justification. It should explain how it defines democratic institutions and also how they will or should function; but it also should explain why democracy, so understood, is desirable. We are all familiar with stories about the fiscal excesses to which democracies are prone, stories about the ignorance of voters, and stories about the venality of legislators. Some of us may also be suspicious of concepts such as "consent" or "the will of the people" associated with traditional arguments for democracy. Against this background, the current interest in deliberative democracy seems promising. This conception of democracy does not rely, for example, on the idea of rational and knowledgeable voters satisfying preferences they have independent of the political process. Nor does it rely on any notion of an independent popular will. Instead, it offers a picture of the democratic process as one in which men and women engage in constructive discussion, seeking a principled resolution of their differences and developing, over time, a conception of the terms on which they will live with one another.

As promising as this idea may seem, however, I believe that it fails to deliver some of what proponents of democracy might hope for. To take one example, on which I will focus a good deal of attention, many democrats have stressed the distinctness and intrinsic attractiveness of the democratic vision, portraying it as fundamentally at odds with a liberalism that seems to stress individual rights against the state, sharply limiting the power of even democratically elected governments. According to these democrats, democratic practice and institutions are valuable in their own right and ought to supersede liberal values when the two conflict. These theorists seem to admire majoritarian institutions and a sometimes messy politics of bargaining and compromise, carried on in legislatures whose power has not been undermined by courts, or other loci of power designed to constrain majorities.

I will survey a bit of this literature in the next section. I will subsequently argue, first, that the democratic ideal as conceived by some

* I thank David Phillips and George Sher for discussing these issues with me and Phillips for commenting on early drafts. I also thank the editors of this volume for their comments on the later versions.

181

theorists of deliberative democracy has come very nearly to coincide with a major strand in contemporary liberal thought. Moreover, despite the quite practical preoccupations of some deliberative democrats, the theory of deliberative democracy, like much contemporary liberal thought, has become quite abstract. Second, as the theory has become more abstract and idealized, its implications for issues of constitutional or institutional design have become less easy to discern. More specifically, the ideal of deliberative democracy does not tell us much about whether, or why, we ought to adopt and respect conventionally democratic institutions;[1] and neither does it offer much support to those democratic theorists who defend more or less majoritarian institutions while strongly opposing the (liberal?) countermajoritarian features of the United States Constitution.

II. Democracy and Liberal Political Thought

A number of contemporary writers,[2] styling themselves as defenders of democracy and democratic rights, have in recent years reacted against what they see as antidemocratic tendencies in political philosophy generally and liberal philosophy in particular. Benjamin Barber, in *The Conquest of Politics*, sees philosophers (and he speaks especially of "liberal" philosophers) as suffering from "the seductions of foundationalism," seeking "to ground politics in something less contingent and less corrigible than politics itself tends to be." Philosophers, as he views them, think they have the truth about what we ought to do, and they assail democratic thinkers like Richard Rorty, Michael Walzer, and Barber himself for "their vulnerability to relativism and subjectivism."[3]

"Progressives [liberals] may emphasize the civil rights of minorities while neoconservatives stress the economic rights of individuals or corporations, but they will concur in opposing the right of the public to try to discover and legislate a common weal," says Barber. "The primary political target of foundationalism is in fact democracy itself. . . ."[4]

Michael Walzer, in his essay "Philosophy and Democracy," similarly criticizes philosophers for a kind of antidemocratic authoritarianism. "The claim of the philosopher . . . is that he knows 'the pattern set up in the

---

[1] It is obviously a matter of controversy which actual institutions, if any, deserve the name "democratic." Thus, one can question whether a particular democratic theory supports what some call democratic institutions. When I want to be neutral about the theoretical credentials of putative democracies, I will speak of conventional democracies or of majoritarian systems or institutions.

[2] See, e.g., Benjamin Barber, *The Conquest of Politics* (Princeton: Princeton University Press, 1988), and Barber's earlier work, *Strong Democracy: Participatory Politics for a New Age* (Berkeley: University of California Press, 1984); see also Michael Walzer, "Philosophy and Democracy," *Political Theory* 9, no. 3 (August 1981): 379–99.

[3] Barber, *The Conquest of Politics*, 5–7, 18.

[4] Ibid., 7.

heavens.' He knows what ought to be done." But this puts him in conflict with the "temporary, shifting and unstable" majorities in real democracies. "Truth is one, but the people have many opinions; truth is eternal, but the people continually change their minds."[5] Yet it is the people, however fickle, who Walzer thinks ought to rule.

The claim of the people to rule, Walzer says, does not rest upon "their knowledge of the truth." It is best put "not in terms of what the people know but in terms of who they are. They are the subjects of the law, and if the law is to bind them as free men and women, they must also be its makers." The people "may not know the right thing to do, but they claim a right to do what they think is right." "[I]t is a feature of democratic government that the people have a right to act wrongly."[6]

When Barber objects to a particular philosopher, as he does in an essay on Rawls, he emphasizes his abstractness and sees him as out of touch with reality. Thus, Barber objects to Rawls's saying that intensity of desire is irrelevant to claims of justice when we know that, in the practice of politics, we must be concerned with intensity both because of its implications for stability and because intensity can be a sign of legitimate grievances. He also thinks Rawls far more sanguine than the evidence of history warrants about the likelihood that, for example, the intolerant will become more tolerant under a free and just regime.[7] In general, Barber seems to be impressed by the messiness of real democratic politics, by the need for compromise and the need to take small steps in the right general direction even as we acknowledge that we will never arrive at any philosophically ideal point. Indeed, he thinks it a mark of any real *"political"* theory "that it eschews the consolation of abstract consensus, the single moment of hypothetical consent, in favor of the realities of conflict and community."[8] Philosophers like Rawls are too quick to reject the best available *democratic* solutions to real-world problems in favor of an unrealistic and impractical ideal.

Though Walzer also comments on the abstract and disengaged character of the philosopher ("he cannot be a participant in the rough and tumble politics of the city . . . he has little taste for bargaining and mutual accommodation"),[9] he is concerned mostly to assert a normative claim about the right of the people to govern themselves. That the people have the right to rule means that, even if the philosopher's political principles are correct, it may be wrong to impose them on society. "[I]t is not at all obvious that a policy's rightness is the right reason for implementing it."[10] One can have the right principles, but not have a right to legislate

---

[5] Walzer, "Philosophy and Democracy," 383.
[6] Ibid., 383, 385.
[7] Barber, *The Conquest of Politics*, 78–80.
[8] Ibid., 90.
[9] Walzer, "Philosophy and Democracy," 381.
[10] Ibid., 386.

them; and one can have the right to legislate, but exercise it wrongly.[11] Only the people can legislate legitimately, even if they fail to get it right.

This attack on political philosophers, it must be said, is not entirely fair. For one thing, if philosophers are to be condemned for trying to work out conceptions of justice or other social ideals, then so also are citizens to be condemned if they think for themselves and vote their own principles. If citizens have a right to offer and vote for their principles in a democracy, then so do philosophers. Philosophers who formulate and defend principles do not necessarily claim some special authority to implement them. As much as Walzer may relish the rough and tumble of real politics, he presumably has a conception at least of better and worse outcomes and would contrive to implement the better ones by whatever means the political process affords.

Walzer, in fact, concedes this point, recognizing that philosophers are, in part, just relatively articulate, book-writing contributors to democratic debate.[12] But he also perceives a tendency, especially among philosophical liberals and the judiciary, to bypass the legislature and seek to implement their policies through the courts. It is here that his criticism acquires substantive bite and coincides with the attacks on the "activist" Supreme Court in the U.S. found also in more conservative writers like Robert Bork and John Hart Ely.[13] Perhaps some of us admire the Court's decisions expanding, for example, rights of personal privacy. But Walzer would reply that it is at least not a sufficient defense of those decisions to show how the rights they uphold can be derived from fundamental, liberal principles of justice. For, even if the principles can be given a strong, philosophical defense, it does not follow that the Court has any right to implement them. Maybe only the people have that right.

That is what Walzer believes, of course, as does Barber. They object to institutional arrangements (like some forms of judicial review) that limit the right of the people to rule. Moreover, though they do not explicitly discuss the obligations of citizens to obey, as distinct from their right to rule, they may also hold, as a matter of individual morality, that the democratic ideal requires of each of us a kind of deference to majoritarian procedures, and that, even when we have the opportunity, we must refrain from trying to circumvent the political process. We must note, though, that a belief in the people's right to rule is a moral belief on the same level as the liberal philosopher's belief in rights to privacy or the libertarian's belief in a minimal state. The alleged right of the people to rule—not to mention any particular institutionalization of this right, such as a system

---

[11] Cf. Jeremy Waldron, "A Right to Do Wrong," *Ethics* 92, no. 1 (October 1981): 21–39.

[12] Walzer, "Philosophy and Democracy," 389.

[13] See John Hart Ely, *Democracy and Distrust* (Cambridge, MA: Harvard University Press, 1980); and Robert Bork, "Neutral Principles and Some First Amendment Problems," *Indiana Law Journal* 47, no. 1 (Fall 1971): 1–35. See also Bork, *The Tempting of America* (New York: The Free Press, 1990).

of representation—thus demands a justification. This is especially so if, as Walzer concedes, it is a right that is sometimes exercised wrongly or foolishly. What, then, is the argument for this right?

It is a central feature of Western political thought, since the seventeenth century, that legitimate authority derives from the people; but this idea is not sufficiently precise to settle the question of how to assign the day-to-day authority to make decisions. My question, in the next sections, is whether the theory of deliberative democracy incorporates an attractive account of the democratic ideal that is also sufficiently specific to provide support for the institutionalized democratic rights Walzer and Barber favor. I go on to ask whether the ideal of deliberative democracy differs sufficiently enough from the ideal underlying contemporary liberalism to support the widespread belief that the two must have fundamentally conflicting institutional implications.

III. Deliberative Democracy

A number of authors have come to use the term "deliberative democracy" in recent years, but while they draw specific implications from the idea, they often fail to offer any general account. An exception is Joshua Cohen, and I will use as my texts here a couple of his essays as well as recent work by Amy Gutmann and Dennis Thompson. Their specific aims are somewhat different from Cohen's, but what they say is compatible with Cohen's more theoretical ideas. All three see democracy as a distinctively legitimate way of organizing social and political relationships.

I start with Cohen.[14] He views democracy as a "fundamental political ideal," in the same way in which, for Rawls, the notion of a "fair system of social cooperation" is a fundamental ideal. Viewing democracy as a fundamental ideal, Cohen does not seek an *independent* justification but, rather, offers deliberative democracy as an interpretation of this ideal which brings out the features that make it attractive. These features are "elements of an independent and expressly political ideal," not something merely contingently valued, as liberty is contingently valued within utilitarian theory.[15] If Cohen succeeds, then, his account might be expected to provide the kind of theoretical underpinning on which democrats like Walzer might call to defend their conventionally democratic predilections.

In explaining the ideal of deliberative democracy, Cohen proceeds by describing what he calls "an ideal legislative procedure": Participants in such a procedure regard themselves as bound only by their own deci-

---

[14] Joshua Cohen, "Deliberation and Democratic Legitimacy," in *The Good Polity*, ed. Alan Hamlin and Philip Pettit (Oxford: Blackwell, 1989), 17–34; and Cohen, "Procedure and Substance in Deliberative Democracy," in *Democracy and Difference*, ed. Seyla Benhabib (Princeton: Princeton University Press, 1996), 95–119.

[15] Cohen, "Deliberation and Democratic Legitimacy," 17, 20.

sions, "not constrained by the authority of prior norms or requirements." But the decisions which are to bind them result from deliberation in which parties advance reasons for their proposals and take one another's reasons seriously. Ideal deliberators are motivated to achieve a consensus which all can find acceptable.[16]

Gutmann and Thompson are clearly more concerned with "real-world" politics, and they do offer what they seem to regard as an independent defense of deliberative practices. "Political decisions," they say, "are collectively binding, and they should therefore be justifiable, as far as possible, to everyone bound by them."[17] Deliberative practices are supposed to serve this end. Gutmann and Thompson may have in mind two different arguments for this conclusion. *In part*, they seem to think that policies adopted in a deliberative democracy are justifiable to everyone *just because* they result from a deliberative process.[18] Policies arrived at deliberatively are automatically justifiable. But this seems most plausible if one has in mind not the actual operation of any actual democracy but, instead, the deliberation of ideally reasonable agents in the sort of ideal procedure which Cohen describes. Gutmann and Thompson also think, however, that policies can be more or less justifiable independent of the process that produced them;[19] and they seem to believe that real-world institutions, operating in a deliberative fashion, are more likely than others to uncover and institute these independently justifiable outcomes. Deliberation, characterized by norms of reciprocity, accountability, and publicity, is then justified instrumentally as an effective method for arriving at justifiable policies.

Gutmann and Thompson's defense of deliberation hovers, it seems to me, somewhat unsteadily, between these two alternatives. What they, and Cohen, clearly do accept, though, is the idea that issues of policy ought ideally to be resolved by reasoned discussion among members of society or their representatives. Discussion should aim not just at policies that can gain a bare majority, but at policies on which there can be a consensus. Just what kind of consensus they require is not clear. At one point Cohen speaks of finding "reasons that are persuasive to all."[20] And that would suggest that we aim at finding a single system of principles everyone can accept. An alternative would be that we seek policies which each member of society can find adequate reason to accept—even if different persons

---

[16] Ibid., 21–23.

[17] Amy Gutmann and Dennis Thompson, *Democracy and Disagreement* (Cambridge, MA: Harvard University Press, 1996), 13, 39, 50.

[18] Ibid., 4, 41.

[19] Ibid., 4, 43.

[20] Cohen, "Deliberation and Democratic Legitimacy," 23. I take the idea to be implicit in Gutmann and Thompson's ideals of "reciprocity" and "accountability"—the former requiring that we seek "mutually acceptable" resolutions of conflicts, and the latter that we be prepared to account for our decisions to everyone. See Gutmann and Thompson, *Democracy and Disagreement*.

have different reasons. The former may be an unreasonably strong requirement, and one which I think all three authors would reject on reflection. For all emphasize that the democratic societies they envision will be marked by considerable moral disagreement—what Cohen refers to as "reasonable pluralism."[21]

In addition to the idea that policymakers should reason with one another and try to resolve disagreements in mutually acceptable ways, Cohen also insists, as noted above, that deliberation should not be "constrained by the authority of prior norms or requirements." The reason, I suspect, is that, otherwise, deliberative democracy would not genuinely constitute a form of *self*-government. For suppose deliberation is constrained by a prior requirement. In that case, we are governed by that requirement regardless of whether we can agree that it is supported by adequate reasons. And Cohen's idea of democratic legitimacy is an idea of self-government in the sense of government in accord with "a free and reasoned agreement among equals." In a recent essay,[22] however, he argues that acceptance of the democratic ideal actually entails accepting certain substantive constraints on outcomes. There seems to be a change in his view, then, though he might well say that the substantive constraints are not *prior* constraints, for they are justified within the democratic perspective. He seems to think that, if we can see in advance that no reason could justify imposing a policy on certain persons, then that policy is ruled out on grounds internal to the idea of democracy. The people remain the final source of authority.

Gutmann and Thompson also accept the idea of substantive constraints on deliberation. In their view, we should not "make deliberation the sovereign guide to resolving moral disagreement in politics." They claim that, in addition to what we might call the "formal" requirements of reciprocity, publicity, and accountability, democratic deliberation ought also to be constrained by "constitutional" requirements of liberty and opportunity. They do not mean that these requirements should be enforced by independent courts. Instead, since the requirements are not determinate, the deliberative ideal requires that they be interpreted and applied only democratically—in light of reasons presented and defended publicly, to everyone. Nevertheless, they do not regard citizens as free to disregard these requirements.[23]

Gutmann and Thompson do not adequately explain why we ought to accept these constitutional constraints. At one point in their book *Democracy and Disagreement*, they say that deliberative democracy "needs" principles determining the "content" of deliberation. At a much earlier point they say that, without such principles, democracy will not "protect basic

---

[21] Cohen, "Procedure and Substance in Deliberative Democracy," 96.
[22] Ibid., 103f.
[23] Gutmann and Thompson, *Democracy and Disagreement*, 17, 199–229.

rights."[24] Perhaps they too think we "need" these principles because policies that do not protect "basic rights" will never be justifiable to everyone, and thus, regardless of the process by which they are adopted, they could not be legitimate. But they do not, to my knowledge, make this argument explicitly. In any case, while they insist on principles of liberty and opportunity, they reject the idea that these ought to be interpreted and enforced by the courts. One of their consistent themes is that, even when we have reason to accept principles or ideals independent of the political process, their application to particular cases is bound to require interpretation, and this is best left to democratic deliberation.[25]

Among defenders of deliberative democracy, then, there seems to be a broad agreement on the value of self-government, relatively unconstrained by further norms, and understood in terms of a process in which reasonable persons attempt to solve political problems and resolve disagreements in ways that are justifiable to each. There is some question in my mind, though, as to just how this idea is supposed to function in moral and political thought about institutions. How much can the theory of deliberative democracy tell us about which actual institutions are justified, whether *their* outcomes are legitimate, and whether we should comply with them? What feature of the theory tells us that constitutional constraints operate best as "self-constraints" rather than as constraints to be enforced primarily by independent courts?

I have tried to indicate that the theory can be understood at more than one level. At its most abstract, as in Cohen's ideal deliberative procedure or his even more abstract "formal conception" of deliberative democracy, the deliberative ideal seems to be something like a metaethical characterization of the idea of legitimacy, just as, say, T. M. Scanlon's contractualism[26] is a metaethical characterization of the idea of moral rightness. At the other extreme, Gutmann and Thompson may view it primarily as a set of specific injunctions concerning how men and women ought to exercise their rights as voters, legislators, and so forth.

However, to begin with, one could consistently accept the theory at one of these levels without accepting it at the other. Moreover, each seems compatible with a variety of ideas about the actual structure of institutions. Though Cohen views the ideal deliberative procedure as inherently attractive, and also asserts that institutions should, so far as possible, "mirror" this procedure, these two claims are also logically independent. Perhaps the institutions that most resemble the ideal procedure will func-

---

[24] Ibid., 200, 17.

[25] Ibid., 35–37.

[26] T. M. Scanlon, "Contractualism and Utilitarianism," in *Utilitarianism and Beyond*, ed. Amartya K. Sen and Bernard Williams (New York: Cambridge University Press, 1982), 103–28. Scanlon takes the idea of contractual agreement, widely invoked in political thought, as part of a basic definition of moral rightness which he contrasts with the utilitarian conception of rightness as maximization of the good. Scanlon defines moral rightness in terms of principles which "no one can reasonably reject."

tion less like this procedure than will other procedures. In some situations, for example, we may do better to invest decision-making authority in a few persons, subject to public scrutiny, rather than to require widespread participation in all decisions. The decisions these persons make may more nearly approximate an ideal deliberative consensus.[27] But if that is right, then the deliberative ideal does not offer much direct support to those who insist on majoritarian procedures and who claim that institutions like judicial review are inherently undemocratic.

IV. LIBERALISM

I turn now to the question of whether contemporary liberal theory gives rise to a serious criticism of deliberative democracy and whether it supports institutional prescriptions seriously at odds with those commonly favored by democratic theorists. I begin with Charles Larmore's useful characterization of liberalism in terms of the kind of problem to which it seeks to respond. The problem is posed by one of the basic facts of "modernity": "that reasonable persons tend naturally to differ and disagree about the nature of the good life."[28] John Rawls, in *Political Liberalism*, proposes a similar account of the defining task of liberalism, though in place of the sometimes misleading phrase "the good life," Rawls speaks of differing and incompatible "religious, philosophical and moral doctrines."[29] This issue of moral conflict and the theoretical understanding of how to respond to it is also central to Thomas Nagel's concerns in his essay "Moral Conflict and Political Legitimacy."[30]

Having characterized liberalism as a response to the problem set by deep disagreement, Larmore, Rawls, and Nagel all describe this response as a requirement, roughly, that the basic institutions of the state must be defensible in terms that are suitably neutral[31] among the conflicting but not unreasonable doctrines held by citizens.

Liberalism, then, is partially a doctrine about limits on the power of the state, but this point has to be put carefully. It need not mean, for example, that the state should do few things, but only that it refrain from doing certain kinds of things—things that cannot be justified, in appropriate

---

[27] See the references in notes 46 and 49 below.

[28] Charles Larmore, *The Morals of Modernity* (New York: Cambridge University Press, 1996), 122.

[29] John Rawls, *Political Liberalism* (New York: Columbia University Press, 1993), xviii.

[30] Thomas Nagel, "Moral Conflict and Political Legitimacy," *Philosophy and Public Affairs* 16, no. 3 (Summer 1987): 215–40.

[31] For a thoughtful critique of this idea, see George Sher, *Beyond Neutrality* (New York: Cambridge University Press, 1997). In my view, Sher makes a better case for the view that liberal premises do not entail neutrality than for the view that we ought to abandon those premises. I might add that Nagel does not, I think, use the term "neutral," though he certainly does accept the idea that state power should be used only in ways that can be justified appropriately even to citizens who otherwise differ radically.

ways, to everyone. Moreover, even the ideal of neutrality is not applied uniformly at all levels of government. In at least some liberal theories, a strong requirement of neutrality applies to issues of constitutional
design—constitutional arrangements must be justifiable, so far as possible, without reference to particular, controversial moral or philosophical
conceptions—but this requirement does not necessarily apply to proposals that might be put forward and adopted in a democratic legislature.[32]

Liberals need to offer an account of just why the requirements of neutrality apply differently in different areas of governmental activity, but I
will leave that issue to one side. I first want to address the question of *why*
the fact of moral, religious, and philosophical disagreement poses a problem that calls for the kind of solution liberals offer. The answer is that it
poses a problem if we also assume that coercive social institutions must
be justifiable *to everyone*, in terms that all can accept without completely
abandoning what is distinctive about their individual points of view.
Finding arguments that are acceptable to each, against the background of
deep disagreement, is the task that liberalism purports to solve.

Liberalism begins, then, with the idea that institutions must be, in some
sense, justifiable to everyone.[33] But this is strikingly similar to the idea
that underlies some theories of deliberative democracy. Gutmann and
Thompson, as already noted, seek "[p]olitical decisions . . . [that are] justifiable . . . to everyone bound by them." And Cohen says that "outcomes
are democratically legitimate if and only if they could be the object of a
free and reasoned agreement among equals."[34] Democrats want citizens
to advance reasons for their policies that everyone can accept, and liberals
advocate neutral reasons just because neutral reasons stand a chance of
being accepted by persons who otherwise disagree. But both share the
conviction of much modern moral and political thought that the ultimate
standard of the right and the legitimate is what men and women can
accept or agree to. Insofar as liberals and democrats differ, their differences evidently do not lie in their deepest aspirations. Do their theories
otherwise commit them to conflicting ideas about the design of political
institutions?

Liberal theorists differ among themselves in the extent to which they
advocate particular institutions or policies. However, some certainly do
make concrete proposals regarding matters of constitutional design and
even economic policy; and it is partly this tendency to prescribe policy
solutions in advance, as it were, that draws the ire of theorists like Barber
and Walzer. These theorists would presumably be content simply to describe the process that we ought to follow in legislating and then await

---

[32] Larmore, *The Morals of Modernity*, 125; Nagel, "Moral Conflict and Political Legitimacy,"
238–39; Rawls, *Political Liberalism*, 214–15.

[33] Nagel, "Moral Conflict and Political Legitimacy," 218; Larmore, *The Morals of Modernity*,
136f., 141; Rawls, *Political Liberalism*, 137, 217.

[34] Cohen, "Deliberation and Democratic Legitimacy," 22.

the results. In current versions of liberal and democratic theory, however, this contrast is far less sharp. In the first place, the substantive principles liberals offer—"equal liberties," "fair equality of opportunity"—are extremely abstract. They seem, as Gutmann and Thompson would certainly agree, hardly more than vague guides to the difficult task of constructing actual policies and institutions.[35] Secondly, contemporary democratic theorists do propose substantive principles: Cohen defends freedom of religion, as does Nagel; and Gutmann and Thompson defend equality of opportunity, as does Rawls.

In *Democracy and Disagreement*, Gutmann and Thompson criticize "constitutional democracy" (Rawls's theory is their main example) for "the priority it gives to principles of justice over processes of deliberation."[36] Of course, they themselves think that democratic deliberation ought to be governed by principles of liberty and opportunity; but what they presumably object to is the idea that these principles ought to be interpreted and applied not by deliberative legislatures but by the courts. That the courts ought to have this power, however, though perhaps widely believed, seems to be something that is not dictated by the fundamental assumptions of liberal thought, any more than it is ruled out by the fundamental premises of deliberative democracy.

V. CONTRACTUALISM AND RIGHTS

To what extent, I have been asking, does the theory of deliberative democracy support the practical and institutional judgments commonly associated with belief in democracy? And to what extent does it rule out ostensibly nondemocratic practices and institutions sometimes associated with liberalism? The answers I have so far suggested have been negative: the rather abstract idea of a deliberative community might, for all we know, be realized to some degree in a great variety of different institutional structures—and perhaps not very well in any.

I do not say this because I reject conventional democratic institutions. I don't. But it seems to me a difficult matter to say why we ought to establish these institutions, work within them, and accept their decisions as legitimate. The theory of deliberative democracy says that government is legitimate when the people govern themselves, meaning that they are governed, as much as possible, in accordance with a consensus achieved by reasonable discussion. As I have noted, however, this does not entail that actual institutions must be conventionally democratic; nor does it

---

[35] Gutmann and Thompson, *Democracy and Disagreement*, ch. 9. It is too seldom remarked how little Rawls actually says about the content of equal opportunity in the one section of *A Theory of Justice* actually devoted to this topic. See John Rawls, *A Theory of Justice* (Cambridge, MA: Harvard University Press, 1971), 83–90. See also William Nelson, "Equal Opportunity," *Social Theory and Practice* 10, no. 2 (Summer 1984): 157–84.

[36] Gutmann and Thompson, *Democracy and Disagreement*, 39.

entail that whatever rights to govern people do have ought to have the force of rights. For example, even if it is thought that majoritarian procedures tend to legislate in accordance with the deliberative ideal, that ideal does not seem to entail that majority decisions ought to be respected. For *particular* decisions may not reflect a reasonable consensus, even if many do.

If belief in democracy is belief in a certain system of rights—if it is the belief, as Walzer puts it, that the people have the right to rule, even if they exercise it badly—then how might those rights be vindicated? The problem of rights is a problem of general interest in moral and political philosophy.[37] To establish majoritarian institutions, or, for that matter, a judicial system, is to establish a system of authority. It is to put the power to make certain decisions in the hands of some and, thereby, to take it out of the hands of others. That is what political rights do. It is for that matter what *all* rights do, from rights of property to rights of the person. The question of how we justify a system of political authority is just an instance of the more general question of how we justify any of these rights.

How ought we to think about this problem of justification? For one thing, we need to look at the issue from a more general moral perspective if we are to consider how these rights relate to other moral considerations. But any moral perspective consistent with the liberal and democratic traditions will hold that legitimate constraints must be acceptable to everyone whom they bind. Within these traditions, there is no ultimate authority beyond what reasonable men and women can justify to one another. Thus, I will try to propose a way to think about rights, and institutions more generally, within a broadly contractualist perspective. In the next section, I consider to what extent the ideas of deliberative democracy significantly affect the specific conclusions we ought to draw about issues of institutional design.

Not all of morality involves rights. A large portion takes as basic the perspective of the choosing agent. It imagines an agent confronted with a choice (or someone giving advice to such an agent) and tries to say something about how the agent should decide what to do. It may, for example, specify certain features of options that make them wrong, or it might merely offer an account of how to rank alternatives on a scale of desirability. In contractualist moral theory—I follow Scanlon[38] here— these moral rules about how to behave, to the extent that there are any, must be justifiable to anyone in the sense that the principles from which they derive must be principles "no one can reasonably reject."

Now much of morality, many think, tells agents to achieve goals, work for ideals, or prevent evils. To the extent that we think this, rights have

---

[37] See, for example, Samuel Scheffler, *The Rejection of Consequentialism* (New York: Oxford University Press, 1994), ch. 4 and appendix 1.

[38] Scanlon, "Contractualism and Utilitarianism."

often seemed problematic. Constitutional rights of free speech or privacy, property rights, democratic political rights, and even personal rights not to be harmed in certain ways can all, at times, stand in the way of our doing what otherwise seems desirable. Why, then, do we recognize rights and think we ought to take them seriously?

I offer a conjecture in the form of an account of the distinctive role rights play in both moral and legal thought. Rights are less directly concerned with *how* agents should decide what to do than with *who* can properly make what decisions in the first place.[39] This helps to explain, of course, why rights occupy such a prominent position in political and legal thought. For, in political society, we need to know which decisions are authoritative and we need to know who is to be held accountable for what decisions. That means it has to be clear who has, or lacks, the authority to make what decisions. One of the reasons for having a government at all, indeed, is just to establish definite answers to questions like these.[40]

But there are also rights in morality. Morality includes requirements and ideals of various kinds. Moral rights belong to an aspect of morality that is more like law than other parts. But why does morality include rights at all? Roughly—assuming a contractualist perspective here—I believe there are significant areas of moral concern within which it is difficult to specify any very definite account of what agents should do that cannot be reasonably rejected by some. This is partly because of conflicts of interest among agents and partly because of reasonable pluralism— permissible differences in values and conceptions of the good. The latter is especially significant, of course, in the case of political principles. Faced with conflicts of both kinds and with the difficulty of resolving them directly, morality itself looks for a quasi-political solution. It shifts its attention from the question of how (any) agent must decide a certain issue to the question of *whose* decision it is. This is what rights are all about. And it is my conjecture that, even when we cannot find nonrejectable substantive principles, we can find nonrejectable answers to the question of who should have authority to decide what questions.

But why should this much agreement be possible? One reason is that the decision about rights does not finally determine what will be done. There remains the possibility of discussion, persuasion, and bargaining.

---

[39] This, again, is the way Walzer sees democratic rights; and I also think that, at an abstract level, what Cohen wants to insist on is that the people should govern themselves. More generally, rights arise, as Hart once suggested, in the portion of morality that is especially concerned with the distribution of human freedom. H. L. A. Hart, "Are There Any Natural Rights?" *Philosophical Review* 64 (1955): 178. I should add that, while my point is that those with rights, unlike others, are properly in a position to make certain decisions, Hart's point is that those with rights are properly in a position to determine what others may or must do.

[40] It is one of the marks of a (mature) legal system that it has rules giving such answers. See H. L. A. Hart, *The Concept of Law* (Oxford: Oxford University Press, 1961), 89–96.

For we can exercise our rights in many ways, and others can have good reason to try to get us to exercise them in one way or another—in some cases even to waive or transfer them to someone else.

Of course, believing in rights is *partly* nothing but believing in certain prohibitions; thus, justifying them requires justifying these prohibitions. We specify who is to make which decisions partly[41] by prohibiting certain actions—by prohibiting the seizure of property, for example, or some instances of coercion. However, we explain prohibitions differently when we say, for example, that a certain decision is this person's to make, as opposed to when we say, in other cases, that one should refrain from an action because it harms. How should we decide, though, who should be empowered to make what decisions subject to what conditions? The most general answer, within contractualist morality, is that principles determining decision-making authority must, like any others, be acceptable to everyone. This I take to be an assumption shared by both deliberative democrats and liberals. But what determines the acceptability or rejectability of such principles?

I see little reason to believe that there is one, uniquely acceptable division of decision-making authority; and it seems highly likely that changes in one part of a system will require changes in another, so that systems will have to be evaluated holistically rather than piecemeal. Moreover, I suspect that justification will be subject to general constraints, analogous to Rawlsian "principles for institutions," such as principles of liberty or opportunity.[42] (Of course, there will also have to be an argument for one or another system of rights for enforcing such constraints.) In what follows, I will try to give examples of the kinds of considerations that are relevant.

1. In general, rights will tend to be justifiable insofar as they enable persons to protect their various interests and values and to achieve their goals. It is important, however, to resist an overly simple picture of how this will work. For one thing, when interests conflict, it may be that no assignment of rights will be able to protect all interests; and any given assignment will tend to favor the interests of one party or the other. (Though it will not *determine* whose interests prevail.) More interestingly, it is a mistake to assume that we advance a person's goals only, or even mainly, by granting rights to that person. Freedom of expression is a case in point. Any one of us probably benefits more from others' having this right than we do from having it ourselves. Arguably, these rights serve primarily the interests of audiences and of the community at large, not just the interests of those who exercise them.

While protecting interests is important, it must be stressed, again, that interests and values conflict. In a society marked by reasonable pluralism,

---

[41] I say "partly" because moral and legal rights are not limited to "claim rights," definable in terms of the obligations of others, but include powers and immunities as well.

[42] See Rawls, *A Theory of Justice*.

it will not in general be possible to justify rights instrumentally by reference to *shared* ends or values. It is true, and worth noting, that, while rights are constraints that enable us to advance our own ends while preventing us from imposing our views on others, they also do not preclude our working to discover commonalities and to develop new ones. Indeed, they can foster this. Still, we must expect profound differences to persist. Given such differences and given the controlling aim of finding institutions justifiable to each, that a system is fair and mutually acceptable is itself an important consideration in its favor.[43]

2. Rights determine a framework within which discussion and negotiation can continue. They make it clear whom we have to persuade or negotiate with, but they postpone the final decision and allow for the possibility of different responses to different situations. This is one of the reasons why we might expect agreement on rights or procedures, even when more substantive agreement escapes us. It also has a couple of corollaries:

2a. We do best to put decision-making authority in the hands of those who will use it in ways that are useful to people generally, or at least are not contrary to their interests. This might depend on who is best positioned, for example, to have the information needed to exercise rights wisely, or it might depend on the motives and attitudes of potential decision makers. After all, any system of rights increases the decision-making power of some while diminishing the power of others. It is natural for those who have less authority to be concerned about what those who have more might do. To take one example, arguments in support of property rights would be considerably weakened if we could not expect owners of capital to seek profits and so invest their capital in productive ways. More to the present point, whether we are willing to establish a system of rights to legislate may well depend on whether we expect those with the rights to be willing to engage actively in discussion with other legislators, and with the populace at large, and whether we expect them to be willing to change their votes in appropriate circumstances as a result. (As a further point, if a system of rights is already in place, anyone who has an interest in the quality of outcomes also has a reason to advocate that persons exercise rights in appropriate ways.)[44]

---

[43] What I say here represents at least a change in emphasis from what I have sometimes said in earlier work. Previously, I have argued against the idea that the intrinsic fairness of procedures justifies them; and I emphasized, instead, the idea that (conventionally) democratic procedures are more likely than others to yield justifiable outcomes. But in the absence of consensus or a serious prospect thereof, I now think that a fair (but not necessarily *equal*) distribution of authority is more important, and I also emphasize that a variety of systems of authority that are fair overall, may contribute in different ways to justifiable outcomes. See William Nelson, *On Justifying Democracy* (London: Routledge and Kegan Paul, 1980).

[44] I suspect that Gutmann and Thompson are little interested in questions about how political rights ought to be assigned in the first place, but more interested in giving an account of how the rights we have should be exercised.

2b. Whether a particular specification of rights can be justified will also depend on the availability of opportunities for those who do not hold the rights to try to influence how they are exercised. If the point of rights is partly to postpone resolving issues in advance, in cases in which many people have a stake in the outcome, this point will be well-served only if the relevant parties have a chance to be heard when a decision must be made. Further rights, like rights of free speech, can play a role here, but so can the removal of economic and social barriers, as well as the cultivation of appropriate attitudes.

3. Rights do not determine outcomes, but they certainly help determine the strategies available to those who are interested in outcomes. Whether it is even in one's own interest to have a certain right can depend on how others are likely to react to your having that right. Anyone who has ever been pressured with an unreasonable request can understand how it can be an advantage to lack the authority to do what is requested. (And, if I lack the authority to do what you want, then not only am I free from unreasonable pressure, but you have an incentive to find a way to solve your own problem. Analogously, then, a good system of rights should reduce "moral hazard" problems, such as the incentives to engage in risky behavior engendered by systems of rights that guarantee compensation for losses.) Russell Hardin has offered a related argument for the inalienability of certain rights: it frees us from the threat of coercive offers.[45] More generally, if we suspect that we will find it difficult to resist temptations, that can be a ground for precommitment strategies; and one form of precommitment is simply to avoid having the right to succumb to the temptation. Constitutional limits on legislative authority can be viewed as precommitment strategies of this sort.[46]

These remarks are incomplete. They are intended simply to illustrate the kinds of argument for or against concrete rights that make sense within a contractualist perspective. For the question about a system of rights, from that perspective, is whether it can be accepted by everyone; and considerations like these are relevant to a system's acceptability.

There are a couple of further points to note in concluding this section. First, rights, as I conceive them, function primarily to determine who gets to make what decisions subject to what conditions. This is true of prototypical democratic rights, but it is also true of prototypical liberal rights. They establish a framework within which men and women make decisions—seeking and receiving advice, discussing the options, making requests, persuading, bargaining, and compromising.

Second, the kind of argument I propose clearly contains consequentialist elements. For example, I see it as an argument against a right if it

---

[45] Russell Hardin, *Morality within the Limits of Reason* (Chicago: University of Chicago Press, 1988), 92f.

[46] Samuel Freeman, "Constitutional Democracy and the Legitimacy of Judicial Review," *Law and Philosophy* 9 (1990): 36.

encourages harmful or destructive behavior, and as an argument for a right that the right may well be used in helpful ways. Surely, however, the rights in a system that we would find acceptable, on the basis of arguments like this, will sometimes be used to what some will see as bad purposes and will stand in the way of what some will see as desirable courses of action. Still, if this is a good way of thinking about rights, then the fact that a system of rights tends to promote what we agree are goods, tends to prevent what we agree are problems, and constitutes a fair and mutually justifiable distribution of control over decisions must be enough to justify the rights—even if, in particular cases, the exercise of the rights has bad consequences. For the rights themselves are seen as the object of agreement.

Finally, while this argument has consequentialist elements, it is not a straightforward utilitarian argument; for it does not begin by specifying an independent account of an obligatory end to be attained. That a right stands in the way of attaining some end in a particular situation, therefore, does not necessarily argue against the right itself or against respect for it. While rights must be justifiable to each member of society, and while this will surely depend partly on the various ends that one or another person deems worthy of attainment, different people may have different ends in mind and may not agree on what these should be. The best we can hope for in this situation is a mutually agreeable, and in that sense fair, distribution of decision-making authority.

VI. Political Procedures

I have sketched, in general terms, an account of the function of rights and a corresponding account of how particular assignments of rights might be evaluated. How does this apply to the case of political procedures? What does the theory of deliberative democracy add to the story?

Cohen offers an abstract ideal of a self-governing community of reasonable persons, living under mutually agreeable terms of cooperation. Perhaps with an ideal like this in mind, Gutmann and Thompson put forward a detailed and nuanced account of what reasonable political deliberation might look like, and they apply it to real political issues. But none of this tells us what actual rights individuals and groups should have, or what the structure of political institutions should be like.

In general, I have claimed, a plausible argument for rights would involve a showing that a certain system of rights would be generally acceptable and not reasonably rejectable by those who must live under it. To argue for this, we would argue that the system of rights constitutes a fair distribution of control over decisions, that it protects or promotes important interests, that rightholders can be expected to exercise their rights in acceptable ways, that their having those rights does not create temptations to bad behavior on their own part or on the part of others, and so on. Accepting a system of rights, though, certainly does not rule out further claims as to how the rights ought to be exercised. Indeed, I am inclined to accept the *ideal* of political behavior that we find in the theory of deliberative democracy. It seems to me plausible that policy outcomes arrived at on the basis of full discussion of alternatives and agreed to by reasonable persons would be justifiable in the sense required by contractualism and would be, in various ways, better than those arrived at without adequate deliberation. It does not follow, however, that we ought to institute conventionally democratic institutions. That certain rights would have good consequences if they were exercised a certain way does not justify them if they will not actually be exercised that way.[47] It is hard to say what institutions would come closest to realizing the deliberative ideal in the world as we know it. Institutions that *look* the most "democratic" may not be appropriate at all.[48]

When I say this, I am not just thinking of the (supposed) problem that some kind of "direct" democracy, with popular assemblies, is impossible in modern states. For one thing, some states in the U.S. do employ direct referenda to decide issues, and it has been seriously proposed that we might use television and computer technologies to enable citizens to listen in on legislative debates and to vote on issues directly. But the referenda we already have seem to do nothing to foster genuine deliberation among citizens. Beyond that, even if we lived in small communities and had town meetings, these might fail to promote ideal deliberation.[49] There are many reasons why actual deliberation falls short of the ideal. We do not need to look beyond a meeting of an academic department to see examples. Some people are just unreasonable. They discount the interests of colleagues and students. Rather than making positive proposals, they remain silent, knowing that the proposals they want to make will look too self-serving and that proposals that might be adopted will not work to their advantage. And others, who may have good but unpopular ideas, are simply afraid to take what they expect will be a minority position.

These are obvious problems, and they are not likely to go away. It may well be that an elected legislature, composed of professional lawmakers

[47] Contrariwise, if we knew that persons would be reasonable no matter what, then, in a kind of analogy with Coase's theorem, we might conclude that it would not matter what system of rights we institute. (From the perspective of a concern with economic efficiency, Ronald Coase argues, it does not matter how we assign initial rights to property. However we assign rights, agents will trade until a Pareto-optimal distribution is reached. See Coase, "The Problem of Social Cost," *Journal of Law and Economics* 3 [1960]: 1–44.)

[48] For this reason, I think Cohen's metaphorical idea that institutions should "mirror" the deliberative ideal is misleading.

[49] Cohen, "Deliberation and Democratic Legitimacy," 30–31. See also Jane Mansbridge, *Beyond Adversary Democracy* (Chicago: University of Chicago Press, 1983). In her long discussion of town-meeting democracy (pp. 39–125), Mansbridge details many factors that discourage individual participation—from lack of education to fear of conflict—as well as factors that lead to inequality.

who can hope for a relatively long term in office, and who operate according to majority rule, is more likely to function in a deliberative manner.[50] If legislators expect to work together over a long period of time, it may be to their advantage to take one another's points of view seriously and to seek mutually agreeable solutions. Reforms like term-limits, on the other hand, often thought to be "democratic," may diminish legislators' stake in fostering long-term relationships of cooperation and mutual respect with one another.

A vigorous and secure free press, and an educated electorate, may help legislators and voters to be more aware of different points of view and of the need to accommodate them. A system for financing campaigns that frees legislators from dependence on large donors may enable legislators to be more independent and thus more flexible and willing to seek mutually beneficial compromises. Strong political parties, with greater control over the nomination process and over platforms, might be less beholden to ideologically committed minority groups and better able to focus on building broad consensus.

But all of this is really speculation. Perhaps, for example, Benjamin Barber is right to be skeptical that the intolerant will become more tolerant under conditions of liberty. We do not know. We do know that we cannot have government, democratic or otherwise, without a specification of some system of legislative and judicial rights. Failing a guarantee of reasonableness, however, no system of rights will be able to *guarantee* results consonant with the deliberative ideal as described by theorists like Cohen, and different systems will make different outcomes more likely. Perhaps, as Gutmann and Thompson may intend, we do better to concentrate our efforts on educating legislators and voters about the possibilities of deliberation than on seeking institutional reforms.

On the other hand, we know a lot about the temptations to which voters and legislators are subject. They range from economic self-interest to racial or religious fears and animosities, and from there to imperialistic moralism. We also know a lot about how the logic of electoral systems can combine with sociological conditions to produce results that will be viewed by many as unjustifiable. Districts represented by a single legislator, for example, against a background of racial prejudice and segregation, can help to perpetuate racially unfair practices. Or, to take another example, systems requiring less than unanimous agreement encourage groups to seek excessive benefits for themselves while spreading the costs over the whole population.

---

[50] For another possibility, see Norman Daniels and James Sabin, "Limits to Health Care: Fair Procedures, Democratic Deliberation, and the Legitimacy Problem for Insurers," *Philosophy and Public Affairs* 26, no. 4 (Fall 1997): 325, 339. While the deliberative ideal informs their approach, they do not argue for (conventionally) democratic methods for deciding about the allocation of scarce resources. Instead, they advocate that those responsible for making decisions, in public or private delivery systems, simply make them in public, according to stated principles, and that they seek to be consistent from one case to another.

Since any institutions create risks as well as opportunities, there is no reason not to try to identify the greatest risks and guard against them. That is certainly one conception of the function of a judicially enforced bill of rights. This need not be a matter of imposing an external moral view, but only a matter of guarding against the potential risks involved in granting less restricted rights to others. The question is just which rights, over which matters, should rest with whom. To construct (or defend) such an arrangement, we will have to think both about substantive outcomes that we have reason to think *could not* be given a reasonable justification[51] and about the temptations and strategic considerations that might make such outcomes likely (and also might make well-meaning legislators *want* limitations on their powers). The ideal of deliberative democracy offers no decisive argument against such limitations in the real world.

Theorists like Gutmann and Thompson, of course, may argue that, independent of any putative general principles of self-government, lawmakers, deliberating in accordance with democratic norms, will do a better job than judges of applying and interpreting norms in a justifiable way. Moreover, if the norms are not enshrined in an independently enforced bill of rights, then further legislative refinements are relatively easy. Of course, that lawmakers will always be guided by democratic norms of reasonableness is doubtful; nevertheless, I think there is some truth in this argument. These are not matters that can be settled *a priori*. Still, it must be pointed out that judicial practice is not without its own deliberative and democratic aspects. For one thing, issues come to the courts when there is a dispute; parties are given opportunities to make a case for their position; and, at least in U.S. appellate courts, judges are expected to issue opinions setting forth, for the public and for other courts, their reasons for deciding as they do. They thereby invite the public, the legislature, and other courts to examine their reasons and to offer counterarguments. Assuming an abstract conception of democracy not unlike the ideal underlying deliberative theory, a plausible case can be made for the desirability of such judicial review.[52]

Let me summarize this section briefly. If we accept the ideas about rights sketched in Section V, then a justifiable system of rights will distribute authority over decisions in a way that is justifiable *to* reasonable persons in an otherwise diverse population. Whether a particular system meets this condition will depend on a variety of things, including the way in which the rights are likely to be exercised and the likely consequences, direct and indirect, of the system.

---

[51] See Cohen, "Procedure and Substance in Deliberative Democracy," 103–4, for arguments that restrictions on religious liberty and on expressive liberties generally *cannot* be justified to those who care about these liberties.

[52] See Freeman, "Constitutional Democracy and the Legitimacy of Judicial Review."

Now, deliberative democrats *might* deny this. They might assert, as Walzer sometimes seems to assert, that the right to rule is a right that the people hold, period, and that there is some definite institutionalization of this right. But I take them not to say this. I take them to hold a more abstract conception of legitimate authority, a more abstract ideal of self-rule. It is compatible with the idea that actual institutions ought to be justifiable to everyone, and it asserts, further, that a system in which collective decisions reflect the deliberation of reasonable persons seeking a reasoned consensus will be justifiable. While I find this claim plausible, however, it does not necessarily imply that conventional, majoritarian procedures are to be preferred in the real world, where, among other things, voters and legislators may be less than reasonable.

VII. Conclusions

One of Cohen's aims, in his essay "Deliberation and Democratic Legitimacy," is to make the case that democracy—conceived in deliberative terms—is an intrinsically attractive idea, not something with mere derivative value as liberty has derivative value within utilitarianism. I am not inclined to dispute Cohen's idea, insofar as he limits it to a claim about the value of something like his ideal deliberative procedure. Indeed, though it is ironic in light of the off-and-on disputes between liberals and democrats, I think the good reasons we have for viewing this kind of procedure as an ideal are not unlike the reasons we have for accepting the liberal contractualism of theorists like Rawls and Scanlon.

For those who identify democracy with the actual electoral procedures of many modern states, and for those who would want to increase reliance on majoritarian procedures or on direct, popular decision-making, it seems to me that the theory of deliberative democracy offers little support. It also offers little support to anyone who wants to claim authority for the actual results of our actual political processes or to anyone who claims that there are special moral reasons always to work within actual democratic institutions. Perhaps, as I suggested in the preceding sections, there are such reasons—at least if contemporary institutions do represent a fair and reasonable distribution of decision-making power and if the exercise of that power does not violate clear, independent moral principles. If there is an obligation to respect democratic procedures, however, I think the ideal of deliberative democracy does not, by itself, explain it.[53]

I do not say that it is irrelevant. If we start with the assumption of reasonable pluralism, together with the idea that institutional constraints or rules must be justifiable to each, we can make a pretty direct case for

---

[53] Jane Mansbridge, if I read her correctly, raises similar concerns about the legitimacy of "real-world" democracies, despite the attractiveness of idealized conceptions, in "Using Power, Fighting Power: The Polity," in *Democracy and Difference*, ed. Benhabib, 46–66.

institutions that are largely majoritarian. For persons who disagree about many matters of morality and religion will have all the more reason to care about just how decision-making authority is distributed. A majoritarian system, with "one person, one vote," and with some judicial protections against excessive governmental intrusion, is just the kind of system that can serve as a natural fallback if we seek a system justifiable to all. However, the fact that we start with wide disagreement is no reason not to seek further agreement where we can get it, and, where we can't, to seek compromises that at least rest on greater mutual understanding and respect. Liberal contractualism can offer direct support for (qualified) majority rule; and majority rule is a framework within which reasonable persons can look for ways to defuse moral conflict and forge moral consensus on formally divisive issues. While reasonable disagreement is not going to go away, its precise extent and locus is not fixed. To the extent that greater agreement can be achieved, that is a gain. But failure to reach agreement does not mean that the system of majority rule is without justification, for the argument I have sketched does not rest on the system's claim to achieve such agreement.

Philosophy, University of Houston

DEMOCRACY AS A *TELOS*

By Kenneth Minogue

I. Introduction

My aim in this essay is to distinguish and comment on a specific movement of thought which I shall call "democracy as a *telos*." This expression
refers to a conception of democracy, cultivated by normative political
philosophers, in which all democratic potentialities have at last been
realized. The result is thought to be a perfected political community.
Democracy as a *telos* must thus be distinguished from the actual liberal
democracies we enjoy at the end of the twentieth century. Indeed, democracy as a *telos* takes off from a specific rejection of such familiar
institutions as elections, political parties, oppositions, a free press, and the
rest, which are regarded, according to taste, as individualistic, bourgeois,
atomistic, formal, and abstract. Democracy as a *telos* refers to the theories
of reformers who, dissatisfied with our present condition, argue that only
a radically transformed democracy can generate a real political community.

A *telos* is the natural completion of some process, and democracy as a
telos suggests that we are *en route* to a better condition in which life
accords as perfectly as may be with democracy. Hence, the term "democracy" in this sense may refer either to the practices that promise to bring
this new condition about (such as participation, constitutional reform,
ideal speech and deliberation, etc.) or to the new condition of human life
itself.

It might be thought that democracy as a *telos* should be understood
as a utopia, but this would fail to register its full weight. Utopias are
constituted by mere desirability. My concern, however, is with desirabilities notionally derived from the ideals to which we are committed.
These ideals are, in fact, constantly transforming the way we live, in
contingent and *ad hoc* ways. The argument of democracy as a *telos* is
thus that this idea brings together and makes sense of political and
intellectual responses to the problems of our time. While it is no doubt
partly a utopia, democracy as a *telos* may claim to be something more
serious: a consistent development of ideals to which we are basically
committed.

The actual content of democracy as a *telos* strikingly overlaps with
other projects for radical transformation of our society, notably communitarianism, socialism, social justice, and republicanism. A great deal of

normative political philosophy crisscrosses this terrain, raising for us the question of whether such an idea should relevantly be considered as conceptual or practical. Still, it is an occupational risk of writing about democracy that the distinction between concepts and practices gets muddled, and what I am calling "democracy as a *telos*" is best understood as a concept hovering between political theory and political practice. Sometimes it is a norm, sometimes a proposal; indeed, exploiting this ambiguity of reference is a hallmark of the genre.

One related feature of contemporary talk about democracy may help to make clear how democracy as a *telos* has come to determine how we think. I refer to a curious and, for most purposes, relatively benign example of the Orwellian memory hole. This is the fact that many of the good things we enjoy in our politics are falsely attributed to democracy. In August 1998, for example, the British prime minister Tony Blair (among others) responded to a car bomb planted by an organization called the "Real IRA" (which killed twenty-nine people in the Northern Irish town of Omagh) by remarking that because Britain is a democracy, it will not violate the rule of law in its pursuit of the culprits. The rule of law is, of course, our anchor, but it derives from long centuries of constitutional development in Britain under monarchy, which is the basic and original form of the modern European (and American) state.[1] Democracy has little to do with it, and indeed the very temptation which Mr. Blair said he was resisting arose precisely because he was (democratically?) tempted to express the outraged feelings of his *dêmos*. Again, Jean Bethke Elshtain, in the course of some sensible remarks about the Violence Against Women Act of 1993 in the United States, talks of "burdensome democratic procedures, including the presumption of innocence. . . ." Her use of "burdensome" here is a piece of irony signifying praise for democracy, as indicating our high standards, but the presumption that concerns her, it hardly needs saying, dates back to medieval times, and was part of the royal system of justice established in English law long before anyone thought seriously about democracy in northern Europe. Professor Elshtain goes on to talk about "democratic jurisprudence, namely, that each case must be looked at individually. . . ."[2] The same point applies. Elshtain's remarks illustrate a widespread tendency to wrap up all our current admirations in the single package of democracy. It is not merely an academic fault. It also corrupts our politics, facilitating the move from "all good things in politics are democratic" to "all democratic things (in whatever sense) are good." Democracy as a *telos* is what generates this mistake.

---

[1] I have elaborated this argument in *Citizenship and Monarchy: A Hidden Fault Line in Our Civilisation* (London: The Institute of United States Studies, 1998). I am here assuming, of course, that America as a civil society has emerged from a thousand years of European, and especially English, political development.

[2] Jean Bethke Elshtain, *Democracy on Trial* (Concord, Ontario: Anasi Press, 1993), ch. 1.

II. Constitutions and Their Consequences

Democracy as a *telos* is, in the first place, a constitutional norm, requiring that our political procedures should more perfectly correspond to a democratic ideal. But we shall find that this constitutional change is in turn favored as a way of achieving a cultural change—perhaps basically the kind of change expressed in Walt Whitman's line "I will make the most splendid race the sun ever shone upon." This normative theory thus exemplifies a familiar ambition in politics: to use constitutional procedures to bring about a political effect, which, in turn, is expected to cause a cultural transformation.

Yet politics is, in important ways, a game, and constitutions are the rules of the game. Changing those rules so as to gain some desirable advantage is hardly playing the game. It is, rather, using constitutions for a political or managerial purpose. It derives from partisanship rather than from political wisdom. A further problem is that those who seek to use constitutional rules to achieve political desirabilities commonly get the causal connections wrong. On *a priori* grounds, Kant concluded that a Europe of republics would be a world at peace.[3] He was evidently wrong, though contemporary theorists are attracted by the similar view that democracies do not go to war with each other.[4] Like all empirical generalizations, this one is hard to confirm. In particular, is it democracy which is the relevant condition of peace, or is it some other feature or features of individualist Western life? A popular recent view was that a dictatorial form of government facilitated prosperity in developing countries better than democracy did, yet most dictators preside over developing impoverishment.

The belief that a country's constitution can determine the development of its culture is clearly not a new one, but we may guess that its runaway modern vogue is a consequence of our current mania for legislation, as measured in the productivity of our legislatures. This Niagara of regulation has so devalued what emerges as to drive activists to seek constitutional entrenchment rather than repealable law as the instrument of their enthusiasms. The problem is that our current passion for improving the world by constitutional diktat seems to be inversely proportional to the evidence for its efficacy.

Democracy, unqualified by the "liberal," is on these grounds popular because it is thought to promote the equalization of society. The link between democracy and equality has been a staple of twentieth-century political theory. Like all such links, it has its deceptive aspects. There have

[3] Immanuel Kant, "Perpetual Peace: A Philosophical Sketch," in *Kant's Political Writings*, ed. Hans Reiss (London: Cambridge University Press, 1970), 100.

[4] For a discussion of the evidence for this view, see James Lee Ray, "Does Democracy Cause Peace?" in *Annual Review of Political Science, 1998*, ed. Nelson Polsby (Palo Alto: Annual Reviews, 1998), 27–46.

been complaints, for example, that in proportion as modern societies have become richer, so the affluent—and selfish—majority has ceased to have an interest in equalizing conditions of life. So, at least, John Kenneth Galbraith has argued.[5]

The most obvious problem in discussing democracy, then, lies in being clear about whether we are concerned with a procedure for arriving at the will of the people, or with whatever the consequences of that will are supposed to be. This ambiguity will be found in most constitutional discussion, but it is particularly acute in discussions of democracy.

When we talk of the various kinds of democracy—for example, "participatory," "representative," "deliberative," even "guided" or "people's"—we are generally concerned to specify conditions of the democratic will. When we refer to aspects of society which test the outcome of that will—as in cultural, or social, or economic democracy—we are referring to the supposed consequences of making real the will of the people. The underlying axiom is that a pure democratic will must generate a pure democratic society, an axiom unaffected by the evident fact that there are huge disagreements about what such a society might be like.

The idea of democracy thus generates two distinct criteria for judging political and social development. The first stems from the will of the people, and the question here is: Has this will clearly emerged from the political process? The second refers to the kind of society generated by democracy: Is it properly democratic?—which for many purposes amounts to the question: Is it egalitarian, inclusive, "diverse," communal, etc.? Each question tests the other. The proof of a pure democratic will is that it generates a desirable society, while a rational society is what would be generated by a pure democratic will. The procedural and substantive criteria are like the blades of a pair of scissors, and they are seldom employed in isolation.

Whether the popular will has emerged in a particular governmental structure is, at least in principle, a technical question, though a highly difficult and contestable one. Whether a society is properly democratic is a normative question. And in modern political thought, norms tend to converge. The norms favored by democratic political theorists would therefore be defective if they diverged from those affirmed by political theorists concerned with justice. That is why much of what might be said by a theorist of democracy converges with the work of a theorist of justice, such as John Rawls.[6] In all of this literature, we inhabit an abstract world of rational human beings solving their problems by negotiation and playing by the rules. Conflict and irrationality are hardly taken seriously.

[5] See John Kenneth Galbraith, *The Good Society: The Humane Agenda* (Boston: Houghton-Mifflin Co., 1996), ch. 2 and passim.
[6] John Rawls, *A Theory of Justice* (Cambridge, MA: Harvard University Press, 1971), sections 11–13.

III. Democracy as the Will of the People

Modern states began as monarchies and have evolved into democracies. Much remained the same, but notionally the will of the people replaced the will of the prince. "The will of the people," however, might best be described, somewhat charitably, as essentially contested.[7] Nonetheless, it remains a touchstone to which all proposals for the reform of actual democracies must be referred. The phrase itself suggests that in politics there is nothing to beat getting the *dêmos* together and deliberating things out. The precedent of Athens beckons,[8] but even if all forty thousand or so citizens of late-fifth-century Athens ever did turn up in the *ecclêsia*, their deliberations would still not plausibly count as "the will of the people." Questions about majorities, inclusion of dissenting opinion, strength of feeling, and other complexities make the whole business of real democratic decision inescapably rough and ready.

In earlier times, European politics used to take the idea of balance between the elements of a civil society as the key to political wisdom. England in the later Middle Ages often prided itself on having a balanced constitution in which the monarchy provided executive decision, the nobles in the House of Lords a certain degree of wisdom and transgenerational stability, and the House of Commons a democratic or representative character. Even this was, of course, to simplify immense complexity. But it was this complex form of government which, in different forms all over Europe and America, became democratized in the course of the last two centuries. The question thus becomes: What is the place of democracy as a relative newcomer in these complex arrangements? The answer that has been given with increasing force in recent times is that only with the emergence of democracy have we discovered the real criterion of what is legitimate in government, and that all aspects of our politics must be brought into line with it. Democracy as a *telos* arises from this widespread conviction.

We have already seen that the problem posed by this conviction is whether we take democracy as a constitutional procedure or as an outcome. The procedure—eliciting the will of the people—is often argued to entail, step by step, the essential features of a good society. Here, however, another logical refinement must be accommodated: Are these features of a good society (many of them forms of equality) a precondition of democracy, or its consequence? In the arguments of democrats, the conditions of democracy and its possible consequences commonly fuse with each other. It is often believed, for example, that wherever the gap in resources between rich and poor is excessive, de-

---

[7] See W. B. Gallie, "Essentially Contested Concepts," in *Philosophy and the Historical Understanding* (London: Chatto and Windus, 1964), 157.

[8] See Gustave Glotz, *The Greek City and Its Institutions*, trans. N. Mallinson (New York: Barnes and Noble, 1969).

mocracy cannot work. On the other hand, democracy itself will, it is
thought, bring about the kind of society it needs for its own operations. In both cases, the underlying value is that of equality. Few democrats regard equality as unimportant.

For the moment, however, let us focus on the issue of how to elicit the
will of the people—the issue of procedure. Democracy provided a critical
cutting edge against the inherited system in which the will of the monarch, or the aristocracy, or the rich who owned property, determined
much of political life. Constitutionally speaking, the politics of the last
two centuries has been driven by the search for a way of actualizing a
pure democratic will. At first it seemed a problem relatively easy to solve:
the restricted franchises of the earlier modern period should be replaced
by the thing called "manhood suffrage." This, however, soon seemed to
constitute the state as an association of patriarchal families, in which
women merely enjoyed what James Mill called "virtual representation."[9]
Manhood suffrage had become widespread by the end of the nineteenth
century, but women complained of their exclusion. Opportunistic conservatives in many countries thought that women were naturally conservative, and soon women also had the vote. The franchise in these times went
to mature persons over the age of legal consent, namely twenty-one in
most countries, but conscription in the two World Wars began at eighteen.
"Is a man who can die for his country at eighteen too young to have a say
in its policies?" the argument went, and opportunistic radicals, figuring
that the young are more radical than the old, reduced the voting age to
eighteen. Somehow even the most mechanical details of the franchise
were stumbling blocks for the perfect representation of the *dêmos*. In
America, voter registration was sometimes a problem, especially in the
South where blacks could find it hard to register. In Britain, the universities of Oxford and Cambridge sent representatives to parliament, and
many graduates thus had two votes, one for the "Oxbridge" candidate
and one for the candidate in the constituency where they lived. Governments could thus gain political advantage in modernizing or democra-
tizing minor impediments to the principle of what in earlier times was
called "one man, one vote." In Britain in the 1970s, in what might well be
taken as the most dramatic disjunction between wisdom and political
participation, the vote was extended to those who were voluntarily living
in mental hospitals.

All of this might seem like a case of dotting the i's and crossing the t's,
but the issue of who should have the vote, and how it should be arranged,
never seems to go away. One only has to spend a few weeks in the United

---

[9] See James Mill, "An Essay on Government," in *Utilitarian Logic and Politics*, ed. Jack
Lively and John Rees (Oxford: Clarendon Press, 1978), 79: "[A]ll those individuals whose
interests are indisputably included in those of other individuals may be struck off without
inconvenience. . . . In this light, . . . women may be regarded, the interest of almost all of
whom is involved either in that of their fathers or in that of their husbands."

States to run into it. Currently, the issue arises from the conduct of the decennial census. Should this be done by the "traditional head-counting" method, or should sampling methods be used? Traditional head-counting is said to favor the white and the rich, while sampling would correct the claimed underrepresentation of the poor, of illegal immigrants, of blacks, and of those who live in rented housing. And why does this matter? A story in the *New York Times* from August 1998 provides the answer:

> "It's the civil rights issue of the next decade," said Representative Carolyn B. Maloney, a Manhattan Democrat who has championed sampling. "If you're not counted, you're not represented. And if you're not represented, you're not getting the dollars."[10]

"Not getting the dollars" is an issue that would have had no significance a century ago: there were no dollars of this kind to get. In contemporary democracy, however, large numbers of voters are also financially dependent on the state. The voter/pensioner[11] in contemporary society is a product of a major transformation of modern society, and raises the question of the changed *scope* of government today. But it is important to recognize that the question of the purity of the democratic will, the question of how to get a collective decision that will be incontestably democratic, remains as difficult as ever. The manhood suffrage that would have satisfied Tom Paine in his search for a form of government that arose "out of the people" rather than "over the people" has long since ceased to satisfy.[12]

Indeed, the very concept of representation has been turned upside down. How can women be "represented" by men (goes one development of democratic thought), or blacks by white legislators, or . . . ? This kind of sociologizing of the process of representation cannot but lead to an endless regress, because there is, in principle, no end to the number of abstract classes into which we might divide society. But the significant point is that each new specification in these terms of the appropriate *form* of democratic representation removes from the activity of representation the general character of being a deliberating political will. For the assumption behind representative parity for sociological groups is that such groups have specific interests, and that these interests, being relatively objective entities, are less matters of judgment than of fact. They require

---

[10] *New York Times*, Metro Section, August 9, 1998.

[11] The term "pensioner" is today yoked to the idea of state payment to the old and the retired, but the word was in earlier centuries used to refer to any sort of *ex gratia* payment, usually intended to generate goodwill. We do not have any general word to refer to those who, for any reason, receive regular payments from the state. Hence, "pensioner" seems to be the best available term to adapt.

[12] See Thomas Paine, "The Rights of Man," in *The Thomas Paine Reader*, ed. Michael Foot and Isaac Kramnic (Harmondsworth: Penguin Books, 1987), 221.

little "deliberation." Representative Maloney, for example, knows that the interest of the New York underclass lies in getting more dollars. No complicated deliberation about political desirabilities is needed. For the voter/pensioner, the economic has become fully subsumed under the political.

In fact, normative political theorists allied to the clients of political activists have created an exploding universe of representational complexities. Applying this theory to self-consciously multicultural societies such as Canada requires that Aboriginal peoples should be federally represented as well as enjoying the benefits of self-government within their own communities. But that apparently democratic advance has collided with the fact that some women in these communities have declared that they do not wish to be subject to tribal determination of female status in communal life. And since all the relevant collectives must be represented within all institutions of government likely to affect them, female and Aboriginal representation even on the Canadian Supreme Court has been demanded.[13] All this would seem to be high comedy; one can easily imagine what the sardonic Hobbes would have made of it. It is by no means the end of the road, however. Some critics have plausibly argued that policy in multicultural societies should be the subject of *continuous* negotiation between the various communities involved.[14]

These are far from being the only problems arising in the quest for the pure democratic will. Political scientists have long been concerned with the psychology of voting. It has been observed that on certain plausible assumptions—such as that voting imposes temporal, physical, and informational costs—it is irrational to go to the trouble of voting unless one's vote promises to determine the outcome. This may be one reason for the prevalence of those who do not bother to vote, something otherwise often interpreted as a sign of alienation from the political process. Critics often charge that low voting rates signify a failure of inclusion in modern democracies. This may or may not be a problem, but in the normative literature, the proposed solution to *all* problems is an enhancement of democracy. Hence the argument for developing more participatory institutions which would, as the cliché has it, give "ordinary people" better opportunities to determine "the conditions that affect their lives."

The problem of how to elicit the pure democratic will also involves the technical question of voting systems. Proportional voting more accurately represents numerical support for parties, but often tends toward a coalitional politics in which clear and decisive changes of policy are difficult. Voting according to constituencies, on the other hand, often produces

---

[13] See Will Kymlicka, "Three Forms of Group-Differentiated Citizenship in Canada," in *Democracy and Difference: Contesting the Boundaries of the Political*, ed. Seyla Benhabib (Princeton: Princeton University Press, 1996), 157ff.

[14] See James Tully, *Strange Multiplicity: Constitutionalism in an Age of Diversity* (Cambridge: Cambridge University Press, 1995).

legislative majorities whose proportions do not correspond to the national vote. A whole literature has grown up on the mechanics of voting.

Even deeper issues hover in the background: What is it to vote? Some votes are positive acts of support, while others are merely strategic moves in keeping some party out of power. And where the voter is convinced that one party is almost certain to win, voting can become a self-referential declaration of some uplifting sentiment.[15]

These are among the problems of securing a pure democratic will, and they are very far from exhausting the field. Further concerns include how the elements of the democracy might arrive at their decisions: by deliberation, for example, or by participating in an "ideal speech situation."[16] The procedural self-understanding of democracies is concerned with how judgments are generated, collectivized, consensualized, aggregated, and operationalized, and there seems to be abundant room to say a great deal on all of these processes, yet, like economists laid end to end, normative theorists never agree on a conclusion. And it is worth going into some of these real-world complexities because much normative political thought, or what is sometimes called "meta-theorizing," adumbrates conditions which are, in practice, quite impossible to make real. Yet making these conditions real, expressing more purely the democratic will, is the fundamental concern of such thought.

IV. Limits on the Democratic Will

Or is it? Here we must broach the delicate question of normative political thought's dedication to the pure democratic will. On the face of it, we have a dogma of popular infallibility, but no one quite believes *that*; indeed, the dogma is often balanced by an almost equally powerful belief, never acknowledged as such, in popular stupidity. The people elect the government, but their power to determine events must be severely constrained by moral, legal, and constitutional restraints (in the form of rights and law, for example) which hobble, and are designed to hobble, the rather deplorable sentiments which sometimes animate majorities. Modern democracies are, in fact, highly managed systems of civil life, and governments do not hesitate to set themselves up in a tutorial relationship to their notional master, the *dêmos*. They engage in public educational campaigns on everything from safety to lifestyle, campaigns which

---

[15] See, for example, Geoffrey Brennan and Loren E. Lomasky, "Large Numbers, Small Costs: The Uneasy Foundation of Democratic Rule," in *Politics and Process: New Essays in Democratic Thought*, ed. Brennan and Lomasky (Cambridge: Cambridge University Press, 1989), 42ff. The argument is that it is almost impossible to justify democracy on the basis of its responsiveness to the preferences of the electorate (ibid., 43).

[16] An "ideal speech situation" is the most familiar formulation of the quest, in the work of Jürgen Habermas, for a conception of public discussion which has freed itself from the distortions of money and power. See Habermas, *The Theory of Communicative Action*, vol. 1 (Boston: Beacon Press, 1984), and vol. 2 (Cambridge: Polity Press, 1987).

not infrequently make sense only on the assumption that the *dêmos* is (as we say these days) severely "intellectually challenged."[17]

This is a problem of increasing practical significance. It suggests the paradox that wise and caring governments are elected by foolish and selfish people—a quite remarkable situation. But there is perhaps a more profound problem which hints at the conclusion to which we are moving. It is a problem which reveals a logical incompatibility between democracy and the modern state itself. Democracy, understood as government reflecting the pure democratic will, contradicts the idea, derived from centuries of monarchy, of *responsible* government. If, *per impossibile*, we could ever achieve a government expressing a pure democratic will, it could not be a responsible government, because (*pace* the famous joke by Bertolt Brecht) the people can hardly dissolve the people and elect a new one. Indeed, what a government purely reflecting the popular will would (in principle) achieve is the end of government altogether. The state would have withered away and the people would act for themselves. This has been the immemorial dream of radicals from Rousseau onward. And this paradox—the basis of the more realistic theories of democracy advanced by the skeptical Joseph Schumpeter and others—forces us to the other term of democratic theory: that of democratic society.[18]

V. Does Democracy Have a Content?

Democracy as the pure expression of the popular will has destroyed all possible competitors to power. It has, as a result, outgrown its constitutional role and turned into something much closer to a utopia. Historically, democracy inherited an intricate system of institutions resting on an idea of divided authority. It was inserted into this system as a new principle of authority: legitimate rulers had to be elected. Yet it is precisely the idea of authority which democracy proceeded to destroy. The resulting political process eroded the formal criterion of authority. Instead of a *dêmos* authorizing a government which uses that authority to take responsibility for public life, the *dêmos* (orchestrated by the media and responding to a cacophony of lobbying groups) comes to be conceived of as a substantive will generating public desirabilities which the government merely expresses. But the democratic will in this form is spectacu-

---

[17] In the United States, the Surgeon General is full of wise advice for the foolish. The British government increasingly crams the school curriculum with courses on parenting, how to manage condoms, and, most recently, a general course for primary schools to be called "preparation for life." The French government has run campaigns to persuade the French to be nicer to foreigners, in order to help the tourist industry. The Austrian government has recently legislated the household duties of males. And the list could be continued endlessly. The interesting question is whether people in need of this kind of instruction have the political sense to vote intelligently.

[18] See Joseph A. Schumpeter, *Capitalism, Socialism, and Democracy* (New York: Harper and Row, 1962), esp. ch. 22.

larly unstable. It commonly seeks to expand the scope of government in all directions, but with this kind of expansion comes the need for constant changes in the law. Enactment and repeal become the rhythm of our legislatures.

The more democracy is believed to be the *dêmos* getting what it wants, the more intolerable its frustration seems to be. When government was a remote source of easily internalized law, the compliance of the people was for the most part effortless. But the more the people develop opinions on public topics and demand action, the more inevitable will be the disappointment. Politics then becomes an oscillation between the democratic will and the inevitably unsatisfactory outcome. And one result is likely to be the conviction that occult forces are blocking the democratic will: what Richard Hofstadter called "the paranoid style of politics."[19]

With the move from authority to desirability, democracy acquires a content, and developing this content becomes the *telos*. Thus, Amy Gutmann explains that democracy needs a justification that can inspire its citizens. What she calls "nonideal democracy," equivalent to Robert Dahl's "polyarchies," ought to satisfy a schedule of basic needs, and this leads her to lament "the failures of every existing democratic government to secure for all its citizens some basic goods such as an adequate income, employment, health care, and education. . . ."[20] Gutmann thus incorporates into her philosophy not merely a procedural norm, but a substantive one as well. It is not merely that she supports both democracy and welfare; it is that she supports democracy *as* welfare. What links both desirabilities is the idea of equality. At a lower level of abstraction, this fusion is what leads Representative Maloney to identify votes with welfare dollars. But the fusion is not empirical. No evidence is advanced, nor really could it be, to show that welfarism must be the outcome of the popular will; indeed, there are many cases where it is not. But the fundamental point is the identification of a procedure with some supposed outcome.

This identification is familiar to us in Marxism, where so-called bourgeois democracy is invalidated because it does not produce the right results, but it can also be found in more sophisticated philosophy. The Rawlsian veil of ignorance is a procedure which notionally produces a universal will, but is merely a deduction from given premises.[21] The effect

---

[19] See Richard Hofstadter, *The Paranoid Style in American Politics, and Other Essays* (Chicago: Chicago University Press, 1979). Hofstadter's target in this essay was primarily, of course, the conspiracy theories of what he recognized as "right-wing" or "pseudo-conservative" movements, but democratic axioms clearly intensify the likelihood of occult forces blocking the people's will. His remark (ibid., xiii) that "[t]he curse of what we call 'second class citizenship' is perennial in American politics" points to the problem to which the search for a pure representation of the popular will would be the solution.

[20] Amy Gutmann, "Democracy, Philosophy, and Justification," in *Democracy and Difference*, ed. Benhabib, 341.

[21] See Michael Sandel, *Liberalism and the Limits of Justice* (Cambridge: Cambridge University Press, 1982).

of identifying a procedure with an outcome is to insinuate some kind of *summum bonum* into the idea of a modern state, and thus to make more manageable the problem of order as posed by Hobbes: namely, how to generate civil order out of a population with radically differing ideas of the good. This is the basis of the liberal principle asserting the priority of the right over the good, but conceptions of what is right tend to foreclose what might be treated as good to the point where the real diversity of actual modern states becomes impossible.

Yet for a government to presume to determine the happiness of the people would be an intolerable interference with freedom. It follows that modern states must be ruled not in terms of some desirable way of life ("virtue" in the classical republics, "happiness" commonly for utilitarians and other modern thinkers) but by abstract laws which largely leave individual aspirations to individual judgment. The business of government is with peace and order, and the range of its concern with justice must *therefore* be limited.[22]

Twentieth-century democracy, then, has acquired both a theory and a practice determining its content; and both theory and practice affirm equalization as the basic demand of the popular will. Equalization is advanced in the name of fairness, and has been implemented by the use of redistributive taxation.[23] This is why Representative Maloney associates votes with welfare dollars. An important question is whether this policy represents the popular will, or reflects other powerful tendencies in modern government.

VI. THE DEMOCRATIC *TELOS*

We need now to analyze what is involved in the program of equalization which lies at the heart of democracy as a *telos*, and we may do this most briskly by invoking Hegel's account of the modern state in *The Philosophy of Right*.[24] On this view, a modern civil association consists of three elements.

First, there is the state itself, the apparatus of government and of law which determines its civic character. Secondly, there is the vast range of links between individuals which this type of association makes possible—

---

[22] The situation reminds one of Beatrice Webb's famous reply when asked whether she or her husband Sidney made the family decisions. "Sidney makes all the big decisions," she is reported to have said, "and I make all the small decisions. But I decide what is big and what is small."

[23] Judgments differ about just how redistributive welfare systems actually are, on the ground that members of the middle class derive many benefits from the system. But we may safely assume that *some* money does pass from rich to poor.

[24] See *Hegel's Philosophy of Right*, trans. and ed. T. M. Knox (Oxford: Clarendon Press, 1952), whose third part on "ethical life" is divided into three sections: one on the family, one on civil society, and one on the state.

churches, clubs, unions, universities, and so on. The slippery term "society" covers this area of our lives, though in common usage today it often includes everything. Society also includes the economy—the activities of entrepreneurs and workers involved in the production and exchange of goods and services. Thirdly, there is the arena of privacy found in family life and individual consciousness.

The crucial consideration for democracy as a *telos* is the place of equality in these three arenas of modern life. The state, as the association of citizens, and of subjects under law, is an arena of equality. In practice, no doubt, many inequalities have long survived, but the unmistakable drive of modern life has been to offer all adults an equal civic status. The democracy for which the old reformers campaigned was itself the most powerful move in this direction. The state is thus equality's beachhead, for in other areas, natural human inequalities—in energy, charm, enthusiasm, inheritance, etc.—were not only reflected but magnified. The new democratic theory has chosen to use the idea of citizenship as a way of subduing the inequalities of society and the economy. Contractual relations such as jobs are—to adapt Sir Henry Maine's terminology, but to reverse his direction of progress—relentlessly converted by legislation into a form of status. Specific conditionalities (racial, sexual, religious, intellectual) have been swept away and replaced by a right based upon mere humanity. This process has even generated such an idea as "social citizenship," in which the receipt of state benefits is construed as an active exercise of citizenship.[25]

Society and the economy are supremely the arenas in which we have the opportunity to succeed, or to fail. These are areas which present the challenge of inequality at its most vibrant. Citizenship among the Greeks was a notional equality superimposed upon what was recognized as a natural inequality. In the modern Christian world, however, a certain equality of manners, largely derived from the Christian doctrine about all being equal in the eyes of God, has diffused a sense of human equality into many areas of life. We think it vulgar to parade some supposed superiority in social relations. Our belief in human rights derives from this, and gave rise to our detestation of slavery, which we abolished, at least wherever our reach extended. On the other hand, most social institutions are functionally hierarchical, and the economy, above all, is an encounter between rich and poor.

Democratization in these areas was a matter of legislating a doctrinal equality of outcome in order to modify spontaneous inequalities.

There remains private and family life. This is the most unlikely candidate for any program of equalization, for differences of strength between men and women, and of wisdom between parents and children, make

---

[25] See, for example, David Marquand, *The New Reckoning: Capitalism, States, and Citizens* (Oxford: Polity Press, 1997).

complementarity the essence of family life. Here the democratization program, in concert with many other tendencies of modern life, has attacked and eroded the complementarity of male and female, and has replaced it as far as possible with a certain homogenization of roles. Children may remain inescapably dependent, though the democratic drive is to get them out of the family and into the public sphere as early as possible. A concern with the dangers of child abuse, and the extension to children of the idea of rights, are among the instruments of this particular homogenization.

The democratic *telos* is thus the program of destroying private and nonpolitical spheres by diffusing the status of citizenship throughout society. It will be clear that the modern project of equality goes vastly further than anything conceived of by the egalitarianism of the Athenians. The state becomes an agent for little less than the transformation of the human condition. Against natural inequality and the modern taste for the cultivation of individuality, democracy as a *telos* poses a universal mode of life, and perhaps in time some universal set of thoughts necessary to sustain such a world. Plato, of course, got there before us:

> [I]f all possible means have been taken to make even what nature has made our *own* in some sense common property, I mean, if our eyes, ears, and hands seem to see, hear, act, in the common service; if, moreover, we all approve and condemn in perfect unison and derive pleasure and pain from the same sources . . . that is a criterion of . . . excellence than which no truer or better will ever be found.[26]

The moral ground advanced for this egalitarian transformation was the move away from power toward justice. And the plausibility of that move has depended upon construing every general type of superiority as some abuse—the rich exercising power to exploit the poor, whites excluding blacks, husbands tyrannizing over wives, parents abusing children, and so on. Each perceived inequality was taken as equivalent to an abuse. Each abuse beckoned the *dêmos* as legislator to improve the condition of the unprotected. And each new form of protection, by identifying the state with the *dêmos*, allowed the state to absorb some new area of society into its control.

We may make two observations relevant to this new situation, even though they cannot be explored here. The first is that this vast change in the role of democratic governments, a change already well underway, implicitly changes the conception of the point of human life. The "pursuit of happiness" is replaced by the civil responsibility to guarantee the satisfaction of human needs.

---

[26] Plato, *Laws*, Book V, 739c–d, in *The Collected Dialogues of Plato*, ed. Edith Hamilton and Huntington Cairns (Princeton: Princeton University Press, 1973), 1324.

The second observation is that responsibility for securing individual happiness has moved steadily away from the striving individuals of early modern times toward governments which guarantee the individual against indigence, job loss, ill health, tyrannical employers, and a great range of other slings and arrows of misfortune. The French expression for "the welfare state" best sums up the situation: *l'état providence*. The state has indeed become the agent of Providence.

Once the issue comes to be formulated as that of justice against power, the project has acquired its own unstoppable momentum, and the democratic will can be plausibly identified, *a priori*, with the moral and rational will. Ideal models of deliberation can be constructed—from Rawls to Habermas—in which an appropriate moral outcome can be guaranteed.[27]

But this identification is, of course, unreal. The actual *dêmos* is perhaps moral in its intentions, but somewhat fitful in following these intentions through. Besides, the just society adumbrated in this *telos* includes some features on which the judgment of the *dêmos* is distinctly unsound. The *dêmos* often prefers capital punishment to therapy, for example. It does not always approve offering the same advantages to ethnic minorities as it does to its own kind, and it may be similarly insouciant about immigrants. As prosperity increases, the people may constitute a majority of the better off who care little for the worse off, some of whom they may regard as lazy or feckless. Thus, the actual democratic will cannot, in fact, be relied upon to produce what normative theorists take to be the right results. And this is the reason for further notable transformations of the modern state, which I discuss in the following sections.

VII. The Scope of Contemporary Government

One reason why actual people may generate tendencies unacceptable to the intellectual vanguard promoting democracy as a *telos* is that most people in modern societies are not fully integrated into its culture. All divisions, beginning with the division of labor, tend to exclude some members of society from its fullest fruits, and hence the project of equality is to overcome what is seen as the cultural barrenness of much modern life. The industrial worker has little to say to the academic; women in domestic circumstances do not experience the camaraderie of the workplace. Democracy as a *telos* aims to integrate all members of society within the same culture. This can only work if people become interchangeable, and that is being achieved by bringing everyone into the workforce. The initial stages of this particular social integration will be found in policies of affirmative action. Men and women, black and white, fit and disabled—

---

[27] Rawls, *A Theory of Justice*, esp. sections 4 and 24; Habermas, *The Theory of Communicative Action*.

all must appear at all levels of society and the economy. To quite a large extent, this homogenization has happened spontaneously, driven both by modern push-button technology and by the many somersaults of popular taste. The modern state takes some of the blind strivings of society and weaves them into a program. It does not lack a general theory which explains what it is doing.

The theory goes as follows: Mankind has, over the centuries, had to pull itself up by its own bootstraps, which required that people should be divided into different classes of person having different privileges and conditions of life—a military nobility to protect the state, for example; a priesthood to deal with necessary consolations and to guarantee contentment and order; a commercial class to trade and encourage technology; and an enclosed order of scientists and scholars to provide the ideas. These people—themselves distorted by specialization—were the owners and proprietors of civilization, disposing of a disproportional quantum of its benefits. But now at last we have reached a point—shall we call it an "end of history"?—at which these divisions, which involved terrible inequalities of power, have become unnecessary. We now understand the secret of progress. Mankind has taken the business of directing civilization under conscious control, and its fruits can be distributed, as a matter of justice, to all. This is a political program which may indeed require the forceful removal of privileges from some people (whites, members of the middle class, males, etc.). Stated in this way, the theory looks like a discovery about the course of historical evolution, but its real point is practical: namely, the teleological doctrine that the conflict and cruelty of history were perhaps necessary in the past, but are no longer so. A just society is therefore the condition of achieving a peaceful world.

It happens that this theory not only underlies democracy as a *telos*, but that it was, earlier in this century, invoked to justify just such a redistribution of civilizational goods. The Bolshevik revolutionaries who overthrew the Czarist empire in Russia in 1917 also believed that they had found the secret of modern dynamism. The secret of Western productivity consisted in electricity, production lines, and heavy industry. The Bolsheviks further assumed that individual initiative was being superseded by teamwork and community. We now know that most of this was nonsense. Western civilization—"capitalism" to its enemies—still had further technological surprises in store, and whole new kinds of technology were developed which eventually destroyed the Soviet regime.

There is little doubt that this theory of human development has appealed to many people in this century, and that the democracies of the West were in the 1970s drifting into a quiet replay of this program by way of growing welfarism and labor regulation. Governments were steadily moving toward spending half or more than half of all the wealth produced in some countries. It became clear, however, that the equalization project in its welfarist form brought diminishing economic returns. Efficiency gets traded off against equity, prosperity diminishes, and the (inegalitarian) market fights (egalitarian) democracy as a *telos* to a standstill. But the conflict remains vibrant.[28]

VIII. Aspects of Social Transformation

The conflict is, in fact, a new version of one of the oldest problems of responsible government: whether the people ought to be construed individually or collectively. Economically, they are for most purposes individuals; politically, they must be treated as some kind of unity. But one of the most powerful implications of the core idea of democracy is that government, as coercion of the people by their rulers, would disappear. If the people rule themselves, the people get what "they" want. One implication of democracy thus contains the seeds of anarchism. Yet the populations of modern democratic Western societies are now governed to within an inch of their lives. By contrast with nineteenth-century people, our contemporaries are required to carry passports and other forms of identification, to report by numbers to various agencies, to get permission to build or modify their houses, to modify their lifestyles in accordance with governmental recommendations, to fit into national strategies of many kinds, to pay a large variety of kinds of taxation, and so on. In their commercial lives they are subject to a whole range of inspectorates. They must conform to increasingly explicit codes, and must work to performance indicators. Far from disappearing, government is everywhere.

Yet, in another sense, each particular government at any given moment can plead a certain innocence. For each government now inherits the fruits of earlier corporatism by which most of the ways we are controlled have been hived off onto independent agencies operating within the law. Hence we hate bureaucrats, but for politicians we only have a certain contempt, seeing them, in part, as no less the victims of a system than ourselves. An increasing quantity of this "governance," as it is tending now to be called, results from the work of international organizations, to which states adhere through treaty.[29]

Such are among the ways in which the program of redistributing the benefits of Western civilization is progressing. It sounds like a beneficent

---

[28] Mark E. Warren, "What Should We Expect from More Democracy? Radically Democratic Responses to Politics," *Political Theory* 24, no. 2 (May 1996): 264.

[29] It is almost as if there were a flight from governments using their power, especially where the decision might cause embarrassment. Thus, the British government, facing in Northern Ireland the conflict between Orange marchers and Republican protesters, handled the issue of whether this or that march through disputed territory should go ahead, by handing it over to an agency whose decisions were to be based upon the prevention of disorder. Such decisions were presented as "the rule of law."

and popular program, and equalization has come to be thought democratic, but like all good things it has its costs. It requires the virtual
destruction of what we have called "society." The world we live in was
created out of the individualistic passions of men—mostly men—who
freely followed their bent. That sometimes involved exploiting and tyrannizing over workers and wives, but it was also the secret of some
elements of creativity and innovation. This is the sense in which democracy as a *telos* is a moral revolution. The sheer space available for individuals to construct worlds of their own shrinks in proportion to the
growth of regulation.

To put the point another way: the democratic program of equalization
makes society a more comfortable place for those who are not very bold
and not very enterprising; by the same token, it makes boldness and
enterprise more difficult.

What is certainly true is that democracy, beginning as a constitutional
innovation in the modern state, has taken over the very assumptions by
which we understand the state itself, and has established a new form of
society in which we are all national resources, required to share in a
widening schedule of appropriate attitudes. "Democracy" functions, in
this particular context, merely as the pretense that a project which comes
from government above comes from the people below.

IX. MOVING TO THE *TELOS*

Something good in moderation may become destructive in excess. Democracy is a vital part of our modern conception of civil society, but as the
principle determining how everything is arranged, it almost insensibly
turns the state into something quite different. The pursuit of a perfect
democracy as the form of a good society would necessarily create something changeless, while a modern state is endlessly dynamic. This dynamism resides, precisely, in the fact that what we have called "society,"
although subject to the rule of law, used to permit the unpredictable
interactions of the individuals composing it. For this very reason, it was
full of imperfections; it was also full of opportunities, and the removal of
the imperfections destroys many of the opportunities.

Political wisdom requires us to recognize that institutions and ideas can
be both negative and positive. The nobles of the early modern ages, for
example, were essential to the protection of feudal kingdoms against
ravaging barbarians; in the later Middle Ages, they became a destructive
burden upon settled life. Rather similarly, in modern life, some ideas and
institutions conducive to freedom have, as it were, reversed their polarities. Consider, for example, an idea such as diversity. It began as an
admiring term for the sheer ebullience and variety of modern societies,
with their wealth of technological innovations, their varied ways of life,
their breadth of ideas, their unregulated artistic striving, and all the other

fruits of human freedom. In recent years, the term has been nationalized, and governments have legislated that clubs, firms, universities, schools, and so on should be "diverse"—by regulatory command. Ethnic and sexual representation is demanded of virtually all activities of any size. This is done for the best of motives, but it turns diversity into uniformity, and our social understanding into a lie. It also destroys the opportunity of excluded groups to make their own spontaneous responses to their situation. Jewish humor and black jazz were alike the fruits of exclusion. Inclusion is no doubt nice, but it is less creative, and state coercion is the quick fix of the attitudinal world.

Again, consider institutions, such as the law, or the academic profession. Constitutionality in previous centuries depended upon distinguishing between what rulers did and what the law decreed. Law was a technical exercise in the maintenance of boundaries. In this century, however, the increasing scope of law in a world of proliferating legislation has combined with the spread of the belief that everything is politics (and the belief is enough to turn itself into a fact) to break down the stiff technicality of law. In liberal terms, before democracy came to reign, the only way to advance a desirability which had been declared illegal was to induce the government to change the law. Today, the straight path to such a desirability is to find a judge who will reinterpret the law. Any fool can, of course, play with words to turn black into white, but in earlier days lawyers were as starchy as the robes they still wear in some countries. They were men (and at that time exclusively men) devoted to form rather than to substance. Of universities we need say less—merely that, in the past, professors generally kept out of journalism and politics and stuck to scholarship. In our democratically expanded academic world, it is rare to find professors who do not have opinions on the whole range of public issues, and who do not conform to whatever are the currently dominant ideas of right thinking.

But perhaps the most striking reversal of polarities is the way in which social enterprise has been undermined, turning relationships into a form of status. In a world of "stress" and "pressures," employers have been made responsible for the happiness of their employees, and can be sued if these are harassed or bullied by workmates. A notional responsibility of the employer has replaced the real responsibility of individual workers in the workplace, largely on the principle that compensation requires a deep pocket. Kinds of sexual harassment which women three generations ago would have dealt with by a supercilious curl of the lip can now lead to litigation and financial settlements. This is often referred to, in an Orwellian way, as "empowerment," but in terms of the moral resourcefulness, courage, and enterprise of the individual, it is part of the enfeeblement resulting from democracy as a *telos*. The political significance of this moral enfeeblement is that it makes the subject of a late-twentieth-century state an easy object to regulate and control.

Democracy as a *telos* exploits the ambiguity between what the people actually want, and what the people might rationally be thought to want. The ambiguity is particularly clear in the area of risk-taking. The risks of unemployment, for example, are unpredictable, and prudence suggests a disposal of one's assets with an eye on this possibility. Just such prudence was a widespread practice in the unions and friendly societies of the nineteenth century in Britain. But the practice has fallen into disuse with the extension of government support for the unemployed, leading to the spread of highly indebted individuals impatient of any gap between desire and satisfaction.

The conclusion to which this argument leads is that the more a state is democratized, the more public authority takes over the responsibilities of individual prudence. Attempts have been made to present dependency on the state as something active—as a form of "social citizenship"—but this seems little more than the exploitation of an honorific word.[30] It might seem that the democratic emphasis on participation supplies the active and enterprising character lacking in welfare dependency, but this is misleading. Totalitarian states were very keen on collective decision-making because in many circumstances it is easy to manipulate. But the real problem in theories of what Benjamin Barber has called "strong democracy" is that they aim to extend collective decision-making into areas which otherwise would be those of individual responsibility. Thus, Barber's objection to vouchers in education is that they "transform what ought to be a public question ('What is a good system of public education for *our* children?') into a personal question ('What kind of school do I want for *my* children?')."[31] Communal judgment is the search for a consensus, for the one right answer to a question posed so as to generate a right answer. Communities, under theories of "strong democracy," would not be particularly friendly to real "diversity."

X. DEMOCRACY AND THE MODERN STATE

There is, I suppose, nothing wrong or even very unusual about advancing a constitution which destroys the very thing it constitutes, but it certainly deserves attention. This is especially the case if it is a destruction which purports to be a fulfillment.

The modern state emerged historically around the sixteenth century, and has continued to evolve as it has responded to the changing tastes of its peoples and the advance of technology among much else. It was an

---

[30] See, for example, "Reinventing Civic Republicanism," in Marquand, *The New Reckoning*, 37.

[31] Benjamin R. Barber, *Strong Democracy: Participatory Politics for a New Age* (Berkeley: University of California Press, 1984), 296.

abstract structure of rights and offices which took much of the personality out of rule, and left self-determining individuals largely free to pursue their own projects. Inevitably, some succeeded and some failed. It was this variation in the destinies of different people which led to the project of transforming the state—either by revolution or through evolution—into something radically different. The hope was that the state might "wither away," to be replaced, perhaps, by something warmer and more communal. We can certainly say that there is nothing sacrosanct about the modern state—a brutish monster with blood on its hands. Such a reaction would be understandable, but it would, in my view, ignore certain important considerations. The modern liberal state is the one civil arena in which widespread freedom and prosperity have been enjoyed, and we should be cautious—in these times when many people think it rational to delegate increasing amounts of authority, either upward to international institutions or downward to more communal ones—about abandoning the complex mixture of distance and intimacy which modern states have evolved. Above all, we need to observe where, under a mist of democratic rhetoric, power is actually moving.

Agatha Christie once wrote a mystery in which ten people isolated on an island are murdered one by one.[32] Arriving at the last victim, one might think one had discovered the murderer, but no, this person too was murdered. The solution to this ingenious problem was, of course, that one of the earlier murders had been a fake. The position of democracy as a *telos* is not dissimilar. For it has killed off inequalities one by one—kings, aristocrats, rich bourgeois, interfering bureaucrats, and so on. At the end, it might seem that we are at last arriving at the promised land of equality. The oppressors are all dead—and yet we still find ourselves under the sway of a government with a finger in every pie. How to explain this remarkable phenomenon?

The project of democracy as a *telos* lies in equalizing society by removing arbitrary power wherever it might be found, subjecting everything to what looks a bit like the rule of law. But the removal of power in the name of equalization (alias democratization) is not what it seems. The crookedness of human timber is such that a program of equalization must have continuous recourse to a class of equalizers: a set of experts in democracy and equality who can readjust the incessant human tendency to generate fresh forms of inequality. The most precise model of this new and less visible adjuster is the social worker, whose business it is to manage the lives of those who cannot manage for themselves—the drugged, the improvident, the unemployable, and so on. This hardly looks like the exercise of power at all. It is merely helping people toward rational standards in conducting their lives. It is, however, the pure model of the tutorial

[32] Agatha Christie, *And Then There Were None* (reprint, London: HarperCollins, 1993).

relationship which has been creeping into government along with the project of democracy as a *telos*. Most of us do not have direct experience of the guidance of the social worker, but we cannot today escape the tutelage of the lawyer and the bureaucrat. And, lured by the image of a perfect society, some normative political philosophers do not think we ought to escape it at all.

Political Science, London School of Economics

RADICAL DEMOCRACY, PERSONAL FREEDOM, AND THE TRANSFORMATIVE POTENTIAL OF POLITICS*

By Steven Wall

I. Introduction

In recent years, theorists of radical democracy have criticized the liberal pluralist model of politics, a model which views the political forum primarily as a space for bargaining and the aggregation of individual preferences.[1] While conceding that some measure of bargaining and preference aggregation is probably an ineliminable feature of democratic politics, radical democrats have charged that this model underestimates or ignores the transformative effects of democratic political interaction. In particular, liberal pluralism does not allow for the possibility that democratic politics can generate new forms of solidarity, enhance personal freedom, and inculcate virtue.

This is an important critique, and so far it has not received the attention it deserves from liberal pluralists. In this essay, I want to examine critically one set of arguments advanced by radical democrats. These arguments concern the claim that there is a tight connection between participation in democratic politics and personal freedom, a connection that is missed by liberal pluralist writers. I will argue that this claim is deeply problematic, and that there are good reasons for holding on to the liberal pluralist view that if there is any connection between personal freedom and participation in democratic politics, it is a weak and contingent one at best.

II. Preliminary Clarifications

I begin by making it clear how I characterize radical democracy and whom I count as a radical democrat. This is necessary, since it is impor-

* I would like to thank Robert Amdur, Ellen Frankel Paul, and Mark Warren for their comments on earlier drafts of this essay.

[1] Writers associated with the liberal pluralist model of politics include empirical political scientists like Robert A. Dahl, *A Preface to Democratic Theory* (Chicago: University of Chicago Press, 1959); and David Truman, *The Governmental Process: Political Interests and Public Opinion*, 2d ed. (Berkeley: Institute of Governmental Studies, 1993); as well as economic theorists of democracy like Anthony Downs, *An Economic Theory of Democracy* (New York: Harper and Row, 1957); William Riker, *Liberalism against Populism: A Confrontation between the Theory of Social Choice and Democracy* (San Francisco: William Freeman Co., 1982); and James Buchanan, "Politics without Romance: A Sketch of Positive Public Choice Theory and Its Normative Implications," in *The Theory of Public Choice*, vol. 2, ed. James Buchanan and R. D. Tollison (Ann Arbor: University of Michigan Press, 1984).

tant not to get bogged down in interpretive disputes about how to classify this or that writer. In this spirit, my remarks here are stipulative. I want to identify a broad body of political thought that includes participatory democrats like Benjamin Barber and Carole Pateman, modern republican writers such as Cass Sunstein and Frank Michelman, and critical theorists like Jürgen Habermas and Seyla Benhabib.[2] While these writers obviously have different objectives in mind, they share a concern that modern liberal societies undervalue democratic political participation and that liberal pluralist theory mischaracterizes its value. For this reason, I will refer to these writers as radical democrats. However, unlike some thinkers in the civic republican tradition,[3] these writers have made peace with modernity. They do not criticize liberal societies for their failure to measure up to premodern ideals. Instead, they seek to articulate a conception of democratic politics appropriate for large, complex pluralistic societies. One consequence of this is that radical democrats often have a broader conception of politics than many civic republicans do. They see the domain of politics as including not just formal political institutions like parliaments and town halls, but also informal public spaces in civil society—a point I shall come back to later in this essay.

Radical democrats, then, can be distinguished from both liberal pluralists and many civic republican writers. Still, radical democracy remains a broad church, sheltering diverse currents of thought. Fortunately, for present purposes, it is not necessary to cut through this diversity and attempt to identify the core or essence of this body of political thought. The reason for this is simply that in this essay I have a relatively circumscribed objective in mind. I am interested in radical democracy only insofar as it presents and defends a distinctive view of personal freedom,

---

[2] See Benjamin Barber, *Strong Democracy: Participatory Politics for a New Age* (Berkeley: University of California Press, 1983); Carole Pateman, *Participation and Democratic Theory* (Cambridge: Cambridge University Press, 1970); Frank Michelman, "The Supreme Court, 1985 Term – Forward: Traces of Self-Government," *Harvard Law Review* 100 (1986): 4–77; Cass Sunstein, "Beyond the Republican Revival," *Yale Law Journal* 97 (1988): 1539–90; Jürgen Habermas, *Between Facts and Norms: Contributions to a Discourse Theory of Law and Democracy*, trans. William Rehg (Cambridge, MA: MIT Press, 1996); and Seyla Benhabib, *Critique, Norm, and Utopia* (New York: Columbia University Press, 1986). Other radical democrats include John Dryzek, *Discursive Democracy: Politics, Policy, and Political Science* (Cambridge: Cambridge University Press, 1990); Iris Marion Young, *Justice and the Politics of Difference* (Princeton: Princeton University Press, 1990); Chantal Mouffe, *The Return of the Political* (London: Verso, 1993); Carol Gould, *Rethinking Democracy: Freedom and Social Cooperation in Politics, Economics, and Society* (Cambridge: Cambridge University Press, 1988); Hannah Pitkin, "Justice: On Relating Private and Public," *Political Theory* 9, no. 3 (1981): 327–52; Mark Warren, "The Self in Discursive Democracy," in *The Cambridge Companion to Habermas*, ed. Stephen White (Cambridge: Cambridge University Press, 1995); and Warren, "What Should We Expect from More Democracy? Radical Democratic Responses to Politics," *Political Theory* 24, no. 2 (1996): 241–70.

[3] See Hannah Arendt, *The Human Condition* (Chicago: University of Chicago Press, 1970); and Alasdair MacIntyre, *After Virtue* (Notre Dame, IN: University of Notre Dame Press, 1984).

one that contrasts with the liberal view.[4] As mentioned above, this view of personal freedom can be stated, albeit broadly and vaguely, as the claim that there is a tight connection between personal freedom and political self-government.

Stated this broadly, however, the radical democratic view is hopelessly fuzzy. To make any headway at all, we must identify more precisely the idea(s) expressed in the claim that there is a tight connection between personal freedom and political self-government. With this in mind, several different possibilities need to be distinguished. For example, it can be, and has been, argued that political self-government is a constituent element of personal freedom. Rousseau famously held that people can be free only insofar as they live in a political community in which they participate in the processes of self-rule and the political community is governed by a general will.[5] Such a view makes political self-government a necessary condition of personal freedom. Less stringently, some have argued that a necessary condition of being free is that one play some active role in the self-government of one's political community. On this less stringent view, there is no further requirement that one's political community be governed by a general will or that one authorize its use of political power.

In contrast to these two views, it is sometimes claimed that political self-government is instrumental to personal freedom. This might be true for one of two reasons. First, it is sometimes argued that active participation in political self-government helps people develop capacities and skills which themselves are integral to personal freedom.[6] On this view, while participation in political self-rule is not strictly speaking a necessary condition for the development of these capacities, it is an important means to their development. Without participating in political self-government, many will fail to develop the capacities and skills integral to personal freedom. Second, it is sometimes argued that participation in political self-government is instrumentally valuable to personal freedom in the sense that the former is an important safeguard to the latter. Given the world in which we live, this view holds, if we are to preserve our liberty we must be self-governing and we must actively participate in

---

[4] It is important to stress that, given this limitation of scope, this essay does not purport to reach a general verdict on radical democracy or on any particular radical democratic theory. The point is not to affirm or reject radical democracy, but to examine and explore one important line of argument that radical democrats have advanced.

[5] Few radical democrats accept Rousseau's ideal of community outright, but identifications with it crop up from time to time in radical democratic writings. See esp. Barber, *Strong Democracy*, and Pateman, *Participation and Democratic Theory*. In discussing this view, I will speak of citizens collectively identifying with the authorization of political power in their political community. I will do this to avoid having to confront the interpretive question of how to understand Rousseau's notion of the general will.

[6] This view has sometimes been attributed to Habermas. See Warren, "The Self in Discursive Democracy," 172–79.

ruling our political communities, for only by so doing can we protect our freedom from potential threats both at home and abroad.[7]

Thus, depending on how the phrase "a tight connection" is construed, there are at least four different interpretations of the claim that there is a tight connection between personal freedom and political self-government. These four interpretations are summarized below.

(A) In order to be free a person must live in a political community in which he participates in processes of political self-rule and he and his fellow citizens identify with the authorization of political power in that political community.

(B) In order to be free a person must live in a political community in which he participates in processes of political self-rule, but it is not also necessary that he and his fellow citizens identify with the authorization of political power in that political community.

(C) Participation in processes of political self-rule is instrumentally valuable to personal freedom because it helps people develop capacities and skills integral to personal freedom.

(D) Participation in processes of political self-rule is instrumentally valuable to personal freedom because it is an important means for safeguarding personal freedom from threats both at home and abroad.

This essay will focus on the first three of these claims. While it raises important issues, (D) does not clearly represent a departure from liberal pluralist theory. With no difficulty, liberal pluralists can concede that if circumstances are such that widespread political participation is the only or the most effective way to preserve liberty, then people ought to value self-government if they value freedom. Accordingly, the dispute between the liberal pluralist and the proponent of (D) is not perspicuously described as a theoretical disagreement about the nature of freedom and self-government. Rather, it is better understood as a sociological dispute over when and how often widespread political participation is necessary to preserve personal freedom.[8]

---

[7] For discussion and defense of this view, see Quentin Skinner, "The Idea of Negative Liberty: Philosophical and Historical Perspectives," in *Philosophy in History*, ed. Richard Rorty, Jerome Schneewind, and Quentin Skinner (Cambridge: Cambridge University Press, 1984).

[8] This is pretty much conceded by the most prominent contemporary proponent of claim (D). Quentin Skinner makes it plain that the writers he draws on in his work all accept a liberal understanding of personal freedom. Their disagreement with liberal writers concerns how this shared understanding of personal freedom can best be promoted and safeguarded. See also Charles Taylor's discussion of this issue in his *Philosophical Arguments* (Cambridge, MA: Harvard University Press, 1995), 302 n. 15.

In contrast, claims (A), (B), and (C), in different ways, all pose an important theoretical challenge to liberal pluralism. It is this theoretical challenge that I want to investigate in this essay. If any of these claims are true, liberal pluralists have failed to grasp, or have underestimated the significance of, political self-government for personal freedom.

III. Radical Democracy: Two Themes

I will discuss these claims in serial fashion, starting with the stronger (A) and (B) and then later turning to (C). First, however, I need to fill in some of the theoretical background to the radical democratic view. Toward this end, in this section, I will identify and discuss two important themes of radical democratic political thought. These two themes I will call respectively *self-transformation through political discussion* and *civic autonomy*. By studying these two themes in some detail, we can come to see why many radical democrats have been tempted to embrace one (or several) of the claims distinguished above.

The basic idea behind the first theme is not difficult to explain. According to radical democrats, politics is not simply a space where we come together to advance our pre-political interests and ends. It is also a space where we subject our understanding of our needs and interests to rational scrutiny. This is a natural consequence of the logic of political discussion. In politics we are called on to express our views and articulate our interests, but in the process of expression and articulation these views and interests can change and be refined. We can discover that our views are mistaken or that we do not have a fully accurate grasp of what is in our best interests. In this way, our understanding of who we are (and other people's understanding of who we are) can be transformed; and more often than not, the radical democrat will contend, this transformation will be for the better.[9]

The second theme is not so easily explained in simple, straightforward terms. Civic autonomy refers to a socially constituted form of freedom that results when citizens collectively identify with the authorization of political power in their society. This can occur in one of two main ways. The first way is the achievement of a rational consensus on political questions. This consensus is made possible when men and women come together to deliberate about and define the common good of their society. Importantly, when such a consensus is reached, persons are bound only by laws they themselves have endorsed. For this reason, consensus in politics is valuable and inspiring. But the consensus must be a rational one to be worthy of respect. Accordingly, radical democrats who invoke

---

[9] For discussion, see Michelman, "The Supreme Court"; Cass Sunstein, "Preferences and Politics," *Philosophy and Public Affairs* 20, no. 3 (1991); and Benhabib, *Critique, Norm, and Utopia*, 313–14.

consensus put great store in the claim that all persons should be allowed to participate on fair terms with others in the formation of the consensus. Only in this way, it is held, can we ensure that no relevant considerations will be overlooked and that no one's interests will be left out in the formation of the consensus.[10] A rational consensus, then, is simply a consensus that has been reached when all have been allowed to participate under fair conditions.[11]

As many radical democrats themselves are quick to stress, however, achieving a rational consensus on political questions is a difficult thing to do in modern pluralistic societies. If this were the only way to realize civic autonomy, it might be fair to conclude that it is a utopian idea. But there is a second way to realize civic autonomy. Unable to reach agreement on the substance of how conflicts ought to be resolved and what collective goals ought to be pursued, citizens might nevertheless come to agree on the appropriate procedures for settling their differences. They might come to share a commitment that certain decision-making procedures—when all participate in them on fair terms[12]—confer legitimacy on the outcomes that flow from them. In this case, despite their disagreements on the substance of politics, citizens would be led to agree that the laws that bind them are legitimate and fair. This would amount to a collective identification with the authorization of political power in their society. Let us call this *second-order civic autonomy*, to distinguish it from the first-order civic autonomy that is realized when a rational political consensus obtains.

Having now sketched these two themes—themes which are given a different interpretation and a different emphasis by different radical democratic thinkers—we can now inquire into how they might bear on the radical democratic view of freedom and self-government. Two answers immediately suggest themselves. The first one holds that the self-transformation that occurs through political discussion is an integral component of personal freedom. The second answer holds that the achievement of civic autonomy is integral to personal freedom because a constitutive element of personal freedom is living in a community in which one can identify with the laws that bind one (as one can in a political community that realizes civic autonomy). These two answers connect the two radical democratic themes to the value of personal freedom. They explain why the radical democrat privileges the domain of politics and exalts the value of political participation. If the first answer is right, then only by

---

[10] See, for example, Jürgen Habermas, *Moral Consciousness and Communicative Action* (Cambridge, MA: MIT Press, 1990); Benhabib, *Critique, Norm, and Utopia*; and Sunstein, "Beyond the Republican Revival."

[11] There are different accounts of what constitutes fair conditions. Different radical democrats have specified them in different ways, but here we need not concern ourselves with these differences.

[12] This qualification is important. Civic autonomy requires active engagement with and endorsement of the relevant decision-making procedures. It is not achieved when citizens acquiesce in political outcomes that follow from procedures they have not participated in.

participating in political self-government can men and women undergo the transformations that make freedom genuinely possible. If the second answer is right, then only by participating in political self-government can men and women come to identify with the authorization of political power in their society. Either way, there is a tight connection between personal freedom and political self-government.

It should not escape notice that these two answers provide justificatory grounds for claims (A) and (B). Recall that these claims read as follows:

(A) In order to be free a person must live in a political community in which he participates in processes of political self-rule and he and his fellow citizens identify with the authorization of political power in that political community.

(B) In order to be free a person must live in a political community in which he participates in processes of political self-rule, but it is not also necessary that he and his fellow citizens identify with the authorization of political power in that political community.

If people must participate in political self-government in order to identify with the authorization of political power in their community, and if this kind of identification is necessary to personal freedom, then (A) is true. Likewise, if they must participate in political self-government in order to undergo the type of transformations that are necessary to personal freedom, then (B) is true. Thus, the two answers suggested above explain how claims (A) and (B) could be true.

Interestingly, some radical democrats accept both of these answers, believing them to be connected. They think that the idea that politics has a transformative dimension explains how civic autonomy is possible. People come to politics with different views and conflicting interests, but through political discussion their views and interests change; and this change makes it easier for them to reach agreement on political questions, or at least on the right procedures for resolving them. However, there is no necessary connection between these two answers. As we shall see later, it is possible that the transformation of beliefs and interests brought about by political discussion might impede, rather than facilitate, the achievement of civic autonomy.

IV. REALIZING CIVIC AUTONOMY IN THE MODERN WORLD

Both (A) and (B) assert a necessary connection between personal freedom and participation in democratic politics. But (A) is the stronger of the two claims. We should start, then, by asking whether there are good reasons for thinking it is true. As I noted above, the idea that in order to be free one must live in a political community that realizes civic autonomy gains support from the thought that living in a political community in which one can identify with the laws that bind one is a constitutive element of personal freedom. This thought, of course, was Rousseau's; and it expresses a powerful ideal.[13]

But while there is little doubt that this ideal is inspiring, doubts have often been voiced about whether it is achievable in practice, particularly in complex, differentiated pluralistic societies. If it is not achievable in practice, then it cannot serve as a valid guide for political action. The ideal would be utopian in the pejorative sense. Given this, radical democrats who accept claim (A) because they accept the ideal that lies behind it need to offer some explanation for how this ideal could be achieved (or at least how it could come closer to being achieved) under modern conditions.[14]

In this section, I will examine and criticize two such explanations that sometimes have been offered by radical democrats. This will put us in a better position in the next section to examine a third explanation, one that draws more explicitly on the transformative potential of politics.

The two explanations to be considered here can be labeled the *universalization strategy* and the *mediation strategy*. In its most general form, the universalization strategy maintains that political discussion has a "disciplining effect." It compels political actors to present their views in public-regarding language. By so doing, it facilitates the achievement of a rational consensus. The basic idea behind this strategy has been well summarized by Benjamin Barber:

> [Political deliberation involves] a kind of "we" thinking that compels individuals to reformulate their interests, purposes, norms and plans in a mutualistic language of public goods. "I want X" must be reconceived as "X would be good for the community to which I belong"—an operation in social algebra for which not every "X" will be suitable.[15]

The force of the universalization strategy turns on how strong this "disciplining effect" actually is. Figuring this out is not just an empirical matter. We cannot judge the disciplining power of political discussion simply by examining actual political discussions, for the radical democrat may claim (and often does claim) that the efficacy of political discussion will only become fully visible once the right background conditions are in place. There is a difference between mere political talk and ideal political dis-

---

[13] As Rousseau famously put it, the ideal is to find a form of political association in which each associate "while uniting with all, nevertheless obeys only himself . . ." (Jean-Jacques Rousseau, *On the Social Contract* [Indianapolis: Hackett Publishing Co., 1988], 148).

[14] By "modern conditions" I mean to refer to certain uncontroversial facts about modern political communities, namely, that they are relatively large, have modern economies, and contain a diversity of social groups.

[15] Barber, *Strong Democracy*, 171.

cussion. Still, even conceding this point, it is fair to inquire into how political discussion is supposed to work its magic once the right conditions are established. And by focusing on this more speculative question, we can come to a judgment about the plausibility of the universalization strategy.

The universalization strategy gets its bite from the idea that in political argument one must present reasons for one's views that relate them to the public good of one's community. Simply asserting that some policy would serve one's own interests normally will not pass muster. This rules out all policies or proposals that cannot be defended in public-regarding language. And, if selfishness obstructs the achievement of a rational consensus (a not implausible idea!), then this constraint would make achieving such a consensus easier. Notwithstanding this, there is a good reason to think that the constraint in question is a weak one. Even if it were in full force, participants in a political discussion would not move much closer to achieving a rational consensus on political questions. The reason for this is not hard to see. Many self-serving political proposals can be expressed in public-regarding language. Participants can circumvent the "disciplining effect" of political argument by repackaging their views in the language of the common good.[16] To be sure, there may be some proposals which it is conceptually impossible to so repackage, but these will constitute a subset, and probably a very small subset, of all self-serving political proposals. We have pretty good reason, then, to think that the universalization strategy will not succeed.

But perhaps more can be said for it than I have so far allowed. Perhaps it is harder to express selfish interests in the language of the public good than I have been assuming. Properly understood, the requirement of expressing political views and preferences in public-regarding language may be a very strong conceptual constraint on political discussion.

How might this be? Up to this point, I have been referring to the idea of public-regarding language as if it were self-explanatory; but this is not the case at all. In fact, the idea is quite vague. It is not obvious what counts as a public good or a public bad; and if this is not obvious, then it is not obvious where the boundaries of public-regarding discussion lie. This vagueness threatens to undermine the universalization strategy. Perhaps recognizing this, some have attempted to sharpen the description of public-regarding language. It is not enough, they argue, for a person to appeal to some public value in order for his views to count as public-regarding; political discussion imposes more discipline than that. They demand that

---

[16] Consider this example. The owner of a domestic factory might be in favor of protectionist legislation because such legislation would likely increase his profits. However, in arguing for the legislation in public debate, he could "repackage" his views by appealing to public values such as the need to protect local jobs from foreign competition.

people express political views that are universalizable.[17] By "universalizable" these theorists have a fairly specific idea in mind. Universalizability means that persons must justify their political views by appealing to reasons that are persuasive to all or could be accepted by all. In other words, participants in political discussion must try to look at things from their own and others' points of view at once in order to discover action-guiding principles which can be accepted from all points of view.[18]

It is not hard to see that this requirement is stronger than the requirement of expressing views in language that refers to public values. Under this stronger requirement, it would be a trickier task to tailor one's conception of the public good to one's private interests. But while the requirement of universalizability provides a way of giving more bite to "the disciplining effect" of public discussion, it runs into several problems.

First, and most importantly, there is no good reason to think that participation in political discussion will in fact motivate people to accept the universalizability requirement. Political discussion may promote "we thinking." It may even induce people to express their views in public-regarding language, but it is hard to see how it could lead them to accept a moral ideal like universalizability. Indeed, the requirement of universalizability will likely be experienced as harsh or overly demanding by many groups of people. It enjoins them to step back from their particular beliefs and values and seek outcomes that all could accept. But even supposing that we could arrive at outcomes that all could accept if we all stepped back, many will not have the motivation to do so. They will not want to step back from their commitments, perhaps viewing this as a form of betrayal.[19] If this is right, then we cannot expect political discussion to move all participants to accept the requirement of universalizability.

---

[17] See, among others, Joshua Cohen, "Deliberation and Democratic Legitimacy," in *The Good Polity*, ed. Alan Hamlin and Philip Pettit (Oxford: Blackwell, 1989); and Seyla Benhabib, "Liberal Dialogue versus a Critical Theory of Discursive Legitimacy," in Benhabib, *Situating the Self* (New York: Routledge, 1992).

[18] See John Mackie's discussion of what he terms the "third stage of universalization in moral thought": John L. Mackie, *Ethics: Inventing Right and Wrong* (Harmondsworth: Penguin, 1977), 93.

[19] This point is a natural extension of what Michael Walzer has termed the problem of particularism:

> Even if [persons] are committed to impartiality, the question most likely to arise in the minds of members of a political community is not, What would rational individuals choose under universalizing conditions of such and such a sort? But rather, What would individuals like us choose, who are situated as we are, who share a culture and are determined to go on sharing it?

See Michael Walzer, *Spheres of Justice* (New York: Basic Books, 1984), 5. See also Georgia Warnake, "Communicative Rationality and Cultural Values," in *The Cambridge Companion to Habermas*, ed. White, where Warnake critically discusses Habermas's views on this issue.

Second, the requirement of universalizability appears to assume that there exists a stock of reasons which are acceptable to all and from which concrete political policies could be derived and justified. However, at least in modern societies, this does not seem to be the case. Many political controversies cannot be resolved by appealing to values or reasons that all could accept.[20] The disagreements in these societies run too deep. Perhaps over time this will change as more people come to accept the same values. If this were to happen, the emerging consensus coupled with general adherence to the universalizability requirement might well yield a rational consensus. But we must first establish this emerging consensus before we can rely on the universalizability requirement to help us achieve a rational consensus. Thinking otherwise threatens to put the cart before the horse.

The requirement of universalizability, therefore, cannot effectively shore up the universalization strategy. We must conclude that this strategy cannot provide a plausible explanation for how the Rousseauian ideal—which stands behind and justifies claim (A)—could be achieved under modern conditions.

Let us turn, then, to the second strategy mentioned at the beginning of this section, the mediation strategy. Some radical democrats concede that all values and ideals cannot be synthesized into a public-regarding language that all can accept. They concede that such an ambition fails to take seriously the deep disagreements that divide people in modern societies. Nevertheless, they maintain, we should not give up on consensus. A rational consensus in politics is possible because political discussion provides a powerful means for mediating and overcoming disagreement. As one writer has put it, the democratic "commitment to universalism amounts to a belief in the possibility of mediating different approaches to politics, or different conceptions of the public good, through discussion and dialogue."[21]

Of course, to be at all successful, this strategy must provide an account of how mediation is supposed to work. We need to be told exactly what is supposed to happen when conflicting views get mediated. In thinking about this matter it may help to distinguish two understandings of mediation. According to the first understanding, the burden of mediation is to identify which views are unreasonable, and then to provide mechanisms by which political discussion could lead people to an awareness of this. Understood in these terms, the mediation strategy is closely related to (or perhaps identical with) the universalization strategy, and there is no need to discuss it further. According to a second understanding, mediation refers

[20] Habermas criticizes civic republican writers on this point; see his *Between Facts and Norms*, 278–79. But the point may cut against Habermas as well, for if disagreements run deep it may not be possible, as he seems to believe, for people to reach agreement on the procedures for resolving them.

[21] Sunstein, "Beyond the Republican Revival," 1554.

to a process that involves empathy and mutual adjustment. When views get mediated, one does not emerge as superior; rather, adherents of both views come to understand one another's views and make concessions.[22]

Can mediation, understood along these lines, explain how civic autonomy could be achieved? The radical democratic literature is pretty sketchy on this point. It is frequently claimed that participation in political discussion is an educative process that teaches people the virtues of compromise. In so doing, it is further claimed, it makes it possible for citizens to reach agreement on more issues.[23] However, it is not always clear what arguments are supposed to support these assertions. To assess the mediation strategy, then, we will need to engage in some rational reconstruction.

There are two basic arguments that have been offered in support of the mediation strategy. One is hinted at, but not fully developed, in the following passage from Hannah Pitkin:

> [A]ctual participation in political action, deliberation and conflict may make us aware of our more remote and indirect connections with others, the long-range and large-scale significance of what we want and are doing.[24]

The important idea in this passage is that persons who hold different political views may nevertheless have shared interests of which they have not yet become fully aware. Participation in political discussion provides an avenue for the discovery of these common concerns.

Consider the following scenario: Two parties, A and B, have different views about political morality. Suppose now that they share, but do not fully realize that they share, a common interest that is compelling for both of them. Further suppose that participation in political discussion would make it more likely that they would come to understand that they share this interest. In this way, participation in political discussion would supply A and B with a motive to make mutual concessions so as to promote their common interest, and this might help them reach agreement on a wide range of political questions.

The second argument in support of the mediation strategy is sketched by Cass Sunstein, among others. "A principal function of a democratic system," he writes, "is to ensure that through representative or participatory processes, new or submerged voices, or novel depictions of where interests lie and what they in fact are, are heard and understood."[25] He then argues that these new voices and submerged interests will have a

[22] For further discussion of this understanding of mediation, see Seyla Benhabib's discussion of Arendt in "Judgment and the Moral Foundations of Politics in Hannah Arendt's Thought," in Benhabib, *Situating the Self*.

[23] See, for example, Sunstein, "Beyond the Republican Revival," 1156.

[24] Pitkin, "Justice: On Relating Private and Public," 347.

[25] Sunstein, "Preferences and Politics," 17.

transformative effect on the political preferences of all participants involved in political discussion. These participants will come to see the one-sidedness of their own views and seek to widen their perspectives to include the standpoint of others.[26] In this way, all are moved closer to substantive agreement.

Both of these arguments present nice stories. And there may be times and contexts in which the stories do capture the truth; but the plausibility of these arguments is severely weakened by their failure to explore the very real possibility that disagreement may become more intense as more people and more groups become active participants in the political process. That this is true is borne out by much historical experience.[27] An active interest in politics is often correlated with passionate convictions about the common good. The passionate convictions motivate the interest in and commitment to political activity. But passionate commitments, whatever their virtues, seldom promote a tolerant, compromising outlook. They bring excitement and tumult to political life, not the quiet and quiescent spirit of compromise and mutual adjustment.

The point being made here can be expressed more sharply if we draw a distinction between civic virtue and civility.[28] The former concerns a citizen's willingness to participate in politics and his commitment to the common good (more precisely, his commitment to his sincere understanding of the common good) of his political community. The latter concerns a citizen's willingness to tolerate disagreement and to seek reasonable accommodations with others. This distinction helps illuminate what is misleading about the arguments for mediation. Radical democrats often write as if civic virtue and civility were complementary, merely different aspects of the same virtue.[29] This allows them to claim that as more people become active in politics and begin to take political discussion seriously, there will be a corresponding increase in the sincere willingness of people to search for shared goals and to adjust their perspectives to accommodate the interests and concerns of others. It is precisely this promise of enhanced civility that gives both of the mediation arguments their force.

But given the common experience of political life in modern societies, this is oddly romantic. Surely it is more plausible to think that an

[26] Sunstein, "Beyond the Republican Revival," 1555.

[27] As a reading of Hobbes makes plain, in the early modern period, one of the central arguments against widespread civic participation was that it tended to divide and polarize a society. See Thomas Hobbes, *Leviathan*, ed. Richard Flathman and David Johnston (New York: W. W. Norton and Company, 1997), 118–19. More recently, one could point to the divisiveness and tumult that went hand-in-hand with increased political participation in the 1960s in the United States.

[28] The distinction has been drawn by others. See, in particular, Michael Walzer, "Civility and Civic Virtue in Contemporary America," in *Radical Principles* (New York: Basic Books, 1980).

[29] For a particularly clear example of this, see Barber, *Strong Democracy*, 223.

increase in political participation, and a concomitant increase in people's commitment to political discussion, will make political life more robust, but also less tolerant and civil. This might be an improvement on the status quo; but at the moment that is not what is at issue. The strategy of mediation asserts that a more participatory, more inclusive form of political life would be more likely to achieve consensus because people would discover shared goals and become more inclined to adjust their views to accommodate the concerns of others. Taking people as we find them, and as they have been in the recent past, this claim is hard to accept.

All of this suggests that the mediation strategy, like the universalization strategy, fails to provide a convincing explanation for how political discussion could make possible, or more likely, the achievement of a rational consensus on political questions. However, this does not yet show that these strategies are unsuccessful in explaining the possibility of civic autonomy, for it might be true that the mechanisms identified by these two strategies, while not leading to a rational consensus on political questions, would nonetheless lead people to accept as fair and legitimate the same decision-making procedures for resolving their disagreements. The two strategies, that is, might be able to account for the realization of second-order civic autonomy, even if they fail to account for the realization of first-order civic autonomy. But while possible, this is unlikely. Substantive disagreement in politics is all too often interwoven with procedural disagreement about how the issues ought to be resolved. Consider, for example, contemporary debates in the United States over abortion. The substantive disagreement about the moral permissibility of abortion is tightly intertwined with disagreement about which institutions—the federal courts, the federal legislature, or the state legislatures—are the appropriate decision-making bodies for resolving the dispute. The fact, then, that substantive and procedural issues are not sharply separable, but often tightly intertwined, strongly suggests that if the universalization and mediation strategies cannot explain the possibility of first-order civic autonomy, they will not be able to explain the possibility of second-order civic autonomy either.

However, notwithstanding this skeptical conclusion, the foregoing analysis of both strategies has taken citizens as we find them, and perhaps this is a mistake. I have tried to show that the universalization and mediation strategies cannot explain how civic autonomy is possible under modern conditions.

But radical democrats can respond to my arguments by insisting that universalization and mediation will become effective mechanisms only after the self-understandings of citizens have been suitably transformed. This brings us to a third explanation of how civic autonomy is possible, one that draws on the following thought. In politics we do not simply argue for policies that advance our interests, nor do we simply seek accommodations with others who are striving to advance their interests. Rather, we seek to gain a better understanding of where our interests really lie. Building on this thought, the third explanation holds that once people come to a better understanding of their own interests, they may be able to reach (or at least move much closer to) a rational political consensus.

This is an intriguing line of argument, and it introduces a number of the issues that I will be grappling with in the remainder of this essay. Let us therefore take a closer look at it.

V. Civic Autonomy and Self-Transformation

The first two explanations of how civic autonomy could be achieved under modern conditions, the universalization strategy and the mediation strategy, take citizens as we find them. The third explanation does not. It appeals directly to (what I earlier identified as) one of the two fundamental themes of radical democracy, the theme of self-transformation through political discussion. Before discussing the third explanation in more detail, then, it may be useful to say a word or two more about the idea of self-transformation through political discussion, since this idea may strike some as mysterious.

People's understanding of their own interests may change in one of two general ways. First, they may come to believe that some interest or concern of theirs is not really their own. That is, they may come to believe that it has been implanted in them by others or generated by processes that they do not identify with. And, for this reason, they may give it up. When this occurs, I shall call it an *autonomous transformation*.[30] Second, people may come to believe that some of their interests are mistaken or that some of their beliefs about what is worthwhile are not sufficiently sensitive to how things really are. And, for this reason, they may change their minds about their interests. When this occurs, I shall call it a *progressive transformation*, since those who change their minds in this way believe that their new interests represent an advance on their old ones.[31]

Both types of transformative experiences can occur through participation in political discussion. By participating in political discussion, a person may come to a better understanding of the origins of his preferences and the conditioning influences on his beliefs. In this way, he

---

[30] It is possible that a person might come to think that some of his interests were implanted in him when this was, in fact, false. In such a case, an autonomous transformation might result (ironically) in the person's becoming less autonomous. Discussing this complication, however, would needlessly complicate my argument. I mention it here just to put it to one side.

[31] It is possible that people could be mistaken in thinking this. We might want to distinguish a genuine progressive transformation from a merely perceived progressive transformation. But again I shall ignore this complication.

can become more autonomous. Likewise, by participating in political discussion, a person can come to a better understanding of what is valuable and worthwhile. In this way, he can form better judgments about how to lead his life.

Properly understood, then, there is nothing mysterious about the idea that politics has a transformative dimension. What we must now ask is: Do radical democrats have a plausible account of such transformation that would explain how a rational consensus in politics could be achieved? Such an account would need to identify the mechanisms that enable people to undergo either autonomous or progressive transformations through political discussion, and it would need to show that such transformations make it more likely that they will converge in their judgments on political questions. More precisely, such an account would need to satisfy two conditions:

(1) It must show that participation in political discussion is necessary if people are to undergo the right type of autonomous and/or progressive transformations. And:
(2) It must show that once people have undergone these transformations, it will be easier for them to achieve civic autonomy.

It should be clear that such an account is necessary if the third explanation is to work. This explanation seeks to vindicate claim (A) by showing how the Rousseauian ideal could be realized in modern societies. If no account of the transformative dimension of politics satisfies both conditions, then the third explanation will fail. This would cast serious doubt on the plausibility of claim (A).

Thus, our initial query can be rephrased in the following way: Do radical democrats have an account of the transformative dimension of politics that satisfies both of these conditions? In the next section, I will argue that no such account exists because no plausible account of self-transformation through political discussion can satisfy condition (2). For this reason, I will conclude that claim (A) should be rejected. Civic autonomy is not a valid political ideal for the modern world.

VI. PLURALISM AND DISTORTED NEED-INTERPRETATIONS

For present purposes, we can assume that radical democrats have well-worked-out and convincing accounts of self-transformation through political discussion. We can assume that these accounts can explain how autonomous and progressive transformations are possible and how they can be identified in practice. Our question is whether there is any reason to think that such transformations could make the realization of civic autonomy possible or more likely.

Before proceeding, I need to introduce one last piece of terminology. Let us say that a person who has undergone either an autonomous or a progressive transformation had a *distorted need-interpretation* prior to the transformation. That is, prior to the transformation he had a distorted understanding of his own needs and interests. With this terminology, we can ask what happens when people overcome their distorted need-interpretations by participating in political discussion. And to this question three general answers can be given: people who overcome their distorted need-interpretations may be no more and no less likely to converge on political questions or to converge on how they ought to be resolved; or they may be less likely to so converge; or they may be more likely to so converge.

The last of the three answers is the one the radical democrat needs if he is to provide an account of self-transformation through political discussion that can vindicate claim (A). Perhaps realizing this, some radical democrats have thought that such an answer is plausible. One writer, for example, has argued that public political discourses should be viewed as "moral-transformative processes," "processes through which new needs and interests, such as can lead to a consensus among the participants, emerge."[32] But here it is necessary to ask why it is that people whose need-interpretations have been tested and refined by political discussion would be any more likely to reach consensus. Why not think the converse is just as likely to be true? After all, it is certainly possible that when people come to a better understanding of their individual needs and interests, they will be driven further apart. They may come to recognize that what is important to them conflicts more violently (than they had previously thought) with what is important to others. We cannot just assume, then, that accurate or refined need-interpretations will bring people closer together. And without this assumption, it is hard to see how participation in political discussion is supposed to bring about the types of transformations in participants necessary to achieve a rational political consensus, or at least make achieving it substantially easier.

Against this, some radical democrats may believe that there exists an underlying social bond between citizens that is disrupted and fragmented only because they suffer, for various reasons, from distorted need-interpretations. If this were right, it would be plausible to think that political discussion under appropriate conditions could bring about transformations in citizens that make it more likely for them to converge in judgment. However, as many have pointed out, such a belief is difficult to sustain for complex modern societies marked by religious, ethnic, and cultural pluralism. For these societies, there is no thick, shared ethical self-understanding that political discussion could bring to the surface and

---

[32] Benhabib, *Critique, Norm, and Utopia*, 314.

articulate. That is why in these societies, even under the best of conditions, politics will remain in large measure a matter of making compromises and striking bargains.[33]

This gives us good reason to conclude that even if democratic politics has a strong transformative dimension (and this is something I have conceded for the purposes of this section), no convincing case exists for thinking that it could make the realization of civic autonomy any more likely. And this means that claim (A) will need to be given up.[34]

VII. LOWERING THE SIGHTS: CLAIM (B)

Thus far, a good deal of my discussion has centered on the first radical democratic theme, the theme of civic autonomy. As I have pointed out, this theme owes much to Rousseau. Yet many radical democrats do not accept the Rousseauian ideal of democratic community. Some have even explicitly advocated a clean break with this ideal,[35] and they perhaps will be able to accept much of the discussion up to this point. Accordingly, we need now to drop talk of civic autonomy and focus exclusively on the second radical democratic theme, the theme of self-transformation through political discussion.

Working with this theme, it is possible to construct important and interesting arguments about personal freedom that do not presuppose the achievement of a rational consensus on political questions. This brings us to claim (B). Recall that this claim holds that participation in political self-government is a necessary component of personal freedom, but it does not add the further requirement that people collectively identify with the authorization of political power in their society. Furthermore, as I pointed out above, claim (B), if true, would give the radical democrat what she needs. It would establish a tight link between political self-government and personal freedom.

In the previous section, I assumed that radical democrats have well-worked out and convincing accounts of self-transformation through political discussion. But is this true? Do any such accounts exist? In this

---

[33] See Jürgen Habermas, "Three Normative Models of Democracy," in *Democracy and Difference*, ed. Seyla Benhabib (Princeton: Princeton University Press, 1996), 24–25.

[34] The alert reader will notice that I have not refuted the ideal that motivates claim (A). That ideal, for all that I have said, may be sound. Instead, I have tried to show that there is no good explanation for how this ideal could be realized under modern conditions, and I have suggested that if it cannot be realized under modern conditions, then it is not a valid guide for political action for modern societies. It is open for someone to accept this and argue that the political problem we face is how to change modern conditions so that the ideal motivating claim (A) can be realized. But my focus in this essay is on those who have made peace with modernity, and this argumentative option is not open to them.

[35] For the views of radical democrats who explicitly distance themselves from Rousseau's ideal of democratic community, see Warren, "What Should We Expect from More Democracy?" 242–43; and Young, *Justice and the Politics of Difference*. See also Habermas's criticisms of civic republicanism in *Between Facts and Norms*, 100–103.

section, I want to consider briefly two candidates for such an account. These have been chosen because both are fairly well-developed, both raise issues that bear on personal freedom, and both bring to light some of the difficulties that confront claim (B). The first account makes use of the phenomenon of adaptive preference formation, the second one relies on the idea that political discussion can provide protection against manipulation.

To begin with the first account, the root idea behind adaptive preference formation is simple: what people want is a function of what they can get.[36] If the options open to them are restricted, their preferences over time may adjust to the restricted option set. Like the fox who comes to express a preference for sour grapes, people become content with their limited options.[37] Moreover, and importantly, this process of preference adaptation is "a purely causal process," and it takes place "behind the back" of the people concerned.[38] Therefore, it is plausible to describe it as an impediment to personal freedom. Other things being equal, those who suffer from adaptive preferences are less free than those who do not.

Applied to the political context, preference adaptation of this sort provides an explanation for why oppressed groups might come to believe in the justice or inevitability of the political order that oppresses them. Given their limited options, they may unconsciously adapt to the social conditions that keep them down, thus becoming content with their lot. In this way their freedom is compromised. This suggests that in assessing how free people are, particularly those who have been oppressed in the recent past, we must not ignore the history of how their preferences have been formed.

This is very sensible; but what, it may be wondered, does it have to do with radical democracy? The answer is provided by the suggestion that the remedy for adaptive preferences is participation in rational political discussion.[39] Such participation can make us more aware of the origins and causal histories of our preferences. For when we participate in political discussion, we come into contact with the views and experiences of others, and we are called on to reflect on and justify our preferences. This

[36] The term "adaptive preference" comes from Jon Elster; he discusses this phenomenon in *Sour Grapes* (Cambridge: Cambridge University Press, 1983).

[37] As the title of Elster's book suggests, the person who suffers from adaptive preferences is like the fox in Aesop's fable who comes not to desire the grapes he cannot have.

[38] Elster is careful to distinguish this type of preference adaptation from self-conscious strategies of preference change; see *Sour Grapes*, 117.

[39] By "rational political discussion" I mean political discussion under fairly good conditions, however these might be spelled out. The suggestion that participation in rational political discussion is the remedy for adaptive preferences is made by Elster, *Sour Grapes*, 33, 140. However, Elster makes it plain that he does not believe that overcoming adaptive preferences (or achieving other beneficial transformative effects) could be the primary point of political participation; see ibid., 91–100. See also Cass Sunstein, "Legal Interference with Private Preferences," *University of Chicago Law Review* 53 (1986).

process of reflection and justification can bring the "behind the back" causal mechanisms that underlie adaptive preferences out into the open, freeing their victims from their grip.

Thus, the phenomenon of adaptive preference formation reveals how participation in rational political discussion could be a necessary component of personal freedom. If citizens suffer from adaptive preferences, and if rational political discussion is necessary to overcome them, then they will need to participate in rational political discussion if they are to be fully free. Of course, one might have doubts about just how effective rational political discussion would be at accomplishing this task, but I want to draw attention to a different problem with this line of argument. Many radical democrats fail to distinguish political from social interaction. This allows them to portray political discussion as the counterpoint to the solitary reflection of the individual. But it is an error to identify the political too tightly with the social, for the former is a subset of the latter. Political activity is simply one kind of social activity. Once this is borne in mind, it is not plausible to claim that participation in rational political discussion is necessary to overcome adaptive preferences. People can learn about the origins and causal histories of their preferences by interacting with others in social, but not necessarily political, contexts.

At this point it might be objected that political discussion, at least under good conditions, is different from other kinds of social discussions, and that these differences are relevant to the matter at hand. In political settings, it might be argued, we must confront the views and perspectives of a wide range of individuals, whereas in other social settings our interaction is often more confined, limited to those who share many of our beliefs and biases. Furthermore, the exposure to a wide range of views and perspectives in political settings might have epistemic value.[40] We might come to learn more about ourselves by confronting the diverse views and perspectives of others; and this self-knowledge might better enable us to overcome adaptive preferences.

There is indeed truth to this objection, and we shall come back to it later. For now, however, it ought to be clear that the objection cannot defeat the point made above. Even if participation in rational political discussion better enables people to identify adaptive preferences than participation in other forms of social discussion does, it would not follow that participation in rational political discussion is necessary for overcoming adaptive preferences. One cannot move from the claim that x is the most effective means for overcoming y to the claim that x is necessary to overcome y. And this stronger type of claim is what must be established if this account is to be relied on to vindicate claim (B).

---

[40] For more on this point, see Iris Marion Young, "Communication and the Other: Beyond Deliberative Democracy," in *Democracy and Difference*, ed. Benhabib, 126–28.

I turn now to the second account mentioned above, the one that relies on the idea that political discussion can provide protection against manipulation.[41] To understand this account, we need first to attend to an insight that is both important and true. The insight is that the identity of human beings is constituted in large part by their interaction with others. The beliefs, needs, and preferences of people are not fixed, but fluid; and they are shaped and structured by the social practices that they find themselves a part of and participate in. These facts warrant the conclusion that the "self" comes to be only within "webs of interlocution."[42]

Granting this basic insight, an insight which has by now become a mere truism, it becomes possible to ask how we know that the socialization processes that have shaped our needs and preferences are not themselves distorted. If the social framework that shapes us is beset with pathologies, how much respect do our self-understandings warrant? How are we to distinguish distorted from authentic self-understandings? The answer given by the second account is that we can only know that our "interpretations" of our needs and interests are not distorted if we have submitted them to a political discussion in which they have been tested. The reason we need to participate in such discussions is that there is simply no better way to ensure that we are not being manipulated by others. Participation can be thought of as a form of insurance against bad faith. As Habermas puts it: "[N]othing better prevents others from perspectivally distorting one's own interests than actual participation."[43] If this is right, then participation in political discussion, at least under the right conditions, is an integral component of genuine self-understanding.

But why, we need to ask again, must we participate in political as opposed to social interaction in order to test our need-interpretations? The argument we have been considering establishes that if people are to be free from manipulation, then it is advisable for them to discuss their needs and interests with others. Yet, by itself, this tells us nothing about the importance of political discussion per se, as opposed to other types of discussions. Thus, by itself, it provides no support for claim (B).

Proponents of the argument do not wish to leave the matter here, however. They contend that the discussion with others that is needed must take place under the right conditions, namely, under conditions in which all have the opportunity to participate on equal terms. And a discussion like this occurs only in public political discourses, where all

---

[41] Proponents of this account include Habermas, *Moral Consciousness and Communicative Action*, and Benhabib, *Critique, Norm, and Utopia*.

[42] The phrase is taken from Charles Taylor, *Sources of the Self* (Cambridge, MA: Harvard University Press, 1992), 36.

[43] Habermas, *Moral Consciousness and Communicative Action*, 67.

are brought together to discuss their common fate.[44] This further step in the argument connects it with claim (B). It shows that participation in rational political discussion is a necessary component of personal freedom.[45]

But is this further step plausible? In thinking about this, we need to attend to the following point: a rational decision to investigate the authenticity of a need-interpretation requires taking into account the costs of doing so. Suppose, for example, that the reliability of a need-interpretation is a function of the relevant information one is aware of, the degree to which that information is representative (not a biased sampling), and the time spent reflecting on it. Participation in ideal political discussion may enable one to score very high along these dimensions; but there are also costs involved in participating in these discussions: time is lost, energy is wasted, and the character of one's commitments may be changed in undesirable ways.[46] For these reasons, it may be rational for some not to want to participate in these discussions. By not participating, even if they become more vulnerable to manipulation, they might be better able to lead the lives they want to lead. This does not mean that it would be rational for such people to forgo all attempts at self-examination. Self-examination—and the scrutiny of one's understanding of one's own needs—can occur in a wide range of social contexts, and it can take many different forms. The point here is only this: It would be a mistake to think that all people, regardless of the character of their projects and concerns, have a compelling reason to participate in rational political discussion so as to insure against possible manipulation.

This undercuts the further step in the argument under consideration. For if participation in ideal political discussion is necessary to get pro-

---

[44] It is true that Habermas distinguishes ethical discourses (discourses which concern cultural values and need-interpretations) from moral and political discourses. And he contends that the former, unlike the latter, take place within the horizon of particular forms of life. This suggests that participation in these discourses is not universal, but limited to those who participate in the way of life in question. Still, within this limited horizon, Habermas insists that all members must be allowed to take part in the discourse on equal terms (*Between Facts and Norms*, 182).

[45] Is this is too strong? Strictly speaking, even if this argument were correct, it might still be the case that some people who did not participate in rational political discussion would, by good fortune, not be subject to manipulation. If so, participation in rational political discussion would not be a necessary component of personal freedom for them. Even so, it could still be argued that such people would lack self-knowledge by not participating in these discussions. They would not know or would not have warrant for believing that their need-interpretations were not manipulated. And the acquisition of this self-knowledge could, without too much of a stretch, be depicted as a gain in freedom.

[46] The very activity of articulating and debating a commitment in public may change its nature; and it is a mistake to suppose that this will always be for the better. Leaving aside the obvious cases of love and loyalty, consider a phenomenon described by Elster. He observes that the successful completion of many goals depends upon a false estimation of their importance, "the belief that one will achieve much is a causal condition for achieving anything at all" (*Sour Grapes*, 158). If Elster is right, then one cost of self-examination is that one will become more aware of one's own limitations and, as a result, will lose the motivation to accomplish even what one is capable of accomplishing.

tection against manipulation, if such protection is necessary for freedom, and if this participation is sometimes irrational, then freedom and rationality can conflict. And this is surely wrong.[47] Leading a free life should not require one to act irrationally. Thus, starting from the idea that participation in rational political discussion provides us with protection against manipulation, we cannot get to the idea that we must participate if we are to be free. And, as I have stressed, this is the idea we need to substantiate claim (B).

Neither this account nor the account that draws on the phenomenon of adaptive preference formation, therefore, can be developed so as to justify the claim that participation in rational political discussion is a necessary component of personal freedom. Both accounts founder on the same problem. If the transformations they identify are possible, they are possible in nonpolitical social contexts as well as political contexts. This negates their potential to provide support for claim (B). However, as I pointed out at the beginning of this essay, many radical democrats have a very broad conception of politics, one that extends well beyond activity in formal political institutions. And it might be thought that this fact takes the edge off some of the points that have been pressed in this section. So before turning to look at the next radical democratic claim, claim (C), I want to say a word or two more about the distinction between the political and the social.

VIII. DELIMITING THE POLITICAL

Here it is not my intention to offer a precise characterization of the political. Any such characterization would likely be arbitrary, downplaying or ignoring features that many think are important. Instead, I will identify three dimensions of politics that help to differentiate it from other forms of social interaction. Taken together, these three dimensions should give us a rough-and-ready way of distinguishing the political from the social, one that is congruent with radical democratic understandings and sufficient for present purposes.

The first dimension is equality. In political interaction, people come together as equals, at least in the sense that they have equal rights to participate in discussions and decision making. This is not to deny that status hierarchies and power differentials mark many actual political relationships. This no doubt is true. Equality is best understood as an ideal internal to political interaction.[48] To the extent that social relationships embody this ideal, particularly in the way in which they respond to

---

[47] I am not claiming that to be free one must be rational. I am claiming only that freedom should not require one to act irrationally.

[48] This point has its roots in Aristotle's attempt (in the *Politics*) to distinguish political relationships from relationships of mastery and dominance.

conflicts and disagreements, they more closely approximate political relationships.

The second dimension refers to the content or purpose of politics. Political interaction is marked by the need to reach collectively binding decisions about what the group should do, particularly when the group in question includes everyone in the community. Of course, we can and do speak of office politics, church politics, perhaps even family politics, but political interaction is first and foremost concerned with decisions that affect the welfare of the entire community.

The third dimension points to the presence of conflict in political relationships. All social groups contain the potential for conflict, but political interaction, more than most other types of social interaction, faces a continual need to confront and respond to conflict and disagreement. This is why we sometimes describe social relationships that have become contested as "politicized."[49] Of course, some hope that in the end discussion and deliberation will be able to resolve much of this conflict, but a good case can be made that conflict is inherent in and endemic to political life.

These three dimensions should not be understood as identifying necessary or sufficient conditions. As I have indicated, they are meant only to provide a rough-and-ready way of distinguishing political from nonpolitical social relations. But while they do not draw a precise line around the political, they have the advantage of not limiting political interaction to formal political institutions. Participation in trade unions, political parties, public interest advocacy groups, and economic enterprises can all qualify as political participation under the account sketched here.

This non-state-centered account of the political, therefore, is fully congruent with radical democratic understandings. Moreover, and importantly, accepting it does not undercut the points made in the previous section. Even if we accept an understanding of the political that is much broader than many traditional accounts, there is still much social space that is not political. Within this social space, citizens can undergo the types of transformations necessary to personal freedom identified by the two accounts discussed above.

With these points behind us, it is now time to consider the third, and most plausible, radical democratic claim about the relation between personal freedom and political self-government.

IX. Democratic Politics and Discursive Autonomy

Thus far I have argued that claims (A) and (B) are suspect. Claim (A) is suspect because there is no good explanation for how the ideal behind it could be realized under modern conditions. Claim (B) is suspect because

---

[49] For discussion of this point see Warren, "What Should We Expect from More Democracy?" 244–50.

there is no account of transformation through political discussion that establishes that people need to participate in politics if they are to be fully free.

Should we conclude from this that the radical democratic view of freedom is thoroughly confused and that there is nothing to be learned from it? That would be premature, at best. The arguments discussed so far, while failing to vindicate either claim (A) or claim (B), have, nonetheless, brought to light some important insights about the contribution political participation and discussion might be able to make to personal freedom. If we drop talk of necessary or integral connections between participation in political discussion and personal freedom, we may be able to construct more convincing arguments. This is where claim (C) enters the picture. Recall that it concedes that participation in political self-government is only instrumentally valuable to personal freedom. Of course, instrumental value is still value. Even though this claim is obviously weaker than claims (A) and (B), it may still be strong enough to vindicate the radical democratic view. It all depends on how tight the instrumental connections are.

We need to ask, then: Are there grounds for thinking there is a tight instrumental connection between political self-government and personal freedom? We have already seen that personal freedom can be diminished by defective preference structures and by manipulation. The source of this kind of unfreedom resides in the causal history of people's preferences and the beliefs that structure their understandings of their interests. But while these phenomena are clearly impediments to personal freedom, we have found no good reason to think that participation in political discussion, as opposed to other kinds of social discussion, is especially helpful in overcoming them. This suggests that if we are to find a tight instrumental connection between political self-government and personal freedom, we will need to look elsewhere.

With this in mind, rather than trying to identify impediments to freedom that democratic political participation could overcome, radical democrats might be better advised to try to identify capacities that are integral to its exercise. They then could argue that democratic political participation does a very good job of developing these capacities. This, in turn, might give them the strong instrumental connection they need.

This is indeed a promising line of argument; and, not surprisingly, a number of writers have taken it up. In what follows, I want to consider this line of argument in what I take to be its most persuasive form. This is an argument that appeals to capacities that are integral to a particular understanding of autonomy.[50] More specifically, the argument I have in mind consists of three steps:

[50] While hints of this argument are present in the writings of a number of radical democrats, it is most carefully set out by Mark Warren. See his "The Self in Discursive Democracy" and "What Should We Expect from More Democracy?"

(i) Autonomy is a component of personal freedom.
(ii) Autonomy includes, among other things, the capacity and the willingness to take up a reflexive[51] attitude toward the interests, commitments, and projects that give meaning to one's life.
(iii) Participation in democratic politics, while not strictly necessary for the development of this reflexive attitude, is especially good at cultivating it.

Each of these steps has to be argued for; but if all could be defended, then it would follow that there is a tight instrumental connection between political self-government and personal freedom.

The first step is not that controversial. Most will agree that being autonomous is part of what it is to be free. The disagreements begin with the second step, for autonomy is a notoriously slippery concept. How it is characterized is often as important as the claims made on its behalf. The second step holds that autonomy demands that one adopt a reflexive attitude toward one's interests, commitments, and projects. Since this is a very important claim, I want to quote from a proponent of the argument under review:

> Autonomy is a kind of freedom. Internally, autonomy implies that one can adopt a reflexive attitude toward one's own internal impulses, interpreting, transforming, censoring and providing names for needs, impulses, and desires, as well as expressing them to others as interests. . . . With regard to the social world, autonomy implies that one can distance oneself from traditions, prevailing opinions, and pressures to conform by subjecting elements of one's social context to criticism.[52]

Notice that on this characterization of autonomy it is crucial that people be able to identify, name, interpret, and discuss their needs and interests with others. A premium is put on reflexive, articulate self-understanding. We shall come back to this characterization of autonomy in a moment; but now that we have a better understanding of it, we can turn our attention to the third step in the argument.

Assuming we characterize autonomy as including the reflexive attitude just discussed, the third step tells us that participation in democratic politics is especially good at cultivating it. Those who participate in democratic politics, at least under fairly good conditions, are much more likely to be autonomous than those who do not. Thus, if we care about promoting autonomy, we should care about expanding opportunities for

---

[51] "Reflexive," as it is used by proponents of this argument, refers to the activity of reflecting critically back on oneself.
[52] Warren, "The Self in Discursive Democracy," 173.

people to participate in democratic politics both within formal political institutions and within informal public spaces in civil society.

Is this true? It might be thought that we could say here what we said earlier. We could agree that participation in democratic politics promotes autonomy, but deny that there is anything special about political participation and discussion per se. Other forms of social discussion and interaction, we could say, develop the capacities necessary for autonomy just as well. However, in the present context, this response is much less persuasive. The reason for this is that there are features of democratic political participation that make it likely to be a good means for promoting the reflexive attitude identified above. Two features in particular should be mentioned here. The first one is that in democratic political interaction we are brought into contact with a wider range of perspectives than we normally are in other forms of social interaction. In democratic politics we must confront difference to a greater degree, for in many forms of social interaction people meet and discuss with others who share many of their own values, beliefs, and preconceptions. The second feature has already been mentioned. Political interaction is marked by a greater degree of conflict than many other forms of social interaction. In democratic politics we are called on to negotiate our way through disruptions and conflicts that demand resolutions.

The fact, then, that in democratic politics we must confront different perspectives and negotiate our way through conflicts suggests that it would be a good means for developing the capacities necessary for autonomy. The reflexive attitude is likely to develop and take root only if we are forced to confront different identities and come to grips with the claims they make on us. This is not to deny that the reflexive attitude could be developed in nonpolitical social interaction. It is just to say that there are reasons to think that participation in democratic politics would be a particularly good means to its development.

If this is right, we have some reason to accept the third step in the argument. Of course, we should welcome empirical research on this matter, but for the purposes of this essay I want to concede the point. Let us return, then, to the issue of the correct characterization of autonomy—the issue raised in the second step. The view that autonomy includes, among other things, the adoption of a reflexive attitude toward one's interests, commitments, and projects sits well with a particular conception of human needs and interests. On this point consider the following remarks by a writer who embraces this understanding of autonomy:

> Epistemically, we cannot say that all needs that permit linguistic expression are true, but only that those which do not permit linguistic articulation cannot be true. It is ultimately the process of discourse, what I have named the moral-transformative experience, that establishes the truth and falsehood of our needs. But even then, we

> must admit that a genuinely fluid and unrepressed relation to inner
> nature consists in the capacity for constant critical reevaluation and
> reconsideration of our most cherished needs.[53]

If we believe, as this passage urges us to, that the truthfulness of our own
needs and interests can only be established in discursive debate with
others, then we will likely be attracted to an understanding of autonomy
that demands of us "constant critical reevaluation and reconsideration of
our most cherished needs." Let us call this understanding the *discursive
conception* of autonomy.

In thinking about this conception of autonomy, it is important to realize
that other conceptions are available. Even if one rejects the discursive
conception, one can still affirm the value of autonomy. To make this point
clear, we can introduce a second conception of autonomy, one that I shall
call the *liberal pluralist conception*. On this conception, the autonomous
person is understood as one who has access to an adequate range of
options, is relatively free from coercion and manipulation, and has (and
exercises) the mental capacities necessary for self-directed action.[54] While
such a person may subject his needs and interests to constant critical
evaluation, this is not an essential condition of autonomous agency. Indeed, on the liberal pluralist conception, the autonomous person may
lead a relatively unreflective life, seldom critically discussing his most
cherished needs and interests with others.

Therefore, on the liberal pluralist conception, we should expect the
instrumental value of participation in democratic politics for cultivating
capacities necessary to autonomous agency to be much less important
than it is on the discursive conception. This, in turn, suggests that an
assessment of the argument under consideration turns heavily on which
conception of autonomy better expresses what is valuable about the concept. Resolving this matter obviously raises a number of difficult issues,
and this is not the place to address them comprehensively. Instead, I want
to conclude by focusing on one important advantage of the liberal pluralist conception, an advantage that may help explain why liberal pluralists are inclined to resist the idea that there is a tight instrumental connection
between participation in democratic politics and personal freedom.

Liberal pluralists are committed to the idea that there exists a wide
range of different conceptions of the good or different ways of life worthy
of respect. This commitment to pluralism accounts for why they are reluctant to say that there is a tight instrumental connection between par-

---

[53] Benhabib, *Critique, Norm, and Utopia*, 338.

[54] For good accounts of autonomy understood along these lines, see Joseph Raz, *The
Morality of Freedom* (Oxford: Clarendon Press, 1986), 369–78; and Stanley Benn, *A Theory of
Freedom* (Cambridge: Cambridge University Press, 1988). I defend a similar account of
autonomy in *Liberalism, Perfectionism, and Restraint* (Cambridge: Cambridge University Press,
1998), 127–61.

ticipation in democratic politics and personal freedom, for the liberal pluralist will think that there are ways of life worthy of respect that do not value (or are incompatible with) a disposition to participate actively in democratic politics. Of course, the radical democrat, as we have described her, is not hostile to pluralism. She concedes that there are many valuable ways of life. But to the extent that she is committed to the discursive conception of autonomy, she must look with suspicion on ways of life that discourage (or do not actively promote) the type of critical self-questioning she prizes. It is here that her pluralism must give way.

To sharpen this point, we can distinguish two levels of pluralism. One level concerns the content of ways of life. It holds that there are a wide variety of projects, pursuits, virtues, and excellences, some of which are incompatible with one another, that could be components of a fully good life. The second level concerns the myriad ways in which people come to acquire and sustain both their beliefs about what are worthwhile projects, pursuits, virtues, and excellences and their preferences about which of these they wish to realize. It holds that it is not unreasonable for people to acquire and sustain these beliefs and preferences under a wide range of circumstances and conditions. The point I am making here is that the liberal pluralist conception of autonomy is more pluralistic at this second level, but not necessarily at the first, than the discursive conception of autonomy. And this, I am suggesting, is an important advantage of the liberal pluralist conception.

To put this point differently, we can cite Hannah Arendt's claim that one of the most important freedoms is the "freedom from politics,"[55] and we can add to this the thought that it ought to be possible for a person to lead a fully free life away from politics. The problem with the discursive conception of autonomy is that it threatens to deny this.

Of course, for some, participation in democratic politics will enhance their freedom. It will help them develop capacities integral to autonomous agency. It is a mistake, however, to exaggerate this valid point, since for others, given their circumstances and their way of life, active engagement in politics or active participation in political discussion may not be instrumentally valuable to their freedom at all. It may even impede their ability to lead their lives on their own terms.

Bearing these points in mind, we can now draw some conclusions. There are good reasons for favoring the liberal pluralist conception of autonomy over the discursive conception. On the basis of this, we can reject the argument under consideration in this section. For without the discursive conception of autonomy the argument does not stand up. Finally, without this argument, we have no good reason to believe there is a strong instrumental connection between participation in democratic politics and personal freedom. We should, accordingly, reject claim (C).

[55] Hannah Arendt, *On Revolution* (Harmondsworth: Penguin, 1963), 280.

X. Conclusion

This completes my examination of the radical democratic arguments in support of the view that there is a tight connection between personal freedom and political self-government. I have tried to show that these arguments do not succeed, and I have suggested that the view they seek to support is mistaken, or at least overstated. However, as I mentioned at the beginning of this essay, it has not been my purpose to examine exhaustively all the criticisms radical democrats have brought to bear against the liberal pluralist model of politics. Each of these criticisms warrants careful study in its own right, and for all that has been said here many of them may be valid.[56] Yet while modest, the conclusions reached here are nonetheless significant. They suggest that the domain of politics, whatever transformative potential it may have, is not an especially important domain of personal freedom.[57]

Philosophy, Kansas State University

---

[56] I have not, for example, sought to deny that active participation in politics and political discussion might bring about other (non-freedom-related) transformations in people that are valuable. Such participation may, as many radical democrats believe, promote virtue, tolerance, and the development of intelligence.

[57] It remains true that for some people, given their projects and goals, active participation in political life will be bound up with their personal freedom. For them, but only for them, will it be correct to say that the political domain is a domain of personal freedom.

DEMOCRACY AND VALUE PLURALISM

By William A. Galston

I. Introduction

My intention in this essay is to open up a question I cannot fully resolve: the relationship between democracy and value pluralism. By "value pluralism" I mean the view propounded so memorably by the late Isaiah Berlin and developed in various ways by thinkers including Stuart Hampshire, Steven Lukes, Thomas Nagel, Martha Nussbaum, Michael Stocker, Bernard Williams, Charles Taylor, John Kekes, and John Gray, among others.[1] I shall define and discuss this view in some detail in Section III. For now, suffice it to say that value pluralism is the view that what we (rightly) value in our lives turns out to be multiple, heterogeneous, not reducible to a common measure, and not hierarchically ordered with a single dominant value or set of values binding on all persons in all circumstances. I use the phrase "value pluralism" rather than "moral pluralism" to indicate that this view encompasses nonmoral as well as moral goods.

My overall thesis is this: If there are good reasons to take value pluralism seriously (and I believe there are), then it becomes impossible to accord democracy normative authority over all other claims, public and nonpublic. Not only is the scope of democratic political authority restricted; certain alternatives to democracy within the sphere of politics must be taken more seriously than they usually are.

This may appear a strange and feckless venture. For many (theorists and citizens alike), the standing of democracy is, like slavery, a settled question. What good can be done by reopening it? Surely twentieth-century experience has taught us that democracy is preferable to any other mode of government. If abstract value theory leads to doubts about

[1] See Stuart Hampshire, *Morality and Conflict* (Cambridge, MA: Harvard University Press, 1993); Steven Lukes, "Making Sense of Moral Conflict," in *Moral Conflict and Politics* (Oxford: Clarendon Press, 1991); Thomas Nagel, "The Fragmentation of Value," in *Mortal Questions* (Cambridge: Cambridge University Press, 1979); Martha Nussbaum, *The Fragility of Goodness: Luck and Ethics in Greek Tragedy and Philosophy* (Cambridge: Cambridge University Press, 1986); Michael Stocker, *Plural and Conflicting Values* (Oxford: Clarendon Press, 1990); Bernard Williams, "Conflicts of Values," in *Moral Luck* (Cambridge: Cambridge University Press, 1981); Charles Taylor, "The Diversity of Goods," in *Utilitarianism and Beyond*, ed. Amartya Sen and Bernard Williams (Cambridge: Cambridge University Press, 1982); John Kekes, *The Morality of Pluralism* (Princeton: Princeton University Press, 1993); and John Gray, *Isaiah Berlin* (Princeton: Princeton University Press, 1996).

255

democratic practice, then it may well be said, so much the worse for theory.

To avoid misunderstanding, I must immediately define terms. My target is democracy seen as what Amy Gutmann calls "populist democracy"—a system that "places no constraints on the substance of popularly supported outcomes *except* those that are required by the democratic procedure of popular rule itself."[2] Robert Dahl has advanced a sophisticated and influential version of the view.[3]

Liberal democracy offers an important amendment to populist democracy, in that some value-claims external to the democratic process are regarded as fundamental rather than derivative. Liberal democracy thus represents an important step toward value pluralism. But I shall argue that it does not go far enough, in two respects. First, careful attention to political experience (including our own in the United States) yields an even broader account of the values to which we may appropriately appeal to justify systems or particular practices of governance. Second, value pluralism grounds a reservation against the claim that the domain of political values (however understood) should be seen as systematically dominating or trumping nonpolitical values.

II. A Methodological Objection

The propriety of my mode of argument may be—has been—questioned. John Rawls argues that it is unreasonable to base claims to political authority on comprehensive doctrines—theological, metaphysical, or ethical—that rational and reasonable people may reject. Political theory must be understood as independent of any particular moral theory, including value pluralism.[4]

It may well be that for practical purposes, it is a mistake to rest political theory on moral theory. The cogency of a political view such as democracy will be more widely evident and accepted than is the truth of any specific moral or theological view that might be adduced in its support. Individuals who disagree with your moral or theological position may nonetheless arrive at your preferred political theory on the basis of very different premises. So understood, Rawls's notion of an "overlapping

---

[2] Amy Gutmann, "The Disharmony of Democracy," in *NOMOS XXXV: Democratic Community*, ed. John W. Chapman and Ian Shapiro (New York: New York University Press, 1993), 129.

[3] Robert Dahl, *Democracy and Its Critics* (New Haven: Yale University Press, 1989).

[4] John Rawls, *Political Liberalism* (New York: Columbia University Press, 1996). Rawls argues that for terms of social cooperation (including democracy) to be justifiable, citizens offering the terms must believe that it would be reasonable for other reasonable citizens to accept them. But it is unreasonable to suppose that citizens holding comprehensive view A would accept terms put forward on the basis of view B—even if B were a view appealing to familiar values such as Kantian autonomy or Millian individuality (ibid., xliv–xlv).

consensus" is nothing more than a description (recognizable to every practicing legislator) of how democratic majorities are built.[5]

On the philosophical plane, antifoundationalism is much in vogue, and with some justification. The mind is not, or not only, the "mirror of nature."[6] Spatial metaphors such as foundations and superstructures are apt to be misleading as guides to philosophical reflection. Priority claims among different branches of philosophy threaten to plunge us into medieval debates over the order of the sciences.

But neither practice nor antifoundationalist theory warrants the conclusion that political theory is detachable from other domains of inquiry. One need not be foundationalist, need not assert the priority of morality to politics (or vice versa), to strive for consistency across domains. If there are good reasons to believe that a particular view of morality is preferable to the alternatives, then it is appropriate (I would say necessary) to ask whether a particular political theory is consistent with that moral view.

III. A Sketch of the Problem

While I cannot present a full exposition of value pluralism, a handful of propositions will clarify its basic thrust.

(1) Pluralism is not relativism. For pluralists, philosophical reflection confirms what ordinary experience suggests—the existence of a wide range of genuine goods that are distinguishable from bads and evils. By contrast, relativists deny that any generally compelling grounds can be offered for attributions of value, which they understand as internal to particular cultures or to individual subjectivity.

(2) The goods identified by pluralism are qualitatively heterogeneous and are not reducible to a common measure of value.

(3) These goods cannot be fully rank-ordered. (There may, however, be partial rank-orderings among subsets of goods.)

(4) No single good or value, or set of goods or values, is overriding in all circumstances.

It might be thought that (2) renders (3) superfluous, that is, that rank-ordering requires some homogeneity of value across goods. But this would be a mistake: it is not necessary to posit a common measure to establish at least a partial rank-ordering. Consider Aristotle's view. He argues against the unity of the good: the various goods we observe are different and distinct.[7] On the other hand, he offers dialectical arguments to the effect that some goods are fuller and higher than others. For example, virtue is

---

[5] See ibid., 385–95.

[6] See Richard Rorty, *Philosophy and the Mirror of Nature* (Princeton: Princeton University Press, 1980).

[7] Aristotle, *Nicomachean Ethics*, 1096b17–26.

a greater good than honor because we pursue honor to be assured of our moral merit, and we desire to be honored on the basis of virtue.[8]

With regard to (4), there is a distinction to be made between an order of value and an order of action. So (on some account) B may be a "higher" value than A. But it does not follow that in circumstances requiring choice, B is always to be preferred and pursued. A may be more urgent, even if not (say) more noble. Value pluralism is generally understood as ruling out dominant or overriding values. But even if the existence of such values is conceded as a contemplative truth, pluralism returns in the sphere of action. Thus, even if we ought to live for the sake of living well, it is also the case that "mere life" is a precondition for the "good life." In specific circumstances, it may be appropriate to choose actions that tend to preserve life over those that emphasize its moral improvement.[9]

I will not argue here for the truth of value pluralism. For the purposes of this essay I will assume what I have come to believe is the case, that value pluralism offers the most nearly adequate account of the moral universe we happen to inhabit.

This may be a questionable point of departure, but it is hardly idiosyncratic. During the past quarter-century, there has been a double shift away from utilitarianism: in political philosophy, through the tenacious efforts of John Rawls; and in moral philosophy, through the widening influence of Isaiah Berlin. If, for Rawls, utilitarianism fails to take seriously the separateness of persons, for Berlin it fails to take seriously the distinctiveness of values. I think it is fair to say that, today, ethical monism is on the defensive.

As a logical matter, the broad implication of value pluralism is clear. If there are no overriding values, then democracy cannot be such a value. If it is not, then statements of the form "X promotes (or sustains, or is most consistent with) democracy" are not sufficient to warrant the conclusion that X is, all things considered, what we should do.

The question is whether in the real world there are any significant concrete phenomena that correspond to the abstract proposition that democracy is not overriding. I think there are, in two categories: limits on the reach of politics, including democratic politics; and alternatives to democracy within the political sphere.

For example, a pluralist outlook is likely to discern core family relationships as goods that limit appropriate democratic action. A policy that systematically separates children from their parents would therefore be deeply suspect. And this would be the case even if that policy were

---

[8] Ibid., 1095b23–30.

[9] This distinction is what Leo Strauss had in mind when he observed that "Aristotle seems to suggest that there is not a single rule, however basic, which is not subject to exception. . . . There is a universally valid hierarchy of ends, but there are no universally valid rules of action." Strauss, *Natural Right and History* (Chicago: University of Chicago Press, 1953), 160, 162.

arrived at through democratic procedures and if it were justified as strengthening democratic institutions.

IV. The Limits of Politics

Democracy is an ordering of the political domain. It is possible, but not easy, to contend that politics is coextensive with the totality of human endeavors and concerns. If, as seems more plausible, politics is not the totality of human life, and if pluralism is correct, then political goods—including democracy—cannot always be overriding. From a pluralist perspective, in specific circumstances it will be possible to say, "X is a procedurally correct determination of a democratic polity, but nonetheless I (a citizen of that polity) have compelling reasons not to do X but to do something else instead." Two such reasons are truth and liberty.

A. Truth

Consider the nature of democratic authority over scientific inquiry. It seems perfectly appropriate for democratic institutions to determine (for example) the distribution of resources devoted to various domains of inquiry.[10] From the standpoint of many physicists, it may be regrettable when a democratic government decides not to invest the billions of dollars needed to construct the next generation of particle accelerators, but it cannot be said that the government has overstepped its bounds. It is legitimate, moreover, for democratic governments to make such decisions based in part on their assessment of the kinds of inquiry that are most likely to sustain democratic institutions. Democracies can impose restrictions on allowable research methods (on human subjects, for example), although these restraints may make it more difficult for research to succeed. And in certain circumstances it may even be legitimate and appropriate for democracies to restrict the public discussion of specific research results.

But distinct from all these actions is direct government intervention to determine the outcome of inquiry. The quest for truth is an autonomous activity guided by its own rules. To be sure, communities of inquiry shape those rules and judge their products, but not on a democratic basis.

One of the sorriest episodes in the history of the Soviet Union was the use of state power to impose the pseudo-Lamarckian views of the quack agronomist Trofim Lysenko on the whole of Soviet biology. Plant scientists of unimpeachable international standing were forced to recant their

---

[10] This is not to suggest that only democratic institutions may do so. The market allocates scientific resources in many areas, especially medical research. And if nondemocratic political institutions are legitimate, then they too may engage in such distribution. My point is simply that when democratic institutions do so, they do not exceed the bounds of their legitimate authority.

adherence to Mendelian genetics and to conduct their research on the basis of an ideological theory of the environmental determination of species change.[11]

This affair is frequently presented as the epitome of totalitarianism. The real point is broader, however: Lysenko's biology would have been no better, and no more legitimate, if it had been imposed by a democratic vote after public deliberation. (Shifting to an example from U.S. history, to the extent that the 1925 Scopes trial moved from the issue of whether evolution was to be taught in classrooms toward a public determination of scientific truth, it crossed a similar line.) The political sphere has no rightful authority over the internal processes that guide the quest for truth.

B. Liberty

In clarifying the scope of democratic political authority, Robert Dahl distinguishes among three different kinds of claims made by individuals regarding the existence of a substantive interest or good. The claim may be about (1) goods integral to the democratic process, such as freedom of speech or assembly; (2) goods external to the democratic process but necessary for it, such as the possession of the basic resources citizens need to take part in politics; or (3) goods external to the democratic process and not necessary to it.[12]

It is possible to argue that all the individual claims that deserve serious consideration fall into the first two categories.[13] This view is deeply implausible, however; and Dahl ultimately rejects it. He acknowledges the existence of important human interests and goods in category (3). And while he is attracted to the view that no interests other than those in categories (1) and (2) should be regarded as binding on democratic publics, he admits that it leaves open a "disturbing question": Can we really assert that human beings "have no inviolable interests beyond their right to the democratic process and whatever is essential to it?"[14]

This question assumes special weight because inviolable interests are frequently thought to include basic individual liberties. Dahl offers the example of the right to a fair trial, the importance of which derives, in large measure, from the permanent threat that state power poses for individual liberty. Legal institutions and procedures (the individual's pre-

---

[11] For a detailed account of this matter, see David Joravsky, *The Lysenko Affair* (Cambridge, MA: Harvard University Press, 1970).

[12] Dahl, *Democracy and Its Critics*, 167.

[13] Jürgen Habermas is an example of this mode of thinking. For a discussion and critique of his view that all valid public claims are inherent in the nature of or conditions for democratic deliberation, see Amy Gutmann and Dennis Thompson, *Democracy and Disagreement* (Cambridge, MA: Harvard University Press, 1996), 17–18.

[14] Dahl, *Democracy and Its Critics*, 182–83.

sumption of innocence, the state's burden of proof, and many others) reflect this understanding of the special status of liberty.

Let me offer another example along similar lines. It is perfectly possible to imagine a procedurally scrupulous democratic public deliberation on the question of which faith should be adopted as the official state religion. (In medieval times there were, in fact, recorded public disputations on this question.)[15] If we are troubled by this prospect, as I think we should be, it is because of our sense that the political order is overriding a fundamental liberty that, in nearly all circumstances, should remain outside the ambit of political power.[16]

To summarize: There are some individual interests that (a) are fundamental human goods, (b) are neither intrinsic to nor necessary for democracy, and (c) are not evidently subject to democratic authority. Among them are basic liberties. These liberties form a second category of activities that challenge and limit the moral scope of democracy.

In so arguing, I do not wish to deny that democracy is an important value or that a wide range of institutions and practices can be justified as promoting democracy. Freedom of speech and of the press are highly valued for this reason. But neither of these freedoms can be understood simply as instrumental to democracy, and neither can be understood as absolute.[17] Both of these considerations point toward an underlying pluralism of basic values.

V. Alternatives to Democracy within the Political Sphere

My thesis in this section is that inspection of our actual practices reveals forms of nondemocratic governance that we have good reasons to believe are justified.

A. Juries

For many purposes, juries are required to reach unanimous judgments. This means that the vote of a single dissenting juror can nullify the votes

---

[15] The disputation represented in literary form by Jehudah Halevi is based on actual events: see Halevi, *Kuzari: The Book of Proof and Argument*, ed. Isaak Heinemann (Oxford: East and West Library, 1947).

[16] I say "nearly all" because it is possible to imagine (indeed, history records) circumstances in which a community is faced with the choice between mass religious conversion and total annihilation. If I found myself in such circumstances, I would certainly argue that the governing institutions should take up this question on an urgent basis, and I would not argue that it would be a moral breach to establish a state religion. (But it would not be mandatory either: the people would be within their moral rights to choose death over the coerced violation of conscience.)

[17] For an authoritative account of these two points, see Laurence H. Tribe, *American Constitutional Law*, 2d ed. (Mineola, NY: The Foundation Press, 1988), ch. 12.

of eleven others—a weighting system that is hard to square with democracy as ordinarily understood.

It could be otherwise. Socrates was tried before a democratic assembly-jury of 501 citizens and (if the Socratic speech presented by Plato is taken at face value) was convicted by a vote of 280 to 221. Each vote counted equally, and a simple majority sufficed to reach a judgment.

But everyone understands why the nondemocratic U.S. jury system exists. Life, liberty, property—these and others are fundamental human goods that government exists to protect and that possess a standing independent of democratic processes. The U.S. jury system crystallizes this pluralistic moral understanding.

B. Expertise

There are some public purposes whose effective pursuit requires specialized knowledge and competence that are not widely shared. When the exercise of such expertise is likely to go against the grain of democratic decision-making, there may be a case for insulating the experts against the vagaries of democracy. Lifetime tenure for judges is one instance of this; the autonomy of the U.S. Federal Reserve Board is another.

To be sure, the element of democratic accountability is not entirely lacking in either case; and both of these institutions are contestable from a democratic point of view. My point is only that good reasons can be adduced in their favor and that these reasons are not straightforwardly democratic. That democratic decision-makers can recognize the claims of expertise does not necessarily mean that these claims rest on a democratic foundation—or that the claims would not exist if they were not democratically recognized.

C. Paternalism

Democracy is thought to give great weight to every citizen's understanding of his or her own interests. From this standpoint, statements of the form "I (we) understand your interests better than you do" are inherently suspect.

Nonetheless, U.S. democratic processes have frequently given standing to paternalistic claims. Amy Gutmann and Dennis Thompson offer a nonexhaustive but representative list:

> safety laws and regulations (mandating seat belts, ignition interlocks, and air bags, or requiring motorcyclists to wear helmets); health regulations (requiring prescriptions for drugs, and banning certain drugs such as laetrile); criminal law (criminalizing suicide, and disallowing consent as a murder defense); and general social policy (restrictions on gambling, prevention of high-risk recre-

ational activities such as swimming in a local quarry, and licensing of professionals).[18]

To be sure, many of these laws and regulations are controversial. For the purposes of this argument, however, I will assume that at least some of them are justifiable, all things considered. My point is that the grounds of their justification are distinct from the bare fact of their democratic authorization. If so, actions consistent with these justificatory reasons may be warranted even in the absence of democratic authorization.

Consider the following case. While walking through a forest, you come upon two men, one kneeling in a submissive posture, the other pointing a gun at the kneeling man's head and tightening his finger on the trigger. As you rush forward to prevent a tragedy, the kneeling man cries out, "Leave us alone. I gave him permission to shoot me, and you have no right to interfere." I want to suggest that you do have that right, even if no democratically enacted law endorses it. Indeed, I want to go farther: you have the right to interfere, even if a democratic law says that you do not.[19] From a pluralist perspective, there are situations (some paternalist, others not) in which the misguided substance of a democratic decision can trump its legitimating form.

D. The common good

Early in 1861, shortly after the beginning of the Civil War, a mob in Baltimore, Maryland blocked the movement of troops from Massachusetts heading south to reinforce the defenses of Washington, D.C. At the same time, President Lincoln received credible information that Maryland was moving toward secession. He asked his Attorney General for a legal opinion concerning his power to impose martial law or suspend various constitutional rights.

The results were not particularly encouraging. The Constitution did provide (Article I, Section 9) for the suspension of the writ of habeas corpus "when in cases of rebellion or invasion the public safety may require it," but the leading authority of the day, Joseph Story, interpreted the Constitution as empowering only Congress to so act. Story was joined in this view by most jurists and judges, as well as by the Supreme Court. Nonetheless, on April 25, 1861, President Lincoln sent General Winfield Scott an order authorizing him to suspend habeas corpus in the event that Maryland moved toward rebellion or secession—the first of several such orders over the next two months.

---

[18] Gutmann and Thompson, *Democracy and Disagreement*, 262.

[19] This is not intended as a parable of Oregon's assisted suicide law, which is distinguishable from the men-in-the-forest case in a number of important respects.

It was not until July that Lincoln presented a formal defense of his action to a special session of Congress. The terms of that defense bring us to the philosophical point:

> The whole of the laws which were required to be faithfully executed, were being resisted, and failing of execution, in nearly one-third of the States. Must they be allowed to finally fail of execution, even had it been perfectly clear, that by the use of the means necessary to their execution, some single law, made in such extreme tenderness of the citizen's liberty, that practically, it relieves more of the guilty, than of the innocent, should, to a very limited extent, be violated? . . . [A]re all the laws, *but one*, to go unexecuted, and the government itself go to pieces, lest that one be violated?[20]

The crux of Lincoln's argument was that his duty to preserve the government he led overrode otherwise binding constitutional and democratic requirements: *Salus populi suprema lex.*[21] While Lincoln informed the Congress of his decision and the reasons for it, he did not ask for their approval. To do so would have been to call into question his right to defend the people's most urgent interests in a moment of supreme danger. Even after the Congress finally passed the Habeas Corpus Act almost two years later, in March 1863, Lincoln continued to defend his conduct on the basis of political and moral obligation rather than positive law.[22]

If we believe (as I do) that President Lincoln acted correctly, it follows that there are considerations based on the common good of a political community that can justify the violation of otherwise binding democratic norms. Just as the "good life" depends on "mere life," so too does a good ordering of the political community depend on the physical existence and integrity of that community.

This limited legitimation of parademocratic leadership is fraught with risk, because it opens the door to the abuse of discretion in the direction of tyranny. But it is even more dangerous to rule it out altogether. A democratic polity is not a suicide pact.

VI. PLURALIST CONSTITUTIONAL DEMOCRACY

The arguments I have sketched thus far are more suggestive than dispositive. I hope they have at least made a plausible case that there is

---

[20] Mark E. Neely, Jr., *The Fate of Liberty: Abraham Lincoln and Civil Liberties* (New York: Oxford University Press, 1991), 12.

[21] "The welfare of the people is the supreme law."

[22] Neely, *The Fate of Liberty*, 68.

something important to be learned about the limits of democracy by viewing it through the lens of value pluralism. I turn now to a brief discussion of constitutional democracy itself within the pluralist framework.

A. Pluralist constitutionalism

From a pluralist perspective, a democratic constitution represents a decision by the people to elevate a subset of worthy ends, purposes, and values above others, at least for the conduct of public life. For example, the preamble to the U.S. Constitution focuses on certain core purposes rather than others: "domestic tranquility" but not "fraternity." The governing institutions established by the Constitution rest on a distinctive balance between the desire for effectiveness and the fear of tyrannical power. The Bill of Rights gives special emphasis to specific liberties, especially those involving the administration of justice. And so forth.

Like every constitution, the U.S. Constitution is characterized by an internal pluralism, that is, by a multiplicity of goods, none of which is overriding in all circumstances. Consider the portion of the Constitution most often viewed as dominant or absolute—the rights enshrined in the First Amendment. As Laurence Tribe makes clear, it proves impossible in practice to evade the task of weighing those rights against competing public interests. For example, the courts have felt compelled to distinguish among more and less protected categories of speech. However, as Tribe observes, "[a]ny exclusion of a class of activities from first amendment safeguards represents an implicit conclusion that the governmental interests in regulating these activities are such as to justify whatever limitation is thereby placed on the free expression of ideas."[23] Constitutional adjudication, then, cannot avoid the essentially deliberative task of weighing and comparing competing values without the guidance of bright lines and lexical priorities.

This does not mean that pluralist constitutionalism is reduced to pure intuitionism. Typically, a line of cases will establish in general terms the kind of test constitutional value A must pass to be regarded as weightier than constitutional value B. Courts are exposed to criticism when a particular test violates a widely shared sense of the relative importance of key values. In 1990, for example, the Supreme Court handed down a decision that lowered the burden of proof that the government had to discharge in order to enact laws that have the effect of restricting the free exercise of religion.[24] This decision triggered a public furor that led to the enactment of a new statute—the Religious Freedom Restoration Act of

---

[23] Tribe, *American Constitutional Law*, 792.
[24] *Employment Division v. Smith*, 110 S.Ct. 1595 (1990).

1993—that, in effect, reinstated the more stringent prior burden on government efforts to impede religious free exercise.[25]

This depiction of pluralist constitutional adjudication leads to a broader point about deliberation within a pluralist framework. It is not necessary (and probably not possible) to begin deliberation with a promiscuous heap of goods to be rank-ordered on a case-by-case basis. There is an important role for the rough-and-ready guidance provided by the rules of ordinary morality. But these rules must be understood (to put the matter in legal terms) as rebuttable presumptions rather than inviolable imperatives of action. Pluralist deliberation must be open to the possibility that even the most deeply entrenched principles of conduct may have to be revised or set aside in unusual circumstances. The nature of the reasons that could warrant this can only be determined with reference to the complex of facts that defines a specific choice-situation.

B. Pluralism and democratic deliberation

In the *Nicomachean Ethics*, Aristotle characterizes the proper sphere of deliberation as an arena of uncertainty and unpredictability. We think through a geometry problem, but we do not deliberate about it; we investigate astronomical phenomena, but we do not deliberate about them. Nor do we deliberate about whether a pot of water will boil when placed over a hot flame.[26]

If Martha Nussbaum is correct, Aristotelian deliberation extends to the specification of ends as well as to the choice of means.[27] That is certainly true for deliberation conducted within the value-pluralist framework. A situation requiring choice will typically present a multiplicity of genuine but heterogeneous human goods, not all of which can be attained (or maximized) simultaneously. Citizens will typically differ among themselves regarding the rank-order or weight to be attached to these goods. But if they are deliberating reasonably, they will at least agree that the goods in question are all ends worthy of pursuit.

Sometimes deliberative agreement can go farther. I suspect we have all had the experience of sitting in a meeting where some matter requiring choice is being debated. Finally someone speaks so cogently that the debate ends: the speaker has somehow enabled us to see the situation in a way such that a particular course of action emerges as clearly preferable, all things considered.

---

[25] Pub. L. No. 103-141 (Stat. 1488, codified at 42 U.S.C.A. sect. 2000bb–2000bb4). This statute was subsequently ruled unconstitutional by the Supreme Court in the case of *City of Boerne v. Flores*, 117 S.Ct. 2157 (1997), and the struggle continues.

[26] Aristotle, *Nicomachean Ethics*, 1112a23–1112b12.

[27] Nussbaum, *The Fragility of Goodness*, 296–97.

The deliberative considerations deployed by successful speakers will themselves vary with the circumstances. It may be urged that B is more urgent than A, or more important, or less risky; or that an increment of A can be obtained only at excessive cost to B. Value pluralism does not rule out the possibility of right answers in specific situations. But these particularized judgments need not flow from, or lead to, general rules of action.[28]

In many circumstances, however, closure cannot be achieved. Where does that leave democratic deliberation? First, it offers a basis for mutual acceptance. While I may believe that a particular choice among, or weighting of, competing goods is best, I understand that it is not unreasonable for others to arrive at different judgments concerning these goods. Disagreement need not degenerate into imputations of error or fault. Those with whom I disagree are not ignorant, or excessively self-regarding, or short-sighted, or blinded by passion; they just happen to see things differently, as I might have under other circumstances.

Second, to the extent that all parties recognize the values at stake as genuine goods, each will have reasons to be cautious about proposed courses of action that, in effect, assign a weight of zero to one or more of these values. Consider the following example: A small town in the Pacific Northwest is divided between 600 committed environmentalists and 400 third-generation loggers. From a pure majoritarian point of view, it would be possible for the environmentalists to impose strict regulations that would throw all the loggers out of work. But if they accept the fact that the logging jobs are part of a way of life that can reasonably be regarded as desirable (its impact on the environment notwithstanding), they will doubt that it is reasonable to press their majoritarian advantage to the hilt and will look for an alternative course of action that does less violence to the most cherished values of the minority. While value pluralism may not entail a politics of inclusion, it certain offers a plausible basis for such a politics.

Another consideration points in the same direction. To believe that it is not manifestly unreasonable for others to see the world differently is to acknowledge that one's own views, while perhaps firmly held, fall short of mathematical certainty. That is, there is some chance that the majority that sees things my way may be, to some extent, mistaken. If so, it is reasonable for the majority to hedge its bets by incorporating some of the minority's views.

Consider an analogy. Suppose there are two cancer researchers pursuing conflicting lines of research: if A's hypothesis is vindicated, B's must be rejected, and vice versa. Even if the National Science Foundation be-

---

[28] For this and related matters, see Brian Barry, "*Political Argument* after Twenty-Five Years," in *Political Argument: A Reissue with a New Introduction* (Berkeley: University of California Press, 1990), xxxix–xliv, lxix–lxxii.

lieves that A is considerably more likely to be correct than B, it is reasonable for the NSF to make an investment greater than zero in B's research.[29]

VII. CONCLUSION

In this essay, I have suggested that three broad political conclusions flow from the acceptance of value pluralism: first, that the legitimate scope of all politics, democratic politics included, is limited; second, that within the political sphere, there are alternatives to democracy that enjoy legitimacy, at least for some purposes in some situations; and third, that democratic deliberation and decision should be guided by mutual acceptance and the quest for inclusive rather than exclusive policies.

My argument is contestable in at least two respects. First, its animating premise may be rejected. I have not presented a case against the possibility of value monism, or against a *summum bonum* theory offering a rationally binding rank-ordering of heterogeneous goods. Value pluralism is consistent with my own experience and, I believe, with the emerging center of gravity in moral philosophy. That does not mean it is true. But it would be helpful for antipluralists to offer affirmative alternatives.

Second, while my conclusions are consistent with value pluralism, I have not established that only value pluralism is consistent with them. I cannot rule out the possibility that, for example, an artful deployment of utilitarianism might produce a similar bottom line. At best, I have offered a plausible case that there is a comfortable fit between recognizing an irreducible multiplicity of goods and acknowledging principled limits to (populist) democracy.

There is one assertion about which I remain steadfast—the propriety of rejoining value theory and political theory. I make no claims as to the priority of either over the other. My point is only that we must strive for consistency between them.

Political Science, School of Public Affairs,
University of Maryland at College Park

---

[29] This example was suggested by a discussion in Joseph H. Carens, "Compromises in Politics," in *NOMOS XXI: Compromise in Ethics, Law, and Politics,* ed. J. Roland Pennock and John W. Chapman (New York: New York University Press, 1979).

THE PROBLEM OF RUSSIAN DEMOCRACY: CAN RUSSIA RISE AGAIN?

By Dmitry Shlapentokh

I. Introduction

While Western political scientists have a variety of opinions on democracy and how its institutions could be improved, they almost never argue about the validity of democracy as a form of government. Of course, it would be unfair here to ignore the presence of an authoritarian streak in Western thought. Thomas Hobbes comes to mind most immediately. Yet the views of those thinkers with an authoritarian bent have become marginalized in present-day discourse; or, to be more precise, it is assumed that their views on the importance of a strong government are irrelevant to the present. The assumption that a strong regime might be necessary in non-Western societies is thought to be the product of these authoritarian/totalitarian societies' elite classes—that is, a justification for imposing the power of the elite upon the people. Most Western political scientists are convinced that democracy is the best of all possible forms of government.

For this reason, in discussions of political reform in Russia and other formerly communist countries, it is taken for granted that democracy is the goal of the present-day political process. Yet democratic institutions are not universally applicable, at least in their Western form. The point here is that the functioning of democratic institutions cannot be separated from civil society. I use the term 'civil society' in the following way. First, I am referring to those institutions that emerge at the grassroots level and exist independently from the state at the grassroots level. By 'state' I mean bureaucratic institutions, such as the standing army, the federal bureaucracy, etc. Second, civil society is characterized by a deep, internalized respect for the law among a majority of a state's citizens. This acceptance of the law, the deeply internalized respect for legalistic discourse in the West, is essentially the reason why the law in the West is not merely promulgated, but is enforceable in most cases.

This is the reason why Western society needs only relatively weak external control (through law-enforcement institutions) to maintain order. This control has been perfected during the process of development of Western society and has corresponded to the rise of democratic institutions. Yet the rise of the power of citizens in Western societies to control government (through the spread of the voting franchise) has not eroded the self-controlling aspect of Western societies. In fact, one could even suggest that this self-controlling aspect of civil society increased during the West's transition from the early modern era to the present day. This, for example, was the point made by Michel Foucault when he asserted that in the process of development, modern Western society had expanded the notion of "deviant" behavior and legitimized the absolute control of society over its members.[1] Taking Foucault's notion to its logical extreme, one can see the development of Western society, from at least the Middle Ages to approximately the middle of the nineteenth century, not as a movement from the autocratic governments of the European monarchs to political liberty—an assumption shared by the majority of Western political scientists, regardless of their political and philosophical leanings—but rather as a transition from comparative liberty to almost totalitarian societies (although control is maintained by society rather than by government).

Foucault, of course, overstated his case, perhaps because he shared the propensity of many French intellectuals to engage in intellectual play and to make paradoxical statements—a characteristic that has allowed France to play the role of stimulator in Western thought. Yet, even when this is taken into account, Foucault's statement has a grain of truth. Indeed, the self-controlling aspect of Western society has made it quite vigilant in checking any form of antisocial behavior or any other form of behavior that might make a person different from others. The United States serves as a good example here. Alexis de Tocqueville, in his classic *Democracy in America* (1835–1840), emphasized the rigidity of American society,[2] and Alexander Herzen, a famous Russian intellectual who was de Tocqueville's contemporary, agreed with his comments. With an air of sarcasm, Herzen stated that in Russia the secret police controlled the life of citizens, while in America society itself did the same work.[3]

One can argue, of course, that these assumptions about the self-controlling nature of civil society do not hold true, for the media in the U.S. is full of information about the high crime rate and about how certain behaviors—homosexuality, for example—are no longer considered deviant. Yet one might still question whether the rates of crime and other deviant behavior have actually risen in the West. As for homosexuality and other

---

[1] While Foucault emphasized the coercive/disciplining nature of Western society in almost all his work, the most important of his books from this perspective is *Discipline and Punish: The Birth of the Prison* (New York: Pantheon Books, 1977). Curiously enough, the title of Foucault's book echoes Fyodor Dostoyevsky's *Crime and Punishment*. The resemblance, of course, is superficial—not only because Foucault probably did not look to Dostoyevsky for guidance (he may or may not have read him)—but because of their dramatically different messages. For Dostoyevsky, restraint and punishment comes from within, from a person's soul. For Foucault, repression and control is external, exclusively societal.

[2] Alexis de Tocqueville, *Democracy in America* (1835–1840; reprint, New York: Alfred A. Knopf, 1994).

[3] Alexander Herzen, *Sobranie Sochinenii* (Moscow: Izdanie Akademii Nauk, 1954–1965), 2:226–27.

forms of sexual behavior, one might state that these forms of behavior have been merely reclassified from "deviant" to "normal." This change in labeling does not mean that deviant behavior per se has gained acceptance, or that there is now a tolerance for behavior most members of the society do not recognize as normal. For example, while homosexuality has been "normalized" in some quarters, cases of marital infidelity and sexual harassment are looked upon with disapproval, or even outright hostility. President Clinton's problems, even though one must acknowledge the political nature of some of the attacks on his character, can serve as an example of this hostility. Moreover, the spread of criminal behavior is usually limited to a few regions in big cities, and, in fact, recent crime statistics show that criminal behavior is not on the increase. In many respects, the idea of a promiscuous and criminalized West is a mirror image of reality. The image of the West as being criminalized and promiscuous, and, in general, morally "rotten," is often taken at its face value, not only by external observers of Western society (for example, Russians) but even by Westerners themselves, who too often ignore their own daily experience and view their society through the prism of the mass media.

The self-controlling feature of Western societies is manifest in people's respect for law, contracts, and legal institutions, a respect which is itself connected with the institution of private property. Indeed, the institution of private property emerged only after property and direct force were separated. The consummation of property rights came through formal legal agreements, not through informal rituals (for example, swearing allegiance to the king). At that point in the transition from premodern to modern, it was legal agreements, not political power, that defined possession. As a matter of fact, the legalistic fabric of Western society, which is implicitly connected with the self-controlling nature of civil society, has been preserved as the foundation of Western society, even when civil society is seemingly submerged by a totalitarian regime, as was the case with Nazi Germany. Moreover, that civil society was never destroyed completely explains the ease with which democratic institutions were restored in the post–World War II era in Germany. Thus, one could come to the conclusion that democratic institutions in the West could not have developed without a self-policed civil society that deeply respected the law, which itself was deeply connected with the institution of private property. All of this, the right of private property most of all, was the result of a long process of development, that is, the transition from a *Gemeinschaft* (community) to a *Gesellschaft* (society or association). Here I am referring to terms developed by Ferdinand Tönnies.[4] According to him, a *Gemeinschaft* is based on informal agreements between its members—

[4] Ferdinand Tönnies, *Gemeinschaft und Gesellschaft* (Community and association) (Berlin: K. Curtis, 1920).

that is, customs, unwritten laws, etc.—while a *Gesellschaft* is based on legally defined relationships and formal law.

In the case of European history, the transition from a premodern society— which I define here as a society with an underdeveloped sense of private property and one in which legalistic relationships are downplayed—was a long one. And this transition from a *Gemeinschaft* to a *Gesellschaft* (to use Tönnies's terms) was a period of great instability that often led to the emergence of authoritarian regimes.

Thus, modern Western democracy was historically conditioned not to allow political liberties to lead to the dysfunction of society, at least in most cases; for Western society enjoyed a strong mechanism of self-control that was anchored in the legalistic fiber of the society. Yet the vast majority of both Western and Russian/Soviet political scientists have ignored this historical conditioning and, as a result, have failed to recognize the limitations of Western democracy. Their reasoning is that a Western-style society can be created in any society, regardless of its historical preconditions. This lack of awareness, which is shared by political leaders, may explain why, when Mikhail Gorbachev introduced reforms aimed at building up democratic institutions in Russia, he did not foresee that the disintegration of the country would be the result. The chaotic condition that now exists, that is, the possible collapse of Russia proper, reminds one of events during the 1917 revolutions. At that time the Bolsheviks were able to restore the state and basic societal order; however, the state was not resurrected through democratic institutions, but rather through the harsh measures of a despotic government. Of course, in the present situation, the revolutionary scenario need not repeat itself, for all events contain possible alternatives. Nevertheless, the events of the Bolshevik Revolution might play out once again—that is, the spread of anarchy could lead to a violent backlash. In this case, with a powerful central authority as the country's foundation, a strong leader might resurrect the country's standing.

The collapse of the Soviet Union—actually the Russian empire, as it was known for centuries—is one of the major events in modern history. And as the event recedes further into the past, it becomes easier for historians to make observations about the nature of the regime and the state. A large body of literature on the regime will undoubtedly develop, although the interpretation of the events will change over the course of time, as is the case with literature about all important events. Currently, both the collapse of the Soviet regime and the regime's history is enmeshed in the political/ideological controversies that divided a great part of the Western intellectual establishment during the cold war era. Present events, however, prove that both those on the left and those on the right of the political spectrum (in the American meaning of the terms 'left' and 'right') had a serious problem in their understanding of the USSR. The problem here stems from their failure to understand the non-Western nature of the Soviet regime, a difference which was not captured by the debate over the applicability of the totalitarian model to Soviet rule that the right and left waged during the cold war.

Western political scientists on the left often saw the Soviet Union as being the same as Western democracies, in the sense that they viewed Soviet leaders as following the will of the populace, as essentially being controlled from below. In their view, there were several signs of popular support that they took to be evidence of the democratic nature of the Soviet regime. Social mobility was one of the more cited examples: political scientists and historians pointed to Stalin's eagerness to place a considerable number of members of the lower classes in the Soviet elite. These commentators stated that the elevation of many of these people to the top would not have been possible in Western societies, and that this indicated that Stalin's regime, despite its abuses, represented the masses and was, in this sense, even more democratic than many regimes in capitalist societies.[5] While many representatives of the masses were indeed elevated to high positions during Stalin's rule, this sort of social mobility needs to be placed outside of the context of the Western tradition. Oriental despots often took the same actions as Stalin: freed from closely defined social stratification and, more importantly, from the restraints imposed by the sanctity of the institution of private property and its accompanying legal hurdles, they could easily send top bureaucrats to lives of slavery and place slaves in positions of leadership.

To explain the Soviet regime, social scientists have applied the 'totalitarian model'. The key element in this model is the distinction between totalitarian and authoritarian regimes: a totalitarian state controls not only the political life but the economic, spiritual, and cultural lives of its citizens, while an authoritarian state exercises political control but leaves the other realms relatively unfettered. This totality of control exercised by the former also implies that the state is detached from its citizens, whose lives in all their aspects are molded by an excessively powerful bureaucracy.[6] Commentators on the left disparaged this model of the totalitarian state and in their studies of the USSR denied its applicability. They insisted that while the Stalinist regime exercised absolute control over Soviet society, Stalin's actions, including the terror, were a reflection of the

---

[5] Professor Sheila Fitzpatrick can be seen as an example of this trend in Western historiography. Until recently she emphasized that social mobility was one of the essential characteristics of Stalin's regime. See, for example, Fitzpatrick, *Education and Social Mobility in the Soviet Union, 1921–1934* (Cambridge: Cambridge University Press, 1979); and Fitzpatrick, *The Commissariat of Enlightenment: The Soviet Organization of Education and the Arts under Lunacharsky, October 1917–1921* (Cambridge: Cambridge University Press, 1970).

[6] On totalitarian states, see, for example, J. L. Talmon, *Myth of the Nation and Vision of Revolution: Ideological Polarization in the Twentieth Century* (New Brunswick: Transaction, 1991).

will of the populace. On this view, it was the desires of ordinary people, not Stalin's regime, that molded Soviet society.[7]

The totalitarian model, at least as it was used to explain Soviet reality, was misleading, but not for the reasons espoused by the left. The real problem with the theory is that it either ignored or marginalized the non-Western aspects of the USSR. Using as their model the relationship of the totalitarian regime of Nazi Germany with its society, advocates of the totalitarian model universalized the relationship between totalitarian states and the societies they ruled. One can see such an approach in the work of Hannah Arendt.[8] Yet the problem here is that the National Bolshevik regime in the Soviet Union and the National Socialist regime in Germany were essentially different.

The idea that there are basic differences between the two regimes, of course, is hardly a novelty. In most cases, however, those social scientists on the left who were loath to see any link between Stalinism and Hitlerism reduced the differences between Soviet and Nazi rule to the moral caliber of the two regimes. They argued, for example, that despite the atrocities committed by the Soviet regime, Soviet ideology still had a positive and humanistic implication—that is, it implied the brotherhood of people and social equality. And after all, the Soviet Union was a major force in the defeat of Nazi Germany. My point here, however, is not the moral differences between the two regimes or the ideological and historical implications of their actions; rather, it is that the regimes were two different social species. In Germany, the Nazi regime was not needed to enforce contractual obligations among those who were recognized as German citizens (those who were not Jews in a racial/ethnic sense or who did not belong to a similarly persecuted group). The regime was not needed to maintain the army as a cohesive unit or to ensure that the bureaucracy performed its important societal functions. In fact, some

---

[7] On the views of revisionists, see Robert W. Thurston, *Life and Terror in Stalin's Russia, 1934–1941* (New Haven: Yale University Press, 1996); and Arch Getty, *Origins of the Great Purges: The Soviet Communist Party Reconsidered, 1933–1938* (Cambridge and New York: Cambridge University Press, 1985). Another theory of the totalitarian state (i.e., a state with unchecked power whose actions are driven by a preconceived quasi-religious dogma) is employed by conservative historians such as Richard Pipes and Martin Malia. See, for example, Martin Malia, *The Soviet Tragedy: A History of Socialism in Russia, 1917–1991* (New York: Free Press, 1996); see also the work by Pipes cited in note 25 below. For these historians, the totalitarian nature of the Soviet regime was directly connected with communist ideology and its utopian overtones. On this view, the totalitarian regime is ideologically inspired, and is for this reason artificial: one would merely need to discredit communist ideology and remove the Communist Party, whose existence was justified only by ideology, and Russian society would immediately return to "normality"—that is, it would become similar to a Western capitalist democracy. This sort of vision of the Soviet regime fits well with Francis Fukuyama's famous theory about "the end of history," a theory that emphasizes present-day Western capitalist democracy as the ultimate goal of humanity. See Fukuyama, *The End of History and the Last Man* (New York: Free Press, 1992).

[8] See, for example, Hannah Arendt, *The Origins of Totalitarianism* (New York: Harcourt, Brace, and World, 1966).

German bureaucrats were so focused on their immediate tasks that they moved smoothly from pre-Nazi to Nazi and post-Nazi eras.

Despite its external similarities to the Soviet regime, and the grinding power of its totalitarian state, Nazi society was still a Western *Gesellschaft* with a strong sense of private property, a legalistic web, and a strong sense of self-control. The totalitarian regime was merely a thin crust, and as soon as that regime was removed, German society (in the Western sector) was restored to conditions that made it indistinguishable from other Western societies. In the Soviet Union, the situation was different. The Soviet regime was based not on the principles of a *Gesellschaft* but on those of a *Gemeinschaft*, and thus is more aptly compared to Oriental despotism than to the National Socialism of Nazi Germany. A strong government was necessary if the society was to continue its existence.

This point is not taken into account by even the keenest observers of Soviet reality. For example, in the early 1960s, Karl Wittfogel aptly pointed out that the Soviet regime was akin to an Oriental despotism;[9] however, perhaps because of prevailing opinion or the intellectual climate of the day (that is, during the coldest part of the cold war), he saw only the repression inherent in these regimes. He clearly saw no positive aspects in them. Yet the strong power of the Oriental despot has not always had negative connotations. In fact, such a powerful leader may be essential in a *Gemeinschaft*, as the collapse of a dynasty and the resulting political vacuum usually leads to a neglect of the agricultural system and often, in the end, to famine, as numerous historical examples have proven. The social fabric then begins to crumble, and there is a rise in antisocial behavior among the populace. The defenseless society is usually plundered by its stronger neighbors, and diseases and other calamities spread throughout the country.[10]

Historically, people living under despotic regimes, or at least a considerable portion of these people, have been well aware of the catastrophic consequences of the collapse of the strong authority. For this reason, even when they rallied against this or that particular authority, they did not want to end the despotic regime: they merely wanted to exchange their "bad" (excessively cruel or particularly inept) ruler for a "good" one. If one were to apply the same principles to the study of the Soviet regime, one would see that a strong rule was, in many ways, essential to the stability of society and was not merely about protecting the power and priv-

[9] Karl Wittfogel, *Oriental Despotism: A Comparative Study of Total Power* (New Haven: Yale University Press, 1963).

[10] Examples can easily be found in ancient history. The collapse of several dynasties in China, the Time of Troubles in Russia in the seventeenth century, and, of course, the collapse of the Roman empire followed the same pattern, in that they were characterized by economic breakdowns, social strife tied in with criminal behavior and other antisocial behaviors, as well as devastating famines and the spread of disease. On the role of catastrophe and its repercussions in world history, see Pitirim Sorokin, *The Sociology of Revolution* (New York: H. Fertig, 1967).

ileges of the party bureaucracy. Chinese leaders have understood well that strong rule is needed to protect the stability of the country. For example, while Deng Xiaoping has dismantled the economic and cultural legacy of Mao, he has never challenged the authoritarian/totalitarian legacy of the Maoist political system. In fact, one could argue that he has perfected it.

Perhaps one reason for this was that the cultural self-centeredness of the Chinese, which borders on xenophobia, has made them reluctant to accept political recipes from the West. Such distancing from the West in the late imperial period (that is, in the later period of the last Chinese dynasty, the Manchu dynasty, which lasted until 1912) proved to be disastrous in that it impeded the country's modernization, which contributed to the country's disintegration and could have led to its absorption by strong neighbors. Today, however, this same cautious approach to the West and its political traditions has secured for China stability and economic growth and has even given it the potential for developing into a superpower in the twenty-first century. In the Soviet Union, with Russia as its dominant republic and Russians as its major ethnic group, the situation was altogether different. In Russia, the trend toward Westernization, an ideology that emphasized the country's similarity to Western nations, eventually stimulated the changes known as *perestroika* (restructuring) in the 1980s, which led to a weakening of the central authority. And this had dire consequences for the USSR.

The economic consequences of the slackening of the control of the state were the most apparent. Those reformers who undertook to dismantle the Soviet state invariably pointed to economic problems as the reason for their actions. Their argument was that a planned economy with the means of production (to use the Marxist term) in the hands of the state was the cause for the USSR's poor performance during the last years of the Soviet regime. In their view privatization was the solution.[11] And privatization was indeed accomplished over the next few years following the collapse of the Soviet regime in 1991. Of course, the method by which the privatization was handled evoked criticism from enemies of the regime. The result of the enterprise was that the lion's share of the property was gobbled up by members of the Soviet bureaucracy and a few semicriminal elements who had managed to gain influence. The majority of the people of the Russian Federation received nothing and are living today in abject poverty. The ethical aspects of privatization, of course, are important; yet they do not constitute the crux of the problem, nor do they explain why privatization and, consequently, modern capitalism do not work in Russia. The problem here is that the *Gemeinschaft* nature of post-Soviet society guarantees that the economy will not function well without a strong central power.

---

[11] Yegor Gaidar and Anatoly Chubais were among the leading Russian economists and politicians who saw privatization as the way out of Russia's economic problems.

While post-Soviet privatization created a rich minority and a poor majority, this is not a phenomenon limited to Russia. Those who support privatization maintain, and not without reason, that the process was similar in all capitalist societies: the United States, for example, underwent the "robber barons" period during the nineteenth and early twentieth centuries. I would argue, in contrast, that the problem in Russia is different and not simply a normal phase of development. The essential problem is not the social polarization between the wealthy and the poor, but some of the other aspects of Russian society. In capitalist societies, private property is protected by law; in fact, it is sacred, and the ability to retain ownership does not depend upon who holds political power. The situation in post-Soviet Russia is different, in the sense that power and property are tightly connected. This is the reason that leading Russian industrial and banking moguls are so concerned with elections: the fear is that changes in the political landscape will lead to changes in property ownership. There is a fear that the property is not absolutely theirs. For this reason, property in Russia is used by its owners as a means of extracting income that can be either consumed or transferred abroad.

Moreover, the transfer of massive amounts of funds outside the country ensures that there will be insufficient investment in the country's industrial complex and infrastructure. This minuscule level of investment is also the primary reason that Russian technology and science continue to deteriorate. The resulting economic system resembles those which existed historically under despotism, where the end of the strong rule of the emperor or pharaoh immediately led to the neglect of the irrigation system and consequently to economic decline.[12] When one notes the pitiful condition of Russian science and of Russia's high-tech industries, one wonders whether the country will ever be able to rise again as an industrial power.

The end of the Soviet authorities' strong rule has led to an erosion of the structure of the government. The lack of funding has led to a deep crisis in the Russian army. A newspaper recently reported that soldiers have been fed dog food because there is not enough money for rations. The prestige of the armed forces started to fall drastically after the collapse of the Soviet empire. In the Western model of development, this sort of humiliation of the armed forces usually leads to a violent backlash or military coup. However, this would require a sense of social cohesiveness, a sense that the army's allegiance is to the society and not to the strong leader. This sort of feeling exists not only in the armies of Western Europe and the United States, but even in those Latin American countries where capitalism is still not fully developed. This is not the case in Russia, where, following the "Oriental model," the strength and cohesiveness of

---

[12] There are numerous instances in the histories of China and Egypt in which breakdowns in the irrigation and economic systems followed the end of a dynasty.

the army was directly related to allegiance to the leader (and the "collective" leader, the Communist Party). As soon as the party was discredited, the army had no anchor to hold onto. For example, the army remained passive in 1991, failing to respond to the dissolution of the state. The decline in Russia's military strength reached its nadir in the military's humiliating defeat at the hands of tiny Chechnya, the culmination of a conflict that raged from 1994 to 1996.

Today the Russian army is no longer a viable military force and has become a haven for criminals; moreover, its cohesiveness is ever weaker, further eroding the power of the Russian state's central authority. And with the decline of centralized supply mechanisms, the army increasingly depends upon local governors. It is clear that the army is merely following in the footsteps of the Soviet army (which was partitioned among the states that arose out of the dissolution of the Soviet Union). It is possible that the Russian army might fragment into splinter groups controlled by local warlords, as the Chinese army did after the collapse of the Manchu dynasty in 1911–1912. Indeed, the fragmentation of the Russian Federation proper is already being predicted by some Western analysts, for example, Zbigniew Brzezinski.[13] Already the far eastern region of the Federation and Krasnodar in the south have begun to behave with increasing independence from Moscow. The Federation has been further weakened by the economic shake-up in August 1998, when the ruble was drastically devalued.

The manifestations of this decline in central authority vary. Some local governors have refused to pay taxes to the central government and have prohibited the movement of food from one region to another. The sense of the Federation's impending demise has led to the fragmentation of the national consciousness. Representatives of the various localities increasingly see Moscow (by which they mean the central government) as a foreign country. This sense of alienation is heightened because the standard of living in Moscow is several times higher than the standard of living in the provinces. Even Russian nationalists have been gripped by this sense of pessimism. Moreover, as Russia has become weaker, the Russian elite, at least those connected with the central government, have become hostile to the West. The steady rise of anti-Western feelings among the elite, and the continuing decline in Russian power and influence, is best understood in the context of the expansion of the North Atlantic Treaty Organization (NATO).

II. CAN RUSSIA ONCE AGAIN POSE A THREAT TO THE WEST?

The incorporation of Poland, Hungary, and the Czech Republic into NATO in March 1999 was the final consummation of the West's victory in

---

[13] Zbigniew Brzezinski, "A Plan for Europe: Russia and the Proposed Expansion of NATO," *Foreign Affairs* 74 (January/February 1995).

the cold war. While this is significant, an even more important aspect of the event is that it heralded one of the most radical changes in geopolitical alignment in the twentieth century. The change is especially dramatic for Russia, which has been thrown back to its seventeenth-century borders. And it goes without saying that these dramatic changes in Russia's geopolitical configuration are the subject of much of the discussion among political analysts when they speculate about the potential impact of NATO expansion.

The problem of NATO expansion cannot be separated from discussions of the cold war and the nature of its resolution. The collective memory of both Westerners and Russian liberals, who briefly dominated the country's political and intellectual milieu, on the topic seems quite selective, almost as if this most recent history is something from the Stone Age. Both groups maintain that the fateful days of August 1991, when the communist coup was turned back, represented the last attempt at saving the Soviet regime and, even more so, the empire. When the red flag was lowered at the Kremlin and replaced by the Russian tricolor four months after the coup attempt, it was still widely believed that the event signified not the end of Russia as a great power, but rather the end of a regime and an ideology that had prevented Russia from being a "normal" country, that is, a country that could be incorporated into the West.

This interpretation of events implied that Russia and the West (here I use the term holistically to include both the United States and Western Europe) were part of the same civilization and that their separation was due only to the communist ideology which had been imposed from above. Moreover, it was assumed that while Russia and the West represented two different shades of this same civilization, they now could be fully integrated. A considerable portion of both Western and Russian intellectuals shared this exalted vision of the relationship between Russia and the West. This sort of thinking is not foreign to the intellectual discourse on the matter even today, when events seem to have conspired against it. A good example of this approach is the recent book by Nicolai N. Petro entitled *The Rebirth of Russian Democracy*.

Petro, a naturalized American citizen and the son of Russian émigrés living in Europe, is loath to see Russia and America/the West as being the products of differing cultural and political traditions. His book apparently was conceived in 1990, while he was a political attaché to the American embassy in Moscow. At the time, he came to the conclusion that his governmental "experience reinforced [his] conviction that the major stumbling block that remained to improving relations with rapidly changing Russia was our inability to recognize the historical roots of Russian aspirations for democracy. The deeply ingrained assumption that Russians were not really prepared for democracy, or worse, actually preferred that an authoritarian leader tell them what to do, clearly conditioned our foreign policy thinking."[14] In Petro's view and that of quite a few Western and Russian intellectuals, the ideological and political immorality of the Soviet regime had prevented the West and Russia from uniting. Here the Soviet regime is seen as a manifestation of certain unhealthy traits (for example, the authoritarian/totalitarian tradition) in Russian political culture. Petro expressed the hope that his book would help reveal the truth about Russians' longing for democracy and would help lead to a new era in Russian-Western relations. He expressed his wish in this way: "May God speed the intertwining of the diverse strands of Russian culture, abroad and at home, that is so essential to Russian democracy."[15]

Watching the collapse of the communist system, Professor Petro became convinced that his vision of Russia's future had begun to take hold. He believed that nonauthoritarian trends had started to take control of the country's political life, a clear signal that the country of his forefathers was about to be incorporated into the Western order—or, to be more precise, a signal that there was going to be a reinvention of the Christian civilization where East and West had once supplemented each other. One could say that Petro saw, at least on a subconscious level, the vision of the great Russian philosopher Vladimir Solov'ev (1853–1900) finally coming to fruition. Early in his career, Solov'ev believed that all branches of Christianity, and even Judaism, the forefather of the Christian church, would merge in holistic unity, heralding the union of all of humanity under the aegis of Christ (though in Petro's case, one could say under the aegis of American democracy). Quite a few intellectuals share Petro's vision; consider, for example, Francis Fukuyama's famous essay on the "end of history," which expressed the notion that the common goal of humanity was democracy.[16]

Among some members of the elite, both in Russia and in the West, Petro's views are still held in esteem, yet adherents to this view are declining dramatically in numbers. The majority of political thinkers are beginning to see Russia as hostile to the West. And here the question arises as to whether America and its allies should commit their resources to confronting Russia in Europe. Pointing out that Russia's similarities to Weimar Germany might mean the rise of a Russian Hitler, some Western analysts regard Russia as a possible threat to the West.[17] Others have pointed to Russia's imperial tradition, which has strong historical roots.

[14] Nicolai N. Petro, *The Rebirth of Russian Democracy: An Interpretation of Political Culture* (Cambridge: Harvard University Press, 1997), vii–viii.

[15] Ibid., ix.

[16] Fukuyama, *The End of History*.

[17] On the fear of a Nazi-style backlash as the result of NATO expansion, see *Moscow News* 49 (December 7–14, 1997). The same ideas can be seen in the work of Alexander Yanov, the well-known Russian émigré author who has explored the nationalistic, Nazi-style movement in the country for some time; see, for example, *Moscow News* 3 (January 25–February 1, 1998). On similar views among Russian intellectuals, see Alexei Arbatov, "When It Comes to U.S.–Russian Relations, the Risks of NATO Expansion Far Outweigh the Rewards," MSNBC, March 3, 1998; and Alexei K. Pushkov, "Don't Isolate Us: A Russian View of NATO Expansion," *National Interest* 47 (1997).

Brzezinski is among those who think that Russia might become an imperial power in the future.[18]

Yet these arguments do not stand up to the facts. The Weimar scenario implies, among other things, that Russians are deeply concerned with the might of the state. The recent example of Chechnya shows that Russians are generally apathetic about nationalistic causes.[19] (Indeed, Chechnya was an integral part of the Russian Federation, and one could argue that Chechnya's secession should have been strongly resisted by the Russian public.) As for the possibility that Russia's tradition of imperialism might reemerge, one might say that historical tradition is not a trustworthy predictor of the future. In fact, there is a belief among some analysts that Russia is now permanently crippled and may not be able to follow an imperialistic path at any time in the foreseeable future, if ever.[20] On this view, the expansion of NATO in Central/Eastern Europe is unwarranted.[21] The sense that Russia has lost its chance to be a strong and viable power has influenced many Western observers, and some of them have come to the conclusion that China rather than Russia should be the focus of American foreign policy. China's bustling economy and developing military potential, these observers argue, will make it America's major political rival in the twenty-first century.[22]

However, historical examples, most notably the Russian Revolution and the Russian Civil War, show clearly, I believe, that Russia has the potential to reemerge as a strong power, if a strong but enlightened elite were to come to power.

III. The 1917 Revolutions and the Reemergence of the Russian State

Historians have provided different interpretations for the revolutionary upheaval of 1917 and the subsequent Civil War in Russia. To briefly

---

[18] On Zbigniew Brzezinski's approach to NATO expansion, see, for example, Brzezinski, "A Plan for Europe," reprinted in *Nezavisimaia Gazeta*, October 24, 1997. For another view of American foreign policy as driven by pragmatic interests, see Charles Krauthammer, "Is NATO Expansion Directed against Russia? Of Course It Is," *Washington Post*, April 17, 1998.

[19] See Anatol Lieven, *Chechnya: Tombstone of Russian Power* (New Haven: Yale University Press, 1997), 6. For more on the weakness of Russian nationalism, see Astrid Tuminez, "Russia in Search of Itself: Nationalism and the Future of the Russian State," Program on New Approaches to Russian Security, Policy Memo Series, No. 20 (Davis Center for Russian Studies, Harvard University, 1997).

[20] David Sutter, "The Danger of Russia's Great Power Illusions," *Prism*, March 6, 1998.

[21] See, for example, *Washington Post*, March 4, 1998; *New York Times*, March 1, 3, and 5, 1998; *Christian Science Monitor*, March 10, 1998; *Los Angeles Times*, March 9, 1998; *Washington Times*, March 9, 1998; and *Boston Globe*, March 8, 1998.

[22] Curiously enough, this view of Russia's decline and China's rise is shared by such seemingly disparate sources as the *New York Times* (Fareed Zakaria, "Let's Get Our Superpowers Straight," *New York Times*, March 26, 1997) and the Russian nationalistic newspaper *Zavtra* (Alexander Prokhanov, "Kitaiskii Otvet," *Zavtra* 43 [1996]).

sketch the sequence of events: Russian society had been in constant crisis since the beginning of the twentieth century. The imperial regime was able to repel the first onslaught of the opposition during the 1905 Revolution. Yet World War I had aggravated social and economic conditions in the country, and this led to the February Revolution of 1917, which overthrew the Russian monarchy. The emerging Provisional Government did not hold power for long, and in October of 1917 the radical Marxist Bolsheviks took power.[23]

Soviet historians, and those from the West who follow them in their major political and philosophical premises, see the Russian Revolution as primarily a social phenomenon. The point of this approach is that the Russian revolutions of 1917 were caused by conflicts between the political and economic elite and the downtrodden masses.[24] According to this view, the Bolshevik Party enjoyed the support of the masses, and this was the reason for the party's victory and its hold over the masses. Those who oppose this view, while they are aware that imperial Russia had experienced social and political problems, do not regard the support of the masses as the major reason for the Bolsheviks' success. They tend to emphasize the fact that the Bolsheviks were not popular among the masses, nor were they able to retain the popular support of even a fraction of the populace for more than several months in 1917. Indeed, these analysts point out, the Bolsheviks retained their hold on power through the machinery of the Red Terror.[25] Their use of terror, on this view, can be explained by two factors. First, they were obsessed with their drive for power: they perpetuated the tradition of radical extremism that had been a part of Russian political culture since the beginning of the revolutionary movement in the late nineteenth century. Second, they were cynical plotters, driven by a lust for power for its own sake. This interpretation of the Russian revolutionary movement had its precursor in similar interpretations of the French Revolution.

These interpretations of Russia's revolutionary process do have valid points and help clarify particular aspects of the revolutionary process. It is clear that the set of ideas inspired by Marxism helped the Russian revolutionaries to organize the state in a way that would ultimately lead to the development of a full-fledged totalitarian regime. It is also clear

---

[23] The February Revolution actually occurred on March 8–12, which was February 23–27 on the Julian calendar in use in Russia at the time. Similarly, the October Revolution began on November 6–7 (October 24–25 on the Julian calendar). These two revolutions are referred to collectively as the Russian Revolution.

[24] For an example of such an approach, see Orlando Figes, *A People's Tragedy: A History of the Russian Revolution* (New York: Viking, 1997).

[25] The Red Terror was launched in September 1918. Officially, it was directed against the members of the imperial elite, i.e., representatives of the middle classes, landlords, intellectuals, officers, etc. Yet it also struck against the various other groups within the populace, as well as the criminal elements. For a conservative view of this subject, see Richard Pipes, *A Concise History of the Russian Revolution* (New York: Vintage Books, 1996).

that the Bolsheviks benefited from conflicts among social classes and that some aspects of the Russian revolutions can be explained through the theory of what is usually called "mass mobilization"—that is, the active participation of a segment of the population in a political party struggling to change society. Yet this explanation misses an essential point. The Russian revolutions involved a disintegration of the country and then a restoration of order.

One of the most potentially confusing aspects of the Russian revolutionary process is this notion of "social mobilization." To begin with, social mobilization, the rallying of supporters around a political leadership, is not solely the prerogative of the left. The enemies of the Bolsheviks, including representatives of right-wing parties, also engaged in the social mobilization of their supporters. In fact, social mobilization is not even unique to modernity, for a similar process can be seen in the past, when this or that charismatic leader has mobilized his supporters behind various causes, such as social change or a simple military expedition. Even more importantly, however, one cannot explain the events in Russia in the context of Western society and Western revolution. Pre-revolutionary Russia was only partially a Western society, and most aspects of Russian political culture were non-Western in nature.

Here is the essential problem. The theory of social mobilization in its present interpretation is in many ways rooted in Marxism, itself the product of Western society and Western political culture. One essential element of this culture is the direct connection between individuals, groups, and political parties. Political life in Western society works in the following way. Particular individuals have a strong sense of association with their group. The members of the middle class, for example, are aware that they belong to a particular category of people and are a class *"für sich"* (for itself), to use the Marxist term. Yet their conscience is not compartmentalized; they feel an allegiance not just to the middle class or to this or that region, but to the entire country. Moreover, their views are universal, in the sense that they believe in the universality of the most important principles of their class; for example, the middle class regards private property as "sacred." The same sort of thing can be said of the workers: they also have a strong attachment to their group on a universal scale.

Both the workers and members of the middle class transmit their desires to the political parties, who, in turn, appeal to their political constituencies. While one can question whether workers have always had their own viable political parties, they (or at least a visible part of them), together with other groups in Western societies, have been involved in the electoral process and have expected those whom they elect to act in accordance with the wishes of the electorate. The electorate also expects that it can count on its representatives. In short, there is a connection between the electorate and its elected representatives. During periods of comparative economic stability, the workers have tended to side with the middle class, especially in those countries where no strong tradition of political division along class lines exists. In cases where living standards fall dramatically, social polarization can lead to political divisions that foster the rise of radical parties, which sometimes can attract a considerable part of the lower classes to their cause. And in this situation, if the slogans of the parties correspond to the masses' desire for direct confrontation with the other social groups, a conflict is likely to take place. The confrontation between two mobilized groups would be what Marx called a "class struggle." In the case of a violent confrontation, this might lead to revolution, the violent end of the established political and social order. This was exactly what Marx saw in the major revolutions of Europe. He, of course, noted the French Revolution's classic case of revolutionary violence, when the Parisian sections[26] were socially mobilized either by the city government or by various parties in the National Convention.

Yet social mobilization is not the only major manifestation of the revolutionary process. To begin with, in Russia "mobilization" did not work exactly in its Western sense, at least not in the way Marx had envisioned. Those who joined the Bolshevik Red Guard and the army did not maintain a direct connection with their class. They did not join in order to carry out certain programs of their class; they joined because in many ways they had "fallen out" of the social structure. Many of them did not join out of an attachment to the cause, even if they felt a strong animosity toward the previous elite; they joined because the Red Guard and the army could provide them with employment. They might also have been attracted to the Bolsheviks as charismatic leaders who could secure them advancement in the future. In this case their attachment would have been to the leadership of the party, not to a class or a cause. At the same time, some of them developed an elite mentality themselves and looked down on the masses, or at least on those sections of the masses that were hostile to the Bolsheviks. In this case it would not be so much a political mobilization as a crystallization of the new elite. The Russian elite was different from the elite of the West; the Russian elite (the party apparatus, the army, etc.) ruled directly. The Russian elite had severed its ties with the electorate almost completely and did little to appeal for the direct support of those (e.g., the workers) who had supposedly placed it in power. (One should add that this aspect of revolutionary change can also be found in Western revolutions, though it was more pronounced in the Russian case, since Russia's revolution was more of a semi-Asiatic one than a strictly Western one.)

From the beginning of their development, the Russian revolutions of 1917, including the Bolshevik Revolution, were not so much revolutions

---

[26] After the French Revolution of 1789, France's large cities were divided into sections for electoral purposes. See William Dole, *The Oxford History of the French Revolution* (Oxford: Oxford University Press, 1989), 127.

of political and social mobilization as they were a melting down of society. Those contemporaries, especially conservative commentators, who watched the events unfold in 1917 have written tellingly of the spread of anarchy throughout Russia.[27]

The decomposition of Russian society manifested itself in various ways. One can start with the overwhelming spread of criminal activity. The increase of crime rates in Russian society may be compared to rising criminal activity in the modern West. High rates of crime can be found in Western societies today, but they are not on the brink of revolution. There is, however, one aspect of criminal behavior at the time of the Russian Revolution that bears special consideration. Although increases in crime followed each new phase of the Revolution, these increases did not follow the patterns typical of Western societies. In modern Western societies, criminal activity tends to be compartmentalized. It is common knowledge that the big cities of the West have higher crime rates than the small provincial cities. It is also common wisdom that crime does not encompass a whole city; it is usually contained within certain areas or neighborhoods. In the Russia of the Revolution, crime spread throughout the country, and the small provincial cities were as affected as the big cities. Drunken pogroms underscored the anarchical nature of events. While the consumption of alcohol does not necessarily lead to outbursts of violence, in the context of the anarchical chaos of the Russian Revolution, drunkenness was often a precondition for anarchical outbursts and antisocial actions. Often the drunken orgies of violence combined criminal behavior with ferocious ethnic violence, such as the bloody pogroms against the Jews.

The Russian army experienced a steady rise in the number of deserters from the beginning of World War I onwards. The army was thrown into further disarray after the collapse of the imperial regime in February 1917. Later, after the Provisional Government also collapsed, having ruled Russia for a few months from the downfall of the Czar in February until the Bolsheviks seized power in October, the army disintegrated almost completely, and many of the soldiers were transformed into roving gangs of bandits. The newly formed Red Army had little credibility, for its troops were inexperienced and without discipline. Even the secret police, the infamous Cheka that the Bolsheviks explicitly created to combat their political enemies and to fight crime and corruption, was not always reliable, since many of its members had ties to criminal elements. The same could be said about the emerging detachments of the Red Guard, the paramilitary organization created on the eve of the Bolshevik Revolution. The Guard was one of the few military forces that the Bolsheviks could

---

[27] See, for example, Ivan A. Bunin, *Okaiannye dnii: Vospominania: Stat'ii* (Moscow: Sovetski Pisatel', 1990); for an English translation, see Bunin, *Cursed Days: A Diary of Revolution*, trans. Thomas Gaiton Marullo (Chicago: Ivan R. Dee, 1998).

deploy in confrontations with its numerous enemies. Yet this force, like the Red Army and the Cheka, was hardly reliable. Many of the guardsmen could hardly be called revolutionary stalwarts; quite a few of them combined the guarding of the Bolshevik regime with looting. The spread of anarchy was combined with the continuing fragmentation of the Russian empire, which itself had several antisocial, anarchical features.

The integration of the Russian empire prior to this time was, of course, a complicated process. The empire was composed of different cultures and different levels of socioeconomic development. Many of these cultural groups had developed a national consciousness of their own, with a strong dose of European-style nationalism. Consider, for example, the various groups in the Baltics. In these regions a considerable portion of the native population expressed a strong desire for independence. In many cases, however, the drive for independence from the central authority had nothing to do with nationalism, at least as it is understood in Europe. In some cases this drive was not even related to the desire of the emerging native elites to boost the nationalistic spirit of their people in order to obtain power. The drive against the center during the revolutionary events of 1917–1921 was often primarily a manifestation of anarchical urges, the result of viewing the central authority, or any authority for that matter, as evil. The spread of anarchy—which was happening all over the empire, and not just in outlying regions with largely non-Russian populations—partly explains the nationality groups' urge to split themselves off from the center.

Indeed, this anarchical behavior was accompanied by a rise in regional separatism throughout the empire. This occurred not only in large regions with a predominantly Russian population (e.g., Siberia) but also in small regions that had seemingly lost any regional differences centuries ago, when the Russian state was created from a number of small principalities. The complete disintegration of the Russian state and society made the situation similar to the situation in present-day Russia. Today the country is on the edge of chaos. Its situation is similar to that of China when the Manchu dynasty collapsed at the beginning of the twentieth century. Sergei Khrushchev (the son of the former Soviet leader), who is currently a fellow at Brown University, has commented on Russia's similarity to the China of that time. Elaborating on how present-day Russia might develop, he writes that the future might hold "clashes of various forces in the struggle for control of the country, something similar to what happened in China a hundred years ago."[28]

In their disregard for the well-being and unity of the state, the Russian people differed greatly from the other Europeans engaged in World War I. Europeans had a strong sense of their countries' national interests and wished to protect the unity of their states. The disintegration of the Rus-

[28] Sergei Krushchev, *Asia Times*, April 24, 1997.

sian state, which actually ceased to exist, led to foreign powers interven-
ing in Russia's affairs. The imperial government and, subsequently, the
Provisional Government had been allies of France, England, and later the
United States in the fight against Germany and the Austro-Hungarian
empire. When the Bolshevik Revolution flared in earnest, the U.S., England, France, and other allies sent troops to various regions in Russia. Ostensibly, the justification for their actions was the Bolsheviks' signing of the
Brest-Litovsk Treaty with Germany, under which Russia agreed to withdraw from the war. The Bolsheviks signed this treaty in March 1918, a few
months after taking power. Lenin understood that Soviet Russia did not
have a reliable military force, and that even Germany, which, as the near
future would demonstrate, was on the brink of defeat, was a mortal threat
to the Bolsheviks' fledgling regime. Lenin convinced his comrades to sign
the treaty only after a prolonged debate, because the agreement led to the
loss of a considerable amount of territory and significant monetary repa-
rations. The treaty was so humiliating that even Lenin called it "obscene."

While the humbling nature of the treaty upset many members of the
Soviet elite, Russia's military allies (France and England first of all) viewed
the accord from a different angle. The treaty supposedly had transformed
Russia into an ally of the Germans. Those countries who sent troops into
Russia asserted that they had no desire to control any part of Russia's
territory, but the reality was far different. At the close of World War I, the
victorious powers absorbed territories from the defeated nations, and in
the case of the weakest loser (Turkey), they appropriated a large chunk of
its territory and divided it among themselves in the form of colonial
possessions. Whether an observer had been cynical or merely had looked
at the logic of the situation, he could have easily assumed that Russia's
fate would have been essentially the same.

In fact, several Russian observers at the time had noted that the country
was extremely weak and marginalized by its new political order and was
in danger of being absorbed by its strongest neighbors.[29] Those with
strong patriotic feelings were pessimistic, seeing nothing but doom ahead
for the country. One of the foremost of these patriotic figures was Vladimir
Got'e, a liberal intellectual. He witnessed the revolutionary upheavals
and the Civil War and recorded his feelings and experiences in a diary
that has been recently translated into English.[30]

In his comments on the anarchy and disintegration of the state, Got'e
did not point to the Bolsheviks or any foreign force as the cause of the
country's maladies. According to him, Russians had no self-control and
lacked a stable civil society. He compared the Russian populace to "go-

[29] See *Vechernii Zvon*, December 9, 1917; *Vechernii Chas*, December 6, 1917; and *Nakanune*,
April 7 and 14, 1918.
[30] Vladimir Got'e, *Time of Troubles, The Diary of Iurii Vladimirovich Got'e: Moscow, July 8,
1917 to July 23, 1922*, ed. and trans. Terence Emmons (Princeton: Princeton University Press,
1988).

rillas," a term he borrowed from historian Hippolyte Taine's description of the French revolutionary populace.[31] At that time, Got'e did not see the Bolshevik government as a despotic government that had placed itself above the populace. He saw the Bolsheviks as a reflection of the organic features of the Russian masses and their penchant for anarchy. Got'e was sure that Russia would perish and be divided by its strongest neighbors. Germany was the major candidate to become the country's master. For Got'e, the idea that foreign powers—especially Germany, Russia's historical enemy—could conquer Russia was abhorrent.

Yet he saw no way the country could avoid such a fate. He was disappointed with Russian citizens' approach to the state, which he saw as a form of self-hatred. He wrote in his diary that while the Germans' possible domination of Russia and the disappearance of the Russian state was troubling, he had come to the conclusion that Russians were not deserving of a great nation like those of the Western powers. He implied that only a tiny cluster of Russia's elite had earned the right to enjoy membership in a great state, but this patriotic elite had been decimated and had no chance for recovery.

The historian Sergei F. Platonov, another observer of the crisis, came to similar conclusions. Watching with both disgust and amazement the zeal with which the Russian populace had engaged in the deliberate destruction of the state, he said that Russians had ceased to be an ethnic group, or at least their disappearance as an ethnic group was ensured. He believed that it was possible that a new ethnic and state entity would emerge in the future; and he thought that, in such a case, the best that could be hoped for would be that pieces of the old Russian ethnic group might be incorporated into this new ethnic entity.[32]

Yet the Bolsheviks were able to reassemble the state and restore political order. This order ensured that the Bolsheviks would enjoy historical longevity, even though no one had believed, at the time of their ascension to power, that they would be able to maintain their position for more than several months at the most.[33] The Bolsheviks arose from the ashes and transformed Russia into a superpower. There are several explanations for how the Bolsheviks were able to accomplish this feat despite their small numbers.[34]

---

[31] Ibid., 31.

[32] It might be added here that Platonov had apparently envisioned this sort of development even before the Revolution, and this was the reason he wrote a book on Russia's history during the seventeenth-century Time of Troubles, when the existence of the Russian state was at stake. See Sergei F. Platonov, *Ocherki po istorii smuty v Moskovskom gosudarstve XVI–XVII* (St. Petersburg: Tip. I. N. Skorokhodovai, 1899).

[33] Gregory Zilborg, *The Passing of the Old Order in Europe* (New York: Thomas Seltzer, 1920), 208.

[34] There were around twenty-four thousand Bolsheviks on the eve of the Bolshevik Revolution. See Woodford McClellan, *Russia: The Soviet Period and After* (New Jersey: Prentice Hall, 1998), 8.

IV. The Bolsheviks' Rise and the Fate of the State

One of the more prevalent theories holds that the Bolsheviks enjoyed the support of the populace. After all, the Bolsheviks provided the peasants with land, allowed the workers to take over the factories, and granted the soldiers the peace they desired. Soviet historians, as well as the many Western historians who were their ideological allies, have argued for this interpretation of the events in revolutionary Russia. In this context, it is also emphasized that the Bolsheviks were the only real Marxists in Russia at that time; and since Marxism (on the view of these historians) was the most advanced theory about how the historical process worked, the Bolsheviks' adherence to this ideology guaranteed that they would understand the interplay of the historical process and ultimately achieve victory. The facts, however, do not support these conclusions.

The Bolsheviks did indeed enjoy the support of a portion of the population as they moved to assume power. It goes without saying that the soldiers were ready to leave the trenches of World War I, in which they had fought alongside France and England against Germany and the Austro-Hungarian empire. Their sense of patriotism had almost disappeared after the collapse of the monarchy, the only institution the peasant soldiery really trusted. A number of soldiers, of course, were under the Bolsheviks' influence, and many of them were given to calling themselves Bolsheviks. For them, the Bolsheviks were the people who had legitimized defiance of the authorities and encouraged their desertion from the army (which is what most had intended to do anyway). And of course, the peasants were happy to see the Bolsheviks promise a partition of the landlords' lands. A considerable portion of the workers were also convinced that the Bolsheviks, who stated repeatedly that they were the workers' champions, would improve their lot.

However, just because some groups within the population believed that the Bolsheviks' program would be beneficial to their interests, this did not mean that these groups would be anxious to render any sort of active support. Their support in no way implied mobilization, as it is understood in Western political culture, where the support of a constituency implies that it will mobilize for action. Although the soldiers might have supported the Bolsheviks, upon their desertion from the army they were transformed into bandits, or they returned to their native villages. If the villages accepted them, they became peasants again. This did not mean, however, that as peasants they would give the Bolsheviks any direct or active support. While the peasants appreciated the authorities' decision to partition the lands and allow the landlords' removable property to be plundered, this did not mean that they were eager to supply the Bolsheviks with bread. They were even less inclined to volunteer to join the Bolshevik army, unless deprivation forced them to do so.

Even the majority of the workers, who constituted a tiny fraction of the Russian population and who were putatively the major force behind the Bolsheviks, lost interest in the Bolsheviks soon after their victory. Their rationale was simple enough. The workers, at least those who had followed the Bolsheviks in the initial stages of the Revolution, had expected that a Bolshevik victory would dramatically improve their well-being. This miracle did not materialize; instead, the workers' economic situation deteriorated, and there seemed to be no force that could change the situation.

One should also not exaggerate the masses' gratitude to the Bolsheviks for their decrees relieving the soldiers from duty at the front and their authorization to partition the lands. The soldiers were deserting en masse already, and the peasants would have plundered the landlords without any authorization from the authorities. More important were the indications that Russian society was collapsing. For the roaming gangs of deserters, bandits, and the other great part of the population that had "fallen out" of the social structure, the presence or absence of a decree made no difference. While it is clear that the Bolsheviks enjoyed a social support that had translated into real mobilization—that is, the desire of some representatives of certain social groups to contribute to the cause— this support was far from decisive in allowing the Bolsheviks to retain power.

Moreover, Marxism did not contain a miraculous formula that was the major reason for the Bolsheviks' salvation. The Bolsheviks would ultimately instill discipline in the society and the army, militarize labor, and extract grain from the peasantry through force; they would also regulate the economy in more general terms. Admittedly, Marxism did provide the Bolsheviks with some clues as to how to organize society. Yet it would be a mistake to assume that Marxism was the only source of guidance for the Bolsheviks. They had an abundant supply of philosophical and historical paraphernalia that they used, depending on the situation. The history of the French Revolution, for instance, was one source. The requirements of the situation, not theoretical or historical examples, dictated the Bolsheviks' behavior.

In fact, the Bolsheviks' policy would become similar to the policies of regimes that had nothing to do with Marxism. All the warring governments during World War I engaged in economic regulation of some sort. Ration cards were the invention of the Germans, not the Bolsheviks or the Russian government. The crucial elements in the Bolsheviks' survival and their ability to resurrect the state were the charisma and brutal decisiveness of their leadership and the sense among the zealots in their ranks, some of whom were willing to sacrifice their lives for the cause, that they were engaged in a quasi-religious mission.

Those who venture to study the Bolshevik Party, or any revolutionary movement, for that matter, can of course find contradictory evidence.

Quite a few Bolsheviks were engaged in drunkenness, debauchery, and corruption. The number of these sorts of fellows had increased substantially by the beginning of the Bolshevik Revolution and the Civil War when the Bolsheviks became the party in power. But the party enjoyed a core of true believers who were ready to die for the cause. Marxism was an important reason for their dedication, and in many ways contributed to their success. Yet it was not Marxism that enabled the Bolsheviks to understand the political reality in a different way from the other contenders for power. The strength of Marxism was not in its sociological methods, but in its emotional implications. Marxism promised humanity a path to real harmony, to the end of history. This is what gives the ideology its strong religious overtones, and this religious aspect of Marxism was reinforced by the strong religious and messianic overtones in Russian culture.

At the time of the Bolshevik Revolution, Marxism was a pure ideology, in many ways similar to Christianity in its incipient stages. The point here is that the Soviet system was still untested, and one could indeed claim that the Bolshevik Revolution was going to open the door for a new society. Moreover, for the true believers, the socialist revolution in Russia was envisioned as more than an isolated Russian phenomenon; it was seen as the beginning of a violent global Armageddon. The revolution was an event of global dimensions and, in Marxist terminology, would close the "prehistory" of human existence and open the era of "real" history, the era of a liberated humanity. This feeling about the historical significance of the event, or actually its meta-historical importance, was an essential element of the psychology of the leaders of the Bolshevik Revolution. Both Lenin and Trotsky believed in their historical importance; and in Lenin's case, this belief actually depersonalized him, in the sense that he began to look at himself from a distance, assuming that he was merely following the ironclad laws of history.

These quasi-religious feelings spread throughout a sizable portion of the ranks of the Bolsheviks and their sympathizers, and were quite important in "mobilizing" them. Many were ready to die for the cause. Yet, although there was a dedicated core of zealots, their numbers were no greater than the first followers of Mohammed or Genghis Khan. This core group of dedicated followers assembled around them those people who had fallen out of the social structure: the unemployed, ex-soldiers, and similar folk. While these people might have professed an allegiance to the masses, their true allegiance was to those who supplied them with a livelihood and the chance for advancement. When necessary, they could easily be used against the various enemies of the regime, including the masses from which they had been drawn. These people were the second level of support for the regime. Their willingness to use repression at the behest of their Bolshevik leaders provided those leaders with the necessary means to maintain power and solidify the Russian state.

V. Terror and the Country's Resurrection

Historians have provided many different explanations for the advent of the Bolshevik Terror. Their vision of the terror, of course, relates to the way they interpret the Bolshevik Revolution itself. Those on the conservative side of the political spectrum see the predatory nature of the Bolshevik regime as the cause of the terror.[35] They also point out that the Bolsheviks' desire to establish a utopian society was transformed over time into a full-fledged totalitarian regime. Those who approach the Bolsheviks from the left see the terror as the Bolsheviks' response to attacks by counterrevolutionary forces from both within the country and outside it.[36] They also imply that since the Bolsheviks represented the subjugated element of the populace, the majority of the Russian masses implicitly supported the terror. This majority saw the terror as the manifestation of their desire to decimate their exploiters, the elite.

While the interpretation of the Red Terror varies, depending on the historian's political viewpoint, all agree about whom the victims of the terror were. The victims included representatives of political parties hostile to the Bolsheviks, as well as representatives of the economic elite of the defunct imperial and provisional governments.[37] Western historians on the political left (who usually call themselves "revisionists," though the term is misleading because they dominate the field) have ignored the study of revolutionary terror almost completely. It was conservative historians who looked at the Bolsheviks' reign of terror as a manifestation of their inherent brutality and ruthless drive for power.[38]

Those commentators who are most strongly opposed to the Bolsheviks add to the list of victims certain elements among the masses, including

---

[35] For examples of this view, see Richard Pipes, *Russia under the Bolshevik Regime* (New York: Vintage Books, 1995); Vladimir Brovkin, *Behind the Front Lines of the Civil War: Political Parties and Social Movements in Russia, 1918–1922* (Princeton: Princeton University Press, 1994); and Martin Malia, *The Soviet Tragedy*.

[36] For examples of this view, see *Soldat Revoliutsii: Voennaia i Politicheskaia Deiatelnost F. E. Dzerzhinskogo*, ed. A. D. Grigorev and S. V. Dzerzhinskaia (Moscow: Voennoe Izdatel'stvo, 1987); and Iurii Dmitrievich Dmitriev, *Pervyi Chekist: Dzerzhinskii—Epizody Geroicheskoi Zhizhi* (Moscow: Molodaia Gvardia, 1968).

[37] Soviet historians paid considerable attention to the Red Terror, interpreting it as the regime's way of repelling the onslaught of internal and external counterrevolutionary forces. Various works dealing with Feliks Dzerzhinsky, the founder of the secret police, portrayed the terror in this way. See, for example, Aleksandr Khatskevich, *Soldat Velikikh Boev* (Minsk: Nauka i Tekhnika, 1987).

[38] Besides the already-mentioned Pipes and Malia (see notes 7 and 25), one could point here to Robert Conquest. His major work, *The Great Terror: A Reassessment* (New York: Oxford University Press, 1990), deals with Stalin's Terror in the late 1930s. He implicitly states that Stalin's Terror was derived from the early terror of the Bolshevik Revolution and the Civil War. Aleksandr Solzhenitsyn, the famous Russian writer, could also be linked ideologically to Conquest, Pipes, and similar Western historians. Solzhenitsyn sees the terror of the Bolshevik Revolution as the central element of the Soviet system from the beginning of the regime to its last years.

disillusioned workers and peasants, some of whom had expressed their support of the Bolsheviks before they took over. The Red Terror undoubtedly affected all of these groups, but these accounts ignore or marginalize the Bolshevik victims found in other groups in Russian society. And it was these antisocial groups (mostly criminals) that either perpetuated anarchical disorder or slowed the Bolsheviks from mastering a strong and reliable machinery of oppression, without which they could not stop the anarchy.

The Bolsheviks started their attack against antisocial elements even before the Red Terror. The fall and winter of 1917–1918 illustrate this point. At the time, the capital, Petrograd (along with other parts of the empire), was overwhelmed with drunken outbursts of violence. The newly born Bolshevik authorities employed machine guns to disperse the drunken crowds and looters. Although the Provisional Government had granted amnesty to quite a few common criminals, the Bolsheviks treated them in a much different way: more and more of them were shot. At the beginning of the reign of terror in the fall of 1918, criminals were shot alongside those who were considered political enemies of the regime. For example, in Penza, a city in the south, the drive against criminals went hand-in-hand with the disciplining of society, the weeding out of antisocial elements. This was the case with prostitutes, who themselves were victims of the economic crises that were the product of Russian wars and revolutions. And while a great many of the prostitutes were drawn from the lower classes, which the Bolsheviks claimed to champion, this did not deter Bolshevik leaders from treating them in the most severe fashion when they saw them as a threat to order. In Nizhny-Novgorod, on Lenin's direct order, hundreds of prostitutes were shot, together with representatives of political parties hostile to the Bolsheviks.[39] The terror solidified the Bolsheviks' power and disciplined the society. It also had an effect on the army, the key element to maintaining power and reorganizing the state.

Although the Bolsheviks relied on volunteers in the beginning to staff the Red Army, they soon abandoned the idea. The new leaders wanted a regular army because the Red Army was hardly a reliable military force. Quite a few soldiers deserted and became bandits, in much the same way as had happened with soldiers of the Imperial Army and the Provisional Government. Those soldiers who did not desert, including members of the Bolshevik party, did not always exhibit a martial spirit. An additional problem was that the Bolshevik leadership had only a few Bolshevik officers at its disposal; because of this, the Bolsheviks had little choice but to conscript officers of the old Imperial Army. To prevent these officers from changing sides again, the party leadership introduced military commissars, political operatives who were to control the military specialists

[39] V. I. Lenin, *Sobranie Sochinenii*, 4th ed. (Moscow: OGIZ, 1941–1958), 41:286.

from the old officer corps and inspire the soldiers to exhibit military valor. The military commissars were also supposed to be in the forefront of attacking troops, in order to show them an example of martial spirit; yet this was far from always being the case.

By applying capital punishment for serious offenses (such as desertion) by both the rank-and-file soldiers and party members in command positions, the Bolshevik leadership was able to discipline the army and the party. Indeed, without at least a partial disciplining of these two key groups, the Bolsheviks would not have been able to crystallize their group of core supporters. And without this core group, which had joined them at the beginning of the Revolution but still wavered from time to time, it would have been impossible for the Bolsheviks to reach their goal. The Bolsheviks began applying the terror with a ruthless decisiveness to discipline the army in the early summer of 1918.

At this point, the Bolsheviks were in a desperate position. The military situation was so critical that a tiny army of Czechoslovaks constituted a mortal danger for the regime. The Czechoslovaks had been trapped in an awkward situation during World War I. They were under the rule of the Austro-Hungarian empire, which had been the prime ally of Germany in the war, but the Czechoslovaks hated the Germans and the Austrians. The reason for the problems with the Czechs was rooted in history. The Czechs had been under German rule for centuries and had been engaged in a struggle with them since the fifteenth century. Later, the Czechs became one of the ethnic groups included in the Austro-Hungarian empire. The Czechs and the Slovaks, as was the case with other Slavic peoples of the empire, were discriminated against by the ruling ethnic groups, the Austrians (ethnic Germans) and the Hungarians.

Naturally, like other ethnic minorities of the empire, the Czechs and Slovaks dreamed of creating an independent state. To them, the Austro-Hungarian state and its ally Germany were their enemies, and they considered the French, British, and Russians as their allies. As Austro-Hungarian subjects, the Czechs and Slovaks were sent to the front. It was clear that they did not want to fight, for they surrendered with little bloodshed. They were prepared, however, to fight the Austro-Hungarians and the Germans, and by the time of the Bolshevik Revolution they were ready to go to the Western front and fight on the French and British side. But with the signing of the Brest-Litovsk Treaty they viewed Russia as an ally of Germany. The Bolsheviks, the Czechoslovaks thought, had prevented them from going to the Western front to fight with the Allies against the Germans and the Austrians. This was the reason behind the Czechoslovak uprising.

The Czechoslovak forces were small, numbering around forty thousand troops and quite possibly less. Yet they were disciplined, and they easily routed the Red Army forces. Trotsky, the Red Army's commander in chief, decided that it was time to induce martial spirit in the army as well as in those members of the party who were attached to the army to maintain discipline. One episode during the campaign against the Czechoslovaks is indicative, for it demonstrates what came to be a pattern in dealing with the army and the party.

In one of the battles, the Red forces were easily routed. Trotsky's response was harsh. Those who had retreated were lined up, and every twentieth man was shot. A detachment of sailors tried to flee on a ship, but the ship was compelled to surrender and the entire detachment was shot. The commanders of the detachments, including members of the party, were not spared. Both the commanders and the party members had committed only one crime—they had not died in the fighting. According to Trotsky, they should have either won or died trying; there was no other alternative. This was not an isolated phenomenon. In several indignant letters that were written by local party leaders to the Central Committee, there were complaints that Trotsky "shot communists" on a regular basis. Trotsky's enemies would, of course, remember this later, during the fierce struggle for succession in the late 1920s which pitted the "right" and Stalin against the "leftist opposition" led by Trotsky.

The Red Terror was quite different than that practiced by the Bolsheviks' opponents—not only in its extent, but in its implications. The Whites never terrorized criminals or those who engaged in drunkenness and prostitution, at least not on a broad scale. One can hardly find even one reported episode in the White movement's history where a large group of drunkards and prostitutes were shot for demoralizing troops on the scale of the Nizhny-Novgorod massacre. Nor did the Whites engage in decimating the ranks of their troops, especially the officers, for cowardice and looting. The White Terror was looser and weaker than its Red counterpart, a sign that the Whites were not "true believers" who would spare no one in the quest for their goal of a "united and indivisible" Russia. The Whites claimed that they were conservative nationalists, while the Bolsheviks were radical extremists; the Whites claimed that they were engaged in a conservative revolution to restore the state, while the Bolsheviks were conducting a revolution of destruction. Yet the paradox of history was that it was the Bolsheviks, in launching the terror that decimated their political enemies and the perpetuators of anarchy, who played the role of a conservative force. It was the Bolsheviks who accomplished not only a "radical revolution"—the changing of the social and economic order—but a deeply conservative revolution that fulfilled the dreams of the most conservative members of the previous elite to restore order to society. The restoration of the Russian state with a strong army was an essential manifestation of this early transformation of Bolshevik ideology into "National Bolshevism," that is, the Bolsheviks' transformation into an essentially conservative nationalist force. During the Civil War, the logic of events forced some representatives of the Whites to understand that this was happening, and some came to the conclusion that the Bolsheviks had stolen the Whites' program of patriotism and order. By doing so, the Bolsheviks had laid the foundation for the transformation of a country that was in ruins into a mighty superpower.

VI. THE BOLSHEVIKS AS RUSSIAN NATIONALISTS

Strangely enough, by pursuing such a radical policy the Bolsheviks actually fulfilled the dreams of Russia's nationalist forces, who had longed for a strong authority to reunify the country. The terror rehabilitated the Bolsheviks in the eyes of some of their most implacable enemies. This was the case with the monarchists. The monarchists did not oppose the Bolsheviks because they saw them as usurpers who had destroyed the old order, but rather because they saw the Bolsheviks as representatives of the populace, or at least as a party that catered to the populace. In the eyes of the monarchists, once the people were liberated from the paternal control of a strong state, they would become an unruly beast that would destroy Russia. Of course, it would be a gross oversimplification to state that the launching of the Red Terror caused all monarchists to become enchanted with the Bolsheviks. Like the French legitimists who recognized no other power but the Bourbons, many Russian monarchists remained bitter enemies of the new regime for the rest of their lives. Yet they did not represent the entire spectrum of the monarchist movement. The Bolshevik Terror enabled some monarchists to look upon the new regime in an altogether different light.

The Bolsheviks certainly did not spare representatives of the monarchist party, and they decimated the old gentry families; of course, it was the Bolshevik government that executed Czar Nicholas and his entire family. Yet the complete story is far more complex. Most of the Bolshevik regime's enemies were the liberals and representatives of more moderate socialist groups, and, of course, the masses, whom the monarchists and conservatives blamed for the end of the Russian state. The Bolsheviks crushed these enemies and reorganized the state apparatus. In the course of the Civil War, many Russian nationalists, mostly from the monarchist camp, discovered that the Bolsheviks had created a formidable army that not only had successfully repelled the White armies but foreign troops as well. Thus, the Bolsheviks were not only a strong dictatorship but one which could be credited, at least in the eyes of some Russian nationalists, with preserving Russia's position as a great power. They appreciated the toughness of the Bolshevik regime. Indeed, for some monarchists, the Bolsheviks were more monarchist than the monarchists themselves. Although the Bolsheviks were supposedly an internationalist force that would lead a worldwide revolution, in actuality they were a nationalist force. The regime Bolsheviks became "National Bolsheviks," whose goal was not so much the creation of a new economic and political order as the upgrading of the country's political standing. And this was the reason that many generals from the Imperial Army joined the Bolsheviks.

For example, General Odinets of the Imperial Army's general staff joined the Bolsheviks the day after their victory. Though he had some problems with the secret police, he was able to prove his loyalty to the regime. He eagerly elaborated upon his reasons for collaborating with the new regime to a trusted friend (a military hero) and his wife, who were both supporters of the Whites. General Odinets stated that the great achievement of the Bolsheviks was ending the anarchy and creating a mighty army. The first and foremost job of this new army would be to unify Russia. In his view, one of the most important aspects of the post-revolutionary conflict was the Bolshevik center's determination to up-hold the unity of the Russian empire against the attempt of its subjects to escape Russian domination. The general also implied that it was the West that wished to see the disintegration of the Russian empire, and that this was the reason that many Western countries assisted the Whites during the Civil War. Elaborating on this topic, General Odinets quoted, in an indirect way, Alexander Pushkin's poem "To the Slanderer of Russia." In this poem, the poet addresses the issue of the Polish uprising of 1830 and states that the uprising was actually incited by the West, which was catering to the "arrogant Poles." Yet despite the West's support, Russia was able to crush both the Poles (in 1830) and the invading Western armies, as it had throughout its history, most notably during Napoleon's invasion. General Odinets pointed out: "And our Russian army, inspired by revolutionary zeal, will restore the Russian state from the cold rock of Finland to the hot Colchis. And please believe me, to all these indepen-dent 'rocks' and Colchis we will give short shrift."[40] Upon unification of the Russian empire, the Russian army would be poised for global con-quest. The general foresaw Europe being incorporated into the empire and predicted endless victory for the Red Army. He discarded the major ideological premise of the Whites: that they were the ones who were destined to make Russia a great state.

The Whites believed that in reality the Bolsheviks had catered to the basest anarchist instincts of the masses and were thus responsible for the destruction of the Russian state. Even worse, the Bolsheviks were inter-nationalists with no concern for Russia's national interests. For the Whites, this amounted to treason. But General Odinets discarded this notion, stating that it was not the Whites but the Reds who were the defenders of the country's interests. It was the Whites, who received much of their support from hostile foreign interests, that were the traitors. The Whites fought the Reds, the representatives of the central government, and helped certain nationalities of the Russian empire to create their own states. The Whites were helping to dismember the empire—which made them

---

[40] Iu. K. Rappoport, "U krasnykh i u belukh," *Archiv Russkoi Revoliutsii* 20 (1930): 244. Colchis was a country bordering on the Black Sea south of the Caucasus Mountains; it is presently part of the Republic of Georgia.

the true traitors. Here the general compared them to the royalists of the French Revolution, who had been unaware that they were traitors.[41] The general described them this way to his friend's wife:

> Traitors! Without understanding this of course. . . . You know, Natal'ia Nikolaevna, what kind of respect I feel for those heroes who forsake everything that is dear to them to withstand the spontaneous anarchy of the populace. Theirs is a heroic act, but unfortunately a harmful one. They are really naive and do not know history at all. They should have read Taine! Their heroism only benefitted their enemies, French and Englishmen. Koblenz, Russian Koblenz! Blind tools in the hand of the perfidious Pitt. They are doomed.[42]

The Bolsheviks, according to the general, were working to build a mighty Russian empire. Those who questioned this had not recognized the real historical meaning of the regime. Even though the players in this historical drama might not be aware of the events' significance, later developments would make this meaning clear. Instead of an international republic of workers, the Bolsheviks' conquest would lead to the emergence of a "Russian empire" that would not be run by a czar but by a "General Bonaparte," that is, a harsh military dictator.

At the time of the conversation I have referred to, Odinets's friend and the friend's wife had no sympathy for the general. They saw him as a simple turncoat who was fighting the Whites for personal advancement. They viewed his "National Bolshevik" ideology as merely a justification for his lack of principle. Yet when they witnessed a parade of Red Army troops, this friend and his wife changed their minds. Watching the disciplined troops, Odinets's friend said: "I have not seen this since 1914. . . . The bayonets in one line. It looks as good as the old companies in the old times." In his mind the enemies became the supporters of the White cause. Moreover, with the Reds' stress on strict discipline, buttressed by terror and enthusiasm, and given that they were poised to reunite the empire and make future conquests, in his mind the Reds became more nationalistic than the Whites. Paradoxically enough, the Bolsheviks' strict discipline and ardent nationalism made them more White than the Whites.[43]

Odinets's friend, who had originally been opposed to the general, later found that these ideas were spreading throughout the country, and were

---

[41] The French monarchists believed that they were fighting against the revolutionary government. Yet in their struggle against the revolutionary regime they actually weakened France as a state, and the revolutionaries pointed this out. Indeed, the revolutionaries emphasized that they themselves were "patriots," fighting for a "united and indivisible" France. At the same time, they viewed their enemies as agents of foreign powers.

[42] Ibid. "Pitt" refers to William Pitt, prime minister of England at the time of the French Revolution. "Koblenz" was the headquarters of the French monarchists in Germany—a symbol of the counterrevolution.

[43] Ibid., 245.

popular not only with renegade generals but with people he had learned to trust. Friends who had participated in the White movement also began to see things in the same way. One friend told him that the White movement was powerless to stop the revolutionary upheaval:

> Everything is much deeper and much more horrible than we thought previously. Twenty thousand officers and Cossacks will not stop this, will not put it down. . . . Everything was turned upside down, the mountains were moved. And should we attempt to put everything in its old order? Everything from the very beginning? But where would we find the force to do all of this?[44]

Odinets's friend came to believe that it would not be the Whites but the Reds who would carry forward the White ideas—that is, would establish strict discipline and create a mighty army that would upgrade the country's international standing:

> Please understand me, please understand: I did not change my political beliefs, I did not become a Bolshevik; I am the same person whom you have known for so many years. Do you remember Petersburg, our discussions? . . . I still believe that the revolution is the greatest calamity, that all Marxists are absolute idiots and that Europe with her limited constitutions is our ideal for the distant future. And with all of this I am stating that we were wrong. Yes, yes, yes, we were mistaken—salvation will not come from that [i.e., the White] side.[45]

In a conversation with a former White officer, Odinets's friend expressed his surprise and indignation that the Bolsheviks, whom he saw as cruel beasts and highway robbers without any real concern for Russia, would be the restorers of the mighty Russian state. The ex-officer, however, stated that the Bolsheviks were in the process of changing their nature. Indeed, the bestiality of the new rulers, their ruthless employment of terror, was the cementing force that would curb the anarchy and build a strong army. "Yes, yes, beasts! Executioners, murderers and highway robbers! But who else could have come to power but executioners! After the cursed 1917 who else could harness [the masses], get rid of the debauchery and madness?"[46]

The ex-officer then added that the Bolsheviks were in the process of creating the type of state that the Whites had always dreamed of. The Bolsheviks had restored discipline in the army and reinstated a structured

[44] Ibid., 246.
[45] Ibid.
[46] Ibid., 247.

bureaucratic society. In its authoritarianism and class division, this regimented Soviet society even outshone its czarist predecessor. "Look at the bureaucracy. Forget that these bureaucrats do not do anything, at the same time look how [the masses] respect the bureaucratic hierarchy. They really respect bureaucratic order! The revolutionary ideas are evaporating and a new revolutionary order is in the process of formation."[47]

The ex-officer also claimed that the new revolutionary order was the old order. According to him, the essence of the revolutionary struggle was not the conflict between different political ideologies, but between those who advocated discipline and order as essential elements of statehood and those who preached anarchy. The Bolsheviks were originally against order and were the party of anarchy, while the Whites were the party of strict discipline and defenders of the state. Formally, the Bolsheviks defeated the Whites. But this was a superficial observation, for when the Bolsheviks had defeated the Whites they had adopted their ideas of discipline and the state. They had essentially become Whites, even though they did not understand this. "And the new order is the old kernel; the order is always the same, only the make up can be different. But if one looks at the very nature of the events, there are only two alternatives: either order or the anarchy of the revolution, and if there is order this means that we [i.e., the Whites] have won." The ex-officer added that the only thing that remained to be done was "the introduction of the institution of private property."[48]

The ex-officer's view of the events was that while it would take some time for Russia to outlive the anarchy of the Revolution, after a long and bloody struggle the day would come. The Bolshevik Revolution would eventually lead to an authoritarian state that would be stronger than the monarchy, more autocratic than the state created by the Russian czars. The ex-officer acknowledged that it might take some time before events played out in this way, but it was inevitable because "the drive for order will be irresistible" in much the same way that the push for anarchy had been. The country was heading to a sort of Russian Thermidor, and those who were on the other side of the barricades needed merely to wait until the impersonal process of social and political evolution returned Russia to its authoritarian normalcy. "And what should we do now? *Exister.* As was the case with Sieyès. *Qu'avez vous fait pendant la terreur? J'existais!* [What have you done at the time of terror? I exist.]."[49]

The idea that the Bolsheviks' terror had solidified the Russian state and laid the foundation for future expansion—that the Bolsheviks had actually done the work of the monarchists—became even more popular as the Civil War neared its end in 1921. Even the most reactionary figures ac-

[47] Ibid.
[48] Ibid.
[49] Ibid., 248. Emmanuel Joseph Sieyès was a prominent figure of the French Revolution.

knowledged this development. This is not that surprising when one considers that the monarchists' feelings about a strong and authoritarian government and their imperialistic vision of Russian foreign policy were more in tune with Bolshevik policy than with the policies of the liberals and social democrats.

The Russo-Polish War of 1920–1921 gave the monarchists more incentive to move along the road to National Bolshevism. In the course of this war, Polish troops invaded the Ukraine, but were ultimately pushed back by a Red Army counteroffensive. In the end, the Soviets were able to retain control of most of the Ukraine. The success of the Bolshevik counteroffensive led the monarchists to see the historical mission of Bolshevism as forging a mighty Russian state and defending the country's national interests. This feeling even spread to anti-Bolshevik émigrés. Discussing the Russo-Polish War, V. V. Shul'gin, a prominent émigré, a monarchist, and a former White, conveyed this point of view to a friend. According to Shul'gin, the most important achievement of the Bolsheviks had been their creation of a formidable fighting force. He also stated that the Whites deserved some of the credit for this because it had been their opposition to the Bolsheviks that had pushed them to create the army. "Of course they [the Bolsheviks] are thinking that they have created a socialist army, which is fighting for the 'International Revolution'—but this is nonsense. They only imagine this. As a matter of fact they have created the Russian army. . . . And this was our achievement as well. We have played the role of the Swedes."[50] Here Shul'gin is referring to Peter the Great, who had created a modern state and army in the eighteenth century because of the Swedes, whom he saw as Russia's major enemy. Shul'gin came to the conclusion that a spontaneous process was going on in the country, and that it really had nothing to do with Bolshevik ideology. As he put it: "The banner of united Russia was raised by the Bolsheviks," though they may not have intended to do so. The same hope—that the Bolshevik dictatorship would finally abandon its internationalist lineage, evolve into a truly nationalistic regime, and use its power and terror to end the anarchy— was shared by others who witnessed the Russian Revolution.[51]

VII. RUSSIA'S PAST AND RUSSIA'S FUTURE

Making predictions about the future, whether on the basis of an analysis of the past or of the present, is a thankless task. Real developments often end up being just the opposite of the predictions. Looked at from afar, these predictions can provide a twisted satisfaction for historians,

[50] V. V. Shul'gin, *Gody, Dni, 1920* (Moscow: Nososti, 1990), 795.

[51] Ibid. Contemporary Russian journalists also admitted that the Bolsheviks had exploited nationalist ideology from the very beginning of their rule. See, for example, *Nezavisimaia Gazeta*, December 10, 1997.

who can point to all the predictions of journalists and politicians as a sign of their collective stupidity—a stupidity which prevented them from seeing the links between events and their internal ironclad logic. The use of analogy to predict Russian history can serve here as a good example. From the beginning of the twentieth century, a growing number of Russian intellectuals of all political persuasions have visualized Russia as following the path of the West. The global predominance of the West provided Russian intellectuals with additional ammunition for this viewpoint. Russian intellectuals historically viewed France as one of the archetypal symbols of the West. Consequently, they regarded the French Revolution as a model to follow.

The French Revolution underwent several stages. The first, from 1789 to 1792, was a period of constitutional monarchy. From 1792 to 1793, France was a liberal republic, and from 1793 to 1794 the radical Jacobins ruled the country. The Jacobins' rule was marked by the Reign of Terror and the so-called Maximum. While the terror decimated the rank-and-file of the regime's real and imaginary enemies, the law of Maximum froze prices on salaries and essential commodities. This law had also legitimized the masses' requisitioning of foodstuffs for the government, mostly to provide supplies for the city of Paris. The terror soon struck against the Jacobins themselves, including Robespierre, the leader of the Jacobins and the *de facto* head of the French government. Robespierre had eliminated those who disagreed with him and those he suspected of being his rivals, either politically or personally. His regime was also harsh on the urban poor, including the population of the capital. As a result, a plot against Robespierre was organized, and he was overthrown on July 27–28, 1794 (known as 9 Thermidor on the French Republican calendar). He and his followers were immediately executed and the scope of the terror was considerably reduced. Shortly thereafter, terror was no longer being employed as a tool to eliminate political enemies, and the law of Maximum was eliminated completely. Robespierre had also been an advocate of a puritanical lifestyle, and this too was put to rest with his defeat.

In the demoralized France of the time, there was only one institution that managed to retain its prestige and cohesiveness: the army. Despite its occasional setbacks, the army soon made republican France one of the strongest countries in Europe. The leader of the army was General Napoleon Bonaparte, and on November 9–10, 1799 (18–19 Brumaire on the Republican calendar), he launched a coup that led to his installation as dictator of France. At the time of the Russian Revolution, it became obvious that there were many parallels between the events of the Russian and French Revolutions. This provided the opportunity for a growing number of Russian intellectuals, from many different political persuasions, to see events in Russia as almost a carbon copy of the events in revolutionary France. In their view, the Russian Revolution of 1905, when the Russian parliament was created, was a Russian variant of the events in France in 1789, when the fall of the Bastille, the major political prison in Paris, heralded the beginning of the French Revolution. Russia's February Revolution in 1917 was seen as a repeat of the fall of the French monarchy in 1792. Logically, the Bolsheviks' advent in October 1917 was regarded as analogous to the rise of the Jacobins, bringing on a quasi-socialist policy and a Reign of Terror.

Following this paradigm, Soviet Russia (the USSR) would have its own Thermidor and, possibly, its own Brumaire. And it seems that events in post-revolutionary Russia did follow this script from history. The New Economic Policy (NEP), initiated in 1921, legitimized private property and trade. The left branch of the party, led by Trotsky, was defeated, and scores of intellectuals both inside and outside Russia were convinced that the Russian Jacobins were on their deathbed. Trotskyites, members of the defeated leftist opposition, were especially convinced that Stalin, who in their view represented the middle, would not be able to hold on for long; and they thought that the right, represented by Nikolai Bukharin, Aleksei Rykov, Mikhail Tomsky, and others, would inevitably triumph and finally legitimize the predominance of private property over socialized property. The right would also legitimize the transition from Marxism, the ideology of the workers, to hard-core Russian nationalism, the ideology of the Thermidorian peasantry. (Luckily for Western historians, the Trotskyites' views were elaborated in letters now located in Trotsky's archives at Harvard University.)

This grand design, however, did not come to fruition, for private property was never fully legitimized. On the contrary, Stalin's "revolution from above" in 1929 eliminated private property completely. The society was thus "Orientalized," and from then on, analogies to Soviet history were sought: in native Russian tradition, with its strong authoritarian strain (comparisons between Stalin and Ivan the Terrible were popular); in Oriental despotism; or in the Roman empire at the time of Rome's decline. For example, comparisons between Leonid Brezhnev's Russia and the Roman empire were quite popular in Russian dissident and semi-dissident poetry. The Nobel laureate Joseph Brodsky alluded quite a few times in his work to the Roman empire in connection with the Soviet Union.[52] While the comparison to Thermidor (the French model) had implied the evolution of the regime into a more moderate form (and later, after Brumaire, into a Western capitalist democracy), the Oriental model implied not just a much more harsh regime, totalitarian in its essence, but also the indefinite stability of the Soviet system. Both models (French and Oriental) proved to be wrong. Not only did the Russian Jacobins become "Orientalized," but the new edition of the Roman empire did not last out the century; rather, it crumbled during Brodsky's lifetime.

---

[52] See, for example, Joseph Brodsky, *Marbles: A Play in Three Acts* (New York: Farrar, Straus, Giroux, 1989).

The reason for the failure of these various predictions is not a sort of collective stupidity of those who observed events in the USSR both in the 1920s and in the post-World War II period. The miscalculations of these observers were of a different nature. They were convinced that there was an ironclad trend of historical development. They were also restrained by the nature of professional discourse, which discouraged polyphony of narrative: it was assumed that good writing followed strictly defined rules which emphasized a linear, logically connected narrative. The observers were also captivated by the seemingly apt analogies with the French, Oriental, and Roman models (many of which were striking), and for this reason were unable to see that there were a variety of alternatives. When alternatives were pictured, they were pictured only in the most general outlines.

Taking these warnings about the limits of prediction as a point of reference, we can address the contemporary problem of the future of post-Soviet Russia: namely, whether a strong and enlightened ruler could assume the helm, and whether he would be capable of implementing a program that would lead Russia to prominence.

The rapid resurrection of the country might be defined as a "Phoenix phenomenon." The term comes from the legend of Phoenix, a bird who engaged in self-immolation only to be resurrected as young and strong. The Bolshevik Revolution and the rise of the Soviet regime, which made Russia a formidable superpower, was seen in the same light. The question here is whether the same phenomenon could happen again in present-day Russia.

To start with, a "Phoenix phenomenon" for Russia is not predestined now; nor was it in the past when a strong state could have failed to emerge. With respect to the Russian Revolution, Western historians on the political left typically thought that the Bolsheviks, who in their view represented the future of humanity and followed the ironclad law of history, were destined to prevail.[53] Soviet historians also made similar pronouncements. Those who saw the Bolsheviks as usurpers, as people who actually subverted the "normal" course of Russian and global history, saw the event in a different light. They assumed that the Bolsheviks could have been replaced by their political opponents: either by the moderate socialists or by conservative and semi-authoritarian rulers such as General Kolchak (one of the leading White generals who fought the Bolsheviks in the Civil War). The result under any of these alternatives, it was thought, would have been the same: Russia would have preserved a viable state authority and would have survived as a state.

Yet all of these scenarios ignored the possibility that the Russian state might simply have collapsed. Indeed, neither the Bolsheviks nor anyone

---

[53] For examples of this view, see Peter Kenez, *Civil War in South Russia, 1919–1920* (Berkeley: University of California Press, 1977); and Diane Koenker, *Moscow Workers and the 1917 Revolution* (Princeton: Princeton University Press, 1981).

else had a sure mandate from the prevailing *zeitgeist* that ensured the survivability of the Russian state: it very well could have fallen apart regardless of the political system. If we apply the same analysis to the situation in present-day Russia, we can see that the emergence of a strong leader and his ability to conduct a policy that would lead to the resurrection of Russia is not predestined. Such a leader would face a number of problems that would make the situation different, in many ways, from that which existed at the time of the Bolshevik Revolution.

The most important impediment to the rise to power of a strong Russian leader is the situation in the capital. The Bolsheviks enjoyed an independent power base: the Soviets—grassroots organizations which emerged after the collapse of the czarist regime in February 1917 and which gradually came to be dominated by the Bolsheviks. The Bolsheviks also had the Red Guards, the paramilitary, at their disposal, and they enjoyed a certain level of acceptance of their rule—if not a popular acceptance, then at least a passive acceptance. A similar situation developed in 1993 when a Russian parliament hostile to Boris Yeltsin might have mustered an independent force.

Indeed, at the fateful moment, in the emerging post-Soviet Russia, the parliament, or Duma, was composed mostly of communists and nationalists who had formed an alliance that would later be aptly called the "red-to-brown" movement. As a matter of fact, most communists were upset not by the end of the Soviet regime but by the disintegration of the USSR, the empire; and from this perspective, the communists were in no way different from hard-core nationalists. The parliament had been adamantly opposed to Yeltsin and the changes that his regime had brought to the country. As a matter of fact, they saw Yeltsin and Gorbachev as the major culprits behind the division of the USSR and the catastrophic decline of the country's international standing and its industrial output. The parliament, which is situated in Moscow, was in a position roughly similar to that of the Petrograd Soviet and the VRK (the Military Revolutionary Council), institutions that were dominated by the Bolsheviks on the eve of their revolution, just as parliament was dominated by the communists in 1993.

The parliament also had military forces at its disposal. To begin with, members of parliament, at least some of them, had toyed with the idea of a military confrontation with Yeltsin for some time. For this reason, they had stored weapons in the parliament building so that they could arm themselves and those Muscovites who might come to their rescue if there were a confrontation. Some of them (and they included people of all political persuasions) also carried personal arms. Yet it was the Russian army that was the major hope of the rebellious parliament. Many members assumed that the army—if not all of it, then at least part of it—would take their side. The reason for their assumption was simple enough: Yeltsin and his policies had been responsible for the end of the USSR and the partition of the mighty Soviet army. Yeltsin was also responsible for the continuous decline of the military officers' and soldiers' standard of living. Members of parliament assumed that many members of the armed forces hated Yeltsin and would be on their side in a confrontation. This pro-parliament military force, it was thought, would play the role of the Red Guards and the pro-Bolshevik soldiers of the Petrograd garrison that had placed the Bolsheviks in power.

These calculations were not groundless. The point here is that Yeltsin, who also relied on the armed forces in this confrontation with the parliament, had a hard time assembling troops against his opposition. In fact, the forces that finally assembled were minuscule. I was told by one Muscovite who witnessed the event that Yeltsin only had four tanks at his disposal. And it was these four tanks that played the decisive role in the confrontation. They shelled the parliament building, compelling the members to surrender. With more determination and organization, or luck, parliament could have had at its disposal an equal or greater force. The Yeltsin regime could have been toppled, and a strong post-Yeltsin regime could have emerged. Indeed, it seems clear that the Yeltsin regime was on the brink of collapse. But the moment was lost.

In the years since the 1993 confrontation, Yeltsin's regime has experienced great difficulties. The most important, of course, was the financial crash in August of 1998, which led to the drastic devaluation of the ruble. With these problems come greater opposition from the communists, who have pressured Yeltsin to resign; yet he has been able to hang on so far. The Russian constitution, which was adopted after the abortive 1993 revolution, has taken many of parliament's powers and placed them in the hands of the president. With the exception of the August 1998 crisis, the parliament has capitulated to Yeltsin time after time. The members of the Duma routinely cave in to Yeltsin, despite their bellicose rhetoric. Therefore, at least at present (in the spring of 1999), Yeltsin's regime is in full control of the capital.

Another factor hampering the emergence of a strong leader is the general situation in the country. Despite all the economic problems, the majority of the Russian population is in no danger of starvation. Moreover, there is no quasi-religious doctrine that would galvanize at least some of the populace as the Bolsheviks' ideology did in 1917. Both Western liberal capitalism and the old socialist doctrine have lost their appeal, and society seemingly is in an existential and political stupor that prevents it from being engaged in revolutionary actions in the manner of the Bolshevik Revolution. There is another problem that a strong leader might face. Long periods of brutal dictatorship have taught Russians to be quite cautious with their political choices. It is clear that the possibility of spilling blood was the reason the country rejected a strong leader in the 1996 elections, especially one who espoused violence as the only way to get out of the present crisis. Moreover, the changes of Gorbachev's *pere-*

stroika and Yeltsin's subsequent reforms have convinced quite a few Russians that any change is actually for the worse and that it is better to preserve the status quo. The idea that the status quo should be preserved is even shared by those members of the populace who were hurt by the reforms. They are seemingly reluctant to try to restore the "good old days," at least as they were realized in the political platform of Gennady Zyuganov, the Communist Party leader, during the 1996 elections. This fear of change was seemingly the major reason why the communists—who, curiously enough, played in this situation the role of a revolutionary force rather than a conservative one—were defeated.

It might be added here that during the last years of the Soviet regime, especially during Brezhnev's tenure (which ended with his death in 1982), the communists played a conservative role, for the very simple reason that they were the supporters of the status quo. It was the dissidents, whom the present-day Yeltsin regime has regarded as its ideological forefathers, who were the force that had pushed for change. The political roles were reversed after the collapse of the Soviet regime. At that time, the anti-communist forces were transformed from the force of revolutionary change to the force of stability, and theirs became the conservative program, the program for preserving the status quo. The communists came to the 1996 elections with a different program and are now, as I have noted, playing the role of a revolutionary force.

Yet the majority of Russians are tired of change. The experiences of Gorbachev's era demonstrated for them that change is usually for the worse. By 1996, the economic situation had stabilized in some aspects—that is, inflation had slowed considerably—and this was one of the major reasons that Yeltsin won reelection. The economic crash of August 1998 shook the populace's belief in the stability of the regime; yet, despite this, a considerable portion of the public is loath to see any radical change and is reluctant to support the rise of a strong leader with dictatorial powers. This aversion to radical change can be seen in the popularity of Russian Prime Minister Yevgeny Primakov. His emergence as a popular figure in the wake of the financial crisis, a popularity which is reflected in the polls, is due largely to the fact that he was able to prevent a drastic and much feared deterioration of the situation without shaking up the country's entire political and economic system. (Perhaps, this popularity explains in part Yeltsin's removal of Primakov in May of 1999, and his replacement by a more compliant figure.)

Finally, some aspiring contenders for the role of strong leader in Russia might be hobbled by other aspects of the country's political and economic culture. Russian citizens expect those political players whom they might regard as a potential replacement for President Yeltsin to be able to change their economic situation for the better; yet at the same time, they do not want any change at all. A few examples will be sufficient to press this point. The nonpayment of salaries has been one of the most serious problems for the majority of the Russian population. The problem apparently stems from entrepreneurs' and government agencies' blatant disregard of a basic element of a capitalist society—that is, payment for work done. To put an end to this situation would require giving law-enforcement agencies the ability to enforce and monitor the payment of salaries. However, this would affect the semi-legal dealings (such as nonpayment of taxes) of the same groups of people who are so upset about the nonpayment of salaries. They want the law-enforcement agencies to be "selective" in their enforcement activities, and, as a result, these groups actually work to hobble any changes in the situation. Finally, there is no force that could change the economy for the better without the enactment of tough measures, and it could not be done overnight even under the best scenario. This, for example, might create problems for General Alexander Lebed, who was elected governor in 1998 of the important Krasnoyarsk region in Eastern Siberia. He can be regarded as one of the major contenders for Yeltsin's job, yet his governorship might preclude him from being successful in any election. Lebed will attempt to use the Krasnoyarsk region as an example of what the population could expect if he were to have the top job. However, if he fails to improve conditions there, he could lose his appeal as a would-be savior.

Thus, today it seems that there is no way for a strong leader to climb to the top of the Russian political pyramid. Yet I would argue that it could happen, for the following reasons. Clearly, there is no easy solution to the crisis, and it is also clear that quite a few Russian citizens have become cynical and that they understand, at least on a subconscious level, that there is no easy solution. Yet their desperation and cynicism have also produced a strong streak of irrationalism in post-Soviet Russian culture. This streak of irrationalism has a variety of manifestations, from the businessmen who promise quick enrichment to the assorted quacks and self-styled magicians who guarantee contact with the afterworld. This streak in Russian culture, which coexists with a deep cynicism, has resulted in the belief of many in a savior, a strong charismatic leader. And indeed, pretenders for this role have emerged throughout Gorbachev's and Yeltsin's reigns. Among them, one should point to the members of the group who tried to replace Gorbachev in August 1991. They were followed by Vladimir Zhirinovsky (a leader of the Liberal Democratic Party), who promised Russians that he would restore the empire and would add new territory besides—Russian soldiers would "wash their boots" in the warm waters of the Indian Ocean. Zhirinovsky was followed by General Lebed, who was followed by General Lev Rokhlin, and, finally, Lebed has once again emerged as the major contender for the role of charismatic savior. And even if Lebed were unable to fix the economic problems in Krasnoyarsk, that would not mean that he absolutely would never have a chance to become president in the future. Some Russian governors, for example, the governors of the Far Eastern regions, continue to be popular with the electorate regardless of the economic problems that their regions encounter. They simply blame Moscow for the problems, playing to the strong animosity that the provinces have toward the more prosperous capital. Last but not least, a political and/or social breakdown could lead to a meltdown and a situation in which the legalistic aspects of the power struggle would be either cast aside or marginalized. In this situation, a strong leader could emerge from an absolutely unpredictable quarter. Indeed, such a volatile situation, where force is the only way to solve the problem, was the case with Yeltsin's confrontation with the parliament in 1993. The possibilities are endless.

The ascension of a strong leader to power does not guarantee that Russian society would move in a direction that would lead Russia out of its present problems. Drastic measures might not be implemented. Or perhaps only the composition of the elite would change: instead of the Moscow elite, it might be a provincial elite that benefits from the change. Yet change is possible, and it is also conceivable that radical change could take place, even without the intention of the leader—or, to be more precise, the ultimate results might be different from what the leader originally planned. Lebed, if his bid for power were successful, might be an example.

Lebed is controversial, as are the statements he makes about the changes he would institute if elected. His rhetoric and his reform proposals seem to play upon the antinomian nature of the country's political and social discourse—the fact that Russian society seems both to desire and to fear strong leadership. Yet even with all the controversy that surrounds him, Lebed enjoys a political style that places him in clear opposition to most of the other political players. This makes him attractive to many Russians. He has stated that his major priority as president would be to bring order to the country, by harsh measures if necessary. Taken in earnest, this course of action might lead to different results than planned. A drive against crime and corruption would lead to the establishment of strict government control over most Russian banks and enterprises, most of which are intimately linked to the underworld. This would be a type of nationalization, even though it would not be described in these terms. The nationalization could be done directly, despite Lebed's occasional statements that he would not challenge the results of Russia's recent privatization. This might just be a political promise, however; for private property is hardly sacred in post-Soviet Russia—even in Moscow, where Western-style capitalism is further developed than it is in the rest of the country. Mayor Luzhkov of Moscow is on record as stating that the results of privatization are not final, and that he would like to reconsider some of them because they were "unfair." In fact, nationalization can be accomplished quite easily in a society where legal restrictions, or any limitations for that matter, are weak. In the new corporate state that would emerge (perhaps even contrary to the original plans), the Oriental streak in Russia's political culture might reemerge—a culture in which the state molds society, rather than business or civil society molding the state.

Developments in early 1999 indicate that Russian society might be ready for change that would reinstate the centrally controlled economy. Indeed, Primakov's government made an attempt to introduce government control over the economy—a move which directly contradicts the International Monetary Fund's prescription for the country. This attempt will most likely fail, but not because it goes against the IMF's recommendations. The reasons for failure will be of a different nature. Success might be achieved only if there is a drastic change of course, coupled with the wide use of repression, as was the case with the Bolsheviks. It is clear that Primakov either has no intention of doing this, or lacks the ability to risk these major changes, or both (the latter is most likely the case, for Primakov is no supreme ruler). It is not Primakov but other rulers who might emerge in the future, such as Lebed or someone like him, who might take on the task of recreating a strong state, without which Russia's reemergence as a strong power would be impossible.

The strengthening of the state with the central authority at the top would lead to a considerable concentration of resources in the hands of the state, and these resources would most likely be used in ways that differ from their current use. Instead of being consumed or transferred to the West, these resources could be used for the development of key industries, science, and technology. The society could replay in some modified way Stalin's five-year plans, under which the concentration of the resources of the state in a truly Oriental manner transformed backward Russia into a mighty industrial state. A strong state, with its repressive machinery, would decimate both the political opposition and the criminal elements in the society, and it seems likely that only such a strong government could bring stability to the country. Although the society would not be completely free from crime, it would be a safer place than it is today. This could help develop the small businesses that would provide an additional prop for a rising economy. Finally, paradoxically enough, foreign investors might also be drawn into the country. This last statement needs some explanation.

One of the assumptions of the present Russian elite was that the transformation of the country along lines more acceptable to the West would lead to massive Western investments. Yet this has not happened, despite the generally positive evaluations of Russian society by the Western press and academia. Indeed, the money given to Russia by the IMF over the last few years has not been given as an investment in the real productive sector of the economy, which would help to boost Russian industrial production and/or to retool Russian industry. Rather, IMF loans have been given to stabilize the country's currency or to close unprofitable enterprises. Moreover, the sums of money Russia has received do not add up to the amounts that it has lost: the flow of capital from the country (estimated at several hundred billion dollars) has exceeded IMF funding many times over.

The situation is quite different from that of China, even though China is experiencing pressure from various groups all over the world because of its continuing human rights violations. Despite the fact that the United States increasingly sees the country as a geopolitical threat, China continues to attract considerable Western investment. The money China receives is quite different from the money the IMF gives Russia. The money received by the Chinese is invested directly in the economy, and this is one of the reasons why the Chinese economy is on the rise. The economic boom in China in itself provides great incentives for foreign investment. The same could be said of the new states that have emerged in formerly Soviet central Asia (such as Uzbekistan and Turkmenistan) and in some of the states of the Caucasus (Azerbaijan, for example) where, despite the clearly authoritarian nature of the regimes, they continue to attract foreign investors. The large deposits of oil in these countries cannot explain this attraction, for Russia's known oil reserves are just as extensive. The explanation of the phenomenon is quite simple. Foreign companies are not concerned with human rights; they are concerned with profits. The repressive regimes in these states provide these companies with the political and social stability they need to conduct their business, so they continue to invest in various "bad" countries despite the angry voices of the press, academia, and, on occasion, the U.S. State Department. Thus, an authoritarian and centrally controlled Russia, even though its relationship with the West might become more tense, could possibly attract more foreign investment than the present regime. Foreign investments could provide additional lubrication of the country's economy and could help ensure Russia's entry into the twenty-first century as a powerful state once again.

VIII. Conclusion

The major problem for quite a few Western social scientists, both on the right and on the left, who have sought to analyze Russia is that they have ignored the Oriental aspect of Russian political culture. This aspect emerged during the imperial period, long before the Bolshevik Revolution, but was shaped and refined under the Soviet regime. Throughout its history, Russia has lacked the kind of self-controlled civil society that is to be found in Western nations, even in those which themselves have totalitarian aspects. The holistic unity of Russian society is based on the authoritarian/totalitarian state. In this context, the state not only drives against all political and social opposition, as it is understood in the West, but actually prevents society from melting down. In the light of these observations, we can see that the experiences of both the Bolshevik Revolution of

1917 and the Yeltsin revolution of 1991 were essentially similar in their structural elements, despite the seemingly different goals set by each revolution's leaders—the creation of a socialist state and the creation of a capitalist state, respectively. In both of the revolutions (or at least in the very beginning of the Bolshevik Revolution), the state was destroyed. The restoration of the economy, the culture, and the military strength of the state was inseparable from the restoration of order in a holistic sense. And this restoration was accomplished by the Bolsheviks upon the solidification of their power and the launching of the reign of terror.

Thus, it is clear from this perspective that the Bolshevik Terror was not just "radical"—that is, aimed against enemies of the regime—but was also "conservative." In their attempt to restore order, the Bolsheviks inevitably struck against a considerable portion of the Russian populace and its antisocial, anarchical tendencies. In this way, the Bolsheviks laid the groundwork for the continuation of the country's authoritarian tradition. Of course, it would be wrong to ignore the role of Marxist ideas (as the Bolsheviks interpreted them) in shaping Russia's post-Revolutionary history. Indeed, it was Marxist ideology that emphasized government control over both the political and the economic life of society. And it was this ideology that provided Stalin with the blueprint to launch his "revolution from above" in 1929, which led to the complete socialization of agriculture and industry. Yet regardless of Stalin's successes or failures at holding onto power (and, of course, his successes were in no way predestined), Russian society developed along authoritarian lines, with a strong state involvement in the country's political, economic, and social life. The Oriental streak in the country's political, social, and economic life—assuming, of course, that the country does not disintegrate—will remain for some time.

The same analysis could be applied to present-day Russia. Most, if not all, observers of the Soviet system (both within the Soviet Union and in the West) rallied against the system's repressive features. Bureaucratic control over the Soviet population, and the brutality with which Soviet leaders ruled over the country during most of Soviet history, evoked nothing but condemnation. The exception, of course, was those Western Sovietologists who took Soviet propaganda at its face value and insisted on denying the Soviet regime's brutal treatment of its citizens and its totalitarian nature. Yet those who rallied against the repressive nature of the state have been unable to see that the repressive nature of the state was the only thing holding the society together. The regime clamped down not only on political dissent but also on the asocial drives of the society, that is, on crime, corruption, and similar phenomena.

Because of their pervasive hatred of the regime and their naive assumptions about the similarity of Soviet society to that of the West, critics of the regime (both Russians and Westerners) failed to see the stabilizing forces in the Soviet government. The critics of the regime repeated the same mistakes as those who attacked the imperial regime at the beginning of the twentieth century. In their belief that the end of the repressive Soviet system would lead to Western-style democracy, they failed to understand the Oriental aspect of the country's political culture. They failed to see that, once left to its own devices, the country, a *Gemeinschaft* rather than a Western *Gesellschaft*, would move toward an anarchy that would threaten its very existence. This is what happened at the time of the revolutions in 1917 and now after the Yeltsin revolution. Since the August 1998 economic crash, the decline of the Russian economy has accelerated. Russians in many regions of the country are fearful of starvation (even though, for the majority, starvation is not a genuine possibility).

The continuous decline of Russia's central authority is manifested by the spread of crime and the increasing push for separation on the part of various components of the Russian Federation. As the situation stands now, the Federation is destined to follow the road of the Soviet Union, where Gorbachev's early attempt to introduce democracy led to a superpower's disintegration. Whether Russia will disappear, at least in the form in which it exists now, or whether it will be transformed into a marginal Third World country, is not predestined. Indeed, the source of Russia's weaknesses (and the weaknesses of other non-Western Oriental states) is at the same time the source of the country's strength, or at least it could be.

The very nature of the Oriental state, a state without a strong civil society, means not only that such a state can easily fall apart, but also that it can easily be reassembled and driven by strong leadership to high economic performance. This happened in Soviet Russia and in Red China. The same thing could happen once again in Russia. However, while the analogies suggest that Russia could restore its economic and military power, they in no way guarantee in themselves that the "Phoenix phenomenon" will repeat itself in Russia. Indeed, both past and present are pregnant with many possibilities, and while Russia could rise again, it could well have missed its chance and may now slide down the road of continuous decline and eventual disintegration. Only time will tell what path Russia will follow. Whatever happens, the Russian example seems to lend support to the idea that a powerful authoritarian/totalitarian state, rather than Western-style democracy, is essential for the strength, and in some cases the very existence, of non-Western societies.

History, Indiana University, South Bend

INDEX

Accountability, 110, 112–18, 120–25, 167, 169–70, 173, 177, 179, 186, 187, 262
Ackerman, Bruce, 152 n. 44, 155 n. 48, 156–58
Against Meidias (Demosthenes), 47
Agency, 13, 58, 81, 252–53
Alienation, 98, 210, 278
Allegiance, 82–83, 283, 291
Amar, Akhil, 9 n. 28, 17, 23 n. 71, 25 n. 78
Amendment, process of, 17, 87–88, 90, 94, 95, 99, 103
American Civil Liberties Union (ACLU), 142
Anarchism, 15, 219, 272, 285–88, 293, 295, 297, 300–301, 312–13
Ansolabehere, Stephen, 148 n. 39, 148–49 n. 40
Apollodorus, 51
Arendt, Hannah, 253, 274
Aristocracy, 7, 13, 34, 37, 40 n. 29, 47, 53, 55–59, 121
Aristophanes, 55, 58
Aristotle, 41, 47, 56, 84, 247 n. 48, 257–58, 266; and citizenship, 42–45, 53–54, 57, 59; and democracy, 32, 44, 53–55; and the *polis*, 34, 37, 42–45
Association, 59, 85, 208, 215, 271, 283; civil, 214; freedom of, 55; political, 232
Athens, ancient, 10, 28, 30–61, 207. *See also* Greece, ancient
Authenticity, 246
Authoritarianism, 130–31, 182, 269, 272–74, 276, 279, 300–301, 311–13. *See also* Dictatorship; Totalitarianism; Tyranny
Authority, 31, 60–61, 140, 185, 189, 193–97, 200–202, 212–13, 222–23, 275–76, 278, 286, 313; and democracy, 255, 259–61; and knowledge, 111; and law, 5, 8, 19, 21, 23–24, 40, 57; moral, 4–5; political, 2–7, 8 n. 21, 13–16, 19–26, 40, 165, 192, 256; and sovereignty, 2, 4–8, 21; and the state, 4–8, 12, 19, 22–24; as ultimate, 4–5, 19
Authorization, 12–15, 17
Autocracy, 28, 30
Autonomy, 27, 102, 108–9, 249–53; civic, 229–31, 236, 238–42

Barber, Benjamin, 182–85, 190, 199, 222, 226, 232

Bargaining, 174–75, 181, 193, 225
Barry, Brian, 68, 70, 73
Bechtle, Gerald, 46 n. 35
Beitz, Charles, 140
Benhabib, Seyla, 226
Berlin, Isaiah, 29, 59, 255, 258
Bill of Rights, U.S., 23, 265
Blackstone, William, 5, 6 n. 15, 7, 21
Blair, Tony, 204
Bodin, Jean, 2, 5 n. 14
Bolshevik Party, 282, 290, 293
Bolshevik Red Guard, 284, 285, 305–6
Bolshevik Revolution, 272, 284, 287, 288 n. 34, 290–95, 304–6, 311–12
Bonaparte, Napoleon, 297, 302
Bork, Robert, 184
Boundaries, 2, 221. *See also* Territoriality
Brady, Henry E., 142
Bramhall, Bishop, 13 n. 38
Brecht, Bertolt, 212
Brest-Litovsk Treaty, 287, 294
Brezhnev, Leonid, 303, 307
Brighouse, Harry, 129 n. 5
Brodsky, Joseph, 303
Brzezinski, Zbigniew, 278, 281
Buckley v. Valeo (1976), 157–58
Bukharin, Nikolai, 303
Bureaucracy, 269, 273–76, 300, 312
Burke, Edmund, 120–21
Bush, George, 71, 114, 116, 117, 119, 123, 125
Butler, Judith, 36 n. 18

Campaign finance reform, 156–57
Canada, 8 n. 22, 119, 210
Capitalism, 218, 273, 276–77, 306, 308, 312
Categorical imperative, 77
Character, 80
Chechnya, 278, 281
Cheka, 285–86
Children, 53–54, 173–74, 179, 216
China, 40 n. 29, 275 n. 10, 276, 277 n. 12, 281, 286, 311, 313
Choice, 19, 27, 108, 128, 143, 164, 170, 192, 266; hypothetical, 141; and ideology, 35
Christian Right, 88, 90
Christiano, Thomas, 129 n. 5, 143 n. 31
Citizens, 88, 117, 121–26, 133, 136–38, 151 n. 43; in ancient Athens, 30–34, 38–40, 42–59; and deliberation, 161, 167–70,